Pro SQL Server 2022 Wait Statistics

A Practical Guide to Analyzing Performance in SQL Server and Azure SQL Database

Third Edition

Thomas LaRock
Enrico van de Laar

Apress®

Pro SQL Server 2022 Wait Statistics: A Practical Guide to Analyzing Performance in SQL Server and Azure SQL Database

Thomas LaRock
East Longmeadow, MA, USA

Enrico van de Laar
Drachten, The Netherlands

ISBN-13 (pbk): 978-1-4842-8770-5
https://doi.org/10.1007/978-1-4842-8771-2

ISBN-13 (electronic): 978-1-4842-8771-2

Managing Director, Apress Media LLC: Welmoed Spahr
Acquisitions Editor: Jonathan Gennick
Development Editor: Laura Berendson
Coordinating Editor: Jill Balzano

Cover designed by eStudioCalamar

Cover Photo by Almas Salakhov on Unsplash

Distributed to the book trade worldwide by Springer Science+Business Media New York, 1 New York Plaza, Suite 4600, New York, NY 10004-1562, USA. Phone 1-800-SPRINGER, fax (201) 348-4505, e-mail orders-ny@springer-sbm.com, or visit www.springeronline.com. Apress Media, LLC is a California LLC and the sole member (owner) is Springer Science + Business Media Finance Inc (SSBM Finance Inc). SSBM Finance Inc is a **Delaware** corporation.

For information on translations, please e-mail booktranslations@springernature.com; for reprint, paperback, or audio rights, please e-mail bookpermissions@springernature.com.

Apress titles may be purchased in bulk for academic, corporate, or promotional use. eBook versions and licenses are also available for most titles. For more information, reference our Print and eBook Bulk Sales web page at http://www.apress.com/bulk-sales.

Any source code or other supplementary material referenced by the author in this book is available to readers on GitHub (https://github.com/Apress). For more detailed information, please visit http://www.apress.com/source-code.

Printed on acid-free paper

This book is dedicated to all the accidental database administrators, developers, and anyone who has written a database query and wondered "what the hell is taking so long?"

Also, for Roy, Moss, and anyone else who decided to turn it off and back on again.

Table of Contents

About the Authors

Thomas LaRock has over 20 years of IT experience holding administrator roles. He is a Microsoft Certified Master in SQL Server and a Microsoft Data Platform MVP since 2009. LaRock has spent much of his career working with data and databases, which led to his selection as a Technical Advocate for Confio Software in 2010 for the software now known as SolarWinds Database Performance Analyzer (DPA).

Currently, he serves as a Head Geek for SolarWinds, a company specializing in software for enterprise infrastructure monitoring. This role allows for LaRock to work with a variety of customers, helping to solve questions regarding network, application, and database performance tuning and virtualization. You can reach Thomas through his blog (thomaslarock.com/blog) and find him on Twitter (@SQLRockstar).

Enrico van de Laar has been working with data in various formats and sizes for over 15 years. He is a data and advanced analytics consultant for DataHeroes where he helps organizations optimize their data platform environment and helps them with their first steps in the world of advanced analytics. He is a Data Platform MVP since 2014 and a frequent speaker on various data-related events throughout the world. He frequently blogs about technologies such as Microsoft SQL Server and Azure Machine Learning on his blog at enricovandelaar.com. You can contact Enrico on Twitter at @evdlaar.

About the Technical Reviewers

Denny Cherry is the owner and principal consultant for Denny Cherry & Associates Consulting and has over two decades of experience working with platforms such as Azure, Microsoft SQL Server, Hyper-V, vSphere, and Enterprise Storage solutions. Denny's areas of technical expertise include system architecture, performance tuning, security, replication, and troubleshooting. Denny currently holds several of the Microsoft certifications related to SQL Server for versions 2000 through 2017 including the Microsoft Certified Master as well as being a Microsoft MVP for over a decade. Denny has written several books and dozens of technical articles on SQL Server management and how SQL Server integrates with various other technologies.

Joseph D'Antoni is a Principal Consultant at Denny Cherry & Associates Consulting. He is recognized as a VMWare vExpert and a Microsoft Data Platform MVP and has over 20 years of experience working in both Fortune 500 and smaller firms. He has worked extensively on database platforms and cloud technologies and has specific expertise in performance tuning, infrastructure, and disaster recovery.

Acknowledgments

There are many people to acknowledge and thank for helping me with this book. I'll do my best to include as many as I can, but please don't be offended if I forget you; it's not on purpose.

I'll start with my wife, Suzanne, for her patience as I spent many off-hours completing this book. Oh, and for all the time I've spent away from home for the past 15 years.

Thanks to Bob Ward of Microsoft for helping uncover new SQL 2022 features, as well as your willingness to share your knowledge on SQL Server for the past 25 years. And thanks for your time in Barcelona in 2006 when you inspired me to want to learn more about SQL Server.

Thanks to my partner in #TeamData, Karen Lopez, for your help, support, and friendship for many years. I became a better technical writer and presenter by learning from you.

Thanks to Kevin Kline for your guidance and support as I left my career as a production DBA to become a Technical Advocate and for providing an example of what proper community leadership looks like.

To Buck Woody, for your support in helping me understand my strengths and your guidance in career opportunities through the years.

To Craig and Vinny, for giving me the opportunity to fail as a DBA, and to Frank and Lori for not letting it happen as much as it should have.

To Rie, Betsy, Rochelle, and everyone on the Microsoft Community team for awarding me the Microsoft MVP status all these years.

Finally, to Jonathan, for thinking of me when it came time to update this book for SQL 2022. Thank you for the opportunity to write another book for you, 12 years later.

Introduction

"Write the book you wish someone else would have written and handed to you when you were starting as a DBA."

Those words were spoken to me by my friend and mentor, Kevin Kline, roughly 13 years ago. At the time I was writing my first book, *DBA Survivor*, and I asked Kevin for advice on how to approach the project. His answer gave me clarity, and I've used the same approach for this book you are now reading.

At the time I started as a junior DBA, Tom Davidson's well-known *SQL Server 2005 Waits and Queues* whitepaper was years away from publication. What I knew about waits I would find using DBCC statements against (the artist formally known as) Sybase ASE and SQL Server 2000 instances.

In other words, I didn't know much.

With the release of SQL Server 2005 and the publication of the Davidson whitepaper, wait statistics became a viable tuning methodology. Administrators and developers could now use waits and queues to understand exactly why a query was running longer than expected. Overnight our team transitioned from **reacting** to query performance issues to being **proactive** in understanding which resources the overall database workload needed most.

Every request sent to a database server has the same constraints: memory, processing, disk, network, and locking/blocking. It doesn't matter if you want to rely solely on execution plans for query tuning; the physical and logical constraints for the query remain the same: they are just presented differently in an execution plan. **The waits and queue tuning methodology reduces the complexity and time necessary for query performance tuning by an order of magnitude**.

Once you understand how the database engine processes requests, how waits happen, and how to track them, you are well on your way to being an expert in query performance tuning.

And that's the goal of this book. When you are done reading, I want you to have all the skills necessary to be an expert in query performance tuning. That's the book I wish someone would have written and handed to me when I was first starting as a DBA.

To reach the goal, this book has been split into two unequal parts. Part I, "Foundations of Wait Statistics Analysis," provides details on how the database engine processes a query (officially called a *request*, which is sent by a *session*, after a *connection* to the instance is established) followed by information on how to query wait statistics information through various SQL Server dynamic management views (DMVs). Part I finishes with an overview of the Query Store feature and guidance on how to create and gather metrics to build your own baselines.

Part II, "Wait Types," dives into specific waits, the causes, some examples, and possible resolutions. The chapters are divided by wait categories, which is a bit tricky as some waits (such as PAGEIOLATCH) have overlap between more than one possible constraint (memory and disk). Therefore, the chapters break down specific waits into categories by CPU, IO, backups, locks, latches, high-availability and disaster-recovery, preemptive, background and miscellaneous, and In-Memory OLTP.

Yes, waits for background and miscellaneous are included, despite their being benign for query performance. It's important for you to know why (and when) these waits happen and when they are safe to ignore (they usually are, but not always).

One thing to note, the examples in this book use a database named GalacticWorks. This is a modified version of AdventureWorks I use for a variety of demos when teaching my classes. The examples in the book will work with AdventureWorks, so don't panic about not having GalacticWorks; you'll be fine with most versions of AdventureWorks.

When you finish this book, I want you to have the confidence to tackle any query performance tuning problem. You'll have the details, information, and knowledge necessary to be an expert. And maybe soon enough, you'll be teaching others and maybe someday write your own book, too.

PART I

Foundations of Wait Statistics Analysis

CHAPTER 1

Wait Statistics Internals

SQL Server wait statistics are an important tool for analyzing performance-related problems and optimizing SQL Server performance. However, they are not always known to many database administrators or developers. I believe this has to do with their relatively complex nature, the sheer volume of different types available, and the lack of documentation for many types of wait statistics. Wait statistics are also directly tied to the specific SQL Server on which they occur, meaning it is impossible to compare wait statistics of Server A to wait statistics of Server B, even with identical hardware and database configuration. Every configuration option, from the hardware firmware level to the configuration of the SQL Server Native Client on the client computers, will impact the wait statistics!

Therefore, we will start this book with a review of SQL Server internals pertaining to wait statistics. We will discuss how wait events are generated, how to view wait events, and how to analyze them as part of a proper performance tuning methodology. Then in Part II of this book, we will explore and examine specific wait events.

This chapter will look at the history of wait statistics through the various versions of SQL Server. Next, we will review the SQL Operating System, or SQLOS. The architecture of the SQLOS is closely tied to wait statistics and to performance troubleshooting in general. The rest of this chapter is dedicated to one of the most important aspects of wait statistics: thread scheduling.

Before we begin, I want to mention a few things related to the terminology used when discussing wait statistics. In the introduction of this book and the preceding paragraphs, I mentioned the term wait statistics. The sentence "compare wait statistics of Server A to wait statistics of Server B" is technically wrong, since we compare the *wait time* (the total time we have been waiting on a resource) of a *specific wait type* (the specific wait type related to the resource we are waiting on). From this point on, when I use the term wait statistics, I mean the concept of wait statistics, and I will use the correct terms wait time and wait type where appropriate.

© Thomas LaRock, Enrico van de Laar 2023
T. LaRock and E. van de Laar, *Pro SQL Server 2022 Wait Statistics*,
https://doi.org/10.1007/978-1-4842-8771-2_1

A Brief History of Wait Statistics

SQL Server has been around for quite some time now. The first release of SQL Server dates back to 1989 and was released for the OS/2 platform. Until SQL Server 6.0, released in 1995, Microsoft worked together with Sybase to develop SQL Server. In 1995, however, Microsoft and Sybase went their separate ways. Both Microsoft and Sybase stayed active in the database world (SAP acquired Sybase in 2010). In 2022, Microsoft will release SQL Server 2022, while SAP released SAP Sybase ASE 16 in 2014 (but is still maintained today), both relational enterprise-level database systems.

Between SQL Server 6.0 and SQL Server 2022, many things have changed, and it is difficult to compare any two versions alongside one another. One thing which has not changed through the years is the concept of wait statistics. Each version of SQL Server stores information about its internal processes. Even though the way we access such information has changed over the years, wait statistics remain an important part of the internal logging process.

In early versions of SQL Server, access to wait statistics required the use of undocumented commands. Figure 1-1 shows how to query wait statistics information in SQL Server 6.5 using the DBCC command.

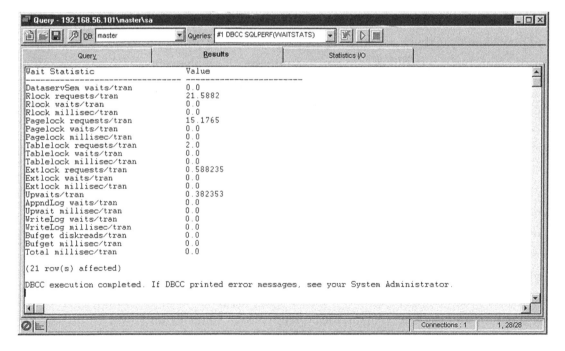

Figure 1-1. *SQL Server wait statistics for SQL Server 6.5*

One of the big changes introduced with SQL Server 2005 was the conversion of many internal functions and commands into Dynamic Management Views (DMVs) and Dynamic Management Functions (DMFs). This made it easier to query and analyze the information returned by functions and commands, including wait statistics information. A new way of performance analysis was born with the release of the SQL Server 2005 Microsoft whitepaper *SQL Server 2005 Waits and Queues* by Tom Davidson.

In the subsequent releases of SQL Server, the volume of new and different wait types grew exponentially whenever new features or configuration options were introduced. If you look at Figure 1-1, you will notice that 21 different wait types were returned. Figure 1-2 shows the amount of wait types, as the number of rows returned, available in SQL Server 2022.

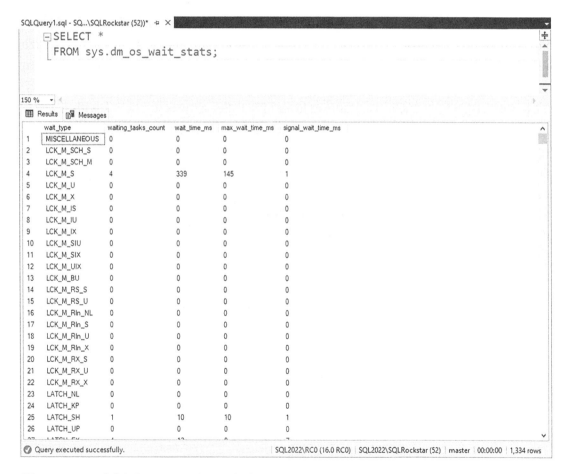

Figure 1-2. *SQL Server wait statistics in SQL Server 2022*

With the release of SQL Server 2022 RC0, the number of wait types increased to more than 1,300 different wait types! The number of wait types will likely continue to grow in future SQL Server releases, as new features are introduced or existing features are changed. Thankfully there is a lot more information available about wait statistics now than there was in SQL Server 6.5!

The SQLOS

The world of computer hardware changes constantly. Every year, or in some cases every month, we stuff more cores inside of processors, increase the memory capacity of mainboards, or introduce entirely new hardware concepts like PCI-based persistent flash storage. Database Management Systems (or DBMSs) are eager to take advantage of new hardware trends. Because of the fast-changing nature of hardware and the need to utilize new hardware options as soon as they become available, the SQL Server team decided to change the SQL Server platform layer starting with SQL Server 2005.

Before SQL Server 2005, the platform layer of SQL Server was restricted, with many operations performed by the operating system itself. This meant it was difficult for SQL Server to keep up with the fast-changing world of server hardware, as changing a complete operating system in order to utilize faster hardware or new hardware features is a time-consuming and complex operation.

Figure 1-3 shows the (simplified) architecture of SQL Server before the introduction of the SQLOS in SQL Server 2005.

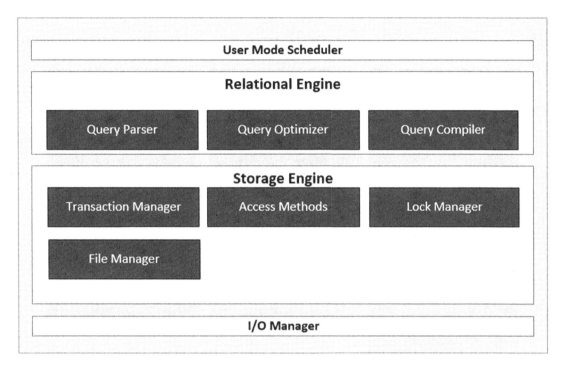

Figure 1-3. *SQL Server architecture before the introduction of SQLOS*

SQL Server 2005 introduced one of the biggest changes to the SQL Server engine seen to this day, the SQLOS. This is a completely new platform layer functioning as a user-level operating system. The SQLOS has made it possible to fully utilize current and future hardware and has enabled features like advanced parallelism. The SQLOS is highly configurable and adjusts itself to the hardware it is running on, thus making it perfectly scalable for high-end or low-end systems alike.

Figure 1-4 shows the (simplified) architecture of SQL Server 2005, including the SQLOS layer.

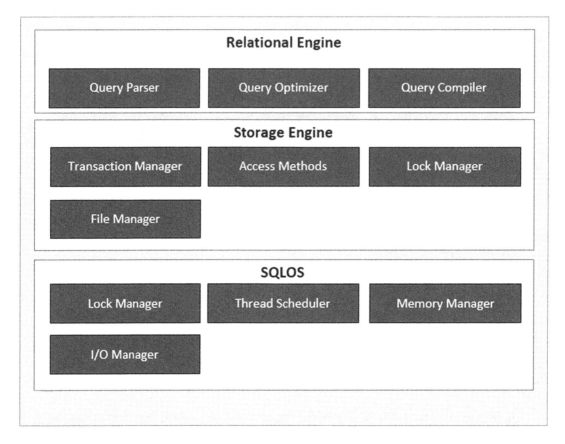

Figure 1-4. *SQL Server 2005 architecture*

The SQLOS changed the way SQL Server accesses processor resources by introducing schedulers, tasks, and worker threads. This gives the SQLOS greater control of how work should be completed by the processors. The Windows operating system uses a preemptive scheduling approach. This means that Windows will give every process that needs processor time a priority and fixed slice of time, or a quantum. This process priority is calculated from a number of variables like resource usage, expected runtime, current activity, and so forth. By using preemptive scheduling, the Windows operating system can choose to interrupt a process when a process with a higher priority needs processor time. This way of scheduling can have a negative impact on processes generated by SQL Server, since those processes could easily be interrupted by higher priority ones, including those of other applications. For this reason, the SQLOS uses its own (cooperative) non-preemptive scheduling mechanism, making sure that Windows processes cannot interrupt SQLOS processes.

Nerd Note   SQL Server 7 and SQL Server 2000 also used non-preemptive scheduling using User Mode Scheduling (UMS). SQLOS brought many more system components closer together, thus enabling better performance and scalability.

There are some exceptions when the SQLOS cannot use non-preemptive scheduling, for instance, when the SQLOS needs to access a resource through the Windows operating system. We will discuss these exceptions later in this book in Chapter 11, "Preemptive Wait Types."

Schedulers, Tasks, and Worker Threads

Because SQLOS uses a different method to execute requests than the Windows operating system uses, SQL Server introduced a different way to schedule processor time using schedulers, tasks, and worker threads. Figure 1-5 shows the different parts of SQL Server scheduling and how they relate to each other.

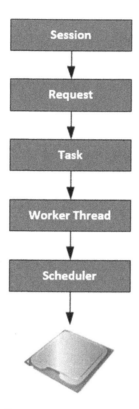

Figure 1-5. *SQL Server scheduling*

Sessions

A session is the connection a client has to SQL Server after it has been successfully authenticated. We can access session information by querying the **sys.dm_exec_ sessions** DMV using the following query:

```
SELECT *
FROM sys.dm_exec_sessions;
```

In older versions of SQL Server, user sessions had a session_id greater than 50; everything lower was reserved for internal SQL Server processes. However, on very busy servers, there was a possibility SQL Server needed to use a session_id greater than 50. If you are only interested in information about user-initiated sessions, it is better to filter the results of the sys.dm_exec_sessions DMV using the is_user_process column instead of filtering on a session_id greater than 50. The following query will only return user sessions and will filter out the internal system sessions:

```
SELECT *
FROM sys.dm_exec_sessions
WHERE is_user_process = 1;
```

Figure 1-6 shows a small part of the results of this query.

	session_id	login_time	host_name	program_name	host_process_id	client_version
1	51	2022-09-26 18:57:56.310	SQL2022	SQLServerCEIP	5644	7
2	52	2022-09-26 18:56:24.513	SQL2022	Microsoft SQL Server Management Studio - Query	1848	7
3	58	2022-09-26 18:56:19.373	SQL2022	Microsoft SQL Server Management Studio	1848	7
4	59	2022-09-26 18:56:19.373	SQL2022	Microsoft SQL Server Management Studio	1848	7

Figure 1-6. *sys.dm_exec_sessions results*

There are many columns returned by the sys.dm_exec_sessions DMV that provide information about each session. Some of the more interesting columns include the following:

> **host_process_id** – The process ID or (PID) of the client program connected to SQL Server will show NULL for internal sessions.

> **cpu_time** – The amount of processor time (in milliseconds) the session has used since it was first established.

> **memory_usage** – The amount of memory (8k pages) used by the session since it was first established.

> **reads** – Number of reads performed by this session since it was first established.

> **writes** – Number of writes performed by this session since it was first established.

> **row_count** – Number of rows returned for this session up to this point.

> **status** – Possible values include "running," "sleeping," "dormant," and "preconnect."

The most common values of the status column are "running," which indicates that one or more requests are currently being processed from this session, and "sleeping," which means no requests are currently being processed from this session.

Requests

A request is the SQL Server execution engine's representation of a query submitted by a session. Again, we will use a DMV to query information about a request; in this case, we query the **sys.dm_exec_requests** DMV:

```
SELECT *
FROM sys.dm_exec_requests;
```

Figure 1-7 shows a portion of the results of this query.

	session_id	request_id	start_time	status	command	sql_handle
1	1	0	2022-09-26 18:56:32.047	sleeping	TASK MANAGER	NULL
2	2	0	2022-09-26 13:42:32.940	background	PARALLEL REDO TASK	NULL
3	3	0	2022-09-26 13:42:32.940	background	PARALLEL REDO TASK	NULL
4	4	0	2022-09-26 18:56:32.047	sleeping	TASK MANAGER	NULL
5	5	0	2022-09-26 13:42:32.953	background		NULL
6	6	0	2022-09-26 13:42:32.970	background	XIO_RETRY_WORKER	NULL
7	7	0	2022-09-26 13:42:32.970	background	XIO_LEASE_RENEWAL_WORKER	NULL
8	8	0	2022-09-26 13:42:33.127	background	XTP_CKPT_AGENT	NULL
9	9	0	2022-09-26 13:42:33.507	background	RECOVERY WRITER	NULL
10	10	0	2022-09-26 13:42:33.507	background	PVS_PREALLOCATOR	NULL
11	11	0	2022-09-26 13:42:33.507	background	POPULATE_LOCK_ORDINALS_TASK	NULL
12	12	0	2022-09-26 13:42:33.520	background	LAZY WRITER	NULL
13	13	0	2022-09-26 13:42:33.537	background	LOG WRITER	NULL
14	14	0	2022-09-26 13:42:35.973	background	SIGNAL HANDLER	NULL
15	15	0	2022-09-26 13:42:33.553	background	LOCK MONITOR	NULL

Figure 1-7. *sys.dm_exec_requests results*

The sys.dm_exec_requests DMV is an incredibly powerful tool for troubleshooting performance-related issues. This DMV has a lot of information about current queries and helps detect performance bottlenecks relatively quickly. Because the sys.dm_exec_requests DMV also displays wait statistics–related information, we will take a thorough look at it in Chapter 2, "Querying SQL Server Wait Statistics."

Tasks

Tasks represent the work to be performed by the SQLOS, but tasks do not perform any work themselves. When a request is received by SQL Server, one or more tasks are created to fulfill the request. The number of tasks generated for a request depends on if the query request is being performed using parallelism or if it's being run serially.

We will use the **sys.dm_os_tasks** DMV to query the task information:

```
SELECT *
FROM sys.dm_os_tasks;
```

Figure 1-8 shows a part of the results of the query.

	task_address	task_state	context_switches_count	pending_io_count	pending_io_byte_count	pending_io_byte_average	scheduler_id
1	0x000001BBAE0784E8	SUSPENDED	684	0	0	0	0
2	0x000001BBAE0788C8	RUNNING	3	0	0	0	0
3	0x000001BBAE078CA8	SUSPENDED	21	0	0	0	0
4	0x000001BBAE079088	RUNNING	7	0	0	0	0
5	0x000001BBAE079848	DONE	NULL	NULL	NULL	NULL	0
6	0x000001BBAE079C28	SUSPENDED	5	0	0	0	0
7	0x000001BBB54F8108	SUSPENDED	5	0	0	0	0
8	0x000001BBB54F84E8	SUSPENDED	36961	0	0	0	0
9	0x000001BBB54F88C8	RUNNING	3	0	0	0	0
10	0x000001BBAE079468	SUSPENDED	8	0	0	0	0
11	0x000001BBB54F8CA8	SUSPENDED	1	0	0	0	0
12	0x000001BBB54F9088	SUSPENDED	37404	0	0	0	0
13	0x000001BBB54F9468	SUSPENDED	988	121	0	0	0
14	0x000001BBB54F9C28	DONE	NULL	NULL	NULL	NULL	0
15	0x000001BBBD814CA8	SUSPENDED	1	0	0	0	0

Figure 1-8. *sys.dm_os_tasks results*

When you query the sys.dm_os_tasks DMV, you will discover it returns many results, even on servers with little user activity. This is because SQL Server uses tasks for its own processes as well.

There are some interesting columns in this DMV worth exploring to see the relations between different DMVs:

> **session_id** – The ID of the session which requested this task.
>
> **worker_address** – The memory address of the worker thread associated with this task.
>
> **task_address** – The memory address of this task.
>
> **task_state** – Possible values include "pending," "runnable," "running," "suspended," "done," and "spinloop."

The most common values of the task_state column are "running," "runnable," and "suspended."

Worker Threads

Every task created has a worker thread assigned, and the worker thread then performs the actions requested by the task.

Nerd Note   A worker thread does not perform the work itself; instead it requests a thread from the Windows operating system to perform the work. For the sake of simplicity, and the fact the Windows thread runs outside the SQLOS, I have left this step out of Figure 1-5. You can access information about the Windows operating system threads by querying **sys.dm_os_threads** if you are interested.

When a task requests a worker thread, SQL Server will first look for an idle worker thread to assign to the task. In the case when no idle worker thread is located and the maximum number of worker threads has been reached, the request is queued until a worker thread finishes its current work and becomes available.

There is a limit to the number of worker threads SQL Server has available for processing requests. This number is automatically calculated and configured by SQL Server during startup. We calculate the maximum number of worker threads ourselves using these formulas:

32-bit system with <= 4 logical processors	256 worker threads
32-bit system with > 4 logical processors	256 + ((# of logical processors – 4) * 8)
64-bit system with <= 4 logical processors	512 worker threads
64-bit system with > 4 logical processors	512 + ((# of logical processors – 4) * 16)

Example: For a 64-bit system with 16 logical processors, we calculate the maximum number of worker threads using the preceding formula:

```
512 + ((# of logical processors - 4) * 16) =
512 + ((16 - 4) * 16) =
512 + (12 * 16) =
512 + (192) = 704
```

which would assign a maximum of 704 worker threads.

The number of worker threads has a default of 0, allowing SQL Server to set the number of max worker threads using the preceding formulas when it starts. We alter the default by changing the **max worker threads** options in SQL Server's properties, as illustrated by Figure 1-9.

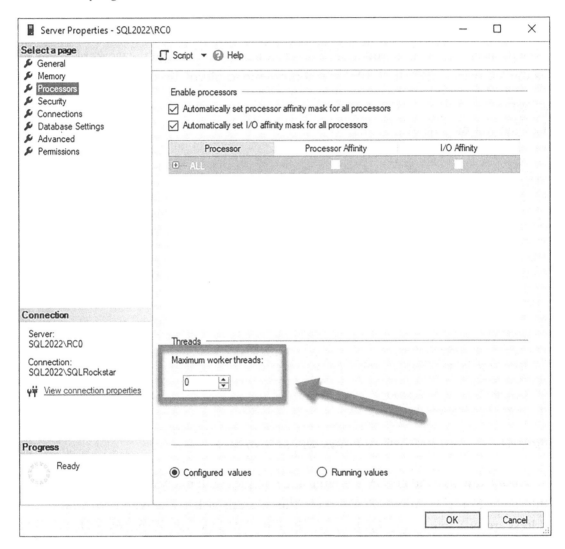

Figure 1-9. *Processors page in the Server Properties*

Generally speaking, you should not need to change the max worker threads option, and my advice is to leave the setting alone, as it should only be changed in very specific cases (I will discuss one of those potential cases in Chapter 5, "CPU-Related Wait Types," when we talk about THREADPOOL waits).

One thing to keep in mind is worker threads require memory to work. For 32-bit systems, this is 512 KB for every worker thread; 64-bit systems will need 2048 KB for every worker thread. Thus, changing the number of worker threads can potentially impact the memory requirements of SQL Server. This does not mean you need a massive amount of memory just for your worker threads – SQL Server will automatically destroy idle worker threads after 15 minutes or if SQL Server is under heavy memory pressure.

SQL Server supplies us with a DMV to query information about the worker threads, **sys.dm_os_workers**. Figure 1-10 shows some of the results of this query:

```
SELECT *
FROM sys.dm_os_workers;
```

	worker_address	status	is_preemptive	is_fiber	is_sick	is_in_cc_exception	is_fatal_exception	is_inside_catch
1	0x000001DA64380180	2	0	0	0	0	0	0
2	0x000001DA64382180	4	1	0	0	0	0	0
3	0x000001DA6438A180	2	0	0	0	0	0	0
4	0x000001DA64400180	4	1	0	0	0	0	0
5	0x000001DA64392180	2	0	0	0	0	0	0
6	0x000001DA64500180	8388608	0	0	0	0	0	0
7	0x000001DA6439A180	2	0	0	0	0	0	0
8	0x000001DA64580180	2097156	1	0	0	0	0	0
9	0x000001DA64582180	8388612	1	0	0	0	0	0
10	0x000001DA64402180	8388608	0	0	0	0	0	0
11	0x000001DA643D4180	4	1	0	0	0	0	0
12	0x000001DA64410180	8388608	0	0	0	0	0	0
13	0x000001DA643E2180	8388608	0	0	0	0	0	0
14	0x000001DA64412180	8388608	0	0	0	0	0	0
15	0x000001DA64510180	8388608	0	0	0	0	0	0
16	0x000001DA6BE02180	8388608	0	0	0	0	0	0

Figure 1-10. Results of querying sys.dm_os_workers

The sys.dm_os_workers DMV is large and complex with many columns marked as "Internal use only" by Microsoft. However, the columns task_address and scheduler_address are available to link together the different DMVs we have discussed so far.

Worker threads iterate through different phases while exposed to the processor, which we observe when we examine the state column in the sys.dm_os_workers DMV:

- INIT – The worker thread is initialized by the SQLOS.

- RUNNING – The worker thread is currently performing work on a processor.

- RUNNABLE – The worker thread is ready to run on a processor.

- SUSPENDED – The worker thread is waiting for a resource.

The states the worker threads go through while performing work is the main focus of this book. Every time a worker thread is not in the "RUNNING" state, it has to wait, and the SQLOS records this information giving us valuable insight into what the worker thread has been waiting on and how long it has been waiting.

Schedulers

The scheduler component's main task is to – surprise – schedule work in the form of tasks on a physical processor(s). When a task requests processor time, it is the scheduler that assigns worker threads to the task, so the request is processed. The scheduler is also responsible for making sure worker threads cooperate with each other and yield the processor when their slice of time, or quantum, has expired. We call this cooperative, or non-preemptive, scheduling. The need for worker threads to yield when their processor time has expired comes from the fact that a scheduler allows only one worker thread to run on a processor at a time. If the worker threads didn't need to yield, a worker thread might stay on the processor for an infinite amount of time, blocking all usage of that processor.

There is a one-on-one relation between processors and schedulers. If your system has two processors, each with four cores, there will be eight schedulers that the SQLOS can use to process user requests, each of them mapped to one of the logical processors.

We can access information about the schedulers by running a query against the **sys.dm_os_schedulers** DMV:

```
SELECT *
FROM sys.dm_os_schedulers;
```

The results of the query are shown in Figure 1-11.

	scheduler_address	parent_node_id	scheduler_id	cpu_id	status	is_online	is_idle	preemptive_switches_count
1	0x000001DA64340040	0	0	0	VISIBLE ONLINE	1	1	777
2	0x000001DA64360040	0	1	1	VISIBLE ONLINE	1	1	37870
3	0x000001DA64480040	0	2	2	VISIBLE ONLINE	1	1	667
4	0x000001DA644A0040	0	3	3	VISIBLE ONLINE	1	0	28884
5	0x000001DA644C0040	0	1048578	0	HIDDEN ONLINE	1	0	0
6	0x000001DA646C0040	64	1048576	0	VISIBLE ONLINE (DAC)	1	1	8
7	0x000001DA6CA00040	0	1048579	1	HIDDEN ONLINE	1	1	6
8	0x000001DA6CA20040	0	1048580	2	HIDDEN ONLINE	1	1	2
9	0x000001DA6BCC0040	0	1048581	3	HIDDEN ONLINE	1	1	0
10	0x000001DA6BCA0040	0	1048582	0	HIDDEN ONLINE	1	1	0
11	0x000001DA6BCE0040	0	1048583	1	HIDDEN ONLINE	1	1	0
12	0x000001DA742C0040	0	1048584	2	HIDDEN ONLINE	1	1	34

Figure 1-11. *sys.dm_os_schedulers query results*

The SQL Server on which I ran this query has two processors with two cores, which means there should be four schedulers to process user requests. If we look at Figure 1-11, however, we notice there are more than four schedulers returned by the query. SQL Server uses its own schedulers to perform internal tasks, and those schedulers are returned by the DMV and marked "HIDDEN ONLINE" in the status column. The schedulers available for user requests are marked as "VISIBLE ONLINE." There is also a special type of scheduler with the status "VISIBLE ONLINE (DAC)." This is a scheduler dedicated for use with the Dedicated Administrator Connection (DAC). This scheduler makes it possible to connect to SQL Server in situations where it is unresponsive, for instance, when there are no free worker threads available on the schedulers processing user requests.

We view the number of worker threads a scheduler has associated with it by looking at the current_workers_count column. This number also includes worker threads not performing any work. The active_workers_count shows us the worker threads that are active on the specific scheduler. This doesn't mean they are running on the processor, as worker threads with states of "RUNNING," "RUNNABLE," and "SUSPENDED" also count toward this number. The work_queue_count is also an interesting column as it provides insight into how many tasks are waiting for a free worker thread. If you see high numbers in this column, it might mean you are experiencing CPU pressure.

Putting It All Together

All SQL Server scheduling parts discussed above are connected to each other, as every connection, session, and query request passes through these same components. The following text is an example of how a query request would get processed:

> A user connects to the SQL Server through an application.
>
> ↓
>
> SQL Server creates a session after the login process is completed successfully.
>
> ↓
>
> When the user sends a query to the SQL Server, a task and a request are created to represent the unit of work that needs to be done.
>
> ↓
>
> The scheduler will assign worker threads to the task so it can be completed.

To see this information in SQL Server, we join some of the DMVs discussed. The query in Listing 1-1 will show you an example of how to combine different DMVs to get scheduling information about a specific session (in this case a session with an ID of 55).

Listing 1-1. Join the different DMVs together to query scheduling information

```
SELECT
  r.session_id AS 'Session ID',
  r.command AS 'Type of Request',
  qt.[text] AS 'Query Text',
  t.task_address AS 'Task Address',
  t.task_state AS 'Task State',
  w.worker_address AS 'Worker Address',
  w.[state] AS 'Worker State',
  s.scheduler_address AS 'Scheduler Address',
  s.[status] AS 'Scheduler State'
FROM sys.dm_exec_requests r
```

```
CROSS APPLY sys.dm_exec_sql_text(r.sql_handle) qt
INNER JOIN sys.dm_os_tasks t
    ON r.task_address = t.task_address
INNER JOIN sys.dm_os_workers w
    ON t.worker_address = w.worker_address
INNER JOIN sys.dm_os_schedulers s
    ON w.scheduler_address = s.scheduler_address
WHERE r.session_id = 70;
```

Figure 1-12 shows the information that the query returned on my test SQL Server. To keep the results readable, I only selected columns from the DMVs to show the relation between them.

	Session ID	Type of Request	Query Text	Task Address	Task State	Worker Address	Worker State	Scheduler Address	Scheduler State
1	70	SELECT	SELECT r.session_id AS 'Session ID', r.com...	0x000001DA7A9ACCA8	RUNNING	0x000001DA7B1D4180	RUNNING	0x000001DA644A0040	VISIBLE ONLINE

Figure 1-12. *Results of the query from Listing 1-1*

In the results, we see Session ID 70 made a SELECT query request. In the query from Listing 1-1, we obtain the text of the query request using a cross apply with the sys. dm_exec_sql_text Dynamic Management Function. The request was then mapped to a task, and the task began running. The task was then mapped to a worker thread, and the task was now in a running state. This meant the query began processing on a processor. The Scheduler Address column shows on which specific scheduler our worker thread was run.

Wait Statistics

So far, we have gone deep into the different components which perform scheduling for SQL Server and how they are interconnected. Now we turn our attention to the main topic of this book: wait statistics.

In the section on worker threads earlier in this chapter, I described the states a worker thread is in while performing work on a scheduler. When a worker thread is performing its work, it goes through three different phases (or queues) in the scheduler process. Depending on the phase (or queue) a worker thread is in, it will enter the "RUNNING," "RUNNABLE," or "SUSPENDED" state. Figure 1-13 shows an abstract view of a scheduler with the different phases.

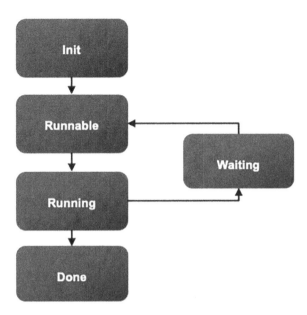

Figure 1-13. *Scheduler and its phases and queues*

When a worker thread obtains access to a scheduler, it will generally start in the Waiter List and be assigned the "SUSPENDED" state. The Waiter List (shown as Waiting in Figure 1-13) is an unordered list of worker threads with the "SUSPENDED" state and is waiting for resources to become available. Here, resources are anything on the system, such as data pages or maybe a lock request. While a worker thread is in the Waiter List, the SQLOS records the type of resource it needs to continue its work (this is the wait type) and the time it spends waiting before that specific resource becomes available (this is the resource wait time).

When a worker thread receives access to the resources it needs, it will move to the Runnable Queue, a first-in-first-out list of all worker threads with access to their resources and ready to be run on a processor. The time a worker thread spends in the Runnable Queue is recorded as the signal wait time.

The top worker thread in the Runnable Queue will move to the "RUNNING" phase, where it will receive processor time to perform its work. The time it spends on the processor is recorded as CPU time. In the meantime, the other worker threads in the Runnable Queue move up the list, and worker threads that have received their requested resources move from the Waiter List into the Runnable Queue.

Nerd Note   The Runnable Queue is a first-in-first-out list (FIFO). If this was not true, a task could theoretically never move from runnable to running on a busy system. The Waiter List, however, is not FIFO.

While a worker thread is in the "RUNNING" phase, there are three scenarios that can happen:

1. The worker thread needs additional resources; in this case, it moves from the "RUNNING" phase to the Waiter List (what we see as SUSPENDED).

2. The worker thread spends its quantum (fixed value of 4 milliseconds) and therefore must yield; the worker thread is moved to the bottom of the Runnable Queue.

3. The worker thread is done with its work and will leave the scheduler.

Worker threads move through the three different phases all the time. It is common for one worker thread to rotate through multiple times until all work is done.

Knowing the different lengths of time a request spends in one of the three different phases makes it possible to calculate total request execution time and also the total time a request waits for either processor time or resource time.

Expressed as a mathematical formula, the total request execution time would look like this:

TotalRequestExecutionTime = Running time + Runnable time + Suspended time

This can also be written as the following:

TotalRequestExecutionTime = CPU time + Signal wait time + Resource wait time

Since there is a lot of terminology involved in the scheduling of worker threads in SQL Server, let's show an example on how worker threads move through a scheduler.

Figure 1-14 shows you an abstract image of the Waiter Queue, the Runnable Queue, and a processor executing a request.

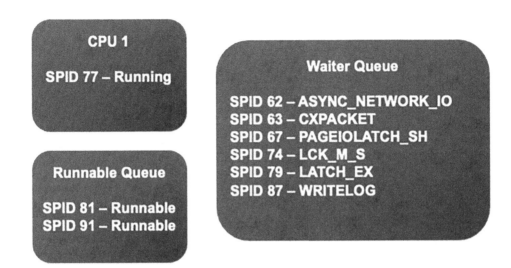

Figure 1-14. *Scheduler with requests*

In this example, we see a request from SPID 77 running on the processor; this request will have the state "RUNNING." There are requests in the Waiter Queue waiting for resources. I won't go into detail about the wait types listed since we will be covering wait types in Part II of this book. While these sessions are in the Waiter Queue SQL Server will record the time spent as wait time, and the wait type will be noted as the representation of the resource they are waiting for. If we query information about these threads, they will have the "SUSPENDED" state. SPID 81 and SPID 91 have their resources ready and are waiting in the Runnable Queue for SPID 77 to complete its work on the processor. While they are waiting in the Runnable Queue, SQL Server records the time they spend there as signal wait time and adds this time to the total wait time. These worker threads will have the status of "RUNNABLE."

In Figure 1-15 we have moved a few milliseconds forward in time; notice how the scheduler and worker threads have moved through the different phases and queues.

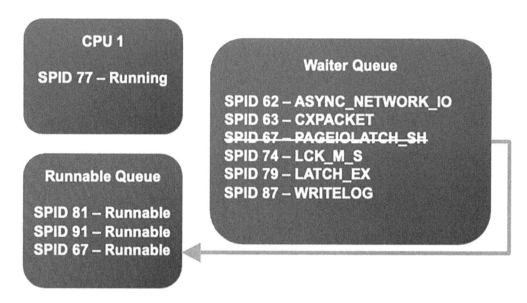

Figure 1-15. *Scheduler with requests after a few milliseconds*

SPID 67 is done waiting for the PAGEIOLATCH_SH wait type and has moved to the bottom of the Runnable Queue. Figure 1-16 shows the next few milliseconds in time.

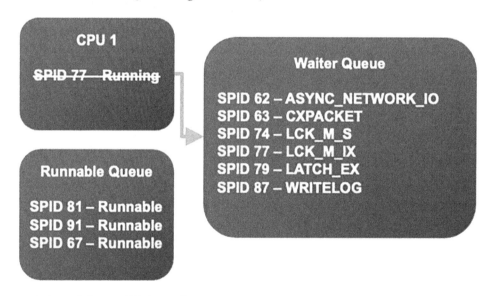

Figure 1-16. *A few milliseconds more*

SPID 77 needs an additional resource and has been placed back into the waiting queue. Here I have chosen to place it in the middle of the image to better represent that the Waiter Queue is not a FIFO queue. Figure 1-17 shows the next few milliseconds.

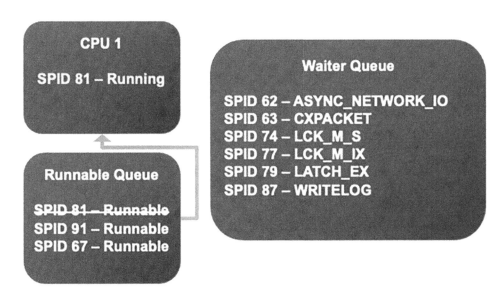

Figure 1-17. *A few milliseconds more*

SPID 81 was the first worker thread in the Runnable Queue, and now with the processor free it moves from the Runnable Queue to the processor, and the state changes from "RUNNABLE" to "RUNNING."

And that is how worker threads move from "SUSPENDED" to "RUNNABLE" to "RUNNING" until the request(s) are complete and they exit the scheduler.

Summary

In this chapter, we reviewed the history of wait statistics throughout various versions of SQL Server. With the introduction of the SQLOS in SQL Server 2005, a lot changed in how SQL Server processed requests, introducing schedulers, worker threads, and tasks. All the information for the various parts are stored in Dynamic Management Views (DMVs) or Dynamic Management Functions (DMFs), which are easily queried and return a lot of information about the internals of SQL Server.

Using these DMVs, we view the progress of requests while they are handled by a SQL Server scheduler and learn if they are waiting for any specific resources. The resources the requests are waiting for and the time they spend waiting for those resources are recorded as wait statistics, the main topic of this book.

CHAPTER 2

Querying SQL Server Wait Statistics

With the introduction of Dynamic Management Views (DMVs) and Dynamic Management Functions (DMFs) in SQL Server 2005, viewing and analyzing wait statistics became easier and less tedious. In SQL Server versions prior to SQL Server 2005, users were limited to the DBCC SQLPERF('WAITSSTATS') command to view wait statistics. Presently, there are a variety of DMVs which return wait statistics related information, and in this chapter, we will take a detailed look at four of the most useful DMVs: **sys.dm_os_wait_stats**, **sys.dm_os_waiting_tasks**, **sys.dm_exec_requests**, and **sys.dm_exec_session_wait_stats**.

Viewing wait statistics information is not only limited to DMVs though. We can also use the Performance Monitor, or Perfmon, to view wait statistics information.

SQL Server 2008 introduced yet another option to view wait statistics, Extended Events. Extended Events were difficult to work with in SQL Server 2008, (you had to write the entire Extended Event session in T-SQL), but Microsoft has drastically improved Extended Events in later versions making them more user-friendly and easier to use.

SQL Server 2016 SP1 introduced two new methods to access wait statistics: through a new DMV called **sys.dm_exec_session_wait_stats** and by adding wait statistics information on a per-query basis inside execution plans.

In SQL Server 2017, Microsoft took recording wait statistics another step forward by including them inside the Query Store. The Query Store is a feature introduced in SQL Server 2016 and acts like a flight recorder for your query workload, logging query statement, performance, and resource utilization.

In this chapter, we will look at the sources which capture wait statistics mentioned in the previous paragraphs, starting with the DMVs. Because the Query Store feature has such a big impact on troubleshooting and analyzing query performance, including wait statistics, we will take a thorough look at it in Chapter 3, "The Query Store."

© Thomas LaRock, Enrico van de Laar 2023
T. LaRock and E. van de Laar, *Pro SQL Server 2022 Wait Statistics*,
https://doi.org/10.1007/978-1-4842-8771-2_2

sys.dm_os_wait_stats

The sys.dm_os_wait_stats DMV is one of the most important DMVs regarding wait statistics. This DMV is the replacement for the DBCC SQLPERF('WAITSTATS') command in use before SQL Server 2005. All the information returned from the DBCC SQLPERF('WAITSTATS') command is included in the sys.dm_os_wait_stats DMV, plus a little bit more.

The **sys.dm_os_wait_stats** DMV shows the total amount of wait time for every wait type since the SQL Server instance was started. It is cumulative, adding wait time to the different wait types, resulting in an ever-increasing total. Querying the sys.dm_os_wait_ stats DMV provides insight into what the query requests were waiting for. This is helpful if you are looking for the grand total of wait time for every wait type, but many times you are interested in the wait time for a specific time segment, or query. In this case, it is possible to reset the sys.dm_os_wait_stats DMV without having to restart SQL Server by using the following command:

```
DBCC SQLPERF('sys.dm_os_wait_stats', CLEAR);
```

This will reset wait statistics information back to 0 again, meaning you lose all information before the reset. In Chapter 4, "Building a Solid Baseline," we will examine a method which will not completely reset the sys.dm_os_wait_stats counters.

As with every DMV in SQL Server, we execute a query against the sys.dm_os_wait_ stats DMV as if it were a table, in this case:

```
SELECT *
FROM sys.dm_os_wait_stats;
```

The results of this query are shown in Figure 2-1.

	wait_type	waiting_tasks_count	wait_time_ms	max_wait_time_ms	signal_wait_time_ms
1	MISCELLANEOUS	0	0	0	0
2	LCK_M_SCH_S	0	0	0	0
3	LCK_M_SCH_M	0	0	0	0
4	LCK_M_S	7	19419	4340	0
5	LCK_M_U	0	0	0	0
6	LCK_M_X	0	0	0	0
7	LCK_M_IS	0	0	0	0
8	LCK_M_IU	0	0	0	0
9	LCK_M_IX	0	0	0	0
10	LCK_M_SIU	0	0	0	0
11	LCK_M_SIX	0	0	0	0
12	LCK_M_UIX	0	0	0	0

Figure 2-1. *sys.dm_os_wait_stats*

Following are the available columns in the sys.dm_os_wait_stats DMV, along with a description of what the column represents:

wait_type – The name of the wait type. The sys.dm_os_wait_stats will return one row for every wait type possible for the specific SQL Server installation.

waiting_tasks_count – The count of how many times a worker thread had to wait for that specific wait type.

wait_time_ms – The total wait time in milliseconds for the specific wait type since the start of the SQL Server instance or a manual reset. This is the time a worker thread has spent in the Waiter List in the "SUSPENDED" state. It also includes the time the worker thread spent in the Runnable Queue in the "RUNNABLE" state while waiting for the scheduler to grant it processor time.

max_wait_time_ms – The maximum wait time in milliseconds a worker thread waited on the specific wait type.

signal_wait_time_ms – The amount of time in milliseconds the worker thread spent in Runnable Queue waiting for an available processor.

Nerd Note   Signal wait times are unavoidable and normal in systems where a large number of queries are being processed, all of them requesting time on the processor. The signal wait time is also an important metric for detecting CPU pressure. Generally speaking, depending on the hardware of your system, seeing signal wait time metrics higher than 15% of the total wait time **MIGHT** indicate CPU pressure, because the worker threads are waiting for a processor to become available.

You may have noticed the sys.dm_os_wait_stats DMV does not return a column for the resource wait time. If we want to display the resource wait time as an additional column, we will need to calculate the value ourselves.

Listing 2-1 shows a query to analyze the sys.dm_os_wait_stats DMV. Besides the regular columns, it will add two more columns for every wait type returned, the resource wait time and the average wait time.

Listing 2-1. sys.dm_os_wait_stats with additional information

```
SELECT  wait_type AS 'Wait Type',
waiting_tasks_count AS 'Waiting Tasks Count',
(wait_time_ms - signal_wait_time_ms) AS 'Resource Wait Time',
signal_wait_time_ms AS 'Signal Wait Time',
wait_time_ms AS 'Total Wait Time',
COALESCE(wait_time_ms / NULLIF(waiting_tasks_count,0), 0) AS 'Average
Wait Time'
FROM sys.dm_os_wait_stats;
```

This query will return results similar to what is shown in Figure 2-2.

	Wait Type	Waiting Tasks Count	Resource Wait Time	Signal Wait Time	Total Wait Time	Average Wait Time
134	LAZYWRITER_...	151605	152949455	4473	152953928	1008
135	IO_COMPLETION	1283	1839	9	1848	1
136	ASYNC_IO_COM...	2	81	0	81	40
137	ASYNC_NETWO...	10449	511	161	672	0
138	PREFAULT_IO_...	0	0	0	0	0
139	SLEEP_BPOOL_...	18	2	0	2	0
140	SLEEP_BPOOL_...	0	0	0	0	0
141	CHKPT	1	715	0	715	715
142	SLEEP_DBSTA...	41	4430	0	4430	108
143	SLEEP_MASTE...	1	69	0	69	69
144	SLEEP_MASTE...	1	113	0	113	113
145	SLEEP_MASTE...	1	209	0	209	209

Figure 2-2. *sys.dm_os_wait_stats expanded with more wait information*

Having both the number of occurrences of a specific wait type and the total wait time makes it possible to calculate an average wait time (represented by the Average Wait Time column in Figure 2-2) for the specific wait type by dividing the wait_time_ms value by the waiting_tasks_count value.

The sys.dm_os_wait_stats is a powerful DMV containing information about the different wait types. It will serve as the basis for the wait statistics baseline methodology outlined in Chapter 4, "Building a Solid Baseline."

sys.dm_os_waiting_tasks

While the sys.dm_os_wait_stats DMV provides cumulative wait statistics information, the **sys.dm_os_waiting_tasks** DMV provides information for the waiting queue of your SQL Server instance. Querying this DMV gives an overview of all tasks with worker threads waiting in either the Waiter List or Runnable Queue for either resource or processor time.

Understanding sys.dm_os_waiting_tasks

Because the sys.dm_os_waiting_tasks DMV shows tasks currently waiting, it is often the first DMV for reviewing the performance of your SQL Server instance. It also supplies additional information for certain wait types which are useful while troubleshooting.

Figure 2-3 shows the results of the following query:

```
SELECT *
FROM sys.dm_os_waiting_tasks;
```

	waiting_task_address	session_id	exec_context_id	wait_duration_ms	wait_type	resource_address	blocking_task_address
1	0x000001DA6407C8C8	21	0	27398	XE_DISPATCHER_WAIT	NULL	NULL
2	0x000001DA6407D848	9	0	40573	DISPATCHER_QUEUE_SEMAPHORE	NULL	NULL
3	0x000001DA6407DC28	11	0	560	SLEEP_TASK	NULL	NULL
4	0x000001DA6C64E108	34	0	153276349	ONDEMAND_TASK_QUEUE	0x0000007BE11FE930	NULL
5	0x000001DA6C64E4E8	20	0	1430	REQUEST_FOR_DEADLOCK_SEARCH	0x0000007BE19FEAE0	NULL
6	0x000001DA6C64F468	37	0	496	SLEEP_TASK	NULL	NULL
7	0x000001DA64386CA8	NULL	NULL	12614	QDS_PERSIST_TASK_MAIN_LOOP_SLEEP	NULL	NULL
8	0x000001DA64387468	3	0	153277370	DISPATCHER_QUEUE_SEMAPHORE	NULL	NULL
9	0x000001DA64387848	6	0	153277370	DISPATCHER_QUEUE_SEMAPHORE	NULL	NULL
10	0x000001DA64387C28	NULL	NULL	153277122	XTP_PREEMPTIVE_TASK	NULL	NULL
11	0x000001DA64387088	33	0	44544018	CHECKPOINT_QUEUE	0x0000007BDF7FED20	NULL
12	0x000001DA6C668108	16	0	449	LAZYWRITER_SLEEP	NULL	NULL

Figure 2-3. *sys.dm_os_waiting_tasks*

Following is a list of columns returned by the sys.dm_os_waiting_tasks DMV and a description of the information they return:

waiting_task_address – The address of the task currently waiting.

session_id – The ID of the session associated with the specific task.

exec_context_id – The ID of the execution context. This value will only change from the default of 0 if the task is being performed using parallelism (the task is using multiple threads instead of a single thread).

wait_duration_ms – The time in milliseconds the task has been waiting. Just like in the sys.dm_os_wait_stats DMV, this time includes both the resource wait time and the signal wait time.

wait_type – The wait type the task is currently waiting on.

resource_address – The memory address information about the resource we are currently waiting for. Not all wait types will log this memory address, so it will frequently be returned as NULL.

blocking_task_address – The address of the task currently blocking the waiting task. When the task is not being blocked by another task, this column will return NULL.

blocking_session_id – The session ID of the session currently blocking the task. Just like the blocking_task_address, this information is only included when this task is being currently blocked by another task. It will return NULL when there is no blocking or when the session information about the blocking task cannot be retrieved or identified. We will explain blocking and locking in Chapter 8, "Lock-Related Wait Types," when we discuss lock wait types.

blocking_exec_context_id – Another column dedicated to information regarding blocking. In this case, it will return the ID of the execution context. This will only return a result other than NULL when a task gets executed using parallelism and one of the threads is responsible for the block. The blocking_exec_context_id can then be used to identify which one of the threads is responsible for the block.

resource_description – Additional information about the resource the task is waiting for. There aren't many wait types for this column – most often parallelism and lock- or latch-related wait types. It is a very useful column when analyzing lock- or latch-related wait types; in those cases, we pinpoint the database object (data page, row, table, etc.) whose availability we are waiting for. Some of the examples later in this book (most notably Chapter 8, "Lock-Related Wait Types," and Chapter 9, "Latch-Related Wait Types") will make use of this column to gather extra information about the resource we are waiting for.

Querying sys.dm_os_waiting_tasks

Because the sys.dm_os_waiting_tasks DMV returns a wealth of information, there are various ways to utilize it depending on what you want to analyze or troubleshoot.

One query found on various forums on the Internet is the following:

```
SELECT *
FROM sys.dm_os_waiting_tasks
WHERE session_id > 50;
```

This query intends to filter out SQL Server internal session IDs and return waiting tasks that originate from user sessions. As mentioned in Chapter 1, "Wait Statistics Internals," we learned you should not filter by session_id for the purpose of identifying user sessions. The results of the query on my test SQL Server are shown in Figure 2-4.

	waiting_task_address	session_id	exec_context_id	wait_duration_ms	wait_type	resource_address	blocking_task_address
1	0x0000007F7453C108	54	0	0	ASYNC_NETWORK_IO	NULL	NULL

Figure 2-4. *sys.dm_os_waiting_tasks where session_id is greater than 50*

While the method of filtering out internal SQL Server processes appears to work fine for many wait types and improves readability, there are specific wait types which will not be returned when running this query.

One example of this is the THREADPOOL wait type, which we will discuss in Chapter 5, "CPU-Related Wait Types." This wait type often has a large negative impact on the performance of your SQL Server but is not returned if you filter for only user sessions. This will impact your analysis because you are missing important facts!

Another reason to not filter on session IDs is the misconception about the relation of the session ID and whether or not the session ID is a user or internal session. There is no guarantee a session ID larger than 50 is a user session. It is possible for SQL Server to have more than 50 internal sessions, in which case there is a chance you will mistake an internal session for a user session.

I believe the best way to query the sys.dm_os_waiting_tasks DMV is by selecting everything and applying a filter when looking for a specific wait type or session. This will return more rows than filtering by session IDs larger than 50, as you can see in Figure 2-5, but it shows the complete picture and minimizes the chance you might miss important wait types. A good idea is to sort on the session_id column to make the results more readable without losing sight of the internal sessions.

	waiting_task_address	session_id	exec_context_id	wait_duration_ms	wait_type	resource_address	blocking_task_address
1	0x000001DA6407C8C8	21	0	3292	XE_DISPATCHER_WAIT	NULL	NULL
2	0x000001DA6407D848	9	0	20559	DISPATCHER_QUEUE_SEMAPHORE	NULL	NULL
3	0x000001DA6407DC28	11	0	290	SLEEP_TASK	NULL	NULL
4	0x000001DA6C64E108	34	0	159025956	ONDEMAND_TASK_QUEUE	0x0000007BE11FE930	NULL
5	0x000001DA6C64E4E8	20	0	2214	REQUEST_FOR_DEADLOCK_SEARCH	0x0000007BE19FEAE0	NULL
6	0x000001DA6C64F468	37	0	845	SLEEP_TASK	NULL	NULL
7	0x000001DA64386CA8	NULL	NULL	1287	QDS_PERSIST_TASK_MAIN_LOOP_SLEEP	NULL	NULL
8	0x000001DA64387468	3	0	159026977	DISPATCHER_QUEUE_SEMAPHORE	NULL	NULL
9	0x000001DA64387848	6	0	159026977	DISPATCHER_QUEUE_SEMAPHORE	NULL	NULL
10	0x000001DA64387C28	NULL	NULL	159026729	XTP_PREEMPTIVE_TASK	NULL	NULL
11	0x000001DA64387088	33	0	50293625	CHECKPOINT_QUEUE	0x0000007BDF7FED20	NULL
12	0x000001DA6C668108	16	0	813	LAZYWRITER_SLEEP	NULL	NULL

Figure 2-5. *sys.dm_os_waiting_tasks*

sys.dm_exec_requests

The **sys.dm_exec_requests** DMV returns information about each request currently executing inside the SQL Server engine.

Understanding sys.dm_exec_requests

Like the previous DMVs, we query **sys.dm_exec_requests** with the following:

```
SELECT *
FROM sys.dm_exec_requests;
```

This returns every query request currently executing. Figure 2-6 shows a small portion of the results on my test SQL Server.

	session_id	request_id	start_time	status	command	sql_handle	statement_start_offset
12	12	0	2022-09-26 13:42:33.520	background	LAZY WRITER	NULL	NULL
13	13	0	2022-09-26 13:42:33.537	background	LOG WRITER	NULL	NULL
14	14	0	2022-09-26 13:42:35.973	background	SIGNAL HANDLER	NULL	NULL
15	15	0	2022-09-26 13:42:33.553	background	LOCK MONITOR	NULL	NULL
16	16	0	2022-09-26 13:42:35.597	background	BRKR TASK	NULL	NULL
17	17	0	2022-09-26 13:42:33.677	background	RESOURCE MONITOR	NULL	NULL
18	18	0	2022-09-26 13:42:33.677	background	XE TIMER	NULL	NULL
19	19	0	2022-09-26 13:42:33.707	background	XE DISPATCHER	NULL	NULL
20	20	0	2022-09-26 19:06:28.843	sleeping	TASK MANAGER	NULL	NULL
21	21	0	2022-09-26 13:42:34.333	sleeping	TASK MANAGER	NULL	NULL
22	22	0	2022-09-26 13:42:34.333	background	RECEIVE	NULL	NULL
23	23	0	2022-09-26 19:06:28.843	sleeping	TASK MANAGER	NULL	NULL
24	24	0	2022-09-26 19:06:28.843	sleeping	TASK MANAGER	NULL	NULL

Figure 2-6. *sys.dm_exec_requests*

The sys.dm_exec_requests DMV returns more columns than the sys.dm_os_wait_stats or sys.dm_os_waiting_tasks DMVs discussed earlier. To keep things readable, I will describe only the columns frequently used for wait statistics analysis. Here is my list:

> **session_id** – The ID of the session this request is associated with.
>
> **start_time** – The date and time the request arrived. This can be different from when you query the DMV, especially with long-running queries.

command – The action the request is performing. The most common commands are query related, like SELECT, INSERT, UPDATE, and DELETE, but there are more commands depending on the request.

sql_handle – The hash value of the batch or stored procedure executed in the request. Not all requests have a handle, and generally you will only see a handle if the request was initiated by a user session and a query is involved. The sql_handle hash is used as input for the sys.dm_exec_sql_text Dynamic Management Function (DMF) to retrieve the query text.

plan_handle – The hash value of the execution plan. An execution plan will show you the operations performed by SQL Server when executing the query and is a great source of query execution information. We use plan_handle the same way as the sql_handle, as input for the sys.dm_exec_query_plan DMF to return the execution plan of the query.

wait_type – The current wait type if the request is in either the "SUSPENDED" or "RUNNABLE" state. This value will be NULL when the request is currently running (i.e., when it is not waiting).

last_wait_type – The last wait type the request encountered if it waited during execution.

total_elapsed_time – The total time, in milliseconds, since the request arrived.

There are more columns available in this DMV, and all have their different uses. A complete description is available on the Microsoft MSDN page at `https://slrwnds.com/f6glon`, and I encourage you to read the article. The sys.dm_exec_requests DMV is a great tool in your DBA toolkit and is one of those DMVs you will use frequently for all kinds of purposes besides analyzing wait statistics.

Querying sys.dm_exec_requests

The sys.dm_exec_requests DMV gives access to query statements and corresponding execution plans by returning the sql and plan handles. If you are interested in this information, and most of the time you probably are, you must pass the sql_handle and plan_handle to their respective DMFs so the hashes turn into something humans can read and understand.

Listing 2-2 shows a query against the sys.dm_exec_requests DMV and also retrieves the query statements and execution plans. I am excluding my current session ID and ignoring session IDs lower than 50 to keep the result set small for this example.

Listing 2-2. Querying sys.dm_exec_requests

```
SELECT
    r.session_id AS 'Session ID',
    r.start_time AS 'Request Start',
    r.[status] AS 'Current State',
    r.[command] AS 'Request Command',
    t.[text] AS 'Query',
    p.query_plan AS 'Execution Plan'
FROM sys.dm_exec_requests r
OUTER APPLY sys.dm_exec_sql_text(r.sql_handle) AS t
OUTER APPLY sys.dm_exec_query_plan(r.plan_handle) p
WHERE r.session_id > 50
    AND r.session_id <> @@SPID;
```

From my system, the results are shown in Figure 2-7.

	Session ID	Request Start	Current State	Request Command	Query	Execution Plan
1	53	2022-09-26 19:07:24.017	sleeping	TASK MANAGER	NULL	NULL
2	54	2022-09-26 18:57:22.187	sleeping	TASK MANAGER	NULL	NULL
3	55	2022-09-26 19:11:24.750	sleeping	TASK MANAGER	NULL	NULL
4	56	2022-09-26 19:13:25.093	sleeping	TASK MANAGER	NULL	NULL
5	57	2022-09-26 19:15:45.907	runnable	SELECT	SELECT * FROM Sales.SalesOrderDetail sod INNE...	<ShowPlanXML xmlns="ht

Figure 2-7. *Results of Listing 2-2*

Using the query in Listing 2-2, we immediately see session ID 64 is performing a SELECT query, and the query column shows the complete statement executed. The Execution Plan column returns the execution plan in an XML format. We can click the XML link to view the graphical execution plan, as shown in Figure 2-8.

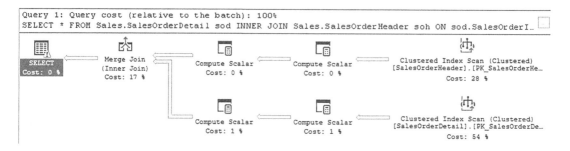

Figure 2-8. *Execution plan*

Using the execution plan, we get insight into how the query is executed by the SQL Server engine. We won't get into the details about execution plans in this book, but you will be using them frequently when you are optimizing query performance, so it is good to know how to access them from the sys.dm_exec_requests DMV.

Nerd Note   When executing a query, the SQL Server engine utilizes the Query Optimizer to determine the most efficient way to return the results. The output of the Query Optimizer is called a query execution plan, sometimes called a query plan, or an execution plan. We discuss execution plans briefly later in this chapter, but if you want more details on execution plans and how to leverage them for performance tuning, check out the series of books by Grant Fritchey.

---

sys.dm_exec_session_wait_stats

One of the latest additions to the wait statistics–related DMVs is the **sys.dm_exec_session_wait_stats** DMV. It was introduced in SQL Server 2016 SP1 and returns wait statistics information on a per-session level. If you remember from Chapter 1, "Wait Statistics Internals," a session is an active connection a user or process has with SQL Server. A session could have multiple requests, which in turn could have multiple tasks performing the actions required to execute a query.

Figure 2-9 shows the columns of the DMV as well as some wait statistics information from my test system.

	session_id	wait_type	waiting_tasks_count	wait_time_ms	max_wait_time_ms	signal_wait_time_ms
1	55	LATCH_SH	3	0	0	0
2	55	PAGELATCH_SH	6	0	0	0
3	55	PAGELATCH_EX	5	0	0	0
4	55	SOS_SCHEDULER_YIELD	1868	503	33	491
5	55	MEMORY_ALLOCATION_EXT	186812	135	0	0
6	55	RESERVED_MEMORY_ALLOCATION_EXT	121913	50	0	0
7	55	LOGMGR_FLUSH	3	0	0	0
8	55	DEADLOCK_ENUM_MUTEX	1	0	0	0
9	55	PREEMPTIVE_OS_QUERYREGISTRY	24	1	0	0
10	55	WAIT_ON_SYNC_STATISTICS_REFRESH	3	4	1	0
11	58	LATCH_SH	40	2	0	0
12	58	LATCH_EX	48	6	0	3
13	58	PAGELATCH_SH	12	0	0	0
14	58	PAGELATCH_EX	12	7	3	0

Figure 2-9. *sys.dm_exec_session_wait_stats*

Does the preceding figure look familiar? It probably does since it is practically identical to the sys.dm_os_wait_stats DMV but with an additional column for the session_id.

But there is more than an additional column. The wait statistics information recorded through sys.dm_exec_session_wait_stats is cumulative *for all requests a specific session performed while it was active.* For instance, if you execute ten different queries inside a single session, the wait times returned by the DMV is the total wait time for those ten queries. This means it is very important to understand what happened during the lifetime of the session. Perhaps the session was executing large batches of queries, or it executed a single query statement. Knowing the workload is important before using this DMV to analyze session wait statistics.

Also, session IDs are reused after a session is closed, meaning you will see commingled wait statistics for both the new session and the old session. When a session ID is reused (or reset when using connection pooling), the wait statistics information inside this DMV for the specific session is reset as well.

With the preceding information in mind, we conclude this DMV is not directly useful as a "first-place-to-look" when performance is reported to be slow. The DMV still has its place though, especially if you reproduce a specific performance issue with a specific action where multiple queries are involved. In this situation, you can zoom in on a specific session ID and reproduce the issue, capturing wait statistics for everything that happens during the execution of the queries.

Combining DMVs to Detect Waits Happening Now

We have reviewed the important DMVs for wait statistics analysis; now, let's see an example of how to use DMVs to find out what is slowing down your SQL Server. Gathering this information will not solve all your problems immediately, but it will provide a clue as to where to start looking for a solution.

Nerd Note   The waits and queue tuning methodology is centered on the idea of resource consumption, where the resources are physical (CPU, memory, disk I/O, network) as well as logical (locking/blocking). As such, the trick here is to understand when it comes to tuning resource consumption you have only two options: *use less* or *buy more*. Once you understand this, it helps guide the actions and solutions possible for your performance issue.

Consider the following scenario: you are the database administrator (DBA) for a large company using a single database to store all sales information. The database is running on a SQL Server instance, and every day, a few hundred users query the database.

Normally everything is running fine – users quickly access the information they want, and everyone who needs to work with the database is happy. Today, however, is not a good day for you as the DBA. The phone hasn't stopped ringing since 10 a.m., and some users are gathering at the door of your office with an angry look in their eyes – querying and inserting sales information is incredibly slow.

Since this book is about wait statistics, let's look at how we analyze wait statistics information regarding the performance problem in the scenario.

We know the sys.dm_os_wait_stats DMV shows cumulative wait statistics information, so for this scenario it wouldn't be much help. A much better starting place would be the sys.dm_os_waiting_tasks DMV, since it will show us all the tasks that are waiting right now.

We run the following query against the sys.dm_os_waiting_tasks DMV:

```
SELECT *
FROM sys.dm_os_waiting_tasks
ORDER BY session_id DESC;
```

While reviewing the results, we see many user sessions with waiting tasks, as shown in Figure 2-10.

	waiting_task_address	session_id	exec_context_id	wait_duration_ms	wait_type	resource_address	blocking_task_address
1	0x000001DA7A9AC108	77	0	28341	LCK_M_S	0x000001DAAEEAEF80	0x000001DA7A9ABC28
2	0x000001DA7A9ABC28	76	0	41595	LCK_M_S	0x000001DAAF3B70C0	NULL
3	0x000001DA7A9AD468	55	0	36520	LCK_M_S	0x000001DAAFBF9840	0x000001DA7A9ABC28
4	0x000001DA6CC01468	38	0	165	HADR_FILESTREAM_IOMGR_IOCOMPLETION	NULL	NULL
5	0x000001DA6C64F468	37	0	817	SLEEP_TASK	NULL	NULL
6	0x000001DA6C65B088	36	0	167947695	BROKER_TRANSMITTER	NULL	NULL
7	0x000001DA6C669088	35	0	167947680	BROKER_EVENTHANDLER	NULL	NULL
8	0x000001DA6C64E108	34	0	167952184	ONDEMAND_TASK_QUEUE	0x0000007BE11FE930	NULL
9	0x000001DA64387088	33	0	997	CHECKPOINT_QUEUE	0x0000007BDF7FED20	NULL
10	0x000001DA6C6684E8	32	0	247616	SP_SERVER_DIAGNOSTICS_SLEEP	0x0000000000000001	NULL
11	0x000001DA74A824E8	31	0	1875	SQLTRACE_INCREMENTAL_FLUSH_SLEEP	NULL	NULL
12	0x000001DA6CC01088	24	0	167947695	BROKER_TRANSMITTER	NULL	NULL
13	0x000001DA64396CA8	23	0	1479	XE_TIMER_EVENT	NULL	NULL
14	0x000001DA6407C8C8	21	0	45555	XE_DISPATCHER_WAIT	NULL	NULL

Figure 2-10. *Results of a query against the sys.dm_os_waiting_tasks DMV*

We notice that the wait times for sessions 55, 76, and 77 seem high, and we also notice they are all waiting with a wait type LCK_M_S. Without going into too many details about this specific wait type (it will be discussed in detail in Chapter 8, "Lock-Related Wait Types") it is enough to know this wait type is related to locking. Sessions 52, 56, and 57 are waiting to place a lock and are blocked by another process with a lock on the same object. We can extract locking and blocking information from the sys.dm_os_waiting_tasks DMF by looking at blocking_columns. For readability reasons, I modified the preceding query to return only blocking information from the sys.dm_os_waiting_tasks DMV. Figure 2-11 shows those columns.

	session_id	wait_type	blocking_task_address	blocking_session_id	blocking_exec_context_id
1	77	LCK_M_S	0x000001DA7A9A9088	76	NULL
2	76	LCK_M_S	NULL	65	NULL
3	55	LCK_M_S	0x000001DA7A9A9088	76	NULL
4	38	HADR_FILESTREAM_IOMGR_IOCOMPLETION	NULL	NULL	NULL
5	37	SLEEP_TASK	NULL	NULL	NULL
6	36	BROKER_TRANSMITTER	NULL	NULL	NULL
7	35	BROKER_EVENTHANDLER	NULL	NULL	NULL

Figure 2-11. *Blocking information from the sys.dm_os_waiting_tasks DMV*

From what we see here, sessions 55 and 77 are blocked by session 76. Session 76, however, is blocked by session 65. We don't see this session ID returned in the sys.dm_os_waiting_tasks DMV, which means the session is not waiting on any resources.

Let's check another DMV, sys.dm_exec_requests, to get information about session 65:

```
SELECT *
FROM sys.dm_exec_requests
WHERE session_id = 65;
```

Figure 2-12 shows the results of this query.

session_id	request_id	start_time	status	command	sql_handle	statement_start_offset	statement_end_offset	plan_handle

Figure 2-12. *Results of a query against sys.dm_exec_requests*

Remember when I wrote the sys.dm_exec_requests DMV returned information about requests currently being processed? Apparently, session 65 doesn't have an outstanding request since no information is being returned.

If we want to find out more information about this session, we can use the sys.dm_exec_sessions DMV discussed in Chapter 1, "Wait Statistics Internals," by executing the following query:

```
SELECT session_id,
    status,
    host_name,
    program_name,
    login_name,
    is_user_process,
    open_transaction_count
FROM sys.dm_exec_sessions
WHERE session_id = 65;
```

This query returns the results shown in Figure 2-13.

⊞ Results 📄 Messages

	session_id	status	host_name	program_name	login_name	is_user_process	open_transaction_count
1	65	sleeping	SQL2022	Microsoft SQL Server Management Studio - Query	SQL2022\SQLRockstar	1	1

Figure 2-13. *Results from sys.dm_exec_sessions*

We therefore assume session ID 65 has no running requests since its status is "sleeping," which is why the query against the sys.dm_exec_requests returns no information. If we look at the program_name column, we can see that this session was initiated from the Microsoft SQL Server Management Studio (SSMS) program by the SQLRockstar user.

I included the is_user_process column to make sure it is a user session, and the open_transaction_count column shows us that this user session has an open transaction.

We now know enough information to take corrective actions. We know the user blocking other tasks, and we decide to give them a call to ask what they are running (or not running). We might then decide to end their session. Ending a user session by using the KILL [session_id] command should always be your last resort because we could be interrupting something important. Ending a session with the KILL command will result in a rollback of the running transaction, undoing all the changes it performed, which can take a long time to complete. In this case, I accept the risk of a rollback and will end the session myself:

```
KILL 65;
```

Immediately after we kill session 65, users report their queries are running again. If we query the sys.dm_os_waiting_tasks DMV, those session IDs are no longer there, meaning they are no longer being blocked.

Nerd Note   This scenario, where the issue is locking/blocking and the solution is to kill a specific user session, is quite common. More than once as a production DBA I was called late at night to solve performance issues where the root cause was a user running reports at an unexpected time of day. Being able to quickly diagnose such issues is valuable, but building your application code to avoid such issues is priceless.

Hopefully, this example has given you insight into how to use the various DMVs available in SQL Server to gather information about currently waiting tasks. In this case, the example consisted of a transaction blocking other queries, and we decided to kill the user session responsible for the blocking lock. In many situations, the solution isn't this relatively simple, but the method of gathering wait statistics information to drill down to the bottom of the problem can be used in almost every performance-related incident.

As I noted in the beginning of this section, just looking at wait statistics alone will not, in most cases, solve a performance problem, but it is a good starting point to begin your investigation. To get a complete picture about the performance of your system, we will often combine the wait statistics information with other metrics, like those from the Performance Monitor, other DMVs, or vendor-specific information (like storage metrics).

Figure 2-14 shows a flowchart of how you might use wait statistics information to analyze a performance problem.

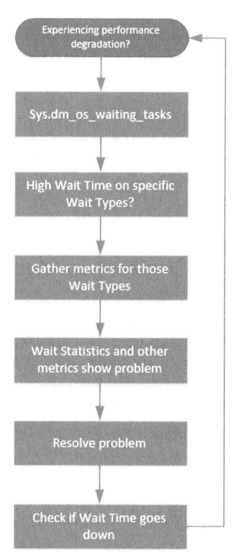

Figure 2-14. *Wait statistics flowchart*

We will expand upon this flowchart in Chapter 4, "Building a Solid Baseline," when we introduce baselines to the wait statistics analysis method.

Viewing Wait Statistics Using Perfmon

One of the tools for accessing necessary extra metrics for analyzing wait statistics is Performance Monitor, or Perfmon. Perfmon is available in the Windows operating system and contains metrics for the operating system, including SQL Server–related performance counters. You start Perfmon by executing the Perfmon command from either a Windows Run dialog or the command line.

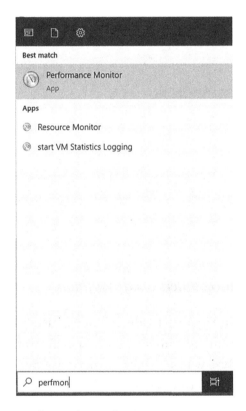

Figure 2-15. *Executing Perfmon from the Start menu*

In addition to giving us information about the performance of our system, Perfmon also displays wait statistics. These counters are located under the SQLServer:Wait Statistics category, as shown in Figure 2-16.

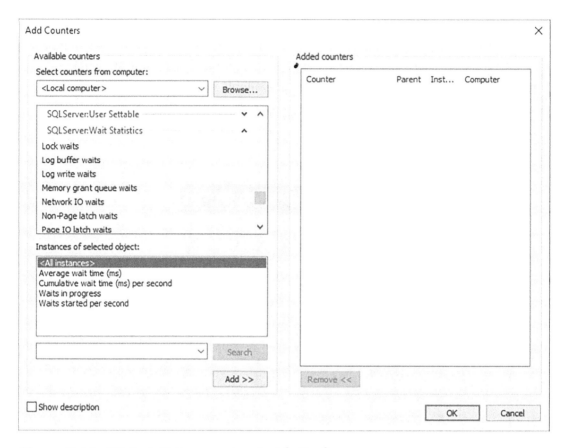

Figure 2-16. *Wait statistics counters inside Perfmon*

One thing you'll notice in Figure 2-16 are the wait statistics inside Perfmon grouped inside categories. We won't find information about specific wait types here, so if we want to use Perfmon to analyze wait statistics, we need a general idea of the category a specific wait type belongs to in Perfmon. Perfmon is able to display an average wait time, cumulative wait time, the current total number of waits, and the amount of new waits started for every wait statistics category. If we are interested in a higher-level view – for instance, we want to know how many tasks are waiting for lock-related wait types – we could use Perfmon to give us that information. If we want to have more detail about specific wait type information for a specific task, we would use the sys.dm_os_wait_stats or sys. dm_os_waiting_tasks DMVs we discussed earlier.

One nice feature of Perfmon is that it can convert the measurements directly into graphs, giving us a more visual way to look at the information without having to create the graphs ourselves. Figure 2-17 is an example of a graph where we are showing the "Average wait time" and "Waits started per second" for the Lock waits category.

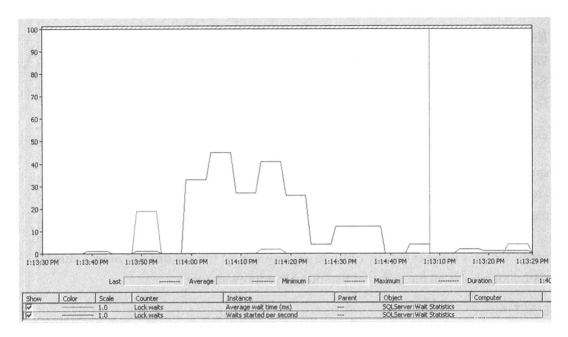

Figure 2-17. *Perfmon graph showing wait statistics information*

For this book, we will use Perfmon for analyzing metrics related to specific wait types, like CPU time, disk latency, and memory usage. We will not make much use of the wait statistics counters inside Perfmon, because the SQL Server DMVs supply the level of detail needed for a complete analysis.

Capturing Wait Statistics Using Extended Events

Most of the wait statistics information in SQL Server is recorded cumulatively, and because so many internal processes also generate wait statistics, it is difficult to detect the impact for a single query. With Extended Events, it is possible to capture the exact wait times a query encountered and on what wait types the query was waiting for. This information will help us analyze the queries with the largest impact on our system, allowing us to optimize query performance so the impact is minimized. Or, if preferred, we might capture queries encountering a specific wait type while executing.

Extended Events were introduced in SQL Server 2008 and are a replacement for the non-security events found inside SQL Server Profiler. Extended Events are more extensible than Profiler, and the number of events included with Extended Events keeps growing with every release of SQL Server.

47

Nerd Note   The death of SQL Server Profiler was thought to be near in 2008 when SQL Server introduced Extended Events (for non-security events) and SQL Server Audit (for security events). At the time of this writing, the year is 2022 and Profiler is very much alive and will never die. #TeamProfiler

Extended Events have a reputation of being difficult to work with, and this was especially true in SQL Server 2008 when they were first introduced. Working with Extended Events became a lot easier in SQL Server 2012 when it was first possible to create Extended Event sessions using SSMS.

There are many different wait-related events available when working with Extended Events. We view these events by running a query against the **sys.dm_xe_map_values** DMV, which holds all the different Extended Events event types:

```
SELECT *
FROM sys.dm_xe_map_values
WHERE name = 'wait_types';
```

Figure 2-18 shows a small part of the results of this query.

	name	object_package_guid	map_key	map_value
15	wait_types	BD97CC63-3F38-4922-AA93-607BD12E78B2	1577	AE_KEYADD
16	wait_types	BD97CC63-3F38-4922-AA93-607BD12E78B2	1443	AELOB_PROCESS_SERIALIZER
17	wait_types	BD97CC63-3F38-4922-AA93-607BD12E78B2	1445	AETM_CALL_SERIALIZER
18	wait_types	BD97CC63-3F38-4922-AA93-607BD12E78B2	1414	AETM_COMPARATOR
19	wait_types	BD97CC63-3F38-4922-AA93-607BD12E78B2	1502	AETM_CRITICAL_SECTION
20	wait_types	BD97CC63-3F38-4922-AA93-607BD12E78B2	1500	AETM_ENCLAVE_WORKER_SLEEP
21	wait_types	BD97CC63-3F38-4922-AA93-607BD12E78B2	1501	AETM_HOST_WORKER_SLEEP
22	wait_types	BD97CC63-3F38-4922-AA93-607BD12E78B2	805	ALL_COMPONENTS_INITIALIZED
23	wait_types	BD97CC63-3F38-4922-AA93-607BD12E78B2	809	AM_INDBUILD_ALLOCATION
24	wait_types	BD97CC63-3F38-4922-AA93-607BD12E78B2	911	AM_SCHEMAMGR_UNSHARED_CACHE
25	wait_types	BD97CC63-3F38-4922-AA93-607BD12E78B2	1633	ARC_IMDS_RESOURCE_INFO
26	wait_types	BD97CC63-3F38-4922-AA93-607BD12E78B2	1218	ASSEMBLY_FILTER_HASHTABLE
27	wait_types	BD97CC63-3F38-4922-AA93-607BD12E78B2	438	ASSEMBLY_LOAD
28	wait_types	BD97CC63-3F38-4922-AA93-607BD12E78B2	206	ASYNC_DISKPOOL_LOCK
29	wait_types	BD97CC63-3F38-4922-AA93-607BD12E78B2	185	ASYNC_IO_COMPLETION
30	wait_types	BD97CC63-3F38-4922-AA93-607BD12E78B2	966	ASYNC_OP_COMPLETION

Figure 2-18.   *Partial results of sys.dm_xe_map_values*

In total, there are about 1500 different wait statistics–related events available in SQL Server 2022 RC0. These events do not map one-on-one against the different wait types, and in some cases the names of the wait types do not match those of the events, even though they have the same meaning. An example of this is the ASYNC_NETWORK_IO wait type, which is named NETWORK_IO by Extended Events. While we won't go into details about Extended Events in this book, I will show you how to use them to capture wait statistics–related information using Extended Events inside of SSMS as well as straight T-SQL.

Capture Wait Statistics Information for a Specific Query

Let's look at how to configure an Extended Event session for capturing wait statistics information for a specific query. We will set a filter on a specific session and then execute the query we want to analyze.

The first thing we do is open SSMS and connect to a SQL Server instance (keep in mind Extended Events was added to versions of SSMS starting with SQL Server 2012). Once connected, we open the Management folder and then choose the Extended Events option. We right-click the Sessions folder and select the option New Session, as shown in Figure 2-19.

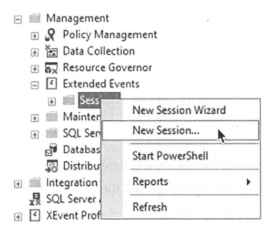

Figure 2-19. *Adding new Extended Event session*

The New Session dialog will appear where we enter a name for this Extended Event session and set additional options. We will ignore those options for now and just fill in the name of the Extended Event session, as shown in Figure 2-20 (note the error message at the top; this is expected until we add events to capture.)

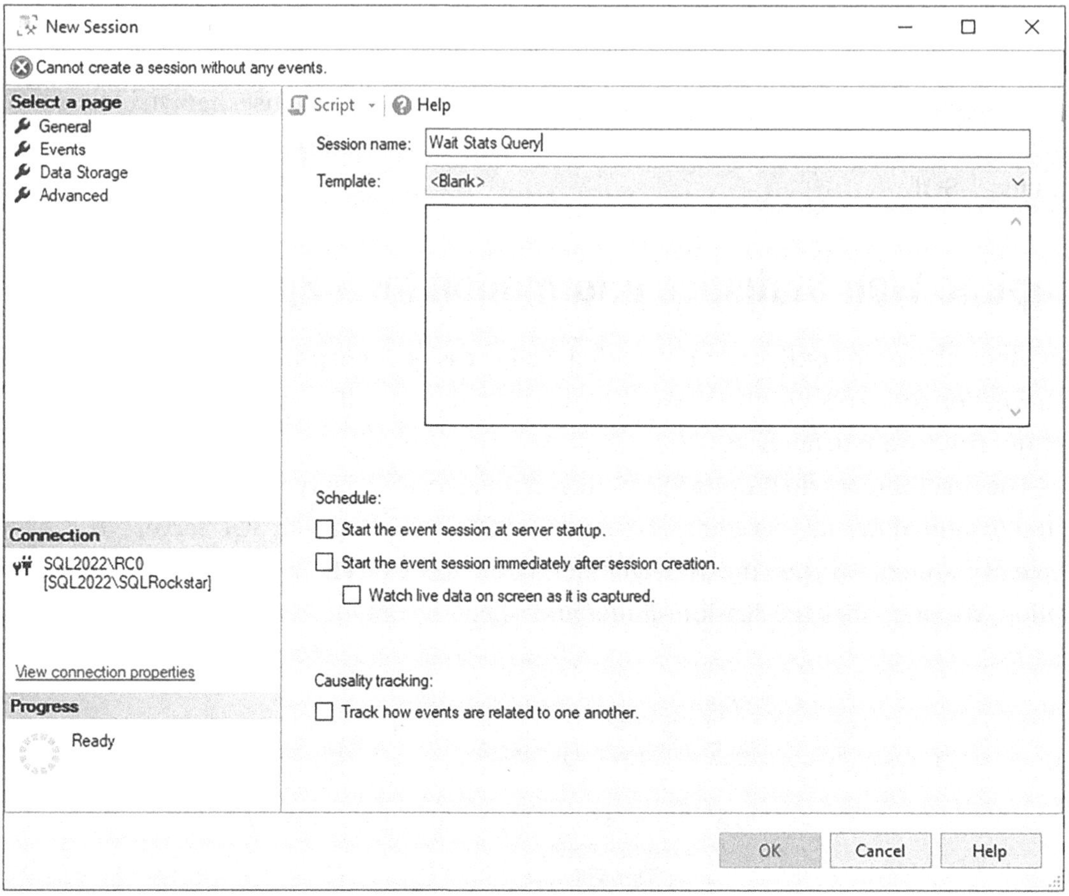

Figure 2-20. *Configuring wait statistics Extended Event session*

The next step is configuring the events this Extended Event session will monitor, which we do by selecting the Events tab (callout number 1 in Figure 2-21) in the New Session dialog.

Since we are interested in wait statistics information, I searched for the wait_info event in the Events Library (callout number 2 in Figure 2-21) and added it to the Selected Events box (callout number 3 in Figure 2-21) as shown here:

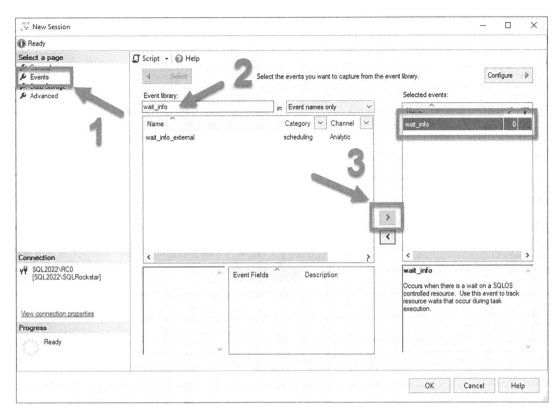

Figure 2-21. *Selecting an event to monitor*

Since we are interested in the wait statistics associated with a specific query, we configure a filter to only return wait statistics information for a specific session. To do this we click the Configure button in the New Session dialog, which opens a new section where we select Global Fields, which will record extra information when a wait_info event is triggered. In this case, I checked the sql_text global field, as shown in Figure 2-22, so we will view the actual query when an event is captured.

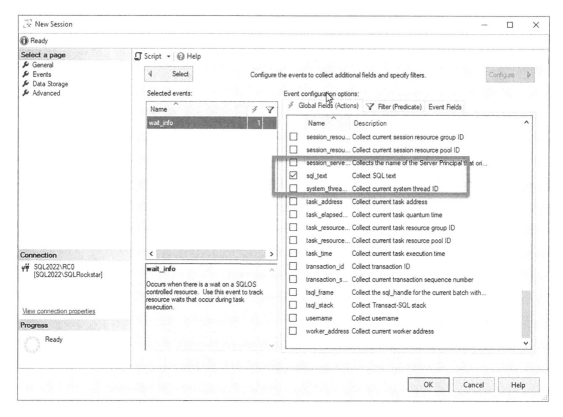

Figure 2-22. *Setting the sql_text global field*

Next is the Filter (Predicate) tab. Here we set the filter to capture events from a specific session ID. We do this by clicking inside the Field box and selecting the sqlserver. session_id field and then setting the Value to the session ID we want to monitor. In this case, I configured the filter to only capture events for session ID 76, as shown in Figure 2-23.

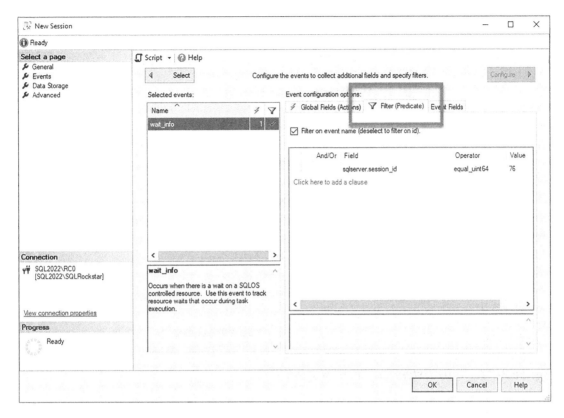

Figure 2-23. *Setting an event filter*

That's all we need to configure for now, so we click OK to close this dialog and save the Extended Event session.

By default, this new Extended Event session will not be automatically started after creation. To start the session, we must open up the Sessions folder again by navigating to the Management ➤ Extended Events folder in SQL Server Management Studio. We right-click the Extended Event session we just created and select the Start Session option, as shown in Figure 2-24.

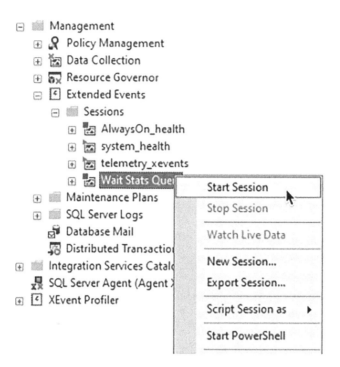

Figure 2-24. *Start Extended Event session*

After we have started the Extended Event session, it will begin collecting information. We view this information by selecting the Watch Live Data option. This will open a new tab in SQL Server Management Studio where we watch the Extended Event session. If you are worried about the overhead of viewing live data, you could choose to write the Extended Event session to an event file by adding a file location inside the Data Storage page of your Extended Event session.

For this example, I executed a simple query against the GalacticWorks database to return everything in the Person.Person table, as follows:

```
SELECT *
FROM Person.Person;
```

I pay close attention when setting the filter in the Extended Event session to match the session ID of the tab in SQL Server Management Studio where I am executing the query. The session ID can be found when looking at the number between parentheses on the tab. The Extended Events Live Data tab returned the information shown in Figure 2-25.

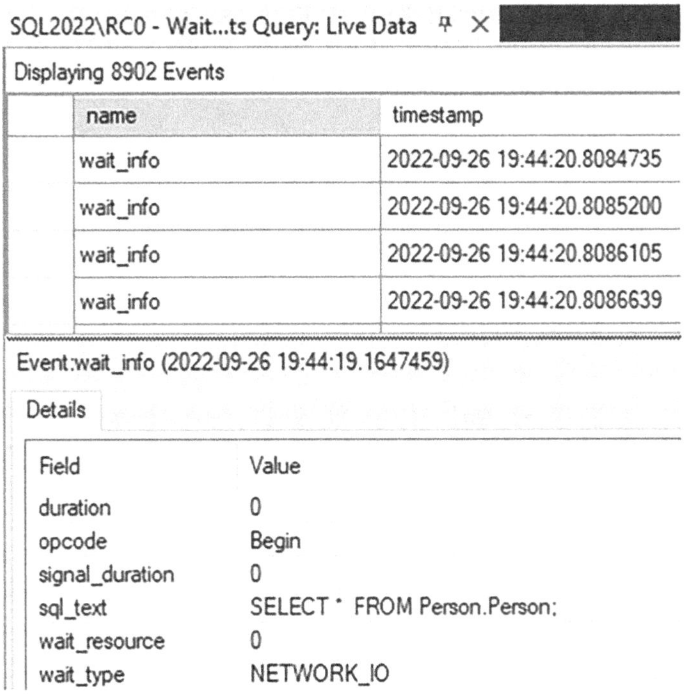

Figure 2-25. *Live wait statistics information from an Extended Event session*

As you see in Figure 2-25, our request encountered a NETWORK_IO wait type. This is one of those examples where the wait name in Extended Events doesn't match the one in the wait statistics DMVs. The NETWORK_IO wait name is the same as the ASYNC_NETWORK_IO wait type the SQLOS uses. We can view the query we executed in the sql_text field.

There are many more global fields you can include in the Extended Event session that might be interesting to capture, like the Execution Plan handle or the Task Execution Time. The global fields will give additional information which is shown when Extended Event session information is returned, giving you an impressive amount of detail.

If, for some reason, you do not want to use SSMS to create and run an Extended Event session or you are running SQL Server 2008, you can use T-SQL to create and configure one. To create the same Extended Event session as above using T-SQL, execute the query seen in Listing 2-3.

Listing 2-3. Create wait statistics Extended Event session

```
CREATE EVENT SESSION [WaitStats Query] ON SERVER
ADD EVENT sqlos.wait_info
  (
  ACTION(sqlserver.sql_text)
  WHERE ([sqlserver].[session_id]=(76))
  )
ADD TARGET package0.event_file
  (
   SET filename = N'E:\Data\WaitStats_XE.xel', metadatafile = N'E:\Data\
   WaitStats_XE.xem'
  );
```

Nerd Note   We included the metadata file in the preceding script by setting the metadatafile parameter. If you are running SQL Server 2012 or higher, this is no longer required.

The easiest way to log the Extended Event session is by saving it to a file; in this case, my filename is E:\Data\WaitStats_XE.xel (SQL Server will add a unique numeric identifier to the filename; in this case, the actual filename is WaitStats_XE_0_132969501905230000.xel). I also included the filter on session ID 76 to capture wait statistics generated by that session.

The next thing we do is start the Extended Event session, which we do by executing the ALTER EVENT SESSION command:

```
ALTER EVENT SESSION "WaitStats Query" ON SERVER STATE = start;
```

We then execute the same query as we did in the original example under the session we are filtering on. After letting the Extended Event session run for a little while, we can stop it using the ALTER EVENT SESSION command:

```
ALTER EVENT SESSION "WaitStats Query" ON SERVER STATE = stop;
```

With the Extended Event session stopped, we next import the information in the file (as XML) into a table to view what the session captured; we do this using the sys.fn_xe_file_target_read_file function. We then parse the XML information to return the results in a more readable format. The query in Listing 2-4 can be used to read an Extended Event file, import it into a temporary table, and return the results as rows.

Listing 2-4. Return Extend Event file as rows

```
-- Check if temp table is present
-- Drop if exist
IF OBJECT_ID('tempdb..#XE_Data') IS NOT NULL
DROP TABLE #XE_Data

-- Create temp table to hold raw XE data
CREATE TABLE #XE_Data
  (
  XE_Data XML
  );
GO

-- Write contents of the XE file
-- into our table
INSERT INTO #XE_Data
  (
  XE_Data
  )
SELECT  CAST (event_data AS XML)
FROM sys.fn_xe_file_target_read_file
  (
'E:\Data\WaitStats_XE_0_132969501905230000.xel',    'E:\Data\WaitStats_
XE_0_132969501905230000.xem',    null,    null    );
GO
-- Query information from our temp table
SELECT
  XE_Data.value ('(/event/@timestamp)[1]', 'DATETIME') AS 'Date/Time',
  XE_Data.value ('(/event/data[@name="opcode"]/text)[1]', 'VARCHAR(100)')
  AS 'Operation',
```

```
XE_Data.value ('(/event/data[@name="wait_type"]/text)[1]',
'VARCHAR(100)') AS 'Wait Type',
XE_Data.value ('(/event/data[@name="duration"]/value)[1]', 'BIGINT') AS
'Wait Time',
XE_Data.value ('(/event/data[@name="signal_duration"]/value)[1]',
'BIGINT') AS 'Signal Wait Time',
XE_Data.value ('(/event/action[@name="sql_text"]/value)[1]',
'VARCHAR(100)') AS 'Query'
FROM #XE_Data
ORDER BY 'Date/Time' ASC;
```

The result of the query in Listing 2-4 can be seen in Figure 2-26.

	Date/Time	Operation	Wait Type	Wait Time	Signal Wait Time	Query
1	2022-09-26 19:53:16.007	Begin	NETWORK_IO	0	0	SELECT * FROM Person.Person;
2	2022-09-26 19:53:16.057	End	NETWORK_IO	49	26	SELECT * FROM Person.Person;
3	2022-09-26 19:53:16.060	Begin	NETWORK_IO	0	0	SELECT * FROM Person.Person;
4	2022-09-26 19:53:16.140	End	NETWORK_IO	80	7	SELECT * FROM Person.Person;
5	2022-09-26 19:53:16.210	Begin	SOS_SCHEDULER_YIELD	0	0	SELECT * FROM Person.Person;
6	2022-09-26 19:53:16.210	End	SOS_SCHEDULER_YIELD	0	0	SELECT * FROM Person.Person;
7	2022-09-26 19:53:16.210	Begin	NETWORK_IO	0	0	SELECT * FROM Person.Person;
8	2022-09-26 19:53:16.377	End	NETWORK_IO	166	10	SELECT * FROM Person.Person;
9	2022-09-26 19:53:16.377	Begin	NETWORK_IO	0	0	SELECT * FROM Person.Person;
10	2022-09-26 19:53:16.397	End	NETWORK_IO	18	9	SELECT * FROM Person.Person;
11	2022-09-26 19:53:16.397	Begin	NETWORK_IO	0	0	SELECT * FROM Person.Person;
12	2022-09-26 19:53:16.397	End	NETWORK_IO	0	0	SELECT * FROM Person.Person;
13	2022-09-26 19:53:16.397	Begin	NETWORK_IO	0	0	SELECT * FROM Person.Person;
14	2022-09-26 19:53:16.400	End	NETWORK_IO	0	0	SELECT * FROM Person.Person;

Figure 2-26. *Results of the query in Listing 2-4*

Most of the columns speak for themselves in terms of the row data they return. Two columns which deserve extra explanation are the Operation and Wait Time columns. The Operation column will show you the beginning or the end of the wait event. The Wait Time column will return the wait time in milliseconds, but it will only be recorded at the end of an operation.

Analyzing Wait Statistics on a Per-Query Basis Using Execution Plans

So far, we have looked at aggregated wait times generated by either various background processes or by the queries we executed ourselves. Since I was the only one executing queries against my test machine, it is easy to correlate wait times to specific queries. Unfortunately, on busy systems where many queries are constantly executed by many concurrent sessions, the various wait statistics DMVs were difficult for analyzing wait types and wait times for specific queries.

Thankfully, the release of SQL Server 2016 SP1 introduced wait statistics captured inside query execution plans. This allows anyone to see the wait types and wait times a query encountered while running. Even though it might seem obvious, this also means per-query wait statistics are only available when looking at the actual execution plan, not the estimated execution plan.

Nerd Note   The actual execution plan is the execution plan used during the execution of the query. There is an option in SSMS to view the estimated execution plan. When used, the SQL Server engine compiles the execution plan *most likely to be used* during the query's execution; however, it does not execute the query itself. Since there is no query execution, there are also no wait statistics to record while compiling the estimated execution plan.

The easiest way to expose per-query wait statistics is by enabling the Include Actual Execution Plan option, shown in Figure 2-27, by clicking the "Query – Include Actual Execution Plan" menu item or by using the key combination CTRL_M and then executing your query.

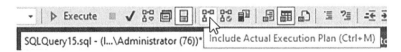

Figure 2-27. *Include Actual Execution Plan option*

When you execute a query with the Include Actual Execution Plan option enabled, the query results return with an additional tab called Execution plan. Clicking the tab will return the visual representation of the execution plan used while executing your query. Figure 2-28 shows an example of an actual execution plan.

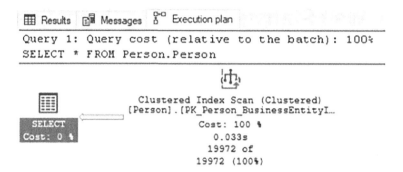

Figure 2-28. *Execution plan*

With the execution plan tab opened, we access the per-query wait statistics by right-clicking the first operator (which in the case of Figure 2-29 is the SELECT operator) and selecting Properties. This opens up the execution plan properties window inside SSMS and reveals a wealth of information, like the degree of parallelism used or the number of rows processed, for the query execution and the various properties of the operator we selected.

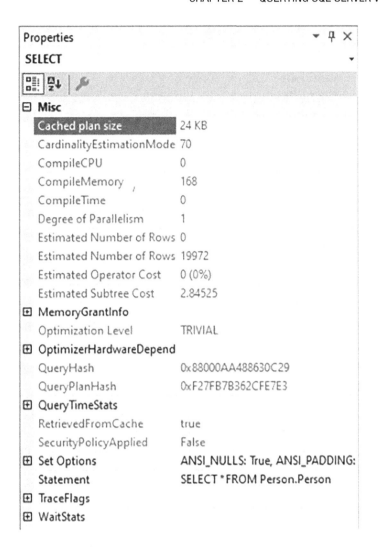

Figure 2-29. *Execution plan properties*

The WaitStats properties are located at the bottom of the properties window. When expanding the WaitStats properties, you find all of the wait types and wait times this specific query experienced while executing. Figure 2-30 shows the per-query wait statistics for this specific example query.

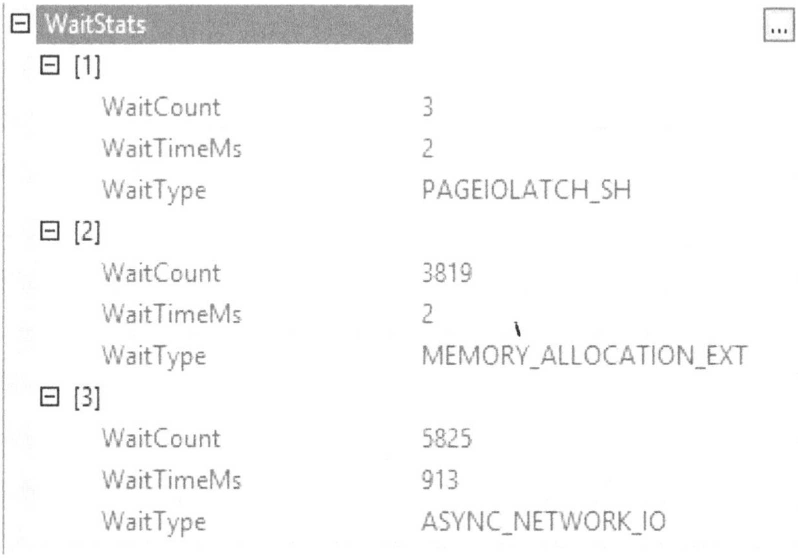

```
☐ WaitStats                                                    ...
   ☐ [1]
         WaitCount              3
         WaitTimeMs             2
         WaitType               PAGEIOLATCH_SH
   ☐ [2]
         WaitCount              3819
         WaitTimeMs             2
         WaitType               MEMORY_ALLOCATION_EXT
   ☐ [3]
         WaitCount              5825
         WaitTimeMs             913
         WaitType               ASYNC_NETWORK_IO
```

Figure 2-30. *Per-query wait statistics in the execution plan properties*

In this case, our query encountered three different wait types while executing: PAGEIOLATCH_SH, MEMORY_ALLOCATION_EXT, and ASYNC_NETWORK_IO. For each wait type, we see how much time was spent waiting and how many times we waited on the wait type. This information is useful when looking at what an individual query encounters in terms of wait statistics during its execution and, perhaps, can give insight for tuning the performance of the query. For instance, if you see a query frequently runs into storage-related wait statistics, it might be worth investigating how to minimize storage access for the specific query so it will execute faster.

One thing that I like to point out again is that the per-query wait statistics are only recorded in the actual execution plan. The reason why I mention this again is the actual execution plan is only available by enabling it before execution of a query. There is no other way to access an actual execution plan, not even through the Query Store as we will see in the next chapter. As a matter of fact, the execution plans stored in the plan cache of SQL Server are the estimated execution plans and not the actual plans. This means that if you are expecting to retrieve per-query wait statistics through the plan cache, you are going to be disappointed.

Thankfully, even though the Query Store feature does not record the actual execution plan, it does (with the release of SQL Server 2017) record wait statistics, and other query runtime information, together with the estimated execution plan. Mixing that information together means that through the Query Store we can look back in time and see what queries encountered in terms of wait statistics!

Summary

In this chapter, we reviewed the various ways we can access information about wait statistics. We took an in-depth look at some of the most important DMVs regarding wait statistics – sys.dm_os_wait_stats, sys.dm_os_waiting_tasks, sys.dm_exec_requests, and sys.dm_exec_session_wait_stats – described their functions and the data they returned, and gave you some example queries you can use against those DMVs. We also went through an example scenario where we combined some of the DMVs to analyze what was slowing down the SQL Server in the example. The steps shown in the example are a good way to analyze performance problems on your system when they are occurring. Briefly, we looked at the Performance Monitor, or Perfmon, and how you can access wait statistics information from inside it. After that, we took a good look at Extended Events and how you can use them to capture wait-related information for specific queries or sessions using the Extended Events GUI or T-SQL. We ended the chapter by looking at the execution plan recorded wait statistics.

CHAPTER 3

The Query Store

With the release of SQL Server 2016, Microsoft introduced a new method to analyze and troubleshoot query performance: the Query Store. The Query Store is often called the "flight recorder" of SQL Server because it provides insights into when queries were executed, how well they performed, and the execution plan used during execution. While the Query Store did not initially expose wait statistics, the release of SQL Server 2017 included that much awaited addition.

Since the Query Store is valuable in terms of query performance analysis and tuning, I believe it deserves some additional attention in order to maximize the benefit of this feature.

What Is the Query Store?

The Query Store feature was first released in SQL Server 2016 and had a goal of exposing and persisting query performance information in an accessible way. Before the Query Store, query performance analysis was a challenging and time-consuming process that required thorough knowledge of how SQL Server processes queries and how to analyze information through the various DMVs. While experience and knowledge of query execution is still helpful, the Query Store helps you retain the necessary performance information without having to roll your own solution.

The Query Store is integrated directly inside the SQL Server engine, capturing and analyzing query executions as they happen. This is a major difference compared to query analysis through other methods, like execution plan cache mining, where query runtime information is only available at a later stage. Another advantage of the Query Store is it persists query runtime information to disk. This allows for a history of runtime metrics for your queries as well as comparison between historic and current runtime statistics. This is a difference compared to the DMVs, which only record information while SQL Server is running and flushes all recorded information at a restart of SQL Server, meaning you start back with all the counters at 0 again. To continue the comparison of the Query Store vs. DMVs, while all the DMVs record information on the

© Thomas LaRock, Enrico van de Laar 2023
T. LaRock and E. van de Laar, *Pro SQL Server 2022 Wait Statistics*,
https://doi.org/10.1007/978-1-4842-8771-2_3

entire SQL Server Instance level, the Query Store allows you to capture query runtime metrics on a per-database basis. This makes analyzing performance for a specific database inside an Instance with multiple databases considerably easier and quicker.

Enabling the Query Store

The Query Store is enabled by default (in READ_WRITE mode) for new databases inside SQL Server 2022 (and is also enabled by default for new Azure SQL Databases). For prior versions of SQL Server, users must manually enable the Query Store to begin collecting information on query executions. Enabling the Query Store can be done in two ways, through the use of SQL Server Management Studio (SSMS) and with T-SQL statements.

Enable the Query Store Using SSMS

As the Query Store is configured on a per-database level, to enable the Query Store, you will navigate to a database inside of SSMS and right-click to select "Properties" as shown in Figure 3-1:

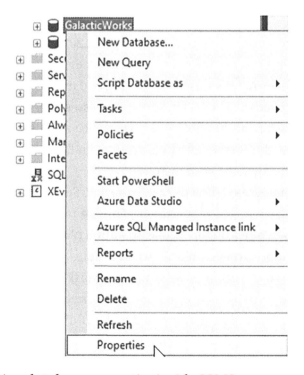

Figure 3-1. *Selecting database properties inside SSMS*

Once selected, the Database Properties screen opens, and from there you will select the Query Store tab (shown as number 1 in Figure 3-2) on the left. When the tab opens, you will select the Operation Mode (Requested) option and select Read Write shown as number 2 in Figure 3-2:

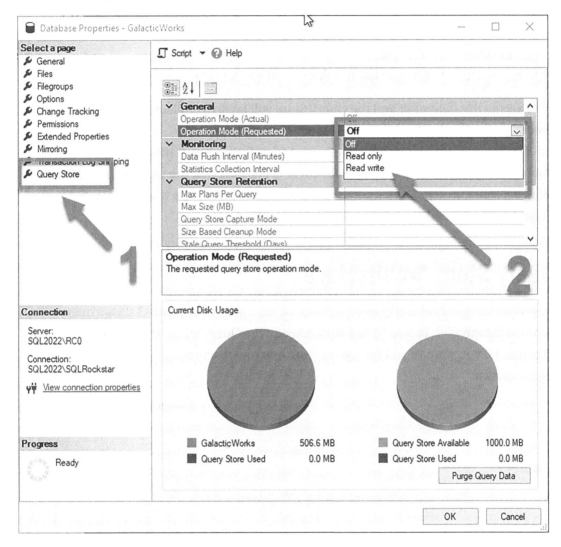

Figure 3-2. *Setting the Query Store to Read Write*

Select OK and the Query Store will begin to collect information for query executions inside the database. For SQL Server 2022, the default maximum size for collecting this data is 1024 MB. If you hit the limit, Query Store will change to Read Only and stop collecting new data. You will want to monitor the space used inside Query Store on a regular basis.

Enable the Query Store Using T-SQL

Enabling the Query Store using T-SQL can be done with the following code as shown in Listing 3-1:

Listing 3-1. Enabling the Query Store using T-SQL

```
ALTER DATABASE GalacticWorks
SET QUERY_STORE = ON (OPERATION_MODE = READ_WRITE);
```

Execute the statement and the Query Store will begin to collect information for query executions inside the database.

The Query Store offers many advantages as well as configuration options. Since this is a book about wait statistics, I will not cover everything that the Query Store has to offer. For more in-depth details of the Query Store, you can review them here: `https://slrwnds.com/bdsxgt`.

Query Store Architecture

To give an idea on how the Query Store works, the image in Figure 3-3 shows query runtime information recorded and stored inside the Query Store. This knowledge is important if you want to add the Query Store as a tool to analyze query performance and wait statistics.

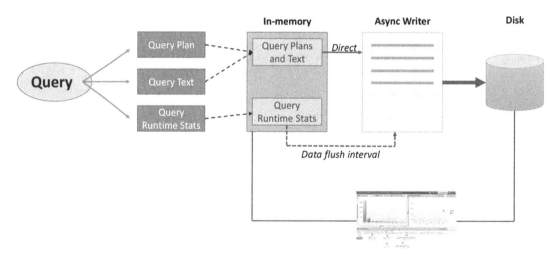

Figure 3-3. *Query Store architecture*

As soon as a query starts execution, the Query Store splits the query runtime information into three parts: the query execution plan, the query text, and the runtime statistics of the query execution. Both the execution plan and the query text are immediately recorded in the Query Store during the compilation of the execution plan. The runtime statistics (including wait statistics information) are added to the Query Store after query execution is complete.

All Query Store metrics are first stored inside a reserved memory area of SQL Server. This means the metrics are directly available through queries or the built-in reports but not hardened to disk yet (one exception is new execution plans; these are hardened directly). Based on a configurable setting inside the Query Store called the "Data flush interval," you configure how fast the Query Store will harden the information to disk.

We access all information in the Query Store through two methods: Query Store DMVs and the built-in Query Store reports. To expose the wait statistics inside the Query Store, we will use both options, though the DMV approach is more useful when looking at wait statistics data.

How Wait Statistics Are Processed in the Query Store

Before we start accessing the wait statistics information recorded in the Query Store, we will examine how the Query Store processes wait statistics because it is different compared to the process described in Chapter 1, "Wait Statistics Internals," of this book. Chapter 1 described the SQL Server engine tracking how long a query spends waiting on a specific resource, or wait type. This information is recorded at a granular level; for instance, the PAGEIOLATCH_SH wait type indicates the query is waiting for data pages to be read from disk to the buffer cache and a PAGEIOLATCH_EX for a query waiting for a data page to be moved to the buffer cache for modification. Instead of recording wait times on a detailed level, the Query Store uses a more high-level wait type overview to minimize performance and resource utilization overhead. The Query Store groups various wait types into categories and records wait times on the category level instead of individual wait types.

This means searching for specific wait types inside the Query Store is not possible and wait types which share the same category cannot be distinguished from each other. To give you an example, both the CMEMTHREAD and the RESOURCE_SEMAPHORE wait types (of which you will learn more in Chapter 6, "IO-Related Wait Types") are recorded inside the Memory category inside the Query Store, even though both wait types indicate different things.

Table 3-1 shows the mapping between wait types and wait categories used in the Query Store. The table is by no means a complete overview of the mappings but should give you a good idea where to expect a certain wait type.

Table 3-1. *Mapping between wait types and categories*

Wait category	Associated wait types
Unknown	Unknown
CPU	SOS_SCHEDULER_YIELD
Worker thread	THREADPOOL
Lock	LCK_M_%
Latch	LATCH_%
Buffer latch	PAGELATCH_%
Buffer IO	PAGEIOLATCH_%
Compilation*	RESOURCE_SEMAPHORE_QUERY_COMPILE
SQL CLR	CLR%, SQLCLR%
Mirroring	DBMIRROR%
Transaction	XACT%, DTC%, TRAN_MARKLATCH_%, MSQL_XACT_%, TRANSACTION_ MUTEX
Idle	SLEEP_%, LAZYWRITER_SLEEP, SQLTRACE_BUFFER_FLUSH, SQLTRACE_INCREMENTAL_FLUSH_SLEEP, SQLTRACE_WAIT_ENTRIES, FT_IFTS_SCHEDULER_IDLE_WAIT, XE_DISPATCHER_WAIT, REQUEST_FOR_ DEADLOCK_SEARCH, LOGMGR_QUEUE, ONDEMAND_TASK_QUEUE, CHECKPOINT_ QUEUE, XE_TIMER_EVENT
Preemptive	**PREEMPTIVE_%**

(continued)

Table 3-1. (*continued*)

Wait category	Associated wait types
Service broker	BROKER_% (but not BROKER_RECEIVE_WAITFOR)
Tran Log IO	LOGMGR, LOGBUFFER, LOGMGR_RESERVE_APPEND, LOGMGR_FLUSH, LOGMGR_PMM_LOG, CHKPT, WRITELOG
Network IO	ASYNC_NETWORK_IO, NET_WAITFOR_PACKET, PROXY_NETWORK_IO, EXTERNAL_ SCRIPT_NETWORK_IOF
Parallelism	CXPACKET, EXCHANGE, HT%, BMP%, BP%
Memory	RESOURCE_SEMAPHORE, CMEMTHREAD, CMEMPARTITIONED, EE_PMOLOCK, MEMORY_ALLOCATION_EXT, RESERVED_MEMORY_ ALLOCATION_EXT, MEMORY_ GRANT_UPDATE
User wait	WAITFOR, WAIT_FOR_RESULTS, BROKER_RECEIVE_WAITFOR
Tracing	TRACEWRITE, SQLTRACE_LOCK, SQLTRACE_FILE_BUFFER, SQLTRACE_ FILE_ WRITE_IO_COMPLETION, SQLTRACE_FILE_READ_IO_COMPLETION, SQLTRACE_ PENDING_BUFFER_WRITERS, SQLTRACE_SHUTDOWN, QUERY_ TRACEOUT, TRACE_ EVTNOTIFF
Full text search	FT_RESTART_CRAWL, FULLTEXT GATHERER, MSSEARCH, FT_METADATA_ MUTEX, FT_IFTSHC_MUTEX, FT_IFTSISM_MUTEX, FT_IFTS_RWLOCK, FT_COMPROWSET_RWLOCK, FT_MASTER_MERGE, FT_PROPERTYLIST_ CACHE, FT_MASTER_MERGE_COORDINATOR, PWAIT_RESOURCE_ SEMAPHORE_FT_PARALLEL_QUERY_SYNC
Other disk IO	ASYNC_IO_COMPLETION, IO_COMPLETION, BACKUPIO, WRITE_ COMPLETION, IO_QUEUE_LIMIT, IO_RETRY
Replication	SE_REPL_%, REPL_%, HADR_% (but not HADR_THROTTLE_LOG_RATE_ GOVERNOR), PWAIT_HADR_%, REPLICA_WRITES, FCB_REPLICA_WRITE, FCB_ REPLICA_READ, PWAIT_HADRSIM
Log rate governor	LOG_RATE_GOVERNOR, POOL_LOG_RATE_GOVERNOR, HADR_THROTTLE_LOG_ RATE_GOVERNOR, INSTANCE_LOG_RATE_GOVERNOR

Accessing Wait Statistics Through Query Store Reports

The most user-friendly way to view the wait statistics that are available inside the Query Store is through the built-in reports available inside SSMS after you enable the Query Store feature on a database. Figure 3-4 shows the default, built-in, Query Store reports that are available at the time of writing this book.

Figure 3-4. *Query Store reports*

As you can see in Figure 3-4, there is a dedicated wait statistics report, query wait statistics. You view this report with either a double-click or a right-click and selecting the name **query wait statistics**. The report will open and look like Figure 3-5.

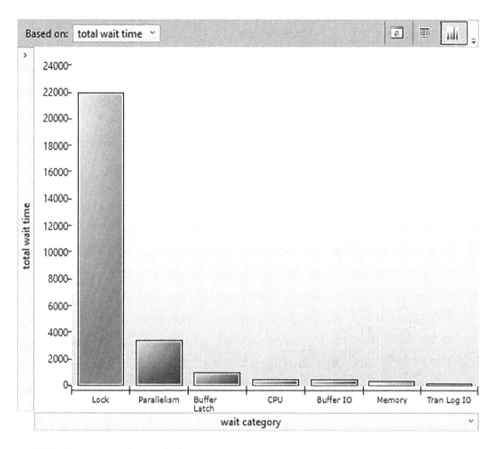

Figure 3-5. *Query wait statistics report*

Notice the waits are organized by categories, as we discussed earlier. Here, the majority of waits belong to the Query Store Lock category, which groups all LCK_M_% wait events together.

In addition to this report, we can also view the wait categories as a query encountered by specifically selecting the Wait Time (ms) metric inside the following three reports:

- Regressed queries

- Top resource consuming queries

- Queries with high variation

To view the wait categories in any of the preceding reports, you first need to configure the metric to Wait Time (ms), as shown in Figure 3-6.

73

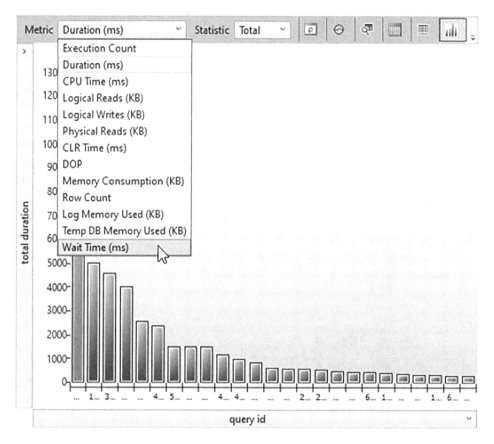

Figure 3-6. *Configuring the metric to Wait Time (ms)*

This changes the graph to return (by default) the top 25 queries ordered by the total wait time.

After changing the metric, we mouseover on any of the columns shown in the graph to retrieve the wait category information, as shown in Figure 3-7.

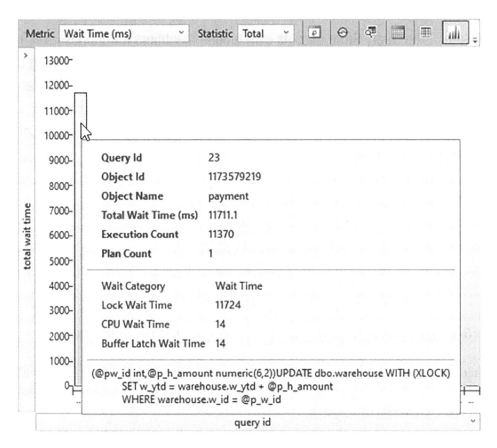

Figure 3-7. *Wait categories exposed in the Query Store*

As you see from Figure 3-7, this specific query ran into Lock, CPU, and Buffer Latch wait categories. We see the wait time per category and the total wait time across all of the categories, but as mentioned earlier, we have no idea about which exact wait types were encountered by the query.

Accessing Wait Statistics Through Query Store DMVs

While the built-in Query Store reports are definitely helpful in visibly identifying queries with high wait times, there is far more information available using the **sys.query_store_ wait_stats** DMV. The columns returned by this DMV show various statistics related to the wait types of the wait categories for a specific execution plan ID.

Nerd Note   The Query Store uses its own unique identifiers for queries, execution plans, and runtime intervals. With that in mind, you identify queries by looking up the Query ID inside the Query Store or execution plans by searching on the plan ID.

Figure 3-8 shows the different statistics recorded for each execution plan ID, split into the different wait categories.

	wait_category_desc	execution_type	execution_type_desc	total_query_wait_time_ms	avg_query_wait_time_ms	last_query_wait_time_ms	min_query_wait_time_ms	max_query_wait_time_ms
1	Lock	0	Regular	4423	0.389006156552331	0	0	51
2	Buffer Latch	0	Regular	1	8.79507475813544E-05	0	0	0
3	Buffer IO	0	Regular	6	0.000527704485488127	0	0	3
4	Tran Log IO	0	Regular	29	0.00255057167985928	0	0	15
5	CPU	0	Regular	3	0.000263852242744063	0	0	3
6	CPU	0	Regular	2	3.94726454566985E-05	0	0	2
7	Lock	0	Regular	2	0.000291502696399942	0	0	2
8	Memory	0	Regular	64	0.00932808628479813	0	0	0
9	CPU	0	Regular	1	8.79507475813544E-05	0	0	1
10	Buffer Latch	0	Regular	5	0.000439753737906772	0	0	3
11	Buffer IO	0	Regular	19	0.00167106420404573	0	0	9
12	Tran Log IO	0	Regular	4	0.000351802990325418	0	0	3

Figure 3-8. *Wait categories statistics inside sys.query_store_wait_stats*

While we query the sys.query_store_wait_stats DMV and look at the various statistics for each, or a specific, execution plan ID, we get more information when joining the various Query Store DMVs together.

As an example, the following query joins various Query Store DMVs to return an overview of queries that encounter high total wait times.

Listing 3-2. Using a Query Store DMV

```
SELECT qsws.plan_id,
    qsq.query_id,
    qsws.runtime_stats_interval_id,
    qsqt.query_sql_text,
    qsws.wait_category_desc,
    qsws.total_query_wait_time_ms
FROM sys.query_store_wait_stats qsws
INNER JOIN sys.query_store_plan qsp
    ON qsws.plan_id = qsp.plan_id
INNER JOIN sys.query_store_query qsq
    ON qsp.query_id = qsq.query_id
INNER JOIN sys.query_store_query_text qsqt
```

```
    ON qsq.query_text_id = qsqt.query_text_id
ORDER BY qsws.total_query_wait_time_ms DESC;
```

The results of this query can be seen in Figure 3-9.

	plan_id	query_id	runtime_stats_interval_id	query_sql_text	wait_category_desc	total_query_wait_time_ms
1	25	23	1	(@p_w_id int,@p_h_amount numeric(6,2))UPDATE dbo....	Lock	11724
2	16	14	1	(@p_w_id int,@p_d_id int,@p_h_amount numeric(6,2))U...	Lock	4423
3	37	37	1	(@no_d_id int,@no_w_id int,@no_d_tax smallmoney,@o...	Lock	4009
4	53	18	1	SELECT StatMan([SC0], [SB0000]) FROM (SELECT TOP...	Parallelism	1058
5	65	69	1	SELECT StatMan([SC0], [SB0000]) FROM (SELECT TOP...	Parallelism	914
6	63	67	1	SELECT StatMan([SC0], [SC1], [SC2], [SC3], [SB0000]) F...	Parallelism	820
7	64	68	1	SELECT StatMan([SC0], [SB0000]) FROM (SELECT TOP...	Parallelism	635
8	27	26	1	(@st_w_id int,@st_d_id int,@st_o_id int)SELECT @st_o_...	Lock	493
9	38	38	1	(@o_id int,@no_d_id int,@no_w_id int,@no_c_id int,@TI...	Lock	474
10	42	42	1	(@no_ol_i_id int,@no_ol_supply_w_id int,@no_s_quantit...	Buffer Latch	388
11	48	50	1	(@d_w_id int,@d_d_id int)DELETE TOP (1) FRO...	Lock	329
12	60	58	1	(@os_d_id int,@os_w_id int,@os_c_id int,@os_o_id int,...	Lock	297
13	41	41	1	(@no_ol_i_id int,@no_ol_supply_w_id int,@no_s_quantit...	Buffer Latch	288
14	38	38	1	(@o_id int,@no_d_id int,@no_w_id int,@no_c_id int,@TI...	Buffer IO	265

Figure 3-9. *Wait statistics information from the Query Store*

Modifying the query by filtering on Query ID allows us to focus on a specific query and analyze its wait behavior. Following is the modified query, and you'll see that I also added some additional columns returning various useful statistics.

```
SELECT qsws.plan_id,
    qsq.query_id,
    qsws.runtime_stats_interval_id,
    qsqt.query_sql_text,
    qsws.wait_category_desc,
    qsws.total_query_wait_time_ms,
    qsws.avg_query_wait_time_ms,
    qsws.last_query_wait_time_ms
FROM sys.query_store_wait_stats qsws
INNER JOIN sys.query_store_plan qsp
    ON qsws.plan_id = qsp.plan_id
INNER JOIN sys.query_store_query qsq
    ON qsp.query_id = qsq.query_id
INNER JOIN sys.query_store_query_text qsqt
    ON qsq.query_text_id = qsqt.query_text_id
WHERE qsq.query_id = 8
ORDER BY runtime_stats_interval_id ASC;
```

In the query and the query results, there is a column called runtime_stats_interval_id. The way in which the Query Store groups runtime (and wait time) metrics is by aggregating based on intervals. By default, these intervals are one-hour blocks, meaning the wait statistics returned for our specific query in the preceding example are the aggregated results of one, or multiple, query executions inside the interval. While you can lower the intervals to smaller time segments by setting the Statistics Collection Interval setting inside the Query Store properties, this will have a negative impact on the performance of your SQL Server Instance, so be careful when changing this setting.

I have only shown a few examples of how to retrieve wait statistics–related metrics from inside the Query Store. With all the information the Query Store collects, there is a whole ocean full of other information to combine with the wait statistics metrics. For instance, filtering on specific wait categories, or detecting queries which generate different execution plans and the impact is on the waits for the specific query. I recommend everyone using SQL Server 2016 or higher to enable the Query Store and explore the metrics it collects.

Nerd Note   While the Query Store is only available from SQL Server 2016 and higher, William Durkin (@sql_williamd on Twitter) and Enrico van de Laar (@evdlaar) released a project called open Query Store which emulates Query Store data collection for SQL Server versions lower than 2016. The project is completely open source and free and available through the project's GitHub page at `https://slrwnds.com/n4mudf`.

Summary

In this chapter, we looked at a new query performance and analysis feature introduced in SQL Server 2016: the Query Store. We looked at how the Query Store works underneath the covers and how we can access query wait statistics information in the built-in reports of the Query Store.

Finally, we looked at accessing Query Store wait statistics using the new Query Store DMVs and showed some example queries that can help you get started on querying the Query Store.

CHAPTER 4

Building a Solid Baseline

In Chapter 2, "Querying SQL Server Wait Statistics," we spent a great deal of time describing and using various methods of accessing wait statistics information. Most of those methods focused on using the information for detecting current performance problems. While it is possible to find the exact cause of a performance problem using these real-time methods, it requires a deep knowledge of the various wait types and – most important – experience in the performance of your specific SQL Server system.

If you manage a single SQL Server instance, you fast become familiar with the way it reacts under different circumstances. If you manage hundreds of SQL Server instances, getting yourself familiar with the way they all perform is next to impossible. Because SQL Server wait statistics are largely based on the workload of the specific SQL Server instance, no two SQL Server instances will have the same wait times for the same wait types. This makes detecting possible problems difficult because we can't just say "hey, the CXPACKET wait type has a wait time of 20,000 milliseconds, so we are having a problem." It all depends on the configuration and workload of your system. One SQL Server instance can have 20,000 milliseconds (20 seconds) of wait time every minute spent on the CXPACKET wait type and experience no performance problems, while another instance has 1,000 milliseconds of wait time and users are constantly complaining about performance.

If we want an in-depth analysis of wait statistics, or any performance-related data, we need a method of collecting performance-related metrics and giving them meaning. Just detecting 10,000 milliseconds waiting for resources doesn't mean anything, since we do not know if it caused performance problems or not. Yes, maybe your users are complaining that performance is horrible while you notice the 10,000 milliseconds wait, but there is no way to be sure if the wait is explicitly causing the specific performance problems users are experiencing. Someone might take a guess and just assume the specific resource wait is the source of the performance problem. As a former production DBA, I can tell you DBAs do not like to take guesses at what's slowing down our database servers. We want to be certain of the source of the performance problem. This is where baselines help.

© Thomas LaRock, Enrico van de Laar 2023
T. LaRock and E. van de Laar, *Pro SQL Server 2022 Wait Statistics*,
https://doi.org/10.1007/978-1-4842-8771-2_4

Baselines help give meaning to performance metrics by providing a definition of the normal state of your system. Without a baseline, we have no idea if the system or application is running optimally or terribly slow. Baselines are incredibly important; in fact, they are so important I decided to write a complete chapter about them in this book. Without a solid baseline, your measurements mean nothing! Even though this book focuses on wait statistics, baselines are useful for every performance-related metric you can capture on your system, giving you a valuable method of performance analysis.

If you read through the previous chapter concerning the Query Store, you might be tempted to think the Query Store can handle all your baselines. While the Query Store is useful for capturing and monitoring the performance of a query inside one database, it doesn't provide a performance overview of your entire SQL Server Instance. I personally consider the Query Store an addition to the regular process of capturing and monitoring baselines, not a replacement.

What Are Baselines?

If we look up "baseline" in the Oxford dictionary, we see the following definition: "A minimum or starting point used for comparisons." This sentence captures the essence of a baseline perfectly by using the important words "starting point" and "comparisons." A baseline is the starting point or, in our case, measurement, with which we compare later measurements against. Ideally, we capture the baseline measurement in a normal or standard situation. If we perform the same measurement again at a later point in time, we compare the measurement against the baseline. If our measurements are not the same during the comparison, something might have changed.

Even if you do not use baseline comparisons when analyzing performance, you are still working with baselines whether you realize it or not. For instance, if you receive a salary every first day of the month, this is your normal situation or, in the context of this chapter, your baseline. If for some reason you didn't receive your salary on the first day of the month, you would notice a deviation compared to the baseline. This might be a reason to investigate why you didn't receive your salary on time. Maybe the day changed from the first to the fifth of the month, or, in the worst case, the company you work for can't pay your salary anymore. In any of these cases, there are actions we can take: either accept the change, and by doing so create a new baseline, or revert the situation back to the baseline state again. Figure 4-1 shows this process.

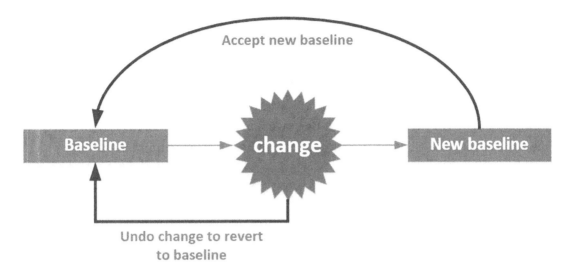

Figure 4-1. Changes impact baseline

Defining and maintaining baselines is an iterative process. Every change occurring on your system could impact your baseline. A new release of an application might change a number of queries, or your company might grant a new department access to the database, increasing the number of connections. In both these examples, we would make adjustments to the baseline, since the normal situation would have changed.

All of these adjusting and measuring baselines with every change to the system sound like a lot of work, and sometimes it is. But believe me – the benefits of having a baseline far outweigh the costs. Baselines help you detect problems faster than just looking at a single measurement, and in the case of wait statistics, it is the only way to find a reliable, definitive answer to your problem. Let's use a more technical example to illustrate this using DBA Jane.

Jane maintains a SQL Server instance hosting a single-user database. This database is used by every sales person in the company and records every financial transaction between the company and its customers. Users access the database through Application X. Application X is running version 2.4 and is very stable. Performance is good, users are happy, and the money keeps rolling in. Everything is great until one day a consultant walks in and wants to upgrade Application X to the brand new 3.0 version. The update to version 3.0 was a breeze and completed without any problems, and all the users love the new features.

Two days later the phone rings. Jane's manager just received word from the sales team that the performance in version 3.0 is horrible and he demands it get resolved right away.

Thankfully, Jane knew the importance of a baseline and created one before the upgrade to version 3.0. Using the version 2.4 baseline, Jane compares the measurements in the baseline to the measurements done in version 3.0 and immediately spots a large difference in the lock wait time measurements. Since other measurements remain roughly the same compared to the 2.4 baseline, Jane focuses on long-running locks and identifies an update query that is locking a table. Jane rolls back the query, and the situation returns to normal. Jane then contacts the application's vendor and learns this behavior was a result of a bug in the software.

Now this example might sound a little far-fetched, but it is a simplified version of the method I use almost every day when measuring the impact of changes or analyzing performance problems. Without a baseline of the lock wait time, Jane wouldn't know that the wait time had increased, since Jane had nothing to compare against. Jane might have chosen to look at other metrics instead of the lock wait time and would have wasted valuable time and money.

The message here is simple: baselines will help you detect abnormal situations and resolve performance problems faster!

Visualizing Your Baselines

Baselines are frequently visualized through graphs. Graphs make it easier to detect measurements with the highest increase or decrease compared to your baseline. Also, visualizing data helps get your point across to prove if a specific configuration is impacting performance, for example, when you need to convince the storage administrator the change in the storage configuration has impacted performance. If you hand them a graph showing normal behavior compared to the behavior after the change, they might be more inclined to help. The graph in Figure 4-2 shows the baseline measurements compared to the measurements done later.

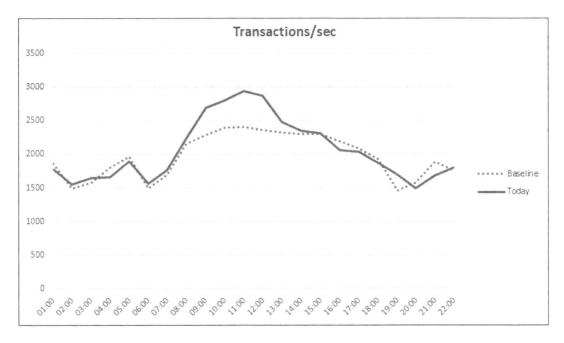

Figure 4-2. *Example of a baseline graph*

As you can see in Figure 4-2, you are able to identify the potential problem quickly. Apparently, between 08:00 and 12:00, the number of transactions per second is higher than the normal situation, and it might be worth taking the time to investigate.

Baseline Types and Statistics

We use different types of baselines depending on the information we collect. There isn't one single baseline to fit all our needs, especially when using baselines for performance-troubleshooting purposes. For example, we could create a baseline for every single wait type, or we could choose to create only baselines for wait types which impact our system the most. We could also choose to create a baseline for specific days or time segments, like business hours, and create another for after business hours.

Next after selecting the metrics we want baselines for, we then make choices on how to calculate the baselines. These choices involve some math and often require calculating aggregates such as averages. In many cases, a baseline consists of an average of many data points, depending on how many measurements performed in each time range. If you collect measurements for a long period of time and calculate the average value from those measurements, you create a more reliable baseline than only one day's worth of measurements. But creating a baseline based on averages also has disadvantages, as averages are heavily influenced by skewed data. Without going too deep into statistical details, skewed data means very high or very low values will impact your average. Consider a group of students and exam scores. We evaluate how the group performed by calculating the average result of the exam (the students are rated between 1 and 10, 1 being very poor and 10 being excellent; a 6 or higher is required to pass the exam). Figure 4-3 shows the exam results in a graph.

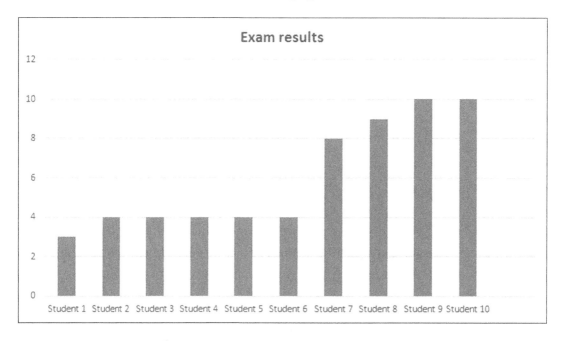

Figure 4-3. *Exam results*

As you can see in Figure 4-3, only four students scored higher than the required 6 to pass the exam. The rest of the group scored below the requirement. However, if we look at the average performance of the group, they scored a 6. We could conclude the group is performing well enough with an average score of 6, but then we would miss how only four of ten students passed the exam. This information is important to keep in mind when you work with average baselines. If you see a spike in the average baseline, it is always something you should investigate, because it impacts your baseline.

There are statistical methods available to deal with skewed data and averages, one being the trimmed (or truncated) mean. This method removes x percent of the highest and lowest measurements in your series, creating a more stable average. Reviewing all possible statistical methods available is beyond the scope of this book. Just be mindful about how the data is collected, if averages are being used and if outliers are possible causing skewness.

Baseline Pitfalls

Hopefully the previous section convinced you baselines are important, but before you go and capture every performance metric and convert them into a baseline measurement, there are some pitfalls to avoid.

Too Much Information

Even though you are free to baseline every possible metric in your environment, this is generally considered a bad idea. Gathering too much information can blind you in your search for answers. Comparing 100,000 different metrics against a baseline every time a performance problem occurs is a colossal waste of time. The advice here is to keep the number of metrics small, including only performance metrics which matter most for your system. For instance, you could include performance metrics related to Availability Groups, but if your system doesn't use this feature, there is no use including them.

Know Your Metrics

Another important aspect in the selection of performance metrics is understanding what a performance metric represents. Without this knowledge, it is difficult to formulate a correct conclusion. For example, if you see a metric named "Locks," you should know if this metric represents the total number of Locks or the number of Locks per second.

Find the Big Measurement Changes

When comparing measurements against a baseline, look for any big increases or decreases. Especially for wait statistics, very small increases in wait time (1–2%) aren't a cause for concern. If one of your wait time measurements goes up 20%, that would be a good signal to start investigating.

Use Fixed Intervals

When capturing wait statistics information, you should use a fixed interval. If we were to capture wait times at random, it would be impossible to build a reliable baseline. One way to automate the capture of wait statistics information is by using the SQL Server Agent and setting a job schedule to a fixed interval, perhaps every 15 minutes.

Building a Baseline for Wait Statistics Analysis

Next, let's get to work and create a baseline we can use for wait statistics analysis. As I mentioned at the beginning of this chapter, baselines are incredibly important for analyzing performance problems using wait statistics. Nobody has the same wait types and wait times compared to your system, so it's up to you to create a baseline you can compare against.

In this section, I will show you a method to create, maintain, and compare baselines and measurements. This is but one example; you could find other methods better suited to your needs.

We will capture SQL Server wait statistics measurements and store them inside a database named "Baseline," so information is not lost. Since wait statistics are logged at the SQL Server instance level, it makes sense to create a separate measurement database inside every SQL Server instance. Figure 4-4 shows you my Baseline database inside SSMS.

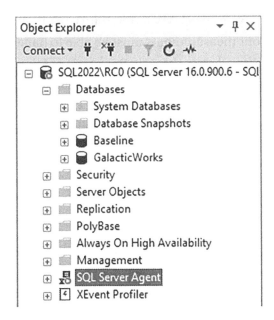

Figure 4-4. *Baseline database*

You can create the database yourself using the script in Listing 4-1, making sure to change the file locations. The database data file will be 1.5 GB when it gets created, which gives enough free space to capture weeks of wait statistics information.

Listing 4-1. Creating the Baseline database

```
-- Create Baseline database
CREATE DATABASE [Baseline]
  ON PRIMARY      (
    NAME = N'Baseline', FILENAME = N'E:\Data\baseline_data.mdf' ,
SIZE = 1536000KB , FILEGROWTH = 10%    )
 LOG ON    (
    NAME = N'Baseline_log', FILENAME = N'E:\Log\baseline_log.ldf' ,
SIZE = 102400KB , FILEGROWTH = 10%    )
GO;
ALTER DATABASE [Baseline] SET RECOVERY SIMPLE
GO;
```

We use the sys.dm_os_wait_stats DMV as the source of our measurements, which means the table holding our measurements must be able to handle the information returned from the DMV. We will store the wait types and wait times and also add additional information to enrich the data, so we can create multiple baselines.

Listing 4-2 shows a query to create a table, named WaitStats, to hold the wait statistics information we will use for creating our baselines.

Listing 4-2. Create a wait statistics table

```
USE [BaseLine]
GO
CREATE TABLE WaitStats
  (ws_ID INT IDENTITY(1,1) PRIMARY KEY,
   ws_DateTime DATETIME,
   ws_Day INT,
   ws_Month INT,
   ws_Year INT,
   ws_Hour INT,
   ws_Minute INT,
   ws_DayOfWeek VARCHAR(15),
   ws_WaitType NVARCHAR(60),
   ws_WaitTime BIGINT,
   ws_WaitingTasks BIGINT,
   ws_SignalWaitTime BIGINT);
```

As you see in the script, we capture the wait type, wait time, signal wait time, and the number of waiting tasks. We also capture the date and time when the wait statistics information is logged. The date and time is split into additional columns to segment the data, making it easier to build specific baselines based on a specific day, hour, month, and so forth, without having to convert the datetime data type every time.

Now that we have our table ready, it is time to capture some wait statistics and insert them into the WaitStats table. Because the sys.dm_os_wait_stats DMV returns cumulative wait times, we must calculate the difference in wait time between the two capture moments. If we were to only capture the information directly from the sys.dm_os_wait_stats DMV, we would always receive ever-increasing wait times, making comparisons difficult. There are two ways to capture the change in wait time between two measurements, and both have their advantages and disadvantages.

The first method, which I call the reset method, will capture the wait statistics information from the sys.dm_os_wait_stats DMV and then reset the DMV using the

```
DBCC SQLPERF('sys.dm_os_wait_stats', CLEAR)
```

command. The main advantage is this method is simple to use, as we only need to capture the information, reset it again, and start the same procedure at the next measurement. There is no need to calculate deltas, because after the first measurement, the counters are reset to 0. The disadvantage is that the DBCC command resets the information inside the sys.dm_os_wait_stats DMV. This means we lose the cumulative information inside the DMV, information we do not want to lose. Figure 4-5 illustrates this method of wait statistics capturing.

Figure 4-5. *Capturing wait statistics using the reset method*

The second option, named the delta method, involves calculating the difference, or delta, in wait time between two measurements. The advantage of this method is we will not lose the cumulative wait times inside the sys.dm_os_wait_stats DMV. The disadvantage is calculating the deltas is more complex compared to the first method. It usually also involves a WAITFOR DELAY command inside the T-SQL script to set the interval. This might mean if you plan to capture wait statistics information using the SQL Server Agent, you could end up with a SQL Server Agent job that is running almost continuously. Figure 4-6 illustrates the delta option of capture wait statistics.

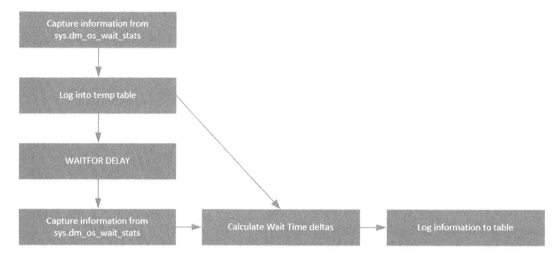

Figure 4-6. *Capturing wait statistics using the delta method*

Nerd Note   A third option would be to grab the metrics without clearing or manually calculating a delta. You would be able to perform any necessary calculations later. Or perhaps only store nonzero metrics on each insert. Or only store metrics if they have changed since the last collection. Use whatever option or method which works best for you and your systems.

There are more methods available with which to capture wait statistics information, but I most frequently see these two, or variations of them. What method you want to use is up to you, as in the end both will return the same results.

Reset Capture Method

The reset capture method consists of a single T-SQL script to capture the information from the sys.dm_os_wait_stats DMV followed by a reset of the counters inside the DMV. Listing 4-3 shows the T-SQL script to fill the WaitStats table we created earlier.

Listing 4-3. Reset capture method

```
USE [Baseline]
GO
-- Insert Wait Stats into Baseline table
```

```
INSERT INTO WaitStats
SELECT
  GETDATE() AS 'DateTime',
  DATEPART(DAY,GETDATE()) AS 'Day',
  DATEPART(MONTH,GETDATE()) AS 'Month',
  DATEPART(YEAR,GETDATE()) AS 'Year',
  DATEPART(HOUR, GETDATE()) AS 'Hour',
  DATEPART(MINUTE, GETDATE()) AS 'Minute',
  DATENAME(DW, GETDATE()) AS 'DayOfWeek',
 wait_type AS 'WaitType',
 wait_time_ms AS 'WaitTime',
 waiting_tasks_count AS 'WaitingTasks',
 signal_wait_time_ms AS 'SignalWaitTime'
FROM sys.dm_os_wait_stats;
-- Clear sys.dm_os_wait_stats
DBCC SQLPERF ('sys.dm_os_wait_stats',CLEAR)
GO
```

Delta Capture Method

The delta capture method also consists of a single T-SQL script, but it is more complex than the reset capture method. It uses a temporary table to store the first measurement, waits for 15 minutes, performs a second measurement, and calculates the deltas. The result is inserted into the WaitStats table. Listing 4-4 shows the T-SQL script you can use if you plan to use this method of collecting wait statistics metrics.

Listing 4-4. Delta capture method

```
USE [Baseline]
GO

-- Check if the temp table already exists -- if it does drop it.
IF EXISTS
  (
  SELECT *
```

```
  FROM tempdb.dbo.sysobjects
  WHERE ID = OBJECT_ID(N'tempdb..#ws_Capture')
  )
DROP TABLE #ws_Capture;

-- Create temp table to hold our first measurement
CREATE TABLE #ws_Capture
  (  wst_WaitType NVARCHAR(60),
wst_WaitTime BIGINT,
wst_WaitingTasks BIGINT,
wst_SignalWaitTime BIGINT   );

-- Insert our first measurement into the temp table
INSERT INTO #ws_Capture
  SELECT wait_type,
wait_time_ms,
waiting_tasks_count,
signal_wait_time_ms
FROM sys.dm_os_wait_stats;

-- Wait for the next measurement
-- In this case we will wait 15 minutes
WAITFOR DELAY '00:15:00'

-- Combine the first measurement with a new measurement and calculate
the deltas
-- Write the results into the WaitStats table
INSERT INTO WaitStats
SELECT
  GETDATE() AS 'DateTime',
  DATEPART(DAY,GETDATE()) AS 'Day',
  DATEPART(MONTH,GETDATE()) AS 'Month',
  DATEPART(YEAR,GETDATE()) AS 'Year',
  DATEPART(HOUR, GETDATE()) AS 'Hour',
  DATEPART(MINUTE, GETDATE()) AS 'Minute',
 DATENAME(DW, GETDATE()) AS 'DayOfWeek',
 dm.wait_type AS 'WaitType',
```

```
 dm.wait_time_ms - ws.wst_WaitTime AS 'WaitTime',
 dm.waiting_tasks_count - ws.wst_WaitingTasks AS 'WaitingTasks',
 dm.signal_wait_time_ms - ws.wst_SignalWaitTime AS 'SignalWaitTime'
FROM sys.dm_os_wait_stats dm
INNER JOIN #ws_Capture ws
    ON dm.wait_type = ws.wst_WaitType;

-- Clean up the temp table
DROP TABLE #ws_Capture;
```

Using SQL Server Agent to Schedule Measurements

After selecting a capture method, we run a T-SQL script to fill our WaitStats table with wait statistics information. As described in the baseline pitfalls section earlier, it is very important to perform measurements at a fixed interval. This makes comparing measurements easier since you are comparing the same time segments. An easy way to do this is by using a SQL Server Agent job set to a fixed interval. The interval can be set to your choosing – the larger you set the interval, the smaller the number of time segments you can compare against. Setting the interval to be shorter will give you more time segments but will also mean an increase in data stored. I personally prefer to set my interval to 15 minutes. This gives enough time segments to compare for most scenarios.

I won't go into details here about how to create a SQL Server Agent job to capture wait statistics information, but I do want to point out how my job looks as an example you can use. I usually end up with a SQL Server Agent job with just one T-SQL script step. In this step, I copy the capture script, depending on which method I want to use. Figure 4-7 shows a screenshot of my SQL Server Agent job.

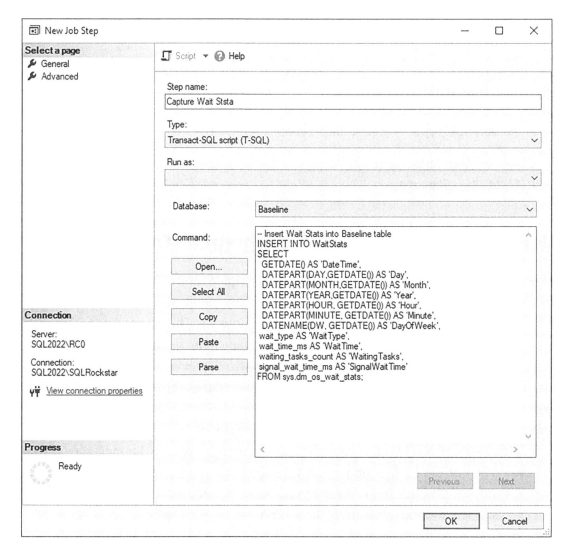

Figure 4-7. *Capturing WaitStats SQL Server Agent job step*

In this case, I used the reset capture method to capture the wait statistics in the WaitStats table.

Figure 4-8 shows the schedule used to capture wait statistics on a fixed interval.

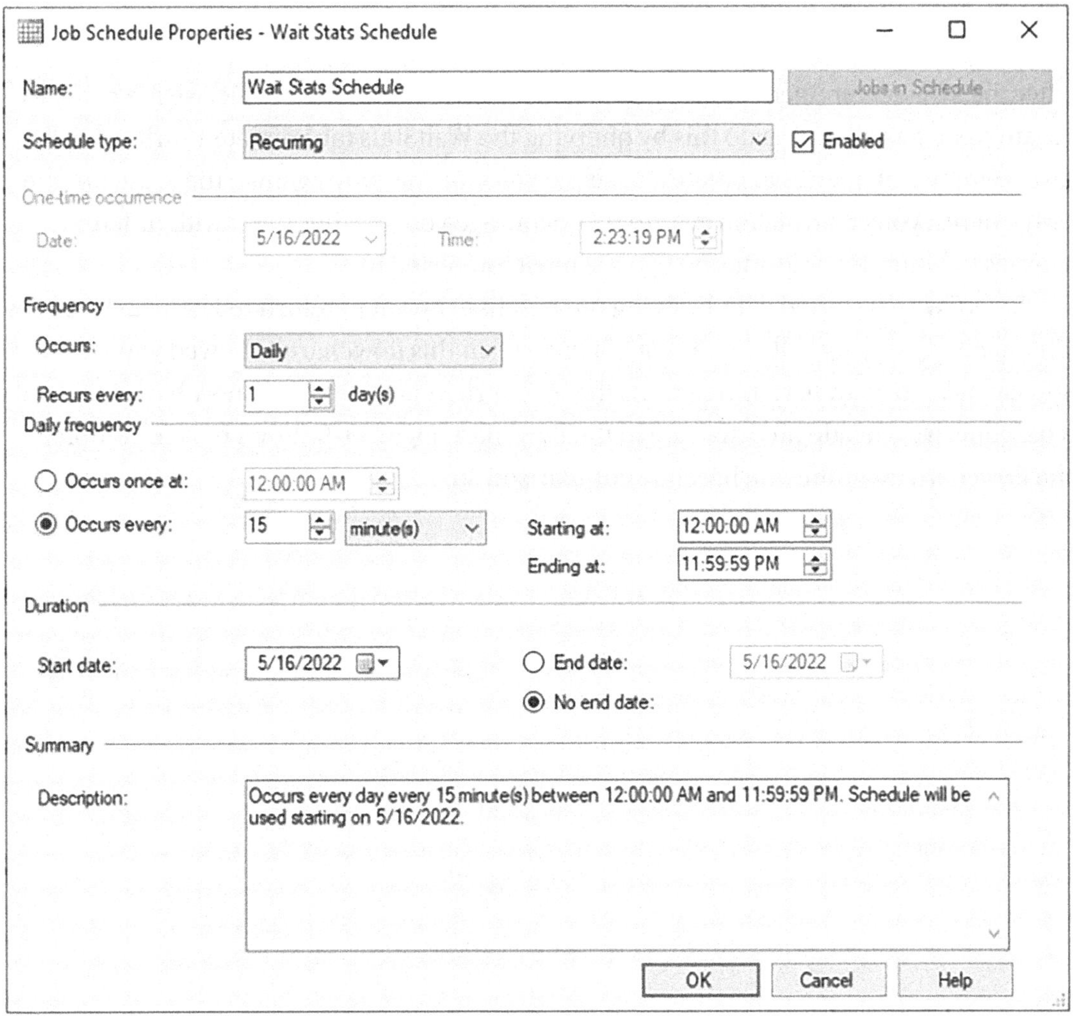

Figure 4-8. *SQL Server Agent job schedule*

As you can see, I have set it to every 15 minutes, every day.

Again, you are free to choose your own capture interval, but make sure to always capture at the same interval length.

After we have created a SQL Server Agent job to gather wait statistics information, we need to let it run for a while. The longer the job runs, the more information we gather, improving the quality of our baselines.

Wait Statistics Baseline Analysis

After the SQL Server Agent job collects wait statistics metrics for a while, we are ready to create some baselines. We do this by querying the WaitStats table created earlier. I will give examples of queries to create a baseline you can compare against; these are not the only queries you can run, however, and I encourage you to experiment with different queries to return the information you are most interested in.

Before we get started with building the baseline, I want to return to Figure 2-14 in Chapter 2, "Querying SQL Server Wait Statistics." In this flowchart, I showed you steps you can take to analyze resource waits that occur right now. Since we now have access to a baseline, we can add an extra step to the flowchart. Figure 4-9 shows how to complete the flowchart, including the baseline comparison step.

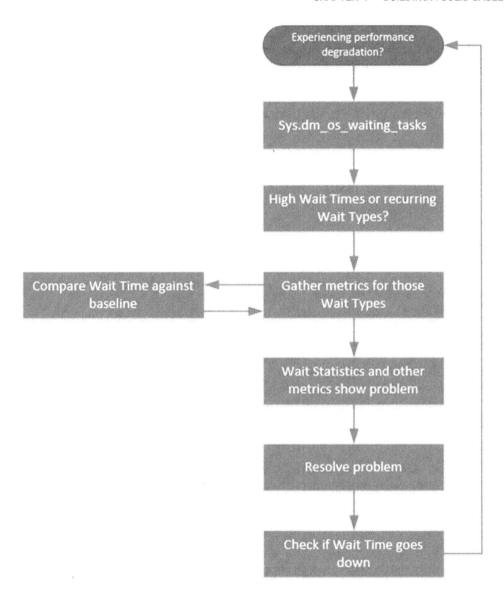

Figure 4-9. *Complete wait statistics performance-analysis flowchart*

The baselines are an extra input to the metrics gathered when researching a performance problem. Baselines are a valuable input because they show information about the period where the performance problem did not exist.

Let's go through an example, using DBA Jane again, where we review all the steps of the flowchart shown in Figure 4-9. In this example, I will show queries against the WaitStats table for building a baseline useful for the performance-analysis process.

Tuesday, around 9 a.m., Jane receives a phone call regarding the daily reporting against the sales database; users complain reports are slower than normal. The problem started around 8 a.m., and users are still experiencing performance problems. The reports are part of a scheduled job that runs every workday, starting at 8 a.m.

The first thing Jane does is query the sys.dm_os_waiting_tasks DMV using the following query:

```
SELECT *
FROM sys.dm_os_waiting_tasks
ORDER BY session_id ASC;
```

Jane focuses on user sessions but does not see any long wait times as shown in Figure 4-10.

	waiting_task_address	session_id	exec_context_id	wait_duration_ms	wait_type	resource_address
20	0x00000039FA027C28	19	0	6347173	ONDEMAND_TASK_QUEUE	0x0000003AC3BBEF50
21	0x00000039F152E4E8	27	0	287001609	HADR_NOTIFICATION_DEQUEUE	0x0000003ACB1EEE00
22	0x00000039EED5D0...	31	0	677	SLEEP_TASK	NULL
23	0x00000039EED5C8...	32	0	7008297	BROKER_EVENTHANDLER	NULL
24	0x00000039EB03E4E8	33	0	287001105	BROKER_TRANSMITTER	NULL
25	0x00000039EB03E8C8	34	0	239	HADR_FILESTREAM_IOMGR_IOCOMPLE...	NULL
26	0x00000039FA027848	2060	0	4	PAGEIOLATCH_SH	0x0000003AC4CAEC90
27	0x00000039FA027848	4002	0	10	PAGEIOLATCH_SH	0x0000003AC50AEA00
28	0x00000039FA027848	4519	0	18	PAGEIOLATCH_EX	0x0000003AC3BBEF50

Figure 4-10. *sys.dm_os_waiting_tasks*

After executing the query against the sys.dm_os_waiting_tasks DMV multiple times, Jane notices that the wait type PAGEIOLATCH_SH is returned every time she queries the DMV. Each time, the wait type is returned with a different session ID but with relatively low wait times.

Jane uses the same T-SQL script to capture wait statistics metrics into the WaitStats table, as we discussed earlier in this chapter. Because Jane has access to historic wait statistics information, she creates a baseline of the PAGEIOLATCH_SH wait times.

The first step is to view the PAGEIOLATCH_SH wait times of today, filtered to show measurements captured between 8 and 9 in the morning, using the query shown in Listing 4-5.

Listing 4-5. Show wait times for PAGEIOLATCH_SH between 8 and 9 a.m. today

```
-- PAGEIOLATCH_SH waits, today between 8 and 9 AM
SELECT
```

```
CONVERT(VARCHAR(5), ws_DateTime, 108) AS 'Time',
ws_WaitTime AS 'Wait Time'
FROM WaitStats
WHERE ws_WaitType = 'PAGEIOLATCH_SH'
AND (ws_Hour >= 8 AND ws_Hour < 9)
AND CONVERT(VARCHAR(5), ws_DateTime, 105) = CONVERT(VARCHAR(5),
GETDATE(), 105);
```

The query returned the results shown in Figure 4-11.

	Time	Wait Time
1	08:00	1528749
2	08:15	1828749
3	08:30	1658974
4	08:45	1698547

Figure 4-11. *PAGEIOLATCH_SH wait times of today*

Now that Jane has the wait times for today of the PAGEIOLATCH_SH wait type, the next step is to create a baseline from the historic measurements of the PAGEIOLATCH_SH wait type to compare today's measurements against the baseline. Jane uses the query shown in Listing 4-6 to build his baseline.

Listing 4-6. PAGEIOLATCH_SH baseline

```
-- Baseline between 8 and 9 on workdays
-- Not including measurements done today
SELECT
  CONVERT(VARCHAR(5), ws_DateTime, 108) AS 'Time',
  AVG(ws_WaitTime) AS 'Baseline'
FROM WaitStats
WHERE ws_WaitType = 'PAGEIOLATCH_SH'
AND ws_DayOfWeek IN ('Monday', 'Tuesday', 'Wednesday', 'Thursday','Friday')
AND (ws_Hour >= 8 AND ws_Hour < 9)
AND CONVERT(VARCHAR(5), ws_DateTime, 105) < CONVERT(VARCHAR(5),
GETDATE(), 105)
GROUP BY CONVERT(VARCHAR(5), ws_DateTime, 108);
```

This query builds a baseline with the following characteristics: return the average wait time of PAGEIOLATCH_SH wait type captured on a workday between 8 a.m. and 9 a.m., excluding today. We exclude today's measurements because they were performed during the performance problem, which might impact the average. Another suggestion would be to filter only data captured in the last x weeks to limit the amount of data calculated in the average.

The results of the query shown in Listing 4-6 can be seen in Figure 4-12.

	Time	Baseline
1	08:00	313038
2	08:15	391444
3	08:30	498923
4	08:45	570782

Figure 4-12. *PAGEIOLATCH_SH baseline*

As you can immediately see when you compare the wait times in Figures 4-11 and 4-12, the measurements done today are a lot higher than those in the historic baseline. To make it a little easier to see the difference, I created a graph of both measurements, as shown in Figure 4-13.

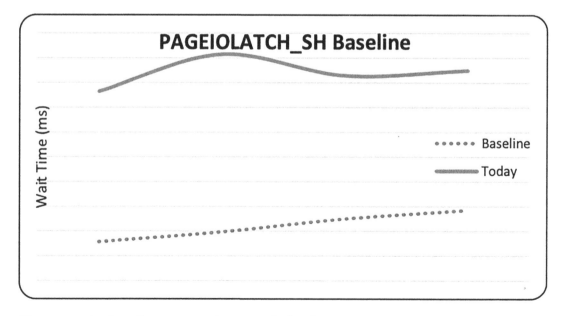

Figure 4-13. *Baseline comparison graph for the PAGEIOLATCH_SH wait type*

Because there is such a difference in wait times for the PAGEIOLATCH_SH wait type between the baseline and today, Jane believes the PAGEIOLATCH_SH wait type needs further investigation.

Nerd Note   We will take a detailed look at the PAGEIOLATCH_SH wait type in Chapter 9, "Latch-Related Wait Types," but to give you a (very) short explanation, long PAGEIOLATCH_SH waits can indicate storage problems.

To investigate further, Jane starts the Performance Monitor to look at metrics related to the storage subsystem and in particular the disk latency counters. As you can see in Figure 4-14, the latency on the disk where the database data file resides peaks to very high values, more than 4,000 milliseconds! For SQL Server to perform optimally, the disk latency should be as low as possible, ideally less than 10ms.

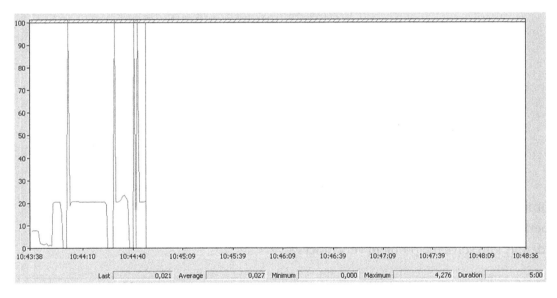

Figure 4-14. *Disk read latency*

With both the wait statistics baseline information and the Perfmon metrics, Jane believes the problem is storage related and contacts the storage administrator. The metrics collected also help the storage administrator, since they can compare their storage-related measurements against those Jane supplied. The storage administrator confirms there is a problem related to the disk that contains the sales database and solves the problem by replacing a faulty disk in the disk array. After the disk gets replaced, the disk latency returns to a 6 milliseconds average, and the high latency peaks disappear. Jane queries the wait times again from the WaitStats table after the disk is replaced and notices the wait times for the PAGEIOLATCH_SH wait type are close to the baseline values again. Users also inform Jane the reports are running normally again.

During this example, Jane went through all the steps of the wait statistics performance-analysis flowchart shown in Figure 4-9:

1. Users experience performance degradation while running reports.

2. Jane queries the sys.dm_os_waiting_tasks DMV to find out if there are high wait times or frequently recurring wait types. The PAGEIOLATCH_SH wait type seems to be recurring frequently.

3. Jane gathers metrics by capturing the PAGEIOLATCH_SH wait times of today and comparing them to the baseline and also gathers additional metrics from Perfmon.

4. All the metrics show the problem is likely storage related, and Jane contacts the storage administrator.

5. The storage administrator replaces a broken disk in the array. Storage latency values drop to 6 milliseconds.

6. Jane checks the wait times of the PAGEIOLATCH_SH wait type again and confirms that they are close to the baseline values.

Even though this example might seem very simple, it is based on a performance problem I encountered in the real world. Using the steps from the wait statistics performance-analysis flowchart combined with the baseline metrics, I was able to identify and solve the problem very quickly.

Nerd Note   Correlation does not imply causation. While replacing the disk seems to have fixed the issue, the reality is your infrastructure architecture is complex. There's a chance the true root cause was something else, perhaps a flooded kernel on a VM host which was showing as a PAGEIOLATCH_SH at that moment in time and was also resolved around the same time the disk was replaced.

In the example, the query in Listing 4-6 creates a baseline for the PAGEIOLATCH_SH wait type. This query is an example of what you can use against the WaitStats table. You should modify it to suit your own needs; for instance, you could choose to not limit the results for weekdays and show average wait times captured on a specific day. Or you could request the actual wait times on a specific date.

If you are capturing wait statistics measurements for a long period of time, it might be a good idea to split the results into multiple tables for easier and faster querying. For instance, you could use the following query to insert all the wait statistics measurements done in March into their own table:

```
SELECT *
INTO WaitStats_March
FROM WaitStats
WHERE ws_Month = 3;
```

This also gives us options to compare specific wait times during different periods of time by joining the different tables together.

Nerd Note   There are many ways for you to slice and dice this data, such as the use of windowing functions, or perhaps use PowerBI and build yourself a proper dashboard. Use whatever works best for you.

Figure 4-15 shows the tables of my baseline database that I usually end up with, sorting the data per month.

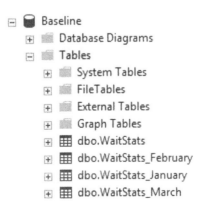

Figure 4-15. *Wait statistics measurement split per month*

You should decide how to split the measurements yourself; maybe you want to store the wait statistics measurements in a separate table for every application version you use or store all the measurements of a specific wait type in a separate table. The choice is yours.

This chapter hopefully gave you some ideas on how to store wait statistics measurements and create baselines from those measurements. I tried to avoid telling you exactly what to do and how to do it, because I believe one single approach doesn't work for everybody. You will need to write and adjust your own queries to create the baselines you are interested in, but I hope this chapter showed you the foundations to further build upon.

Summary

In this chapter, we took a close look at baselines from both a theoretical and a practical point of view. Baselines are incredibly important for any type of performance analysis you perform. In the case of wait statistics, baselines are frequently required if you want to troubleshoot SQL Server–related performance problems. Since wait statistics are unique for your system, there is only one method by which to compare wait times – baselines.

I gave you some examples and T-SQL scripts to create your own wait statistics baseline table, so you can start capturing wait statistics information right now. We also went through an example of how you can query that baseline information and compare it to actual measurements to troubleshoot a performance-related incident.

PART II

Wait Types

CHAPTER 5

CPU-Related Wait Types

Processors have evolved enormously in the last few decades, and processor manufacturers manage to build faster processors on a yearly basis. And while the speed of processors is hitting a ceiling, the number of cores manufacturers manage to build inside their processors has grown. At the time of writing this book, you can buy a single processor with 64 cores inside to power your system. Processors are also one of the difficult parts of your system to replace. While expanding your system's memory is relatively easy, replacing a processor for a faster one or more cores requires you to change the system's motherboard due to CPU socket incompatibility. This means we are often stuck with the current processors until we replace the system altogether.

Processors are important for SQL Server. Higher processor speeds will accelerate processor-related instructions, and more cores means more schedulers for SQL Server to use for request executions. But even these upgrades in speed and cores cannot prevent the fact we will sometimes wait on processor resources. In this chapter, we will look at some wait types with a relation with your system's processor.

CXPACKET

By far the most common CPU-related wait type in SQL Server instances deployed uses default, out-of-the-box, configuration options. It is also one of the most misunderstood wait types and sometimes has little impact on your query performance. In fact, lowering CXPACKET wait times may degrade the performance of your query! If you are running SQL Server 2016 SP2 or later, there are changes in how to handle CXPACKET waits. We will discuss the impact of the changes, including the parallelism-related wait type CXCONSUMER, at the end of this section.

© Thomas LaRock, Enrico van de Laar 2023
T. LaRock and E. van de Laar, *Pro SQL Server 2022 Wait Statistics*,
https://doi.org/10.1007/978-1-4842-8771-2_5

What Is the CXPACKET Wait Type?

The CXPACKET wait type occurs when a query is executed in parallel (i.e., on multiple CPU cores) instead of serial (a single CPU core). Parallel execution of queries has a performance advantage compared to serial execution if the work is divided among multiple worker threads. This advantage would apply to queries returning large result sets; queries returning only a few rows benefit far less from parallelism, and in many cases parallelism slows down those queries. This doesn't mean we turn off parallelism as I have yet to see a true OLTP database where every query only returns a handful of rows. Many systems have a mixed workload, dealing with short duration queries but also large, longer-running, reporting, and analytical queries.

Parallel queries use multiple worker threads to execute a request. Along with the worker threads created to perform the work requested, a parallel query will also use a control thread, also known as the Thread 0. This Thread's 0 task is to coordinate the other worker threads. While the Thread 0 is waiting for the other worker threads to finish the work they were assigned to perform, it records total wait as the CXPACKET wait type. To understand this relation a little bit better, look at Figure 5-1.

Figure 5-1. *Parallel query threading*

As soon as the SQL Server Query Optimizer decides on an execution plan which uses parallelism, you will see CXPACKET waits occur. This is completely normal and nothing to worry about if you are expecting queries to run in parallel and they perform as expected. In those cases, you can ignore long wait times on the CXPACKET wait type. There are, however, cases where you don't want to use parallelism or when parallelism is negatively impacting the performance of your queries because of skewed workloads.

Because the CXPACKET wait type is directly related to the parallelism settings of your SQL Server instance, we can influence it by adjusting server configuration settings. We find the parallelism settings in the Server Properties ➤ Advanced ➤ Parallelism section of your SQL Server instance, as shown in Figure 5-2.

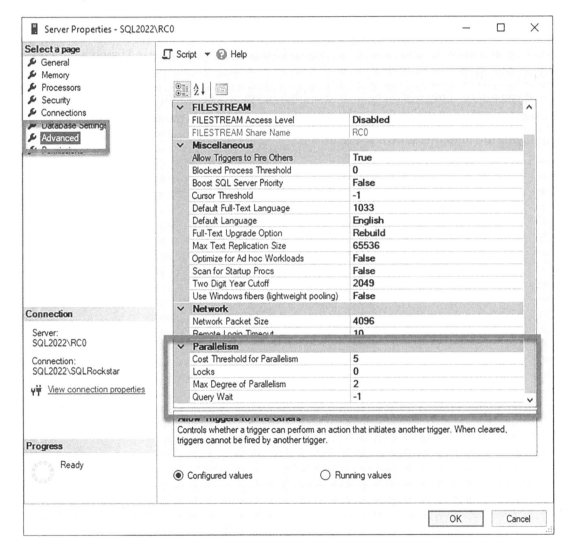

Figure 5-2. *Parallelism configuration for entire SQL Server instance*

Of these settings, the Cost Threshold for Parallelism and Max Degree of Parallelism settings will have the most impact on parallel queries.

The **Cost Threshold for Parallelism** setting configures the cost threshold for a query executed in parallel by the Query Optimizer. If a query has a cost higher than the value configured in the Cost Threshold for Parallelism, the Query Optimizer might decide to generate a parallel plan instead of a serial one. By default, the setting has a value of 5 and can be configured to have a value between 0 and 32,767.

The **Max Degree of Parallelism** setting configures the maximum number of schedulers used by each operator when executing a parallel plan. By default, this setting is configured to be 0, which means all available schedulers may be used when a parallel plan is executed.

If you are running SQL Server 2016 or higher, you are also able to configure the MAXDOP parallelism settings on a database level through database scoped configuration items, as shown in Figure 5-3.

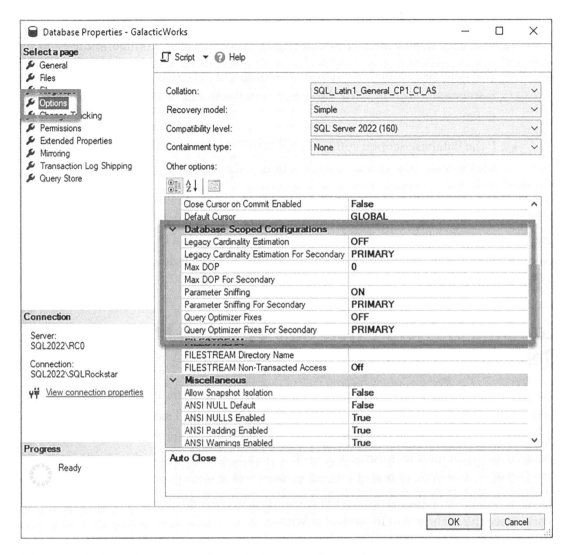

Figure 5-3. *Database scoped parallelism configuration*

The introduction of database scoped configuration settings for parallelism is a welcome change. Consider, for instance, when you have multiple databases inside the same SQL Server instance. Ideally each of those databases will use configuration settings tuned for their specific workloads. Before SQL Server 2016, we couldn't configure that on a per-database level, so generally you would stick with generalized configuration values. Now with database scoped configurations possible, it is easy to configure the optimal setting for each individual database.

With the ability to add database scoped configuration values for parallelism settings, there is a difference in how the SQL Server engine processes these configurations:

- The database scoped configuration setting will overwrite the current instance setting only if the database scoped setting is set to a non-default value.

- If the database scoped configuration setting is set to its default value, the instance-wide configuration setting will be used.

As an example, if the Max Degree of Parallelism setting is configured to be 4 on the instance level and 0 (default) on the database level, queries executed in parallel may use four schedulers. If the database scoped setting is changed to be a value of 2, queries executed against the database may use a maximum of two schedulers overwriting the instance setting of 4.

Lowering CXPACKET Wait Time by Tuning the Parallelism Configuration Options

There are various methods you can use to lower CXPACKET wait times, but you must first determine if CXPACKET waits are causing your issue. Like I said earlier, CXPACKET waits are normal whenever parallelism is enabled for the SQL Server instance. One solution found on Internet forums is to disable parallelism by setting the Max Degree of Parallelism option to a value of 1. In most cases, this is not a good idea. Disabling parallelism will make the CXPACKET waits disappear, but some queries might perform worse since they cannot run in parallel anymore.

A better approach to lowering CXPACKET waits is to tune the Cost Threshold for Parallelism and Max Degree of Parallelism options, so they match with your workload. This way only the queries which benefit the most from parallelism will be run in parallel. A way to find this parallelism sweet spot is by comparing the runtime of a query when it ran serially vs. in parallel. You should generally focus on queries that access a lot of information and have a longer runtime in general, as those will be the queries that benefit the most from parallelism.

Consider this example where we have a query against our GalacticWorks database requesting information from the Sales.SalesOrderDetail table:

```
SELECT *
FROM Sales.SalesOrderDetail
ORDER BY CarrierTrackingNumber DESC;
```

To determine if this query is a candidate for parallel execution, we will check the estimated cost of the query. To view this information, we look at the estimated execution plan for if the query were executed serially. To make sure the query runs serially, we add the query option MAXDOP 1:

```
SELECT *
FROM Sales.SalesOrderDetail
ORDER BY CarrierTrackingNumber DESC
OPTION (MAXDOP 1);
```

We select the Display Estimated Execution Plan (or press CTRL+L) and hover over the SELECT icon in the execution plan window:

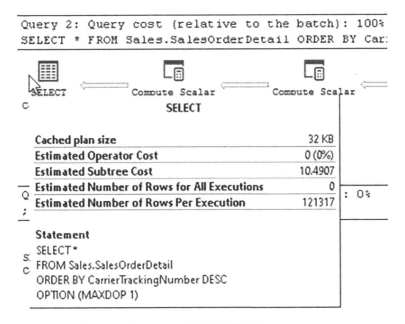

Figure 5-4. *Estimated cost of query with MAXDOP 1*

In this case, the estimated cost is 10.4907. Because the Cost Threshold for Parallelism is still the default value of 5 for this instance, I am confident the query will run in parallel if I remove the MAXDOP query hint.

Figure 5-5 shows the actual execution plan after executing the query without the MAXDOP 1 option.

```
Query 1: Query cost (relative to the batch): 100%
SELECT * FROM Sales.SalesOrderDetail ORDER BY CarrierTrackingNumber DESC
```

Figure 5-5. *Actual execution plan without MAXDOP 1 option*

As you can see, the query ran using parallelism, just as we expected, since the estimated cost was higher than the value configured for the Cost Threshold for Parallelism option. If we look at the properties of the SELECT operation in the actual execution plan, we find additional information, as shown in Figure 5-6.

SELECT	
Cached plan size	40 KB
Estimated Operator Cost	0 (0%)
Degree of Parallelism	2
Estimated Subtree Cost	7.08005
Memory Grant	21 MB
Estimated Number of Rows for All Executions	0
Estimated Number of Rows Per Execution	121317

Statement
SELECT*
FROM Sales.SalesOrderDetail
ORDER BY CarrierTrackingNumber DESC

Figure 5-6. *SELECT operation properties*

The properties of the SELECT operation show the query was executed using two threads and the estimated cost decreased to 7.08005.

If we changed the Cost Threshold for Parallelism value to a higher number rather than the default of 5, queries like this example may not use parallelism, but larger cost reporting queries will. Remember, this option is for the entire instance and will affect queries in every database.

Even though the estimated cost decreased, the improvement in execution time is small (about 300 ms) for this example query. You will want to consider the execution time (using SET STATISTICS TIME) when tuning for parallelism using the Cost Threshold for Parallelism option and decide if altering this setting is a benefit or not.

Nerd Note   The default Cost Threshold for Parallelism value of 5 is antiquated for modern database workloads. You will want to test to see what value is right for your specific system, but for most out-of-the-box installs, I recommend setting this value to a higher number, such as 50, and adjust as necessary from there.

Another setting to keep in mind is the **Max Degree of Parallelism** option. When left at the default of 0, all available schedulers may be used when a query runs in parallel. But using more schedulers doesn't necessarily mean the query executes faster. The benefits of using more schedulers decrease after using more than 8. Microsoft recommends the following configuration (from `https://slrwnds.com/xtvmvp`):

- For servers with > 8 cores, set the Max Degree of Parallelism option to 8.

- For servers with < 8 cores, set MAXDOP at or below the number of logical processors.

This is a general recommendation, and your mileage will vary. The KB article also discusses the use of NUMA (Non-Uniform Memory Access) nodes, how SQL Server configures soft-NUMA nodes, and the recommended settings.

Nerd Note   In an ideal world, you would configure your SQL Server instance to run inside of a single NUMA node. This includes not only the number of logical processors assigned to each node but the amount of memory as well.

The setting of both the Cost Threshold for Parallelism and Max Degree of Parallelism options depends on the workload of your system and requires careful testing to find out what works for you and what doesn't. They will impact your CXPACKET wait time though, so compare the CXPACKET wait times against a baseline after changing the Cost Threshold for Parallelism or Max Degree of Parallelism options to measure the impact of the change.

Lowering CXPACKET Wait Time by Resolving Skewed Workloads

A skewed workload is a workload where the parallel worker threads do not receive the same amount of work to perform. This is not an optimal situation, as the Thread 0 will wait for the longest-running worker thread to complete, logging CXPACKET waits while waiting. Figure 5-7 shows an abstract example of a skewed workload.

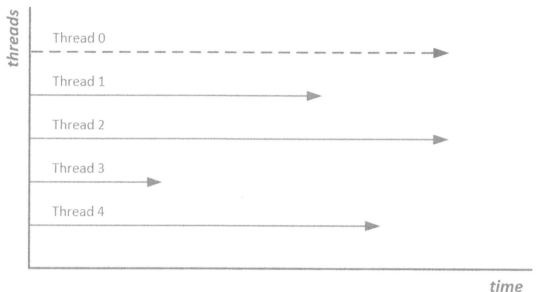

Figure 5-7. *Skewed parallel query threading*

If we assign some of Thread 2's work to Thread 3, the query would perform faster and result in lower CXPACKET wait times.

We view the thread distribution in the actual number of rows property of the parallel operation inside the actual execution plan. Figure 5-8 shows the properties of a clustered index scan that has been performed using parallelism. The operation occurred in the example query we used in the previous section against the Sales.SalesOrderDetail table.

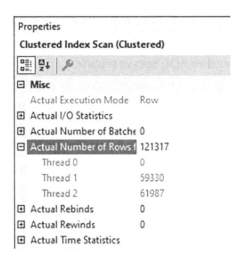

Figure 5-8. *Parallel thread distribution*

In this example, we see the clustered index scan returned 121317 rows that were distributed among two threads (notice that Thread 0, the coordination thread, doesn't process any rows). The distribution of the number of rows is relatively even in this case, so we probably aren't running into a skewed workload problem.

Skewed workloads are often caused by outdated statistics. If the Query Optimizer believes there are fewer (or more rows) in the table than the true amount, it might distribute the work unevenly across the threads. Make sure to regularly perform maintenance on your statistics to prevent skewed workloads.

Introduction of the CXCONSUMER Wait Type

As described earlier, parallelism consists of two parts: producers and consumers. The easiest way to understand this is to consider the Thread 0 as a producer. It is the job of Thread 0 to distribute work to all available parallel worker threads. Those worker threads are consumers and perform the actual work the producers send to them.

With the release of SQL Server 2017 CU3 (and later SQL Server 2016 SP2), Microsoft changed how parallelism waits are recorded. The main goal was to make the CXPACKET parallelism wait more actionable.

Before SQL Server 2017 CU3 and SQL Server 2016 SP2, there was no way to distinguish if consumers were spending time waiting on producers to send work to them. Everything was recorded as CXPACKET wait time internally. The SQL Server development team split up the wait times for parallelism into two different categories: **CXPACKET** and **CXCONSUMER**. With this change, the meaning of those two wait types also changed compared to earlier SQL Server releases.

CXCONSUMER waits will occur whenever a consumer thread is waiting for a producer thread to send rows. This is expected behavior and in many cases safely ignored when analyzing wait statistics information.

CXPACKET waits are now recorded without the CXCONSUMER wait time, meaning CXPACKET wait times not only indicate parallelism occurring but also indicate an issue regarding parallelism operations (for instance, threads are running into issues with required buffer or thread synchronization). Effectively, this means if you are running SQL Server 2017 CU3 or SQL Server SP2 or higher, the CXPACKET wait indicates parallelism issues better than lower SQL Server versions, thus making the CXPACKET wait type more actionable as the development team intended. The advice in dealing with high parallelism wait times described earlier in this chapter is still valid, though it now has a more direct impact on CXPACKET wait times.

CXPACKET Summary

The CXPACKET wait type is directly related to the usage of parallelism during query execution. If queries are executed with parallelism, you will always see CXPACKET waits. Normally this is nothing to worry about, so avoid the knee-jerk reaction to turn off parallelism completely. Instead, focus on tuning the Max Degree of Parallelism and Cost Threshold for Parallelism options so that the thresholds are high enough that your large queries can benefit from using parallelism but your small queries do not experience a negative impact. Also, avoid skewed workloads by making sure your statistics are up-to-date.

If you are running SQL Server 2017 CU3 or SQL Server 2016 SP2 (or higher), the CXPACKET wait time meaning has changed a bit resulting in that CXPACKET waits are far more likely to indicate a parallelism issue occurring than in SQL Server versions that are lower than those mentioned.

SOS_SCHEDULER_YIELD

Just like CXPACKET, the **SOS_SCHEDULER_YIELD** is a wait type that will frequently show up in the top 10 of total wait time on your system. And just like the CXPACKET wait types, SOS_SCHEDULER_YIELD wait times do not necessarily indicate there is a problem with your SQL Server instance. SOS_SCHEDULER_YIELD waits occur as soon as queries execute on your SQL Server instance and are closely related to SQL Server scheduling.

What Is the SOS_SCHEDULER_YIELD Wait Type?

Before we answer what the SOS_SCHEDULER_YIELD wait type means, we have to go back to Chapter 1, "Wait Statistics Internals," where we discussed SQL Server scheduling. Remember how the SQLOS uses its own cooperative non-preemptive scheduling model to make sure Microsoft Windows processes do not interrupt SQL Server's own processes. The SOS_SCHEDULER_YIELD wait type has a direct relation with the SQLOS's cooperative, non-preemptive scheduling model. To make it easier to understand, I have included Figure 5-9, which should be familiar to you as it represents a scheduler that we discussed in Chapter 1.

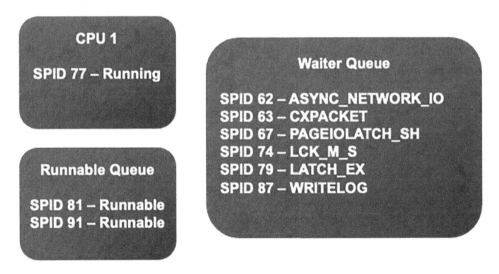

Figure 5-9. *Scheduler and its phases and queues*

If you remember from Chapter 1, "Wait Statistics Internals," worker threads move through the different phases and queues in a fixed order. Generally, a worker thread starts on the Waiter List while it waits for resources, and it then moves to the Runnable Queue waiting for its turn to be run on the processor and finally receives processor time to execute its request, receiving the "RUNNING" state. If the worker thread needs additional resources while it is in the "RUNNING" state, the worker thread moves back to the Waiter Queue list and starts a new trip through the different queues and phases.

There is one exception to this behavior, and it occurs when a worker thread is in the "RUNNING" state and doesn't need additional resources to complete its work. If the SQLOS allowed for a worker thread to stay on the processor for as long as it didn't need any additional resources, the processor could be "hijacked" by one single worker thread for an infinite amount of time. To make sure a situation like this cannot occur, the scheduler gives every worker thread a specific slice of time in which they need to perform their work. We call this slice of time a **quantum**, and it is a fixed, unchangeable, 4 milliseconds. If a worker thread spends its quantum, it must yield the processor, and it moves back to the bottom of the Runnable Queue. It will skip the Waiter List because the worker thread doesn't need additional resources. While the worker thread is waiting to move back to the processor again, the SOS_SCHEDULER_ YIELD wait type is recorded. Figure 5-10 shows this behavior.

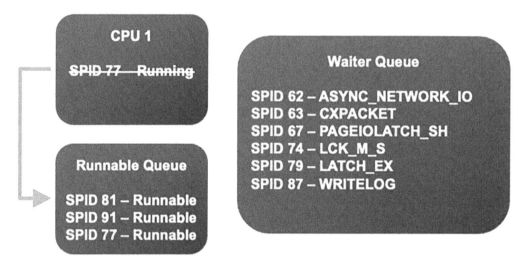

Figure 5-10. *Worker thread voluntarily yielding the processor*

As you can probably guess, worker threads are voluntarily yielding all the time, especially on long-running queries where there is no need for additional resources. But keep in mind wait times for the SOS_SCHEDULER_YIELD wait type are only logged when the worker thread was in the Runnable Queue. If there is no other worker thread in front of the yielding worker thread, it will move directly back to the processor without waiting (it will still move through the Runnable Queue though). To show you an example of this, I executed the following queries against the GalacticWorks database on my test SQL Server, where there is no concurrency whatsoever:

Listing 5-1. Sample queries to show SOS_SCHEDULER_YIELD waits

```
-- Clear Wait Stats
DBCC SQLPERF('sys.dm_os_wait_stats', CLEAR);

-- Simple select
SELECT *
FROM Sales.SalesOrderDetail
ORDER BY CarrierTrackingNumber DESC;

-- Check for SOS_SCHEDULER_YIELD waits
SELECT *
FROM sys.dm_os_wait_stats
WHERE wait_type = 'SOS_SCHEDULER_YIELD';
```

Figure 5-11 shows the results of this query against the sys.dm_os_wait_stats DMV.

	wait_type	waiting_tasks_count	wait_time_ms	max_wait_time_ms	signal_wait_time_ms
1	SOS_SCHEDULER_YIELD	30	0	0	0

Figure 5-11. *SOS_SCHEDULER_YIELD waits*

As you can see in Figure 5-11, the query encountered the SOS_SCHEDULER_YIELD wait type 30 times during execution. It did not spend any time waiting for another worker thread in the Runnable Queue since this was the only query executing at the time. If it spent any time waiting for another worker thread, the wait_time_ms column would have returned a value higher than 0.

As I said at the start of this section, the SOS_SCHEDULER_YIELD wait type is generally not a cause for concern. If, however, the wait times are significantly higher than those in your baseline, it can be a reason to perform some additional research. There are basically three situations you can encounter when dealing with SOS_SCHEDULER_ YIELD waits, as shown in Figure 5-12.

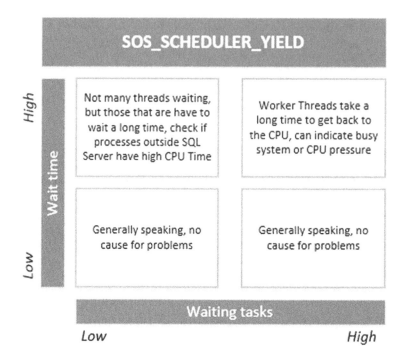

Figure 5-12. *SOS_SCHEDULER_YIELD situations*

Let's look at how we can analyze and resolve the SQL Server CPU pressure problem.

Lowering SOS_SCHEDULER_YIELD Waits

If you are experiencing higher-than-normal SOS_SCHEDULER_YIELD wait times along with a large number of waits overall, you could, potentially, have a CPU-related problem on your system. To lower the SOS_SCHEDULER_YIELD waits, we will focus on the top-right section of Figure 5-12, where there are a high number of waiting tasks and high wait times.

If you are experiencing high wait times for the SOS_SCHEDULER_YIELD wait type together with a high number of waiting tasks, you probably have a very busy SQL Server instance. Worker threads will yield, but it takes a long time to get back on the processor again because there are many other threads waiting in the Runnable Queue. As we discussed earlier in Chapter 1, "Wait Statistics Internals," the Runnable Queue is a first-in-first-out list, meaning the more worker threads waiting inside the Runnable Queue, the longer it takes for worker threads to move through it. You will usually see a high CPU usage on the system by the SQL Server process.

To show an example of this problem, we will use the Ostress utility to execute a specific query simultaneously from a number of threads. The Ostress utility is part of the RML utilities for SQL Server, which are available here https://slrwnds.com/ixhxj4.

After the utilities are installed, we start by saving a script to a local file. In this case, we save to a folder C:\TeamData\sos_scheduler_yield.sql on the test server:

Listing 5-2. Sample Ostress script

```
WHILE (1=1)
  BEGIN
    SELECT COUNT(*)
    FROM Sales.SalesOrderDetail
    WHERE SalesOrderID BETWEEN 45125 AND 54185
END;
```

This query counts the number of rows between two SalesOrderIDs in the Sales. SalesOrderDetail table of the GalacticWorks database. It will do this in an endless loop. After saving the query to a local file, we start the Ostress utility using the following command as shown in Listing 5-3 and Figure 5-13:

Listing 5-3. Ostress sample code

```
"C:\Program Files\Microsoft Corporation\RMLUtils\ostress.exe" -S.\RC0 -E
-dGalacticWorks -i"C:\TeamData\sos_scheduler_yield.sql" -n20 -r1 -q
```

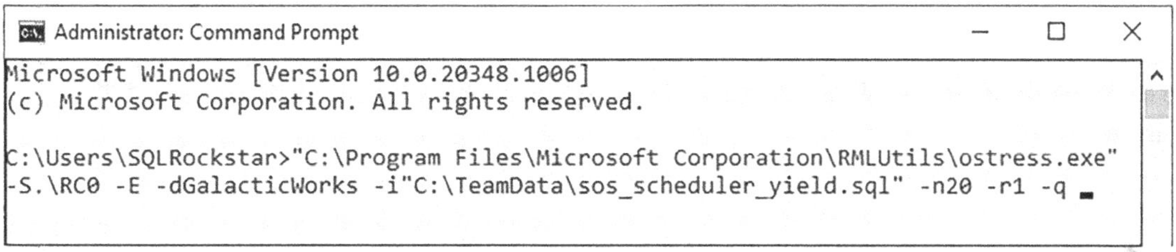

Figure 5-13. *Ostress sample code executed using Command Prompt*

This starts the Ostress utility, which connects to the GalacticWorks database and executes the sos_scheduler_yield.sql script using 20 threads.

As soon as we start Ostress, the CPU of the test SQL Server hits 100%, as shown in Figure 5-14.

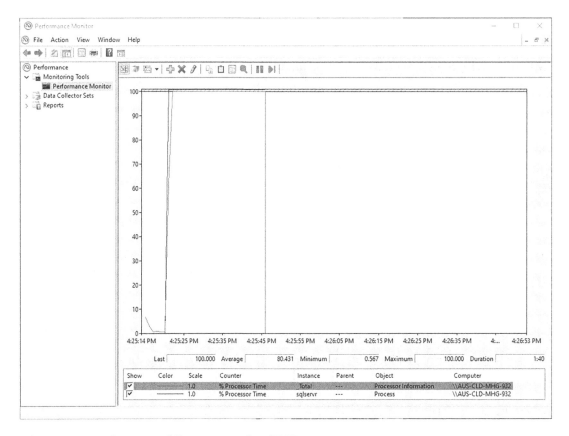

Figure 5-14. *Impact of Ostress on the CPU*

As you see in Figure 5-14, the CPU load is generated from the sqlservr process, which is the SQL Server instance we are running the Ostress query against. If we query the sys.dm_os_waiting_tasks DMV to check if the SOS_SCHEDULER_YIELD wait type is responsible for the CPU usage, we would be in for a surprise, as you can see in Figure 5-15.

```
SELECT *
FROM sys.dm_os_waiting_tasks
WHERE wait_type = 'SOS_SCHEDULER_YIELD';
```

200 %

⊞ Results Messages

waiting_task_address	session_id	exec_context_id	wait_duration_ms	wait_type	resource_address	blocking_task_address	blocking_session_id	blocking_exec_context_id	resource_description

Figure 5-15. *No SOS_SCHEDULER_YIELD waits occurring*

This is the tricky part of the SOS_SCHEDULER_YIELD wait type, as it frequently won't get returned by the sys.dm_os_waiting_tasks DMV – another reason to capture and use that wait statistics baseline!

To show the high CPU usage is related to the SOS_SCHEDULER_YIELD wait type, we look at the cumulative wait statistics DMV, sys.dm_os_wait_stats. We use the following query to show the top 5 wait types ordered by wait time, while we run the Ostress utility (reset the DMV before starting the Ostress utility to keep the numbers small):

```
SELECT TOP 5 *
FROM sys.dm_os_wait_stats
ORDER by wait_time_ms DESC;
```

The results of this query are shown in Figure 5-16.

	wait_type	waiting_tasks_count	wait_time_ms	max_wait_time_ms	signal_wait_time_ms
1	SOS_SCHEDULER_YIELD	18175	706614	94	706570
2	SOS_WORK_DISPATCHER	74	352646	30012	770
3	SLEEP_TASK	74	50370	2002	34
4	LOGMGR_QUEUE	298	38986	141	0
5	SQLTRACE_INCREMENTAL_FLUSH_SLEEP	5	20030	4008	0

Figure 5-16. *Top 5 wait types during Ostress execution*

As you see, the number 1 wait type is SOS_SCHEDULER_YIELD with a high amount of waiting_tasks_count and total wait_time_ms. But in second place, we find the SOS_WORK_DISPATCHER wait, a new wait introduced with SQL2019. The SOS_WORK_DISPATCHER wait is recorded for the time a thread is idle, waiting for work to be assigned.

If you experience a CPU problem with a production SQL Server instance, you might first focus on very small, very quick queries like the ones we executed in this example. If the volume of those queries increased, or if the number of user connections to the SQL Server executing those queries increased, then you could see high CPU usage. Sudden growth in transactions or user connections can also lead to high SOS_SCHEDULER_YIELD wait times.

Another cause of high SOS_SCHEDULER_YIELD waits, together with very high CPU usage, can be a phenomenon called spinlock contention. Spinlocks are defined as "lightweight synchronization primitives which are used to protect access to data structures" and are a very advanced topic. Appendix II, at the back of this book, goes into a little bit more detail about spinlocks for those who are interested in learning more about them.

Very large, complex queries may also lead to higher SOS_SCHEDULER_YIELD wait times. Try looking for active queries consuming a lot of CPU time and have complex calculations or data type conversions inside them. One query I use frequently to identify CPU-heavy queries is the one in Listing 5-4.

Listing 5-4. Detecting expensive CPU queries

```
SELECT TOP 10
  QText.TEXT AS 'Query',
  QStats.execution_count AS 'Nr of Executions',
  QStats.total_worker_time/1000 AS 'Total CPU Time (ms)',
  QStats.last_worker_time/1000 AS 'Last CPU Time (ms)',
  QStats.last_execution_time AS 'Last Execution',
  QPlan.query_plan AS 'Query Plan'
FROM sys.dm_exec_query_stats QStats
CROSS APPLY sys.dm_exec_sql_text(QStats.sql_handle) QText
CROSS APPLY sys.dm_exec_query_plan(QStats.plan_handle) QPlan
ORDER BY QStats.total_worker_time DESC;
```

The results of the query in Listing 5-3 on my test SQL Server can be seen in Figure 5-17.

	Query	Nr of Executions	Total CPU Time (ms)	Last CPU Time (ms)	Last Execution	Query Plan
1	WHILE (1=1) BEGIN SELECT COUNT(*) FROM Sa...	578152	2610483	4	2022-05-19 16:38:53.360	<ShowPlanXML xmlns="http://schemas.microsoft.com...
2	WHILE (1=1) BEGIN SELECT COUNT(*) FROM Sa...	9555	40217	5	2022-05-19 11:29:06.770	<ShowPlanXML xmlns="http://schemas.microsoft.com...
3	WHILE (1=1) BEGIN SELECT COUNT(*) FROM Sa...	6180	26390	3	2022-05-19 11:29:06.763	<ShowPlanXML xmlns="http://schemas.microsoft.com...
4	WHILE (1=1) BEGIN SELECT COUNT(*) FROM Sa...	5832	24731	3	2022-05-19 11:29:06.757	<ShowPlanXML xmlns="http://schemas.microsoft.com...
5	WHILE (1=1) BEGIN SELECT COUNT(*) FROM Sa...	5859	24726	3	2022-05-19 11:29:06.750	<ShowPlanXML xmlns="http://schemas.microsoft.com...

Figure 5-17. *Expensive CPU queries*

As you see, the query used with the Ostress tool is the query that executed the most and took the highest total CPU time. This query is a good starting point for an investigation. Maybe the query can be optimized or rewritten, so it doesn't consume as much CPU time.

Another method to identify expensive CPU queries is with the Query Store. The Query Store offers a built-in report called "Top Resource Consuming Queries" allowing you to filter on CPU time, as shown in Figure 5-18.

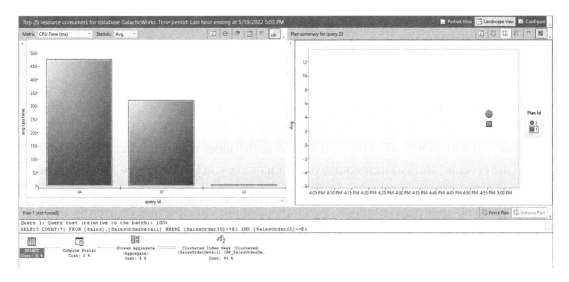

Figure 5-18. *Visualizing expensive CPU queries through the Query Store*

SOS_SCHEDULER_YIELD Summary

The SOS_SCHEDULER_YIELD wait type will occur on every SQL Server instance since it is directly related to the scheduling model that SQL Server uses to grant worker threads access to the processor. It might indicate a problem if the total wait time or total amount of waiting tasks suddenly increases compared to your baseline measurements. Most of the time a large increase in SOS_SCHEDULER_YIELD waits also means an increase in the CPU load. This increase is caused either by the SQL Server process itself or by another process outside of SQL Server that requires a large amount of processor time, limiting the time SQL Server can access the processor. If the SQL Server process is responsible for the increase in CPU load, you should try to correlate the increase in SOS_SCHEDULER_YIELD waits with an increase in user activity. Another option is to query the sys.dm_exec_query_stats DMV, as shown in Listing 5-1, or use the Query Store to find the queries that require the most processor time and focus on optimizing those queries.

THREADPOOL

One of the most notorious wait types is THREADPOOL. Unlike CXPACKET and SOS_SCHEDULER_YIELD which occur even when your SQL Server instance isn't experiencing any issues, high **THREADPOOL** wait times frequently indicate a performance problem. Just as with the other two CPU-related wait types discussed earlier, the THREADPOOL wait type is closely related to the way SQL Server scheduling works.

What Is the THREADPOOL Wait Type?

If you see THREADPOOL waits on your system with longer wait times than normal, and your SQL Server is (almost) unresponsive, chances are you have an issue called **thread pool starvation**. Thread pool starvation occurs when there are no more free worker threads available to process requests. When this situation occurs, tasks currently waiting to be assigned to a worker thread will log the THREADPOOL wait type.

SQL Server provides a number of worker threads to the schedulers with which to process requests. The number of worker threads available for your system depends on the number of processors and the processor architecture. Table 5-1 shows the maximum number of worker threads available for systems with up to 64 logical CPUs.

Table 5-1. *Maximum number of worker threads*

CPU number	32-bit architecture	64-bit architecture
≤4	256	512
8	288	576
16	352	704
32	480	960
64	736	1472

You can also calculate the maximum number of worker threads available by using these formulas:

32-bit with <= 4 logical processors: 256 worker threads

32-bit with > 4 logical processors: 256 + ((number of logical processors − 4) × 8)

64-bit with <= 4 logical processors: 512 worker threads

64-bit with > 4 logical processors: 512 + ((number of logical processors − 4) × 16)

Even though SQL Server calculates the maximum amount of available worker threads automatically (only once during startup), you can choose to overwrite the default by changing the Maximum Worker Threads option inside the Processors properties of your SQL Server instance, as shown in Figure 5-19. By default, the value of the Maximum Worker Threads option will be 0, which means SQL Server will calculate and assign the maximum amount of worker threads available using the preceding formulas.

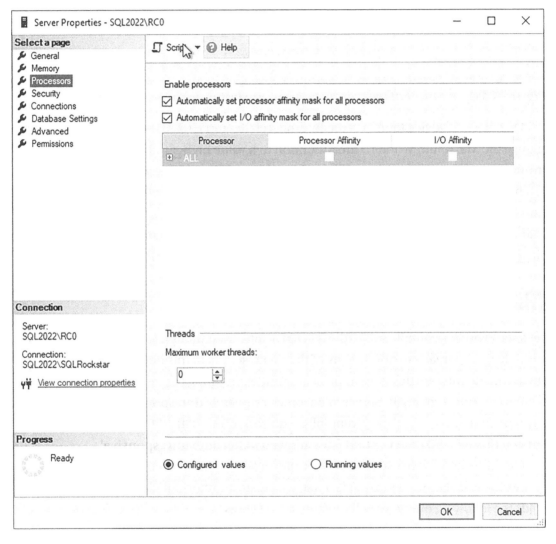

Figure 5-19. *Processors configuration of a SQL Server instance*

You can also query the number of worker threads assigned to your SQL Server instance by running the following query:

```
SELECT max_workers_count
FROM sys.dm_os_sys_info;
```

For my 64-bit test SQL Server with 4 logical processors, I have 512 worker threads available, as you can see in Figure 5-20.

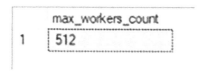

Figure 5-20. *Amount of worker threads on my test machine*

One piece of advice found on the Internet related to THREADPOOL waits is to change the Maximum Worker Threads option to a value higher than the default. I strongly advise against changing this option from its default value. Changing the setting to a higher value than the amount of worker threads may degrade the performance of your SQL Server because context switching occurs far more often. Another reason not to change the setting is that every worker thread requires a bit of memory to operate; for 32-bit systems, this is 512 KB per worker thread, and for 64-bit systems, it's 2048 KB.

THREADPOOL Example

Let's start with an example of THREADPOOL waits. Even though I have warned you multiple times already to not run any of the demo scripts in this book in a production environment, this one deserves a special reminder. Running the demo scripts in this section can cause your SQL Server to become completely unresponsive, not accepting any new connections, and can eventually require a restart of the SQL Server service! **Do not run this on a SQL Server that isn't allowed to become unresponsive**!

For this example, we use the Ostress utility again to simulate concurrency and load against the test SQL Server instance. First, we create another .sql file (select_rnd.sql) that holds the following query we will execute using Ostress:

```
SELECT TOP 1 *
FROM Sales.SalesOrderDetail
ORDER BY NEWID()
OPTION (MAXDOP 1);
```

This query will select one random row from the Sales.SalesOrderDetail table in the GalacticWorks database. There is a reason I included the query option to serially run this query, and I will explain later.

Now, before we launch Ostress to execute the query, we are purposely going to lower the maximum amount of worker threads available on the test SQL Server. To do this, we execute this query:

```
EXEC sp_configure 'show advanced options', 1;
GO
RECONFIGURE
GO
EXEC sp_configure 'max worker threads', 128;
GO
RECONFIGURE
GO
```

This will set the maximum number of worker threads available to 128, the minimum value for a 64-bit SQL Server instance.

Let's fire up Ostress and execute the .sql script we created earlier:

```
"C:\Program Files\Microsoft Corporation\RMLUtils\ostress.exe" -S.\RC0 -E
-dGalacticWorks -i"C:\select_rnd.sql" -n150 -r10 -q
```

In this case, we start 150 different threads to execute the query in the select_rnd.sql file 10 times. The reason for spawning 150 threads is because 150 is now higher than the maximum number of worker threads available on the test SQL Server instance, but not so high that we cannot execute queries anymore.

While the script is running, let's take a look at the number of worker threads running and waiting using the sys.dm_os_schedulers DMV:

Listing 5-5. Querying sys.dm_os_schedulers

```
SELECT scheduler_id,
    current_tasks_count,
    runnable_tasks_count,
    current_workers_count,
    active_workers_count,
    work_queue_count
```

```
FROM sys.dm_os_schedulers
WHERE status = 'VISIBLE ONLINE';
```

The results of this query are shown in Figure 5-21.

	scheduler_id	current_tasks_count	runnable_tasks_count	current_workers_count	active_workers_count	work_queue_count
1	0	54	34	43	42	11
2	1	54	33	42	41	12
3	2	53	32	41	41	12
4	3	55	34	43	42	12

Figure 5-21. *Tasks and worker threads per scheduler*

The most important columns here are the current_workers_count, active_ workers_ count, and work_queue_count columns. The current_workers_count column shows the number of worker threads associated with this scheduler; this number also includes worker threads that are not yet assigned to a task. The active_workers_count column returns the number of worker threads that are in the "RUNNING," "RUNNABLE," or "SUSPENDED" states. The big difference between the current_workers_count and the active_workers_count columns is that the active_workers_count is the number of worker threads that have been assigned to a task, while the current_workers_count returns all the worker threads. The work_queue_count column shows us the number of tasks that are currently waiting to get a worker thread assigned to them. If you see values higher than 0 in this column for a longer period and for all schedulers, you are experiencing thread pool starvation.

Let's check the sys.dm_os_waiting_tasks DMV for waiting tasks that originate from a user session. Notice that we filter out all the sessions that have a session ID lower than 50, even though I told you to not do this in Chapter 2, "Querying SQL Server Wait Statistics":

```
SELECT *
FROM sys.dm_os_waiting_tasks
WHERE session_id > 50;
```

If we check the results on the test SQL Server instance, we could conclude that nothing is waiting, as you can see in Figure 5-22. The test SQL Server is responding incredibly slowly though, and querying anything requires multiple seconds.

waiting_task_address	session_id	exec_context_id	wait_duration_ms	wait_type	resource_address	blocking_task_address

Figure 5-22. *No tasks are waiting*

Let's check the sys.dm_os_waiting_tasks DMV without filtering out session IDs:

```
SELECT *
FROM sys.dm_os_waiting_tasks;
```

As you see in Figure 5-23, THREADPOOL waits are not logged as user sessions but have an empty session ID. This is one reason I always recommend to not filter the sys.dm_os_waiting_tasks DMV on session ID numbers.

7	0x000001DA8364D468	NULL	NULL	370	THREADPOOL	NULL	NULL
8	0x000001DA8364DC28	NULL	NULL	348	THREADPOOL	NULL	NULL
9	0x000001DAE8B8D848	NULL	NULL	347	THREADPOOL	NULL	NULL
10	0x000001DACAD8C8C8	NULL	NULL	347	THREADPOOL	NULL	NULL
11	0x000001DAE2FB28C8	NULL	NULL	345	THREADPOOL	NULL	NULL
12	0x000001DAE8B8DC28	NULL	NULL	263	THREADPOOL	NULL	NULL
13	0x000001DA6CDE44E8	NULL	NULL	147	THREADPOOL	NULL	NULL
14	0x000001DAD48408C8	NULL	NULL	18	THREADPOOL	NULL	NULL

Figure 5-23. *THREADPOOL waits*

There are quite a lot of THREADPOOL waits, with various wait times, some running into seconds of wait time. Things get worse than this though. Figure 5-24 shows an error I encountered when I tried to connect to my test SQL Server instance while running the Ostress tool.

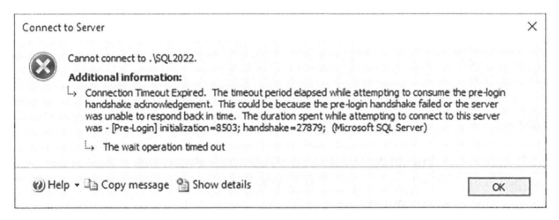

Figure 5-24. *Timeouts are occurring and SQL Server is unresponsive*

This error is the result of SQL Server unable to handle any additional login requests.

Now that we have seen the kind of problems thread pool starvation can create, let's look at how we can lower, or even resolve, THREADPOOL waits.

Gaining Access to Our SQL Server During THREADPOOL Waits

THREADPOOL waits are difficult to troubleshoot, mostly because there are many possible reasons why your SQL Server doesn't have any free worker threads available. Also, THREADPOOL waits can completely lock down your SQL Server instance, making connections to it (and troubleshooting it) almost impossible, as you have seen in the earlier example.

The first step is to make sure you do not get into a situation where you cannot connect to your SQL Server instance for troubleshooting is to enable the Dedicated Administrator Connection (or DAC). If you remember the section about schedulers in Chapter 1, "Wait Statistics Internals," you might recall a special type of scheduler reserved for the DAC. This dedicated scheduler, shown in Figure 5-25, is strictly reserved for the DAC and has access to its own worker threads.

	scheduler_address	parent_node_id	scheduler_id	cpu_id	status	is_online	is_idle	preemptive_switches_count
1	0x000001DA64340040	0	0	0	VISIBLE ONLINE	1	1	777
2	0x000001DA64360040	0	1	1	VISIBLE ONLINE	1	1	37870
3	0x000001DA64480040	0	2	2	VISIBLE ONLINE	1	1	667
4	0x000001DA644A0040	0	3	3	VISIBLE ONLINE	1	0	28884
5	0x000001DA644C0040	0	1048578	0	HIDDEN ONLINE	1	0	0
6	0x000001DA646C0040	64	1048576	0	VISIBLE ONLINE (DAC)	1	1	8
7	0x000001DA6CA00040	0	1048579	1	HIDDEN ONLINE	1	1	6
8	0x000001DA6CA20040	0	1048580	2	HIDDEN ONLINE	1	1	2
9	0x000001DA6BCC0040	0	1048581	3	HIDDEN ONLINE	1	1	0
10	0x000001DA6BCA0040	0	1048582	0	HIDDEN ONLINE	1	1	0
11	0x000001DA6BCE0040	0	1048583	1	HIDDEN ONLINE	1	1	0
12	0x000001DA742C0040	0	1048584	2	HIDDEN ONLINE	1	1	34

Figure 5-25. *Dedicated Administrator Connection scheduler*

If you connect through the DAC to your SQL Server instance, your session will be mapped to the DAC scheduler. This makes it possible to connect and execute queries even if all the other schedulers have massive task queues.

You can enable the DAC by executing the following query:

```
sp_configure 'remote admin connections', 1
GO
RECONFIGURE
GO
```

If you want to connect to your SQL Server instance using DAC, you need to add the ADMIN: prefix to the server name you are connecting to, as shown in Figure 5-26. You can only connect using the DAC when you execute a new query from inside SQL Server Management Studio without being connected to the server.

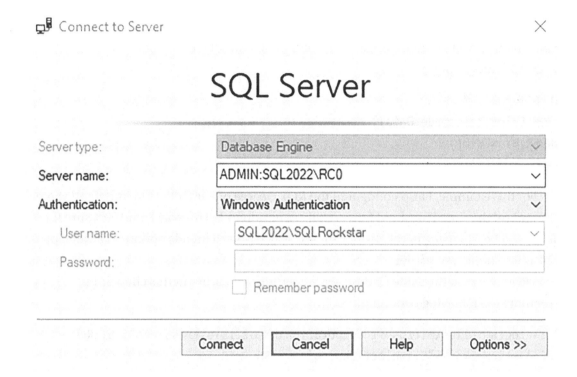

Figure 5-26. *Connect using the Dedicated Administrator Connection*

You can also connect using DAC with SQLCMD, either by using the ADMIN: prefix when declaring the server instance name or with the -A parameter flag. Once you are able to connect to your SQL Server instances using the DAC, you always have a way in, even when the SQL Server instance won't accept any new connections.

With the DAC enabled, let's discuss some common causes for THREADPOOL waits.

Lowering THREADPOOL Waits Caused by Parallelism

One of the most common causes for THREADPOOL waits is related to the extensive use of parallelism during query execution. During the execution of a parallel query, multiple worker threads are used to perform the work needed. If you left the configuration options related to parallelism – Max Degree of Parallelism and Cost Threshold for Parallelism – at the default values, it might cause more queries to run in parallel than was intended. Depending on how many processors your SQL Server has access to, and the number of worker threads used during a parallel query, one single parallel query can require many worker threads.

To show this behavior, I have modified the query we used to generate THREADPOOL waits so that it will execute using parallelism. In this case, I commented out the MAXDOP query option:

```
SELECT TOP 1 *
FROM Sales.SalesOrderDetail
ORDER BY NEWID()
-- OPTION (MAXDOP 1)
```

For this example, I also configured the Max Degree of Parallelism to its default value of 0 and set the Cost Threshold for Parallelism option to 1. This way I am 100% sure the query will be run using parallelism. I left the Max Worker Threads option on a value of 128 as we configured earlier.

We now repeat the same Ostress test we performed earlier in this chapter by executing the following command:

```
"C:\Program Files\Microsoft Corporation\RMLUtils\ostress.exe" -S.\RCO -E
-dGalacticWorks -i"C:\select_rnd.sql" -n150 -r10 -q
```

If we query the sys.dm_os_waiting_tasks DMV, we should see THREADPOOL waits occur again, but this time, because our test query is executed in parallel, we will also find many CX* waits returned by the sys.dm_os_waiting_tasks DMV, as shown in Figure 5-27.

8	0x000001DA7A833468	173	0	2577	CXSYNC_PORT	0x000001DA94FE2EB0	0x000001DAA2AA0CA8
9	0x000001DAA2AA0CA8	173	1	1280	CXSYNC_PORT	0x000001DAD3D406F0	0x000001DACAD8C108
10	0x000001DA797A9C28	126	2	637	CXSYNC_PORT	0x000001DB5F38C6F0	0x000001DA7CA7D468
11	0x000001DACC66CCA8	114	0	1803	CXSYNC_PORT	0x000001DAEC7CEEB0	0x000001DAE8B8DC28
12	0x000001DA7384ECA8	150	0	1705	CXSYNC_PORT	0x000001DAE307CEB0	0x000001DA7A9ACCA8
13	0x000001DAE3535088	NULL	NULL	914	THREADPOOL	NULL	NULL
14	0x000001DAD2C87C28	NULL	NULL	784	THREADPOOL	NULL	NULL
15	0x000001DA7A9AD848	NULL	NULL	97	THREADPOOL	NULL	NULL

Figure 5-27. *CXSYNC_PORT and THREADPOOL waits*

If you see a combination of THREADPOOL and parallelism waits occurring on your SQL Server instance, it is worth the effort to check your parallelism configuration. The first section of this chapter discussed CXPACKET waits and how you can lower them.

Another hint that might steer you in this direction is the CPU load during this particular case is higher than normal. In the case of my test SQL Server instance, all my CPUs went to 100%.

Lowering THREADPOOL Waits Caused by User Connections

Another common cause of THREADPOOL waits is a sudden increase in users connecting and executing queries against your SQL Server instance. This problem can occur if, for instance, the application connecting to your SQL Server instance uses multiple connections. The main problem here is that those connections stay active and keep acquiring worker threads.

To give you an example of this problem, we will again use Ostress to connect and execute queries against my test SQL Server instance. In this case, we will use a different .sql file, saved as wait.sql, as input for Ostress, with the following query inside it:

```
WAITFOR DELAY '00:05:00'
```

The only thing this query will do is wait for 5 minutes. After those 5 minutes, the query will end and the connection will disconnect. Let's run Ostress using the wait. sql file:

```
"C:\Program Files\Microsoft Corporation\RMLUtils\ostress.exe" -S.\RC0 -E
-dGalacticWorks -i"C:\TeamData\wait.sql" -n140 -r1 -q
```

We change the number of threads generated by Ostress to 140 and again leave the Max Worker Threads option set to 128 worker threads.

When we query the sys.dm_exec_sessions DMV using the following query, we see that many new user sessions, generated by the Ostress utility, are active, as shown in Figure 5-28.

```
SELECT *
FROM sys.dm_exec_sessions
WHERE is_user_process = 1;
```

	session_id	login_time	host_name	program_name
119	172	2022-09-27 18:48:06.820	SQL2022	OStress
120	173	2022-09-27 18:48:06.817	SQL2022	OStress
121	174	2022-09-27 18:48:06.827	SQL2022	OStress
122	175	2022-09-27 18:48:06.823	SQL2022	OStress
123	176	2022-09-27 18:48:06.827	SQL2022	OStress
124	177	2022-09-27 18:48:06.833	SQL2022	OStress
125	178	2022-09-27 18:48:06.860	SQL2022	OStress
126	179	2022-09-27 18:48:06.863	SQL2022	OStress
127	180	2022-09-27 18:48:06.870	SQL2022	OStress
128	181	2022-09-27 18:48:06.873	SQL2022	OStress
129	182	2022-09-27 18:48:06.877	SQL2022	OStress
130	183	2022-09-27 18:48:06.880	SQL2022	OStress
131	184	2022-09-27 18:48:06.880	SQL2022	OStress
132	185	2022-09-27 18:48:06.887	SQL2022	OStress
133	186	2022-09-27 18:48:06.897	SQL2022	OStress
134	187	2022-09-27 18:48:06.887	SQL2022	OStress

Figure 5-28. *Ostress user sessions*

If we query the sys.dm_os_waiting_tasks DMV, we see THREADPOOL waits are also occurring, as shown in Figure 5-29.

| 7 | 0x000001DA7A9A8CA8 | NULL | NULL | 1653 | THREADPOOL | NULL | NULL |
| 8 | 0x000001DACC66D468 | NULL | NULL | 1652 | THREADPOOL | NULL | NULL |

Figure 5-29. *THREADPOOL waits inside the sys.dm_os_waiting_tasks DMV*

The big difference between THREADPOOL waits caused by excessive parallelism and an increase in user connections is that the CPU of my test SQL Server instance remains low in the latter case, as shown in Figure 5-30.

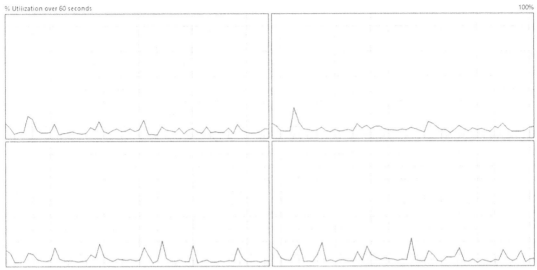

CPU

Intel(R) Xeon(R) Gold 6254 CPU @ 3.10GHz

% Utilization over 60 seconds   100%

Figure 5-30. *CPU usage*

The small spike in the CPU usage history graph is caused by starting up the Ostress utility. After that, the CPUs remain at a constant low usage percentage.

Resolving THREADPOOL waits caused by an increase in user connections should start at the source. Analyze where the user connections are coming from, and look at the queries those connections are executing. I have seen cases where an application suddenly used hundreds of active user connections after an update, and as the SQL Server instance was not designed to handle that amount of concurrent, active, connections, THREADPOOL waits appeared.

Keep in mind user connections should only cause THREADPOOL waits when they are executing queries. User connections connected to a SQL Server instance but not executing anything should not be a reason for THREADPOOL waits.

Also, having many different user connections active against a database can create many locks on rows or tables. If you notice high lock-related wait times together with THREADPOOL waits, the problem could be the high amount of locking and blocking occurring. In this case, you should try to find the queries that are causing the lock waits and see if you can optimize them. We will discuss lock-related wait types, and what you can do about them, in Chapter 7, "Lock-Related Wait Types."

THREADPOOL Summary

THREADPOOL waits are one of the most alarming wait types to see on your SQL Server instance. They occur because there are not enough free worker threads available to process requests, so tasks that request a worker thread will have to wait until a new worker thread becomes available. Thankfully, THREADPOOL waits are not very common, as they have the potential to completely lock you out of your SQL Server instance. The only way to connect in those cases is by using the Dedicated Administrator Connection (or DAC), which I urge you to enable on all your SQL Server instances.

Excessive use of parallelism and a large increase in active user connections are two of the most common causes for THREADPOOL waits. The former has a direct relation to the CXPACKET wait type we discussed earlier, so methods to resolve the CXPACKET wait type can also help to resolve THREADPOOL waits. The latter requires a deeper investigation into why the number of active user connections suddenly increased. Maybe they are the result of a bug in the application connection to the SQL Server instance. We also briefly touched on locking and blocking behavior as a possible cause for THREADPOOL waits. We will take a deeper look at how we can resolve lock-related waits in Chapter 7, "Lock-Related Wait Types."

CHAPTER 6

IO-Related Wait Types

In this chapter, we will examine IO-related wait types in the broadest sense of the term. I say "broadest" because the selected wait types are also related to storage, memory, or network components of your system. One could argue how the majority of wait types could fit multiple categories and you are right, but I need to prevent this chapter from covering 90% of all wait types available.

I consider the wait types in this chapter to have a direct relation to storage, memory, or network but to not relate directly to a functionality or concept in SQL Server. For instance, the PAGEIOLATCH_xx wait types are frequently related to storage, but they are not included in this chapter. The reason for this is because they are also a latch wait type, and I believe latch wait types deserve a separate chapter because of their function in SQL Server.

The performance of IO-related components is incredibly important for SQL Server. Practically every part of SQL Server interacts with IO components in one way or another, whether it is a data page that needs to be read from disk into memory or the results from a query that need to be transported across the network to your end users. If one of these components can't handle the workload generated on your SQL Server instance or isn't configured properly, your performance will decline.

The wait types in this chapter will help you track down which of your IO components is slowing you down, so you can take appropriate action to prevent or resolve performance-related incidents.

ASYNC_IO_COMPLETION

The **ASYNC_IO_COMPLETION** wait type is a common wait type which occurs when SQL Server performs a file-related action on the storage subsystem and waits for the action to complete. You will see this wait type when you are performing actions interacting with the storage subsystem, like database backups, mirroring, or log

T. LaRock and E. van de Laar, *Pro SQL Server 2022 Wait Statistics*,
https://doi.org/10.1007/978-1-4842-8771-2_6

shipping. Just like with most wait types, if you are seeing this wait type occur, it doesn't necessarily mean there is a problem with your storage subsystem. It is only a problem when the wait time is longer than you expect it to be compared to your baseline values, which we discussed in Chapter 4, "Building a Solid Baseline."

What Is the ASYNC_IO_COMPLETION Wait Type?

If we look up the ASYNC_IO_COMPLETION wait type in Books Online (BOL), we will see the following definition: "Occurs when a task is waiting for asynchronous non-data I/Os to finish." This is a rather short and vague definition, so let's add a little more detail.

ASYNC_IO_COMPLETION waits occur when a task is waiting for a storage-related action to finish. The task is initiated and monitored by SQL Server. Figure 6-1 shows this as a visual representation of the wait type.

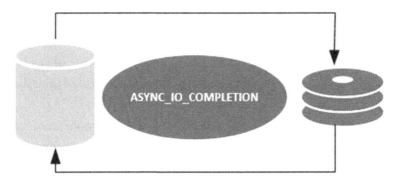

Figure 6-1. *ASYNC_IO_COMPLETION wait occurring*

As long as the storage-related action is running, the ASYNC_IO_COMPLETION wait time is logged. As you can imagine, the faster your storage subsystem (or larger your network bandwidth), the lower your ASYNC_IO_COMPLETION wait times will be. It warrants mentioning here the key word is asynchronous; the task is handed off to the operating system and returns control to SQL Server, allowing SQL Server to be free to execute other logic and come back later to check if the IO request is complete.

As I said earlier, usually ASYNC_IO_COMPLETION waits are no cause for concern. They will happen normally during many SQL Server operations which need access to the storage subsystem, like backups or the creation of a new database. It is a cause for concern if the wait times are higher than expected when compared to baseline measurements.

ASYNC_IO_COMPLETION Example

Let's go through an example which generates ASYNC_IO_COMPLETION waits. We won't need any extra utilities for this; just running a database backup will trigger ASYNC_IO_COMPLETION waits.

In this case, I will perform a backup of the GalacticWorks database on my test server.

To perform this action, I will use the query in Listing 6-1. This query will reset the sys.dm_os_wait_stats DMV, perform the database backup, and then query the sys.dm_os_wait_stats DMV for the ASYNC_IO_COMPLETION waits.

Listing 6-1. Generate ASYNC_IO_COMPLETION waits

```
USE [master];

DBCC SQLPERF('sys.dm_os_wait_stats', CLEAR);

BACKUP DATABASE [GalacticWorks]
TO DISK = N'C:\TeamData\GalacticWorks.bak'
WITH
  NAME = N'GalacticWorks-Full Database Backup',
  STATS = 2;

SELECT *
FROM sys.dm_os_wait_stats
WHERE wait_type = 'ASYNC_IO_COMPLETION';
```

The backup operation took <1 second on my test SQL Server instance. Figure 6-2 shows the results of the query in Listing 6-1.

	wait_type	waiting_tasks_count	wait_time_ms	max_wait_time_ms	signal_wait_time_ms
1	ASYNC_IO_COMPLETION	4	863	862	0

Figure 6-2. *ASYNC_IO_COMPLETION wait time*

As you can see, for almost the entire duration of the database backup, ASYNC_IO_COMPLETION waits were logged.

Lowering ASYNC_IO_COMPLETION Waits

A common cause of high ASYNC_IO_COMPLETION wait times is database backups, as you just saw in the example. If you want to know if your ASYNC_IO_COMPLETION waits are occurring because backups are running, look for backup-related waits occurring at the same time.

If we modify the last sys.dm_os_waiting_tasks query in Listing 6-1, we would see backup-related wait types being returned by the DMV.

Listing 6-2. Modified query

```
SELECT *
FROM sys.dm_os_wait_stats
WHERE wait_type IN
  (
  'ASYNC_IO_COMPLETION',
  'BACKUPIO',
  'BACKUPBUFFER'
  );
```

Figure 6-3 shows the result of the query in Listing 6-2.

	wait_type	waiting_tasks_count	wait_time_ms	max_wait_time_ms	signal_wait_time_ms
1	ASYNC_IO_COMPLETION	4	863	862	0
2	BACKUPBUFFER	377	823	6	9
3	BACKUPIO	365	23	4	4

Figure 6-3. *ASYNC_IO_COMPLETION waits together with backup-related waits*

If you see both waits occurring at the same time, chances are a database backup is causing your ASYNC_IO_COMPLETION waits. One way to lower the wait times is to enable backup compression.

Another method of lowering ASYNC_IO_COMPLETION waits is by configuring instant file initialization. Instant file initialization was introduced in Windows 2003 and speeds up the process of allocating space on a disk tremendously by removing the need to zero out files (writing zeros inside files before the files are used). This does not affect the speed of your backup but will give increased performance when creating a database, adding files to a database, or restoring a database. Instant file initialization is not enabled by default, unless you are running your SQL Server service under an account that has local administrator privileges. Starting with SQL Server 2016, Microsoft added an option to enable instant file initialization during SQL Server setup, as shown in Figure 6-4.

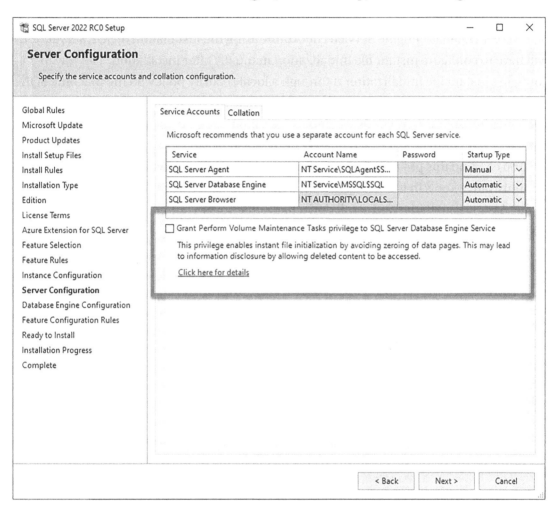

Figure 6-4. *Grant Perform Volume Maintenance Task privilege to the SQL Server Database Engine Service checkbox in SQL Server setup*

Nerd Note   The use of instant file initialization removes the zeroing out of data pages in exchange for faster file creation. This is a classic example of trading speed and convenience for security. By avoiding the zeroing out, you open up the possibility for data leakage by allowing deleted data on disk to be accessed.

While the risk is minimal, it is still a risk and one you should discuss with your audit team.

If you did not enable the Grant Perform Volume Maintenance Task privilege to the SQL Server Database Engine Service checkbox during the installation of SQL Server, you will have to configure instant file initialization manually after installation. The way to configure instant file initialization is through a local security policy on the machine SQL Server is running on by adding the account your SQL Server service is running under. Larger organizations may choose to deploy a Group Policy Object to ensure this setting is automatically configured for all their SQL Server instances.

You can find this policy by opening the local security policy MMC under Administrative Tools in the Configuration Panel. Open up the Local Policies ➤ User Rights Assignment folder and scroll down to the "Perform Volume Maintenance Task" policy, as shown in Figure 6-5.

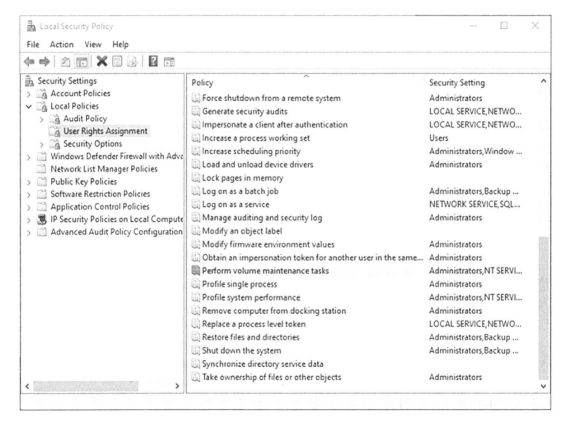

Figure 6-5. *Perform Volume Maintenance Task local policy*

Double-click the policy to open it, and add the account your SQL Server service is running under. The last step is restarting your SQL Server service. After the restart, SQL Server can make use of instant file initialization.

To show you the impact of instant file initialization, I used the query in Listing 6-3. This query clears the sys.dm_os_wait_stats DMV and then creates a new database with a 500 MB data file and a 100 MB log file. It then queries the sys.dm_os_wait_stats DMV for the ASYNC_IO_COMPLETION wait type.

Listing 6-3. Measure the impact of instant file initialization on ASYNC_IO_COMPLETION waits

```
DBCC SQLPERF('sys.dm_os_wait_stats', CLEAR);

CREATE DATABASE [IO_test]
ON  PRIMARY
  ( NAME = N'IO_test', FILENAME = N'E:\Data\IO_test.mdf' , SIZE = 512000KB ,
  FILEGROWTH = 10% )
LOG ON
  ( NAME = N'IO_test_log', FILENAME = N'E:\Log\IO_test_log.ldf' , SIZE =
  102400KB , FILEGROWTH = 10% );
SELECT *
FROM sys.dm_os_wait_stats
WHERE wait_type = 'ASYNC_IO_COMPLETION';
```

Figure 6-6 shows the wait statistics information both before and after configuring instant file initialization.

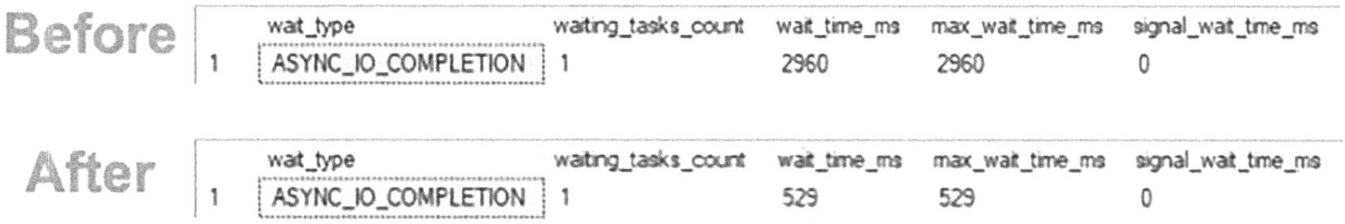

Before

	wait_type	waiting_tasks_count	wait_time_ms	max_wait_time_ms	signal_wait_time_ms
1	ASYNC_IO_COMPLETION	1	2960	2960	0

After

	wait_type	waiting_tasks_count	wait_time_ms	max_wait_time_ms	signal_wait_time_ms
1	ASYNC_IO_COMPLETION	1	529	529	0

Figure 6-6. *Impact of instant file initialization on ASYNC_IO_COMPLETION waits*

Even for this relatively small database, the gain of using instant file initialization is pretty big, as you see in the difference in wait times. Before enabling instant file initialization, the query in Listing 6-3 took 3 seconds to complete; after the change it went down to half a second.

If you configured instant file initialization and checked no backups are performed at the same time you see high ASYNC_IO_COMPLETION waits, the problem might be your storage subsystem. One method of analyzing potential storage problems is by using Perfmon to monitor the Physical Disk Avg. Disk/sec Read and Avg. Disk/sec Write counters on the disks on which your database resides, as shown in Figure 67. These counters show you the read and write latency to your disks in seconds (this means a value of 0.005 means 5 milliseconds). SQL Server performs optimally with a maximum latency of 5 milliseconds. The higher the latency value, the higher the wait time of storage-related wait types.

Nerd Note   These Perfmon counters are returning values showing how long SQL Server waited for the read or write operation to complete. These values include the total round trip time, which means they include time for network latency, or an overloaded VM kernel, so be advised to examine all layers of infrastructure between the SQL Server engine and the data stored on disk.

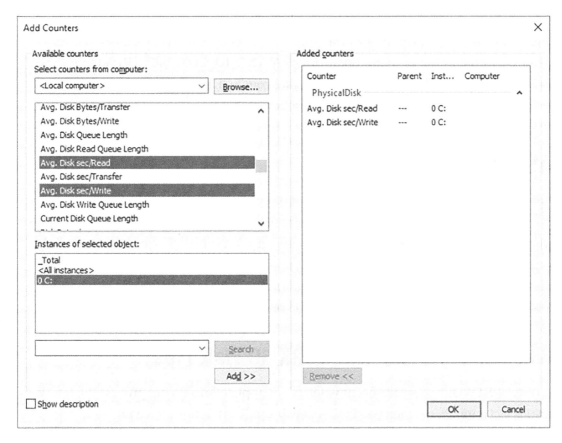

Figure 6-7. *Avg. Disk sec/Read and Avg. Disk sec/Write Perfmon counters*

Be careful about jumping to conclusions regarding your storage performance. Always talk to your storage administrator (if you have one) and show them your measurements before you decide the storage subsystem is the bottleneck. Storage is the domain of the storage administrator, and they can help you analyze and resolve performance problems.

ASYNC_IO_COMPLETION Summary

The ASYNC_IO_COMPLETION wait type occurs when you perform actions related to the storage subsystem from your SQL Server instance, such as database backups and the creation of new databases. While ASYNC_IO_COMPLETION waits are completely normal, they can indicate storage-related problems if wait times are higher than normal. Before you run to your storage administrator, make sure there is actually a performance problem. One possible way to do this is by checking your storage latency, as high latency values will impact ASYNC_IO_COMPLETION wait times as well. Also check whether the higher ASYNC_IO_COMPLETION wait times are directly related to database backups being performed. One great method to lower ASYNC_IO_COMPLETION wait times is by enabling instant file initialization by adding your SQL Server service account to the Perfmon Volume Maintenance Task local policy.

ASYNC_NETWORK_IO

Just like the ASYNC_IO_COMPLETION wait type, **ASYNC_NETWORK_IO** is related to throughput. But instead of storage subsystem throughput, the ASYNC_NETWORK_IO wait type is related to the network connection between your SQL Server instance and your client connections. Again, seeing wait times for this specific wait type does not necessarily mean there is a network-related issue, since ASYNC_NETWORK_IO waits always occur, even if you query your SQL Server instance on the SQL Server itself.

What Is the ASYNC_NETWORK_IO Wait Type?

ASYNC_NETWORK_IO waits occur when client applications do not process the query results fast enough, or when you have a network-related performance problem. The former is most likely, since many applications process SQL Server results on a row-by-row basis or improperly handle the volume of data returned. SQL Server will wait for the client application to acknowledge it has received the current result set before it will send additional results. While SQL Server is waiting to send the requested data, the ASYNC_NETWORK_IO wait type is logged. Another situation in which ASYNC_NETWORK_IO waits can occur is when you are using a linked server to query remote databases. Figure 6-8 shows a graphical representation of this.

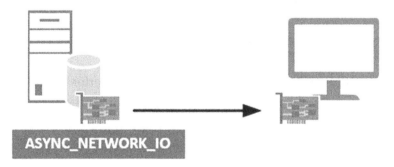

Figure 6-8. *ASYNC_NETWORK_IO*

ASYNC_NETWORK_IO Example

Showing an example of the ASYNC_NETWORK_IO wait type doesn't require a complicated test environment. Listing 6-4 shows a query that will generate ASYNC_NETWORK_IO waits when run against my test SQL Server instance from another computer using SQL Server Management Studio (SSMS), which should be enough. The query is going to clear the sys.dm_os_wait_stats DMV and then perform the actual query against the GalacticWorks database. The last statement will show us the wait times of the ASYNC_NETWORK_IO wait type.

Listing 6-4. Generate ASYNC_NETWORK_IO waits

```
DBCC SQLPERF ('sys.dm_os_wait_stats', CLEAR);

SELECT *
FROM Person.Person;

SELECT *
FROM sys.dm_os_wait_stats
WHERE wait_type = 'ASYNC_NETWORK_IO';
```

Figure 6-9 shows the wait times for the ASYNC_NETWORK_IO wait type.

	wait_type	waiting_tasks_count	wait_time_ms	max_wait_time_ms	signal_wait_time_ms
1	ASYNC_NETWORK_IO	6332	999	45	107

Figure 6-9. *ASYNC_NETWORK_IO wait times*

In this example, the results of the query against the GalacticWorks database couldn't be processed by the SSMS application as fast as the SQL Server instance supplied the results, and ASYNC_NETWORK_IO waits occurred.

Nerd Note   In this example, it is worth mentioning again how this is a single server; therefore, there was no outbound network traffic. However, to SQL Server, it is considered a network wait, as SSMS is an external client to the database engine, even with SSMS installed on the same machine.

Lowering ASYNC_NETWORK_IO Waits

One way to lower ASYNC_NETWORK_IO waits is to identify queries returning a large result set back to the application. A common example is a query using SELECT * and returns all columns from a wide table where only a few columns were needed. In our example, if we modify the query to return only the first 100 rows, SSMS might be able to keep up with the information returned.

Listing 6-5. Limit to 100 rows

```
DBCC SQLPERF ('sys.dm_os_wait_stats', CLEAR);

SELECT TOP 100 *
FROM Person.Person;

SELECT *
FROM sys.dm_os_wait_stats
WHERE wait_type = 'ASYNC_NETWORK_IO';
```

The resulting wait times after this modification can be seen in Figure 6-10.

	wait_type	waiting_tasks_count	wait_time_ms	max_wait_time_ms	signal_wait_time_ms
1	ASYNC_NETWORK_IO	10	73	47	0

Figure 6-10. *ASYNC_NETWORK_IO wait times after modifying the query*

As you can see, we have less ASYNC_NETWORK_IO waits. SSMS was able to keep up with the results returned, so the SQL Server instance did not delay sending the results back to the client.

Another way to limit results returned is by filtering out information using WHERE clauses. Smaller results will result in lower ASYNC_NETWORK_IO wait times.

If you believe that ASYNC_NETWORK_IO waits are not caused by large results being returned to an application, or by the speed at which an application can process the results, there is a possibility the network configuration is slowing you down. In this case, you should first check your network utilization. Sadly, there isn't a counter in Perfmon that directly shows the network utilization without having you perform some math to calculate it. Instead, use the Networking tab of the Task Manager to view your network-card utilization, as shown in Figure 6-11.

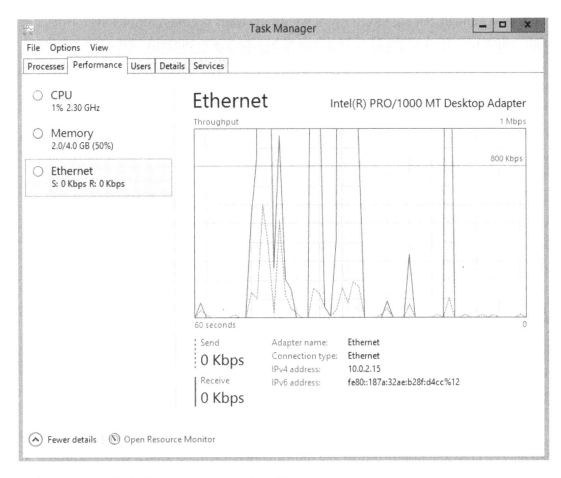

Figure 6-11. *Task Manager network utilization*

If you notice that the network utilization is high while also experiencing higher than normal ASYNC_NETWORK_IO wait times, it is possible the network is slowing you down. In this case, it is a good idea to talk to your network administrator. Usually a network configuration consists of many parts, like switches, routers, firewalls, network cables, drivers, firmware, potential virtualization of the operating system, and so on. All of these parts can slow down your network throughput and can be a potential cause of ASYNC_NETWORK_IO waits.

ASYNC_NETWORK_IO Summary

The ASYNC_NETWORK_IO wait type occurs whenever an application requests query results from a SQL Server instance over the network and does not process the returned results fast enough. Seeing ASYNC_NETWORK_IO waits occur is completely normal, but higher than normal wait times can be caused by changes in the returned query results or network-related problems. Lowering ASYNC_NETWORK_IO wait times that are application related can be achieved by decreasing the number of rows and/or columns returned to the application.

CMEMTHREAD

Waits of the **CMEMTHREAD** wait type indicate a pressure on SQL Server–related memory objects. These memory objects allocate memory for the various parts of SQL Server like both the buffer and procedure cache. Whenever CMEMTHREAD waits occur, it means multiple threads are trying to access the same memory object at the same time.

What Is the CMEMTHREAD Wait Type?

To explain how CMEMTHREAD wait type generation works, we have to dig a little deeper inside some programming terminology, specifically the terms **critical sections**, **mutual exclusions,** and **thread safety**. These three concepts play a direct role in the CMEMTHREAD wait type generation.

A **critical section** consists of a piece of code accessing a shared resource which can only be accessed by one thread at a time. In our case, the shared resource would be a SQL Server memory object (perhaps a data page). SQL Server memory objects are accessed by a single thread at a time to minimize the risk of corruption to the memory object. Because there are many threads wanting to access memory objects, we use a method to allow only one thread access at a time. This method is called **mutual exclusion (mutex)**. SQL Server uses a mutex object to make sure concurrent threads are not in their critical sections at the same time when accessing the memory object. A mutex does this by serializing the thread access to the memory object. Only a single thread can be the owner of a mutex object, and while a thread has ownership, it can access the shared resource. When the thread is done, the mutex object will move to the next thread in line. By using these objects, we have created **thread-safe** code, where multiple threads do not have concurrent access to memory objects. Figure 6-12 shows this situation.

threads   mutex object   shared resource

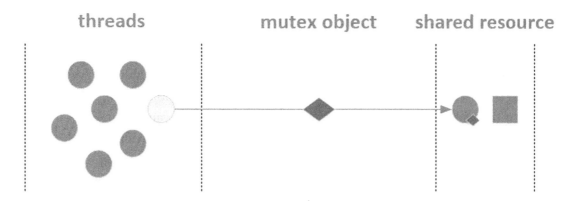

Figure 6-12. *Thread waiting for a mutex object to access a shared resource*

A simplified example of this behavior is when you and a large group of other people are waiting for a single ticket dispenser to buy a ticket to see your favorite rock band. In this case, the ticket dispenser is the shared resource, and only a single person can access the ticket dispenser at a time. When we reach the ticket dispenser, we can get a ticket, and the people behind us have to wait until we are done. After we have bought a ticket, the next person in line gets access to the ticket dispenser.

We can also view this behavior in SQL Server, but to do this we have to make use of a debugger (like WinDbg). Figure 6-13 shows how a thread in SQL server waits for a mutex since access to the memory object was granted to another thread. To capture this image, I used an Extended Event session which created a SQL Server mini-dump when a CMEMTHREAD wait occurred. I then used WinDbg to open the mini-dump and returned the stack. For details on how to use SqlDumper, go to `https://slrwnds.com/32n2up`.

```
0:170> ln 0x000007FEF9F86059;ln 0x000007FEF9F4219C;ln 0x000007FEF9F41F03;ln 0x000007FEF9F437AB;
(000007fe`f9f41400)    sqldk!XeSosPkg::wait_info::Publish+0x138    |  (000007fe`fa020930)    sqldk
(000007fe`f9f41f70)    sqldk!SOS_Scheduler::UpdateWaitTimeStats+0x2bc    |  (000007fe`f9f42250)
(000007fe`f9f41e90)    sqldk!SOS_Task::PostWait+0x9e    |  (000007fe`f9f4db60)    sqldk!SOS_Task::
(000007fe`f9f437e0)    sqldk!EventInternal<SuspendQueueSLock>::Wait+0x2ca    |  (000007fe`f9f43a6
(000007fe`f9f6e1a0)    sqldk!SOS_UnfairMutexPair::LongWait+0x191    |  (000007fe`f9f6e400)    sqld
(000007fe`f9f455d0)    sqldk!SOS_UnfairMutexPair::AcquirePair+0x46    |  (000007fe`f9f45640)    sq
(000007fe`f9f45970)    sqldk!CMemThread<CMemObj>::Alloc+0xb6    |  (000007fe`f9fdee40)    sqldk!CM
```

Figure 6-13. *Example of a CMEMTHREAD wait occurring in a mini-dump*

The important line here is the **SOS_UnfairMutexPair::LongWait**, which generates the CMEMTHREAD wait because the thread we are monitoring has to wait for another thread which currently has access to the memory object. The line after that, **SOS_UnfairMutexPair::AcquirePair**, means the thread received the mutex, followed by access to the memory object represented by **CMemThread<CmemObj>::Alloc**.

Lowering CMEMTHREAD Waits

Since there are many different memory objects present in SQL Server which could potentially generate CMEMTHREAD waits, there are many possible solutions to lowering CMEMTHREAD wait times depending on the memory object being accessed.

One of the more common situations where CMEMTHREAD wait occurs is when large amounts of short, concurrent, ad hoc queries are executed. Every time an ad hoc query is executed (one which could not be parameterized), the Query Optimizer generates a new execution plan for the query. All these new execution plans are saved to the plan cache, and a memory object for allocating cache descriptors is accessed. Since the memory object is thread-safe, CMEMTHREAD waits can occur if the rate of insertion is high enough. A good place to start looking if you suspect CMEMTHREAD waits are going to occur because of ad hoc queries is the procedure cache. The query in Listing 6-6 will give you information about the number of execution plans in the procedure cache.

Listing 6-6. Query procedure cache

```
SELECT  objtype,
  COUNT_BIG (*) AS 'Total Plans',
  SUM(CAST(size_in_bytes AS DECIMAL(12,2)))/1024/1024 AS 'Size (MB)'
FROM sys.dm_exec_cached_plans
GROUP BY objtype;
```

The results of this query should look like Figure 6-14, though the numbers will be different on your system.

	objtype	Total Plans	Size (MB)
1	Prepared	23	8.570312
2	View	87	25.109375
3	Adhoc	38	6.429687
4	Rule	2	0.085937
5	Trigger	1	0.078125
6	Proc	10	4.062500

Figure 6-14. *Results of querying procedure cache*

We will focus on the number of ad hoc execution plans. If you see this number growing rapidly and experience CMEMTHREAD waits, it is worth the effort to analyze those ad hoc queries. If possible, try to optimize the queries so they generate a reusable plan. If your application uses many dynamic queries, then try to use the sp_executesql system stored procedure instead of the EXECUTE (EXEC) command. Using the EXEC command will most likely result in a plan that will only be used once.

Microsoft has released various fixes (most notably the partitioning of certain memory objects across CPUs) for this problem in SQL Server 2005 SP2, making it less common these days. Even if you are using newer SQL Server editions than SQL Server 2005, it might be a good idea to upgrade to the latest available Service Pack since there have been various memory-related bug fixes in every SQL Server edition.

CMEMTHREAD Summary

The CMEMTHREAD wait type is a memory-related wait type. CMEMTHREAD waits occur when multiple threads try to access memory objects which are only accessed by a single thread at a time. The time other threads spend waiting for their turn to access the memory object is recorded as CMEMTHREAD wait time. One of the more common cases where CMEMTHREAD waits can occur is when your system uses a high amount of ad hoc queries. Every time a new execution plan is generated, SQL Server will access a memory object; if many execution plans are generated, this will lead to a queue of threads wanting access to the memory object, resulting in CMEMTHREAD waits.

IO_COMPLETION

Just like the ASYNC_IO_COMPLETION wait type, **IO_COMPLETION** waits occur when SQL Server is waiting for storage-related actions to complete. And just like the ASYNC_IO_COMPLETION wait type, seeing high wait times of the IO_COMPLETION wait type doesn't necessarily mean there is something wrong with your storage system. IO_COMPLETION waits occur normally, while your SQL Server instance is running and should only be a concern if wait times are a lot higher than normal.

What Is the IO_COMPLETION Wait Type?

While the ASYNC_IO_COMPLETION wait type is recorded when database-related actions are performed, like a database backup, IO_COMPLETION waits occur when non-data pages are involved, like the restore of a transaction log backup or when bitmap allocation pages, like the GAM page, are accessed. IO_COMPLETION waits can also occur when queries are being executed that perform read or write operations to storage, like a Merge Join operator.

IO_COMPLETION Example

Let's generate some IO_COMPLETION waits by restoring a transaction log backup. For this example, we will make use of the GalacticWorks database again. The query in Listing 6-7 will perform a full backup of the GalacticWorks database, make some changes, and perform a transaction log backup. When complete, we will restore the full backup again, clear the sys.dm_os_wait_stats DMV, restore the transaction log backup, and check for IO_COMPLETION waits.

Listing 6-7. Generate IO_Completion waits

```
-- Make sure GalacticWorks is in Full recovery model
ALTER DATABASE GalacticWorks SET RECOVERY FULL;
-- Perform full backup first
-- Otherwise FULL recovery model will not be affected
BACKUP DATABASE [GalacticWorks]
TO DISK = N'C:\TeamData\GalacticWorks.bak';

-- Make some changes to AW database
USE GalacticWorks;
UPDATE Person.Address
SET City = 'Portland'
WHERE City = 'Bothell'
-- Backup Transaction Log
BACKUP LOG [GalacticWorks]
TO DISK = N'C:\TeamData\GalacticWorks_Log.trn'
-- Restore the previous full backup with NORECOVERY
USE [master];

RESTORE DATABASE [GalacticWorks]
FROM DISK = N'C:\TeamData\GalacticWorks.bak'
WITH NORECOVERY, REPLACE;
-- Clear sys.dm_os_wait_stats
```

```
dbcc sqlperf ('sys.dm_os_wait_stats', CLEAR);
-- Restore last Transaction Log backup
RESTORE LOG [GalacticWorks]
FROM DISK = N'C:\TeamData\GalacticWorks_Log.trn';
-- Check IO_COMPLETION waits
SELECT *
FROM sys.dm_os_wait_stats
WHERE wait_type = 'IO_COMPLETION'
```

The results of this query against the sys.dm_os_wait_stats DMV on my test system can be seen in Figure 6-15.

	wait_type	waiting_tasks_count	wait_time_ms	max_wait_time_ms	signal_wait_time_ms
1	IO_COMPLETION	535	13	0	1

Figure 6-15. *IO_COMPLETION waits*

We only modified a few records using the query in Listing 6-7, so the total wait time is low since the restore of the transaction log backup occurred fast.

IO_COMPLETION wait times also occur when starting up your databases after a restart of the SQL Server service. This means you should expect IO_COMPLETION waits after a restart or a failover; these are completely normal. Also when AUTO_CLOSE is enabled and the database is starting, you should experience IO_COMPLETION waits.

Lowering IO_COMPLETION Waits

Most of the time, IO_COMPLETION waits shouldn't be a cause for concern. When they are a lot higher than the wait times in your baseline, you should analyze the storage subsystem performance like I described in the "Lowering ASYNC_IO_COMPLETION" section. While certain query operations can also cause IO_COMPLETION waits, these are frequently not the cause for higher-than-normal wait times.

IO_COMPLETION Summary

Just like the ASYNC_IO_COMPLETION wait type, IO_COMPLETION waits occur when accessing your storage subsystem. IO_COMPLETION waits occur when SQL Server is waiting on non-data page operations to complete, like a transaction log restore operation or the reading of bitmap pages, like the GAM page. Seeing waits of the IO_COMPLETION type occur is completely normal, and these frequently do not require deeper analysis unless the wait times are a lot higher than the values in your baseline. In those cases, focus on the performance (and especially latency) of your storage subsystem first.

LOGBUFFER and WRITELOG

I have combined both LOGBUFFER and WRITELOG in this section. This is because both wait types have a close relation to each other, to the transaction log, and to the storage subsystem.

What Are the LOGBUFFER and WRITELOG Wait Types?

To understand what the **LOGBUFFER** and **WRITELOG** wait types represent, we need to have some understanding of how SQL Server writes to the transaction log. In short, the following events happen whenever we change or add data inside a database:

1. Data page is modified in the buffer cache; if the page wasn't already in the buffer cache, it is read into the buffer cache first.

2. The data page is marked as "dirty" inside the buffer cache.

3. The log records which represent the modification are saved to the log buffer.

4. A log flush (we will discuss in more detail later) occurs, writing the log records from the log buffer to the transaction log.

5. The dirty data page is written to the data file.

To show this behavior, I have included Figure 6-16.

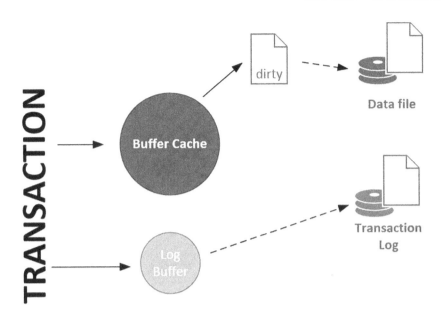

Figure 6-16. *How a transaction moves*

The action representing the movement of a dirty data page and the action of writing the log records to the transaction log are shown as dashed lines. I did this on purpose to illustrate how these actions do not necessarily happen directly.

Dirty data pages are updated inside the buffer cache first and are written to the data file when a checkpoint operation occurs. Therefore, a dirty page can stay inside memory (i.e., buffer cache) even after the transaction is committed.

This is not true for the log records inside the log buffer. As soon as the transaction commits, and the transaction has an active log record in the log buffer, all the log records inside the log buffer are written (or *flushed*) to the transaction log on disk. But a log flush is also triggered in a different way. The log buffer has a fixed size of 60 KB, and as soon as the log buffer is full, it will flush all the records inside to the transaction log.

Since this section is about WRITELOG and LOGBUFFER, now is a good time to bring them into this story. The WRITELOG wait type occurs when SQL Server is flushing the contents of the log buffer to the transaction log on disk. The LOGBUFFER wait type occurs when SQL Server has to wait for free space inside the log buffer to insert the log record. I have added both the wait types at the parts where they can get generated in Figure 6-17.

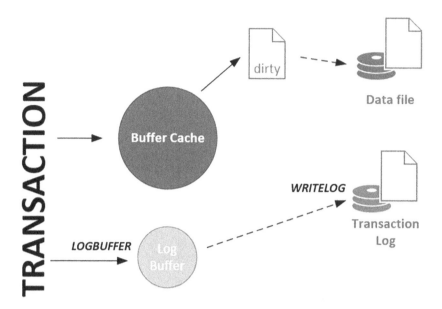

Figure 6-17. *Transaction movement and the LOGBUFFER and WRITELOG wait types*

This is why I said these wait types are related. Whenever WRITELOG waits occur, chances are you will also find LOGBUFFER waits if the process flushing the log records to the transaction log cannot process them as fast as new log records are entering the log buffer.

This situation frequently occurs on systems with a high volume of concurrent data modifications, resulting in transactions which are written to disk. Another common cause is the performance of the storage subsystem where the transaction log file resides. If the storage subsystem has suboptimal performance, your WRITELOG wait times will increase, with the possibility existing that LOGBUFFER waits can occur if the volume of transactions is high enough.

The performance of your transaction log is critical for the performance of your entire database. Slow transaction log performance will have an impact on every change you perform inside your database, as every modification has to be written to the transaction log before it can get committed.

LOGBUFFER and WRITELOG Example

To give you an example of LOGBUFFER and WRITELOG waits occurring, I am creating a new database using the script in Listing 6-8.

Listing 6-8. Create TLog_demo database

```
USE master;
-- Create demo database
CREATE DATABASE [TLog_demo]
ON PRIMARY  (
  NAME = N'TLog_demo', FILENAME = N'C:\TeamData\TLog_demo.mdf' , SIZE =
  153600KB , FILEGROWTH = 10%)
LOG ON  (  NAME = N'TLog_demo_log', FILENAME = N'C:\TeamData\TLog_demo.ldf'
, SIZE = 51200KB , FILEGROWTH = 10%);
-- Make sure recovery model is set to full
ALTER DATABASE [TLog_demo] SET RECOVERY FULL;
-- Perform full backup first
-- Otherwise FULL recovery model will not be affected
BACKUP DATABASE [TLog_demo]
TO  DISK = N'C:\TeamData\TLog_demo_Full.bak';
-- Create a simple test table
USE TLog_demo;
CREATE TABLE transactions  (
  t_guid VARCHAR(50) );
```

Now that we have created a brand new database, I will use the Ostress utility to generate load against the TLog_demo database. I will execute the query in Listing 6-9, which I saved to the logbuffer_impl.sql file, with 200 concurrent connections using the following command:

```
"C:\Program Files\Microsoft Corporation\RMLUtils\ostress.exe" -S.\RC0 -E
-dTLog_demo -i"C:\TeamData\logbuffer_impl.sql" -n200 -r1 -q
```

Listing 6-9. Insert rows inside the TLog_demo database

```
DECLARE @i INT
SET @i = 1
WHILE @i < 10000
  BEGIN
    INSERT INTO transactions
        (t_guid)
```

```
    VALUES
         (newid())
  SET @i = @i + 1
END
```

Before I started the Ostress utility, I cleared the sys.dm_os_wait_stats DMV.

After about 1 minute on my test SQL Server, the Ostress utility finished executing the workload. If I query the sys.dm_os_wait_stats DMV and look for the LOGBUFFER and WRITELOG wait types, I get the results shown in Figure 6-18.

	wait_type	waiting_tasks_count	wait_time_ms	max_wait_time_ms	signal_wait_time_ms
1	WRITELOG	832990	4193437	78	423653
2	LOGBUFFER	96	9	1	3

Figure 6-18. *WRITELOG and LOGBUFFER waits*

Lowering LOGBUFFER and WRITELOG Waits

There are generally two approaches you can take to lowering LOGBUFFER and WRITELOG waits, keeping in mind WRITELOG waits occur normally and this wait time should only be a cause for concern if it is a lot higher than normal.

The first approach is to take a good look at how your transactions are being executed. In the preceding example, we implicitly committed every INSERT statement. This means that as soon as the log record for the INSERT statement entered the log buffer, it needed to be flushed again. If we would explicitly commit the whole WHILE loop, we would have larger writes to flush to the transaction log, resulting in better performance. This is because writing small blocks frequently is generally slower than writing large blocks at a larger interval. Cursors can also have the same effect as the example we used, so use them as little as possible.

The other approach is based on the storage subsystem. If SQL Server cannot write the log records fast enough, you can encounter LOGBUFFER and WRITELOG waits. As a best practice, make sure to split your transaction log and database data files on separate disks, so they do not impact each other in times of heavy load. Also monitor the disk the transaction log is located on using the disk-performance counters in Perfmon, like Avg. Disk sec/write, to show you the write latency, and Disk Writes/sec, to show the write IOPS and check if the values are inside the acceptable range.

If your SQL Server instance is running SQL Server 2014, you could choose to make use of the Delayed Durability option, which was introduced in SQL Server 2014. In short, enabling this option will no longer flush the log buffer content to disk when a transaction commits but rather will wait until the log buffer is full (60 KB) before flushing the contents to the transaction log. By enabling this option, you are running a risk that committed transactions not yet written to the transaction log will be lost during a failure since they are written only to the transaction log when the log buffer is full.

LOGBUFFER and WRITELOG Summary

Both the LOGBUFFER and WRITELOG wait types are related to the way SQL Server processes transactions. The WRITELOG wait type occurs every time a log record is written to the transaction log and generally isn't a cause for concern. When paired with high LOGBUFFER wait times, high WRITELOG wait times can indicate transaction log pressure. To lower those wait times, try to avoid cursor and WHILE statements, since the statements inside the cursor or WHILE clauses will often get implicitly committed, creating a large amount of small writes. Also check your storage configuration to make sure the transaction log isn't on the same drive as the database data file. If high wait times still occur, analyze the performance of the disk on which your transaction log is located.

RESOURCE_SEMAPHORE

The **RESOURCE_SEMAPHORE** wait type is a memory-related wait type which occurs when a query memory request cannot be granted immediately. These waits occur on servers experiencing memory pressure, or when a large number of concurrent queries request memory for expensive operations like sorts or joins.

What Is the RESOURCE_SEMAPHORE Wait Type?

When a query is executed in SQL Server, a series of steps occur before the actual execution. The first step is a compiled plan is generated. This plan contains the logical instructions, or operations, needed to fulfill the query requests. During the generation of the compiled plan, a calculation is performed to determine the amount of memory needed to execute all the query operations in the compiled plan. Some of the operations requiring memory are sorts and joins, which temporarily store row data in the memory of the SQL Server. The minimum amount of memory needed to perform these sorts or joins is known as the required memory, without which the query simply cannot get executed. If more memory is needed to store row data in-memory during a sort, for instance, it will be calculated as additional memory. Without this additional memory, a query can still get executed, but instead of writing the temporary row data to memory, it will write it to disk.

When the query is executed, a memory grant is determined based on the required and additional memory values calculated in the compiled plan. This memory grant is needed to perform a memory reservation of an internal object called the **resource semaphore**. The resource semaphore is responsible for reserving the memory a query needs for execution, but it also manages memory throttling when too many queries concurrently ask for memory reservations or when there is not enough memory available. It does this by maintaining a queue of the queries requesting memory. If there are no queries inside the queue and a new query requests memory, the resource semaphore grants it to the query (if enough free memory is available). However, if there is a queue, the new query will be put at the end of the queue, and it has to wait for its turn to receive a memory grant.

Before the resource semaphore will grant the requested memory to a query, it will check whether there is enough free memory available. If, for some reason, there is less memory available than the amount requested by the query, the query will be put in the queue again until enough memory is available. When a query is inside the resource semaphore queue waiting for its requested memory, the time it spends inside the queue will be recorded as the RESOURCE_SEMAPHORE wait type.

There is a maximum amount of memory available for the resource semaphore to use, and it is allocated from the buffer cache. The resource semaphore can allocate up to 75% of the memory from the buffer cache for memory grants, but a single query can never get more than 25% of that amount. For instance, if we have a SQL Server with a buffer cache that can grow to 500 MB, we would have a maximum of 375 MB for memory grants. A single query in this example can never receive more than 93 MB. Having so much memory being possibly granted to queries can be problematic, since the memory is not being used for the buffer cache, meaning more IOs to the storage subsystem are needed to retrieve and write data pages.

RESOURCE_SEMAPHORE Example

For this example, we are going to execute a query against the GalacticWorks database that involves a sort operation. As I mentioned in the previous section, a query that involves a sort will request memory from the resource semaphore so as to perform the sort operation. We will also use the Ostress tool to create a situation where multiple queries are requesting memory, creating a queue at the resource semaphore.

Let's take a look at the query and the memory grant information that we will be executing in Listing 6-10.

Listing 6-10. Sort query against the GalacticWorks database

```
SELECT
  SalesOrderID,
  SalesOrderDetailID,
  ProductID,
  CarrierTrackingNumber
FROM
Sales.SalesOrderDetail
ORDER BY CarrierTrackingNumber ASC
```

As you can see, this is a relatively simple query returning information from the Sales.SalesOrderDetail table, ordered by the CarrierTrackingNumber.

If we enable the Include Actual Execution Plan option and execute the query, we find the amount of memory required to execute it. The results on my test SQL Server are shown in Figure 6-19. You can access these properties by showing the Properties window (View ➤ Properties Window) or by pressing F4 and selecting the SELECT operator.

```
⊟ MemoryGrantInfo
    DesiredMemory          13568
    GrantedMemory          13568
    GrantWaitTime          0
    MaxQueryMemory         545712
    MaxUsedMemory          8608
    RequestedMemory        13568
    RequiredMemory         512
    SerialDesiredMemory    13568
    SerialRequiredMemory   512
```

Figure 6-19. *MemoryGrantInfo inside the properties of the execution plan*

Because we requested the actual execution plan, we see the amount of memory granted to the query for execution. In this case, the query got 13,568 KB (13.5 MB) granted by the resource semaphore, as shown in the GrantedMemory property. The minimal amount of memory needed to execute the query, the required memory, was 512 KB, shown by the RequiredMemory property. The query asked for 13,568 KB, as shown in the DesiredMemory property, which is the sum of the required and additional memory. We can see the query received what it asked for, since both the GrantedMemory and DesiredMemory have the same value.

There are two other properties in Figure 6-19 I would like to point out, the SerialDesiredMemory and the SerialRequiredMemory properties. In the case of this query, both these properties have the same values as the DesiredMemory and RequiredMemory properties. This is because the query was performed without using parallelism. When you use parallelism in your queries, more memory is needed to perform the sort operation since work is split up among threads. Figure 6-20 shows the MemoryGrantInfo properties when I forced the query in Listing 6-10 to use parallelism, spreading the work among four threads.

MemoryGrantInfo	
DesiredMemory	14272
GrantedMemory	14272
GrantWaitTime	0
MaxQueryMemory	535264
MaxUsedMemory	8816
RequestedMemory	14272
RequiredMemory	1216
SerialDesiredMemory	13568
SerialRequiredMemory	512

Figure 6-20. *MemoryGrantInfo properties when executing a parallel query*

As you can see, the SerialRequiredMemory has the same value as when we executed the query serially. The RequiredMemory and RequestedMemory have increased in size so that the sort operation can be completed using parallelism. You should keep this information in mind when you run into memory-related issues and when many of your queries involve sort and join operations that are performed using parallelism, since parallelism simply requires more memory.

Now that we know how much memory is needed to execute the query in Listing 6-10, let's use Ostress to execute the query using multiple connections. Before I start Ostress, I will change the maximum server memory value to 512 MB using the following query:

```
EXEC sys.sp_configure N'max server memory (MB)', N'512'
GO
RECONFIGURE WITH OVERRIDE
GO
```

I saved the query in Listing 6-10 to a file named resource_semaphore.sql and executed Ostress using the following command line:

```
"C:\Program Files\Microsoft Corporation\RMLUtils\ostress.exe" -S.\RC0 -E
-dGalacticWorks -i"C:\TeamData\resource_semaphore.sql" -n200 -r1 -q
```

This will execute the resource_semaphore.sql script against the GalacticWorks database with 200 concurrent connections, with each connection performing the query one time.

While Ostress is running, I query the sys.dm_os_waiting_tasks DMV, looking for RESOURCE_SEMAPHORE waits; some of the results are shown in Figure 6-21.

	waiting_task_address	session_id	exec_context_id	wait_duration_ms	wait_type
1	0x00000230EE083468	152	0	4286	RESOURCE_SEMAPHORE
2	0x00000230EE083468	152	0	4286	RESOURCE_SEMAPHORE
3	0x00000230EE083468	152	0	4286	RESOURCE_SEMAPHORE
4	0x00000230EE083468	152	0	4286	RESOURCE_SEMAPHORE
5	0x00000230EE083468	152	0	4286	RESOURCE_SEMAPHORE
6	0x00000230EE083468	152	0	4286	RESOURCE_SEMAPHORE
7	0x00000230EE083468	152	0	4286	RESOURCE_SEMAPHORE
8	0x00000230EE083468	152	0	4286	RESOURCE_SEMAPHORE
9	0x00000230EE083468	152	0	4286	RESOURCE_SEMAPHORE

Figure 6-21. *RESOURCE_SEMAPHORE waits in the sys.dm_os_waiting_tasks DMV*

Because we set our maximum server memory to 512 MB, and each query requests 13.25 MB memory, we do not have enough memory free to grant all the memory requested. This will result in the RESOURCE_SEMAPHORE wait type you can see in Figure 6-21.

There are various other resources we can use to analyze RESOURCE_SEMAPHORE waits. The resource semaphores themselves have their own DMV, sys.dm_exec_query_resource_semaphores, which will return information about their memory consumption and outstanding and waiting grants. Figure 6-22 shows the results of the query that follows against the sys.dm_exec_query_resource_semaphores DMV while running the Ostress workload:

Listing 6-11. Query the sys.dm_exec_query_resource_semaphores DMV

```
SELECT
    target_memory_kb,
    max_target_memory_kb,
    total_memory_kb,
    available_memory_kb,
    granted_memory_kb,
    grantee_count,
    waiter_count
FROM sys.dm_exec_query_resource_semaphores
WHERE pool_id = 2
```

I am filtering out pool_id 1 because this pool does not handle user queries.

	target_memory_kb	max_target_memory_kb	total_memory_kb	available_memory_kb	granted_memory_kb	grantee_count	waiter_count
1	236328	381528	271360	0	271360	20	117
2	12432	NULL	12432	12432	0	0	0

Figure 6-22. *sys.dm_exec_query_resource_semaphores*

As you might have noticed, two rows are returned. This is because there are two different resource semaphores. The top row is the "regular" resource semaphore. This will handle queries requesting more than 5 MB memory. The second row (identified by the NULL value of the max_target_memory_kb column) returns information for the "small" resource semaphore, which handles queries smaller than 5 MB. Because our query requested more than 5 MB of memory, we receive our memory grants from the regular resource semaphore.

Let's go through the various columns that are returned by the query against the sys.dm_exec_query_resource_semaphore DMV:

- The **target_memory_kb** column returns the amount of memory in KB that this resource semaphore plans to use as a maximum amount of memory it can grant to queries.

- The **max_target_memory_kb** column returns the maximum amount of memory this resource semaphore could grant.

- The **total_memory_kb** column returns the total memory held by the resource semaphore and is the sum of the **available_memory_kb** and the **granted_memory_kb**.

- The **granted_memory_kb** returns the amount of memory that is granted to queries at this time.

- The **grantee_count** and **waiter_count** columns return the amount of grants that have currently been satisfied or are waiting in the resource semaphore queue.

From this information, we see the information returned by the granted_memory_kb column is correct, and our test queries are requesting the memory grants. We know from the execution plan that our test query will request 13,568 KB. Since the grantee_count column shows us that two memory requests are granted, we can multiply the amount of memory requests with the amount of memory per query (20 × 13,568 KB), which ends up being 271,360 KB, the amount of granted memory in Figure 6-22.

We can also use Perfmon to monitor the total size of the granted memory by looking at the SQLServer:Memory Manage\Granted Workspace Memory (KB) counter, as shown in Figure 6-23.

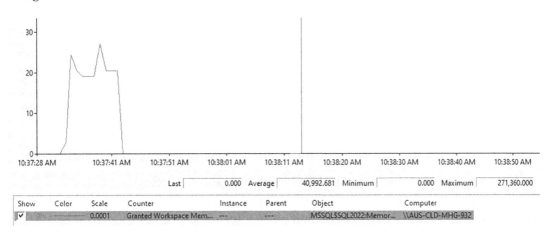

Figure 6-23. *Granted Workspace Memory (KB) Perfmon counter*

Notice the spike in Figure 6-23, which occurred when I executed the Ostress workload, and just as in the results in Figure 6-22, the amount of memory granted was 271,360 KB.

Lowering RESOURCE_SEMAPHORE Waits

There are various possible methods you can use to lower, or resolve, the wait times of the RESOURCE_SEMAPHORE wait type. The most obvious one would be adding more memory, but this might be an expensive solution, while other less expensive options exist.

The first possible solution would be to look at the queries requesting large amounts of memory for their execution. You should focus on the queries performing large sorts or joins (especially hash joins) and check whether you can lower the number of rows needing to be sorted or joined or avoid the sort or join completely. One way to avoid a sort operation is to add an index to the table where the sort is performed. If the order of values inside the index is the same as the sort operation, a sort operation would no longer be necessary, since the index would already have ordered the results.

Another solution involves parallelism. If queries use parallelism during sort or join operations, more memory is requested than when the query is executed serially. Modifying queries so they don't use parallelism, by either using query hints or changing the parallelism configuration for the whole SQL Server instance, will result in lower amounts of memory being required to execute the queries.

Another possible solution is the use of the MAX_GRANT_PERCENT query hint, limiting the amount of memory a query is granted as a percent of the configured maximum for the instance.

Starting with SQL Server 2017+, the Enterprise Edition has a memory grant feedback feature which recalculates the memory required for a query and then updates the grant value for the cached plan. The next time the query is executed, the revised memory grant size is used.

Finally, if you are running an Enterprise Edition of SQL Server, you could use the resource governor feature to configure the memory usage of each resource pool. By configuring the amount of memory a certain resource pool can use, you can also set the amount of memory a resource semaphore can grant. We won't go into detail about the resource governor feature in this book, but more information can be found on the MSDN page of the resource governor here `https://slrwnds.com/lc8dmc`.

RESOURCE_SEMAPHORE Summary

The RESOURCE_SEMAPHORE wait type is related to the amount of memory a query needs to perform certain operations, like sorts and joins. An object, named a resource scmaphore, is responsible for managing and throttling the memory requests of queries.

If a query requests more memory than the resource semaphore can grant, the memory request will be moved into the resource semaphore queue. While the memory request is inside the resource semaphore queue, RESOURCE_SEMAPHORE wait times are recorded. There are various methods to lower or resolve RESOURCE_SEMAPHORE waits. You can choose to add more memory to the SQL Server instance or optimize the queries, so sorts and joins do not require as much memory. Another option is using the resource governor, where you define resource pools so as to minimize the impact of large memory requests.

RESOURCE_SEMAPHORE_QUERY_COMPILE

In the previous section, we discussed the RESOURCE_SEMAPHORE wait type, which indicates there is not enough free memory available for certain query operations like sorts and joins. Just like the RESOURCE_SEMAPHORE wait type, the **RESOURCE_SEMAPHORE_QUERY_COMPILE** wait type is also related to the memory of your SQL Server instance. But instead of indicating a shortage in query memory, the RESOURCE_SEMAPHORE_QUERY_COMPILE wait type indicates a memory shortage during the compilation process of the query.

What Is the RESOURCE_SEMAPHORE_QUERY_COMPILE Wait Type?

In the explanation of the RESOURCE_SEMAPHORE wait type, we discussed what resource semaphores are and what they do. For the explanation of the RESOURCE_SEMAPHORE_QUERY_COMPILE wait type, we are going to dive a little deeper into the inner workings of the resource semaphore.

You should think of resource semaphores as "gateways" that throttle direct access to memory resources, as there are different tasks a resource semaphore can perform. In the previous section, we discussed the resource semaphores are responsible for granting memory for certain operations, like sorts and joins. We also noted that there are two resource semaphores responsible for granting this memory – the regular resource semaphore handles queries requesting 5 MB or more memory, and the small resource semaphore handles memory grants for queries requesting less than 5 MB memory.

The resource semaphores related to the RESOURCE_SEMAPHORE_QUERY_COMPILE wait type are responsible for memory grants needed during the compilation process of a query, *excluding* the memory needed for query execution. Just like the resource semaphores in the previous section, the ones responsible for memory grants during the compilation process have different gateways. Figure 6-24 shows the different gateways for the compilation-memory resource semaphore.

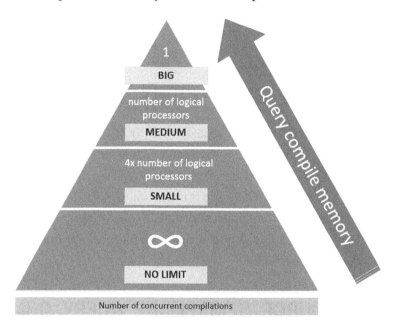

Figure 6-24. *Compilation-memory resource semaphore*

By default there are three gateways: small, medium, and big. Depending on the amount of memory the compilation of a query needs, it is assigned to one of the three. If the amount of memory needed for compilation is less than the memory threshold for the small gateway, the query does not pass through a gateway. The amount of concurrent compilations, or queries, allowed to move through the gateway simultaneously is calculated by the number of logical processors available for your SQL Server instance. For example, if your SQL Server instance has 4 logical processors, the small gateway will allow 16 concurrent compilations and the medium gateway 4. The big gateway will always allow only one query at a time to compile.

The memory threshold for the small gateway is static, but for the medium and big gateways, the thresholds are dynamic. This means the compilation memory needed to reach the medium or big gateways will change during the runtime of your SQL Server instance.

The whole purpose of these gateways is to ensure the need for compilation memory stays under control. This avoids out-of-memory situations in cases where many large compilation-memory requests would automatically be granted and would drain the SQL Server instance of its memory.

Before we continue, let's review an example of a query compilation.

Say we have a query that needs 1560 KB of compilation memory. The query will start by requesting a gateway. Our small gateway has a threshold of 370 KB, and our medium gateway has a threshold of 5346 KB, so this query will end up in the small gateway. If there are any queries currently in a queue at the small gateway, the query will enter the queue and wait until its turn, all the time logging RESOURCE_SEMAPHORE_QUERY_ COMPILE wait time. While the query is compiled, the amount of memory used during the compilation is tracked; if the query ends up using more memory and reaches the threshold of the medium gateway, it is moved to the medium gateway. When the query compilation is finished, it is removed from the gateway.

We can access information about the resource semaphore gateways from inside SQL Server by executing the DBCC MEMORYSTATUS command. Somewhere in the enormous amount of results, you will find the gateway information as shown in Figure 6-25.

Small Gateway (default)	Value
1	Configured Units	16
2	Available Units	16
3	Acquires	0
4	Waiters	0
5	Threshold Factor	380000
6	Threshold	380000

Medium Gateway (default)	Value
1	Configured Units	4
2	Available Units	4
3	Acquires	0
4	Waiters	0
5	Threshold Factor	12
6	Threshold	-1

Big Gateway (default)	Value
1	Configured Units	1
2	Available Units	1
3	Acquires	0
4	Waiters	0
5	Threshold Factor	8
6	Threshold	-1

Figure 6-25. *Gateway information returned by the DBCC MEMORYSTATUS command*

Let's go through the results that are returned for the gateways.

The Configured Units row returns the maximum amount of concurrent compilations allowed for this gateway. This is determined by the number of logical processors available for your SQL Server instance. Because my test SQL Server has 4 logical processors, I have 16 slots for the small gateway (4 × logical number of processors) and 4 for the medium gateway. The Available Units row shows the number of currently free slots for this gateway, while the Acquires row shows the slots currently taken by compilations. The number of queries that have to wait for a free slot is shown in the Waiters row. The Threshold value is the amount of memory in bytes that a query compilation would need in order to enter the gateway. For my test SQL Server system, the small gateway has a threshold of 380,000 bytes, or 371 KB. As you might notice in Figure 6-25, the medium gateway has a threshold of −1. This is because of the dynamic nature of the thresholds of the medium and big gateways. Since there is no activity at the gateway below the medium one, there is no need to set a threshold yet.

RESOURCE_SEMAPHORE_QUERY_COMPILE Example

To show you an example of RESOURCE_SEMAPHORE_QUERY_COMPILE waits in action, I am going to execute the query in Listing 6-12 multiple times, using many concurrent connections. The query is a dynamic query that selects a random row from two joined tables inside the AdventureWorks database. In this case, it doesn't matter if any results are returned or not – the thing we are trying to achieve here is the creation of compilation-memory contention.

Listing 6-12. RESOURCE_SEMAPHORE_QUERY_COMPILE wait query

```
DECLARE @ID VARCHAR(250)
DECLARE @SQL VarChar(MAX)
SET @ID = FLOOR(RAND()*(20000-1)+1);
SET @SQL =
  '
  SELECT
    ' + @ID + ',
    SUM(soh.SubTotal),
    COUNT(soh.SubTotal)
  FROM sales.SalesOrderHeader soh
  INNER JOIN person.Person p
    ON soh.SalesPersonID = p.BusinessEntityID
  WHERE p.BusinessEntityID = ' + @ID + '
  '
EXEC (@SQL)
```

Before we execute the query with many concurrent connections, let's check how much compilation memory would be needed. We can do this by executing the query in Listing 6-12 in SQL Server Management Studio and enabling the actual execution plan.

After executing the query and opening the actual execution plan, we need to look at the CompileMemory property. You can access these properties by showing the Properties window (View ➤ Properties Window) or by pressing F4 and selecting the SELECT operator. Figure 6-26 shows the actual execution plan properties on my test SQL Server.

⊟ **Misc**

Cached plan size	40 KB
CardinalityEstimationModelℕ	70
CompileCPU	2
CompileMemory	464
CompileTime	2
DatabaseContextSettingsId	1
Degree of Parallelism	1

Figure 6-26. *Miscellaneous execution plan properties*

The value returned by the CompileMemory property is the amount of compile memory needed expressed in KB. For this query, 464 KB is needed for compilation. The threshold for the small gateway on my test SQL Server was 371 KB, so I am pretty sure the query will access the small gateway.

Again, we will use the Ostress utility to generate the needed concurrent connections to execute the query. I saved the query in Listing 6-12 to the resource_semaphore_ compile.sql file and then used that file as input for the following Ostress command. Because the query is very fast, I let every connection execute it 100 times so that we have some time to look at the wait statistics.

```
"C:\Program Files\Microsoft Corporation\RMLUtils\ostress.exe" -S.\RC0
-E -dGalacticWorks -i"C:\TeamData\resource_semaphore_compile.sql" -n200
-r100 -q
```

After a few seconds, many RESOURCE_SEMAPHORE_QUERY_COMPILE waits can be seen in the sys.dm_os_waiting_tasks DMV, as shown in Figure 6-27.

	waiting_task_address	session_id	exec_context_id	wait_duration_ms	wait_type
1	0x0000020E9B6EBC28	148	0	96	RESOURCE_SEMAPHORE_QUERY_COMPILE
2	0x0000020E9542ACA8	240	0	96	RESOURCE_SEMAPHORE_QUERY_COMPILE
3	0x0000020E9A8CB088	124	0	32	RESOURCE_SEMAPHORE_QUERY_COMPILE
4	0x0000020E98BE8CA8	249	0	83	RESOURCE_SEMAPHORE_QUERY_COMPILE
5	0x0000020E960848C8	170	0	83	RESOURCE_SEMAPHORE_QUERY_COMPILE
6	0x0000020E98D4D848	254	0	83	RESOURCE_SEMAPHORE_QUERY_COMPILE
7	0x0000020E94514CA8	207	0	76	RESOURCE_SEMAPHORE_QUERY_COMPILE
8	0x0000020E92B27C28	110	0	82	RESOURCE_SEMAPHORE_QUERY_COMPILE
9	0x0000020E95599C28	120	0	76	RESOURCE_SEMAPHORE_QUERY_COMPILE
10	0x0000020E9B9E84E8	233	0	81	RESOURCE_SEMAPHORE_QUERY_COMPILE

Figure 6-27. *RESOURCE_SEMAPHORE_QUERY_COMPILE waits*

If we now execute the DBCC MEMORYSTATUS command, we should be able to find out at what gateway the compilation contention is occurring. Figure 6-28 shows the gateway output of the DBCC MEMORYSTATUS command on my test SQL Server.

	Small Gateway (default)	Value
1	Configured Units	16
2	Available Units	0
3	Acquires	1
4	Waiters	50
5	Threshold Factor	380000
6	Threshold	380000
	Medium Gateway (default)	Value
1	Configured Units	4
2	Available Units	4
3	Acquires	0
4	Waiters	0
5	Threshold Factor	12
6	Threshold	14022656
	Big Gateway (default)	Value
1	Configured Units	1
2	Available Units	1
3	Acquires	0
4	Waiters	0
5	Threshold Factor	8
6	Threshold	-1

Figure 6-28. *DBCC MEMORYSTATUS during compilation contention*

As you can see in Figure 6-28, if we look at the number of Available Units, there are no available slots left for new compilation-memory requests. As a matter of fact, we have 50 compilation-memory requests waiting in the resource semaphore queue. Also note that the threshold of the medium gateway has now changed from −1 to 14,022,656 bytes (13,694 KB). Now that contention is occurring on a lower gateway, the threshold for the medium gateway is dynamically determined, even though there are no compilation-memory requests being processed by this gateway.

Lowering RESOURCE_SEMAPHORE_QUERY_COMPILE Waits

The methods you can use to lower the wait times of the RESOURCE_SEMAPHORE_QUERY_COMPILE wait type are in many cases the same as those that you would use to lower or resolve RESOURCE_SEMAPHORE waits. Just like the RESOURCE_SEMAPHORE wait type, the RESOURCE_SEMAPHORE_QUERY_COMPILE wait type is memory related, so if you can increase the total amount of memory available for query compilation, chances are you will lower or resolve RESOURCE_SEMAPHORE_QUERY_COMPILE wait times.

Because we can access very specific information about the gateways of the resource semaphore dealing with the compilation memory by using the DBCC MEMORYSTATUS command, a good first step is to analyze the usage patterns of the gateways. If you notice one specific gateway constantly has waiting memory requests, then the memory threshold of that gateway, or the maximum allowed amount of concurrent compilation-memory requests, should give you some hints about the root cause. For instance, if you notice many queued compilation-memory requests at the big gateway (which only allows one query at a time), the source of your RESOURCE_SEMAPHORE_QUERY_COMPILE wait times may be the queries requesting a large amount of compilation memory. Another cause may be a large number of concurrent queries all needing access to the small gateway, which was the case in our example, causing a queue at the gateway.

In these cases, you should find the specific queries causing the queues at the gateways and try to optimize them, either by lowering the amount of compilation memory or by making sure fewer compilations happen. The latter can be done by making sure your queries are being parameterized correctly. Queries that generate ad hoc plans every time they are executed can be a cause of RESOURCE_SEMAPHORE_QUERY_COMPILE waits, especially if they are executed very frequently and concurrently.

If your SQL Server is under memory pressure, it is also possible to see RESOURCE_SEMAPHORE_QUERY_COMPILE waits occur. This happens because of the dynamic compilation-memory thresholds of the medium and big gateways. If SQL Server is under memory pressure, the thresholds of both these gateways will lower, giving more queries the chance to use the medium or big gateways. But because the medium and big gateways allow fewer concurrent compilations, in the small gateway, the available concurrent slots will be filled faster.

Just as with the RESOURCE_SEMAPHORE wait type, you can use the resource governor to split workloads into specific resource pools. Each resource pool will have its own resource semaphores responsible for granting compilation memory, making it possible to split heavy compilation-memory usage across multiple resource pools.

RESOURCE_SEMAPHORE_QUERY_COMPILE Summary

Just like the resource semaphores that are needed to grant memory requests for specific query operations, resource semaphores exist for access to compilation memory. These resource semaphores throttle access to compilation memory through the usage of gateways. When a query is compiled, it will approach a gateway based on the amount of compilation memory it needs. The gateway can then grant the compilation memory requested or put the request in a queue if there are more requests that concurrently want to access the gateway. When a query is waiting inside one of these queues, the RESOURCE_SEMAPHORE_QUERY_COMPILE wait type is recorded.

Resolving or lowering RESOURCE_SEMAPHORE_QUERY_COMPILE wait times is commonly achieved by either freeing up more memory or by lowering the compilation-memory needs of queries.

SLEEP_BPOOL_FLUSH

The **SLEEP_BPOOL_FLUSH** wait type is directly related to the checkpoint process inside SQL Server. The checkpoint process is responsible for writing modified, or "dirty," data pages from the buffer pool to the database data file on disk. SLEEP_BPOOL_FLUSH waits also have a relationship with the performance of your storage subsystem. If we search for the definition of the SLEEP_BPOOL_FLUSH wait type on Books Online, Microsoft describes the wait type as occurring "when a checkpoint is throttling the issuance of new I/Os in order to avoid flooding the disk subsystem."

It is pretty common to see SLEEP_BPOOL_FLUSH waits occur, and frequently they will not indicate a problem. There are, however, cases where SLEEP_BPOOL_FLUSH waits can indicate performance problems that are related to either the checkpoint process or the storage subsystem.

What Is the SLEEP_BPOOL_FLUSH Wait Type?

To get a better understanding of how the SLEEP_BPOOL_FLUSH wait type gets recorded, we need to understand how the checkpoint process works inside SQL Server.

The checkpoint process is an internal SQL Server process responsible for writing modified (dirty) pages from the buffer cache to the database data file. One of the main reasons for the checkpoint is to speed up recovery of a database when an unexpected failure occurs. When an unexpected failure occurs, SQL Server needs to revert to the state which existed before the failure. It will do this by using the contents of the transaction log to redo, or undo, changes made to data pages. If the data page was modified, but the change was not yet written to the database data file, SQL Server will need to redo the change to the data page. If a checkpoint already wrote the changed data page to the database data file, this step is not needed, which speeds up the recovery process for the database because SQL Server knows the data was written to the database data file. Figure 6-29 shows the (simplified) process that happens when a data page gets modified.

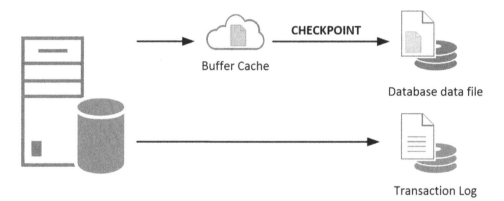

Figure 6-29. *Data modification process*

The first thing that happens when a data page is modified by a committed transaction is the change will be recorded in the transaction log (first in the log buffer and then to disk as described in the WRITELOG and LOGBUFFER wait types section). The modification of the data page will happen in the buffer cache, and the data page will be marked as dirty (red page icon). When a checkpoint occurs, which can be for multiple reasons as we will discuss later, all of the data pages marked as dirty since the previous checkpoint is written to the physical database data file on your storage subsystem, regardless of the state of the transaction which created those dirty pages (green page icon).

The checkpoint process is executed by SQL Server automatically roughly once every minute, which is the default recovery time interval for versions of SQL Server earlier than SQL Server 2016. This does not mean a checkpoint will occur every minute exactly. The values you specify for the recovery interval are the upper time limit at which a checkpoint should occur, the checkpoint process analysis of the outstanding I/O requests, and latency; throttle checkpoint operations to avoid overloading the storage subsystem.

The following list will describe the various checkpoint types available in SQL Server:

- The internal checkpoint type is not configurable and occurs automatically when certain actions are performed, for instance, a database backup.

- **Automatic** – These are the default checkpoints, on SQL Server version lower than 2016, which occur roughly every minute when left at their default value of 0. We can change the interval of the checkpoint process by changing the recovery interval configuration option under the Server Properties ➤ Database Settings page in SQL Server Management Studio. We can only change it to a value in minutes, and it will be used for all databases inside the SQL Server instance.

- **Manual** – You can manually cause checkpoints to occur by issuing the CHECKPOINT T-SQL command. Optionally, you can specify the time in seconds at which the checkpoint must be completed. If you do issue a manual checkpoint, it will run in the context of the current database. For example, executing CHECKPOINT 10 in a query window will perform a checkpoint within 10 seconds of the time you executed the query.

- **Indirect** – SQL Server 2012 added an extra option to configure checkpoint intervals on a per-database level. Configuring this option to a value greater than the default 0 will overwrite the automatic checkpoint process for the specific database. You can use indirect checkpoints for a specific database by using the following command:

- `ALTER DATABASE [db name] SET TARGET_RECOVERY_TIME = [time in seconds or minutes]`

- With the release of SQL Server 2016, indirect checkpoint became the new default setting of the checkpoint process (with the value of 60).

As I mentioned before, SQL Server will attempt to throttle the checkpoint process to avoid overloading the storage subsystem if it believes this is necessary. It monitors the number of outstanding requests to the storage subsystem and tries to detect if there is any latency. Using this information, it will throttle the amount of IOs the checkpoint process generates so as to avoid a too-heavy load on the storage subsystem. When the checkpoint process is getting throttled, the SLEEP_BPOOL_FLUSH wait type will be recorded.

SLEEP_BPOOL_FLUSH Example

The following example shows the impact of the SLEEP_BPOOL_FLUSH wait type on SQL Server versions lower than SQL Server 2016. As mentioned earlier, in SQL Server 2016, the way SQL Server handles the checkpoint process has changed which means it is far less likely for the wait type to show up in an example like the following.

Generating SLEEP_BPOOL_FLUSH waits is relatively simple, and the script in Listing 6-13, which is almost the same one as we used for the LOGBUFFER and WRITELOG wait types, will put pressure on the checkpoint process such that SLEEP_BPOOL_FLUSH waits will occur.

Listing 6-13. Generate SLEEP_BPOOL_FLUSH waits

```
USE TLog_demo;
DECLARE @i INT
SET @i = 1
WHILE @i < 100
  BEGIN
    INSERT INTO transactions
        (t_guid)
    VALUES
        (newid())
  SET @i = @i + 1
  -- Force a checkpoint to occur within 1 second
  CHECKPOINT 1
END
```

Since we are also using the same database as in the LOGBUFFER and WRITELOG wait types example, Listing 6-14 shows the script to create the database if it doesn't exist already.

Listing 6-14. Create TLog_demo database

```
USE master;
-- Create demo database
CREATE DATABASE [TLog_demo]
ON PRIMARY  (
  NAME = N'TLog_demo', FILENAME = N'C:\TeamData\TLog_demo.mdf' , SIZE =
  153600KB , FILEGROWTH = 10%)
LOG ON  (  NAME = N'TLog_demo_log', FILENAME = N'C:\TeamData\TLog_demo.ldf'
, SIZE = 51200KB , FILEGROWTH = 10%);
-- Make sure recovery model is set to full
ALTER DATABASE [TLog_demo] SET RECOVERY FULL;
-- Perform full backup first
-- Otherwise FULL recovery model will not be affected
BACKUP DATABASE [TLog_demo]
TO  DISK = N'C:\TeamData\TLog_demo_Full.bak';
-- Create a simple test table
USE TLog_demo;
CREATE TABLE transactions  (
  t_guid VARCHAR(50) );
```

What the script in Listing 6-13 will do is perform an insert of a random GUID into the transactions table inside a loop that is executed 100 times. Every time it enters a new GUID, it will issue a CHECKPOINT command with a time limit of 1 second. This forces the checkpoint process to perform a checkpoint within the 1-second time limit.

Before running the script in Listing 6-13, I cleared the sys.dm_os_wait_stats DMV using the DBCC SQLPERF('sys.dm_os_wait_stats', CLEAR) command.

After almost 70 seconds, the script completed on my test SQL Server. I then executed the following query to take a look at the SLEEP_BPOOL_FLUSH wait times:

```
SELECT *
FROM sys.dm_os_wait_stats
WHERE wait_type = 'SLEEP_BPOOL_FLUSH';
```

The results of the query can be seen in Figure 6-30.

	wait_type	waiting_tasks_count	wait_time_ms	max_wait_time_ms	signal_wait_time_ms
1	SLEEP_BPOOL_FLUSH	311	60415	938	26

Figure 6-30. *SLEEP_BPOOL_FLUSH waits*

As you can see, the SLEEP_BPOOL_FLUSH wait time has a very high amount of wait time after running the script in Listing 6-10. Normally you would expect those wait times to be either very low or close to zero. If we were to remove the CHECKPOINT command from the script completely and let SQL Server decide on when to run the checkpoint process, we not only get a completely different result, as shown in Figure 6-31, but also the script's runtime is decreased to just a few milliseconds.

	wait_type	waiting_tasks_count	wait_time_ms	max_wait_time_ms	signal_wait_time_ms
1	SLEEP_BPOOL_FLUSH	0	0	0	0

Figure 6-31. *SLEEP_BPOOL_FLUSH wait times after removing CHECKPOINT*

Lowering SLEEP_BPOOL_FLUSH Waits

Even though it is not very common to run into performance problems caused by the SLEEP_BPOOL_FLUSH wait type, there are various methods to lower the wait times.

The most obvious one would be to check the various configuration options available to manually configure the recovery interval that we discussed earlier. The lower the value of the recovery interval, the more often checkpoint processes will take place, and the bigger the chance of running into SLEEP_BPOOL_FLUSH waits. Also, as you noticed in the example, performing frequent CHECKPOINT commands inside transactions can lead to SLEEP_BPOOL_FLUSH waits.

Another possible cause can be the storage subsystem on which your database data file resides. As explained earlier, the checkpoint process calculates the load of the storage subsystem and then decides if throttling its throughput is needed. If there is a frequent need of throttling because your storage subsystem is busy, you are more likely to see SLEEP_BPOOL_FLUSH waits occur.

If you are running SQL Server 2016, chances are you will never run into very high SLEEP_BPOOL_FLUSH wait times since the default way SQL Server handles the process has been changed.

SLEEP_BPOOL_FLUSH Summary

The SLEEP_BPOOL_FLUSH wait type is closely related to the checkpoint process in SQL Server. The checkpoint process is responsible for writing modified, or dirty, data pages from the buffer cache to the database data file. The checkpoint process analyzes the performance of the storage subsystem before it writes the dirty pages to disk, and if the storage subsystem is busy, the checkpoint process will throttle its throughput, resulting in SLEEP_BPOOL_FLUSH waits. It is not very common to see very high SLEEP_BPOOL_FLUSH wait times, but they can impact performance nonetheless. Queries that frequently execute the CHECKPOINT T-SQL command, or a recovery interval that is configured to a very low value, can be possible causes for seeing SLEEP_BPOOL_FLUSH waits occur. The performance of your storage subsystem can also impact the checkpoint process if it is forced to throttle its throughput.

WRITE_COMPLETION

As with the ASYNC_IO_COMPLETION and IO_COMPLETION wait types, the **WRITE_COMPLETION** wait type is related to specific actions SQL Server performs on the storage subsystem. Again, it is very normal to see WRITE_COMPLETION waits occur on your SQL Server instance, and they should only be a cause for concern if the wait times are way higher than normal.

What Is the WRITE_COMPLETION Wait Type?

The WRITE_COMPLETION wait type is a relative of the IO_COMPLETION wait type. But where the IO_COMPLETION wait type is logged for specific read and write operations, the WRITE_COMPLETION wait type is only logged for some very specific write operations. Some of these write operations are growing a data or log file or performing the DBCC CHECKDB command.

Since the WRITE_COMPLETION wait type is related to writing SQL Server data to the storage subsystem, the performance of it can have an impact on the wait times.

WRITE_COMPLETION Example

To show you an example of a WRITE_COMPLETION wait occurring, I am going to perform a CHECKDB against the GalacticWorks database after clearing the sys.dm_os_wait_stats DMV using the DBCC SQLPERF('sys.dm_os_wait_stats', CLEAR) command.

Keep in mind that this example is a completely normal situation in which WRITE_COMPLETION waits can occur, and it shouldn't stop you from performing regular database consistency checks!

Listing 6-15 shows the query I executed to generate a few WRITE_COMPLETION waits.

Listing 6-15. Generate WRITE_COMPLETION waits

```
DBCC SQLPERF('sys.dm_os_wait_stats', CLEAR);
DBCC CHECKDB ('GalacticWorks');
SELECT * FROM sys.dm_os_wait_stats
WHERE wait_type = 'WRITE_COMPLETION';
```

The results of the last query in the batch are shown in Figure 6-32.

	wait_type	waiting_tasks_count	wait_time_ms	max_wait_time_ms	signal_wait_time_ms
1	WRITE_COMPLETION	2	3	2	3

Figure 6-32. *WRITE_COMPLETION waits*

As you can see, the amount of wait time is so low that it would not be a cause of any concern. This is also partly due to the fact that the GalacticWorks database is very small and the storage performance of my test machine is very fast. Running CHECKDB against larger databases can result in higher wait times.

Lowering WRITE_COMPLETION Waits

If you see high WRITE_COMPLETION wait times, try to find out what process is generating the waits. In many cases, it will be caused by a CHECKDB or database data or log file growth.

One thing worth checking is the instant file initialization option discussed in the ASYNC_IO_COMPLETION section earlier in this chapter. Not using this option can impact the duration of the WRITE_COMPLETION wait time.

Another, far less common cause for a higher WRITE_COMPLETION wait time is when you are experiencing page latch contention on your Page Free Space (PFS) page. The PFS page tracks the amount of free space in data pages. If a process needs to modify the PFS page very frequently, it is possible to see WRITE_COMPLETION waits occur along with many PAGELATCH_UP waits, which we will discuss in Chapter 9, "Latch-Related Wait Types." To give you an example of such a scenario, consider a high amount of concurrent queries that all create a temporary table, insert a few rows, and remove the temporary table again. In this case, the PFS page of the tempdb database needs to get updates very frequently to reflect the creation and removal of the temporary tables.

WRITE_COMPLETION Summary

The WRITE_COMPLETION wait type, just like the ASYNC_IO_COMPLETION and IO_COMPLETION wait types, is related to specific storage-related actions performed by SQL Server. Seeing WRITE_COMPLETION waits is very normal and won't be a cause for concern in many situations. Operations such as CHECKDB and database data or log file growth can cause WRITE_COMPLETION waits.

CHAPTER 7

Backup-Related Wait Types

Backups are a very important part of database administration, and they are essential for the survival of the company you work for. **Data is the most critical asset a business owns**, and if a disaster causes data to be lost, companies can lose large amounts of money or even go out of business.

There are many possible methods to minimize data loss during a disaster. We could use a SAN instead of direct attached storage and perhaps leverage SAN replication. Or we could utilize cloud storage. Perhaps we create a SQL Server Always On Availability Group to replicate our data across datacenters and global regions. But the first step we must do, and hopefully have already taken, is performing regular backups of the data inside our SQL Server databases.

Implementing and scheduling SQL Server backups is not a very difficult task, and there is no excuse not to perform regular backups. The type of backup and the interval of backup operations are dictated by the needs of the organization you work for and are frequently expressed in "RTO" (Recovery Time Objective) and "RPO" (Recovery Point Objective) times. These times represent the amount of time it should take to recover from a disaster and the amount of data loss that is acceptable when a disaster occurs. These two times should be the primary input for your SQL Server backup strategy.

Nerd Note   I said "backup strategy," but in reality what you want to build first is a **recovery strategy**. This is where RTO and RPO are vital. Once you know your recovery strategy, you then configure your database backups.

Thankfully, SQL Server has different options available for meeting RTO and RPO requirements right out of the box. We can use SQL Server's own backup mechanism to

T. LaRock and E. van de Laar, *Pro SQL Server 2022 Wait Statistics*,
https://doi.org/10.1007/978-1-4842-8771-2_7

fulfill our company's RTO and RPO times; we are not dependent on third-party backup software. Since the SQL Server backup operation is an internal process, there are different wait types associated with it, and in this chapter, we will take a look at three of the most common wait types directly related to performing backups and restores.

Noticing high wait times on these backup-/restore-related wait types will not likely lead to a performance degradation of your SQL Server instance. However, we do have options to optimize the SQL Server backup process that can result in faster backup and restore times. And since backups/restores of your database(s) are vital for the survival of your company, optimizing backup and restore throughput is well worth the effort.

BACKUPBUFFER

The first backup-related wait type to discuss is **BACKUPBUFFER**. If we look up the definition of this wait type on Books Online, we get the following text: "Occurs when a backup task is waiting for data, or is waiting for a buffer in which to store data. This type is not typical, except when a task is waiting for a tape mount." The way this is worded sounds as if we would only see this event when writing our backups to a tape device, which is not true. BACKUPBUFFER waits will always be logged during a backup operation, no matter the destination of the backup file. The reason for this is in the way the SQL Server backup operation uses buffers to read data from the database and write it to the backup file.

What Is the BACKUPBUFFER Wait Type?

To understand how BACKUPBUFFER waits are generated, we will dive into the internals of the SQL Server backup process. These internals are mostly the same regardless of the backup method you use (i.e., transaction log, differential or full backup), and as such, they will encounter the same wait types.

SQL Server allocates buffers for the backup process. These buffers will be filled with data from your database and will be moved through the backup process as they are written to the backup file (or vice versa for a restore operation). The buffers are allocated inside the memory of your system but outside the buffer cache so as to avoid stealing memory from the buffer cache. The size and the amount of the backup buffers are automatically calculated by SQL Server, but we can configure these values ourselves as parameters of the backup/restore command. Figure 7-1 shows how these backup buffers are ordered and moved through a "reader," which reads the data from your database or backup file to a buffer, and a "writer," which writes the data from the buffer to the backup file or database.

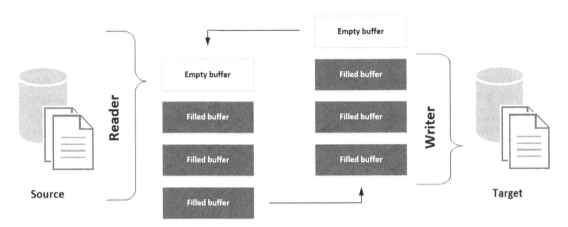

Figure 7-1. *Backup buffers moving through reader and writer*

We can view information about the buffer amount and size during a backup or restore operation by enabling two trace flags, 3213 and 3605, which will output backup/ restore information to the SQL Server error log. The query in Listing 7-1 enables both trace flags and performs a full database backup of the GalacticWorks database on my test SQL Server.

Listing 7-1. Full database backup with backup-information trace flags

```
-- enable trace flags
DBCC TRACEON (3213);
DBCC TRACEON (3605);
-- backup database
BACKUP DATABASE [GalacticWorks]
  TO  DISK = N'C:\TeamData\GWorks.bak'
WITH NAME = N'GalacticWorks-Full Database Backup';
-- disable trace flags
DBCC TRACEOFF (3213);
DBCC TRACEOFF (3605);
```

Keep in mind that trace flags inside SQL Server should only be used under the guidance of Microsoft Support. I am enabling them now to show me backup information on my test SQL Server, but I would advise against using them on a production system.

Inside the SQL Server error log, additional information about the backup we just performed is logged, as you can see in Figure 7-2.

6/6/2022 3:23:50 PM	spid73	DBCC TRACEOFF 3605, server process ID (SPID) 73. This is an infor...		SQL Server
6/6/2022 3:23:50 PM	spid73	DBCC TRACEOFF 3213, server process ID (SPID) 73. This is an infor...		SQL Server
6/6/2022 3:23:50 PM	Back...	BACKUP DATABASE successfully processed 24889 pages in 1.188 s...		SQL Server
6/6/2022 3:23:50 PM	Back...	Database backed up. Database: GalacticWorks, creation date(time): 2...		SQL Server
6/6/2022 3:23:49 PM	spid73	Media Buffer size:	1024 KB	SQL Server
6/6/2022 3:23:49 PM	spid73	Media Buffer count:	7	SQL Server
6/6/2022 3:23:49 PM	spid73	Filesystem i/o alignment:	512	SQL Server
6/6/2022 3:23:49 PM	spid73	TXF device count:	0	SQL Server
6/6/2022 3:23:49 PM	spid73	Filestream device count:	0	SQL Server
6/6/2022 3:23:49 PM	spid73	Fulltext data device count:	0	SQL Server
6/6/2022 3:23:49 PM	spid73	Tabular data device count:	1	SQL Server
6/6/2022 3:23:49 PM	spid73	Total buffer space:	7 MB	SQL Server
6/6/2022 3:23:49 PM	spid73	Min MaxTransferSize:	64 KB	SQL Server
6/6/2022 3:23:49 PM	spid73	MaxTransferSize:	1024 KB	SQL Server
6/6/2022 3:23:49 PM	spid73	Sets Of Buffers:	1	SQL Server
6/6/2022 3:23:49 PM	spid73	BufferCount:	7	SQL Server
6/6/2022 3:23:49 PM	spid73	Memory limit:	511 MB	SQL Server
6/6/2022 3:23:49 PM	spid73	Backup/Restore buffer configuration parameters		SQL Server
6/6/2022 3:23:49 PM	spid73	DBCC TRACEON 3605, server process ID (SPID) 73. This is an inform...		SQL Server
6/6/2022 3:23:49 PM	spid73	DBCC TRACEON 3213, server process ID (SPID) 73. This is an inform...		SQL Server

Figure 7-2. *Additional backup information*

In this case, the backup operation created seven buffers, shown by the **Buffer count** parameter, with a size of 1024 KB each, as shown by the **Buffer size** parameter. The total memory needed to create the buffers is shown by the **Total buffer space** parameter, 7 MB (Buffer count * Buffer Size). Another interesting bit of information returned is the memory limit. This shows the maximum amount of memory outside of the buffer cache which the backup operation could access.

Now we have an idea of how the backup process works inside SQL Server, let's take a look where the BACKUPBUFFER wait type comes in.

As we described earlier, the SQL Server backup process uses buffers to store data that needs to be written to the backup file. Whenever a buffer is not directly available, the BACKUPBUFFER wait will occur, making the process wait until a full buffer is written to the backup file and it becomes available again.

BACKUPBUFFER Example

Generating BACKUPBUFFER waits is very simple - just perform a backup operation. For this example, I ran the query shown in Listing 7-2. The query will first reset the sys. dm_os_wait_stats DMV, then perform a full backup of the GalacticWorks database, and finally will return the wait statistics information for the BACKUPBUFFER wait type.

Listing 7-2. Generating BACKUPBUFFER waits

```
-- clear sys.dm_os_wait_stats
DBCC SQLPERF('sys.dm_os_wait_stats', CLEAR);
-- backup database
BACKUP DATABASE [GalacticWorks]
  TO DISK = N'C:\TeamData\GWorks.bak'
WITH
  NAME = N'GalacticWorks-Full Database Backup';
-- Query BACKUPBUFFER waits
SELECT *
FROM sys.dm_os_wait_stats
WHERE wait_type = 'BACKUPBUFFER';
```

The results of the query against the sys.dm_os_wait_stats DMV are shown in Figure 7-3.

	wait_type	waiting_tasks_count	wait_time_ms	max_wait_time_ms	signal_wait_time_ms
1	BACKUPBUFFER	376	890	19	12

Figure 7-3. *BACKUPBUFFER waits*

The total duration of the backup operation was around 1 second on my test SQL Server. Of that 1 second, 890 milliseconds were spent waiting on free backup buffers.

Lowering BACKUPBUFFER Waits

As stated in the introduction of this chapter, backup-related waits aren't normally a cause for concern since they typically don't impact the performance of your SQL Server instance. However, we can improve backup performance by using the wait statistics information of the various backup-related wait types.

One of the most common ways to lower BACKUPBUFFER wait times is by adding more buffers for the backup operation to use, overwriting the automatic allocation of buffers. We do this by specifying the BUFFERCOUNT option inside the BACKUP T-SQL command. There is, however, a catch to altering the number of buffers the backup operation can use. Every buffer created will allocate the value of the MAXTRANSFERSIZE option; this value is automatically calculated by SQL Server itself or by setting the value yourself inside the BACKUP command (up to a maximum of 4,194,304 bytes). Since the backup operation allocates memory outside of the buffer cache, there is a chance that using too many or too large buffers can result in out-of-memory problems. So, be careful when testing what the optimal value for your SQL Server instance is.

Listing 7-3 shows a modification of the query in Listing 7-2, which we used to demonstrate BACKUPBUFFER waits occurring. In this case, we added the BUFFERCOUNT option and configured it to a value of 200.

Listing 7-3. Database backup with BUFFERCOUNT configured

```
-- clear sys.dm_os_wait_stats
DBCC SQLPERF('sys.dm_os_wait_stats', CLEAR);
-- backup database
BACKUP DATABASE [GalacticWorks]
  TO DISK = N'C:\TeamData\GWorks.bak'
WITH
  NAME = N'GalacticWorks-Full Database Backup',
  BUFFERCOUNT = 200;
-- Query BACKUPBUFFER waits
SELECT *
FROM sys.dm_os_wait_stats
WHERE wait_type = 'BACKUPBUFFER';
```

The results of the query against the sys.dm_os_wait_stats DMV are shown in Figure 7-4.

	wait_type	waiting_tasks_count	wait_time_ms	max_wait_time_ms	signal_wait_time_ms
1	BACKUPBUFFER	2	0	0	0

Figure 7-4. *BACKUPBUFFER waits*

As you can see, the amount of time spent on the BACKUPBUFFER wait time went down to 0 milliseconds instead of the 890 milliseconds it spent when we did not supply the BUFFERCOUNT parameter. This happens because the number of buffers we specified was enough to process the backup operation without a need to allocate additional buffers. Since no additional buffers were required, we do not spend time waiting on their allocation.

Another option is to configure the MAXTRANSFERSIZE option inside the BACKUP T-SQL command. This will allow buffers to be filled with larger units of work, up to a value of 4,194,304 bytes, or 4 MB. Again, allocating more space for the buffers will result in a larger reservation of memory.

BACKUPBUFFER Summary

BACKUPBUFFER waits occur normally during backup or restore operations when the backup/restore operation has to wait for free buffers to become available again. Because they occur normally, they shouldn't be a cause for concern. We do have some options for lowering BACKUPBUFFER wait times which will also impact the duration of the backup/restore operation. They should be configured and tested thoroughly though, because setting those parameters too high can result in out-of-memory errors.

BACKUPIO

Just like the BACKUPBUFFER wait type, the **BACKUPIO** wait type occurs when a part of the backup or restore operation runs into contention problems. Interestingly enough, the description of the BACKUPIO wait type is **identical** to BACKUPBUFFER in Books Online: "Occurs when a backup task is waiting for data, or is waiting for a buffer in which to store data. This type is not typical, except when a task is waiting for a tape mount." The same description, but for two different wait events, is not confusing at all. Again, this wait type is common when performing a backup or restore operation, even when the backup target, or restore source, is not a tape device.

What Is the BACKUPIO Wait Type?

To better understand how BACKUPIO waits are generated, we have to take a look at Figure 7-5, which we showed earlier as Figure 7-1.

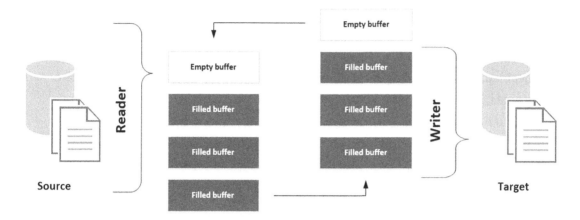

Figure 7-5. *Internals of a backup operation*

In the previous section where we discussed the BACKUPBUFFER wait type, we explained the BACKUPBUFFER wait type occurs when waiting for a free (empty) buffer to become available. For the most part, the BACKUPBUFFER wait type is situated on the left side of Figure 7-5, at the reader. The BACKUPIO wait type occurs for the most part on the right side of Figure 7-5, at the writer section. When BACKUPIO waits occur, there is a delay in the time the writer is writing data. This delay can be caused by many different things, for instance, when writing a backup to a slow disk, when writing a backup to a network location, or when restoring a database.

The BACKUPIO wait type will frequently be accompanied by ASYNC_IO_COMPLETION waits when a database backup or restore is performed.

BACKUPIO Example

We will make use of the same example used to demonstrate the BACKUPBUFFER wait type. I did modify the query to return BACKUPIO waits instead of BACKUPBUFFER waits, and I also included the ASYNC_IO_COMPLETION in the results of the query against the sys.dm_os_wait_stats DMV. Listing 7-4 shows the modified backup query.

Listing 7-4. Generating BACKUPIO waits

```
-- clear sys.dm_os_wait_stats
DBCC SQLPERF('sys.dm_os_wait_stats', CLEAR);

-- backup database
```

```
BACKUP DATABASE [GalacticWorks]
  TO DISK = N'C:\TeamData\GWorks.bak'
WITH
  NAME = N'GalacticWorks-Full Database Backup';
-- Query BACKUPIO waits
SELECT *
FROM sys.dm_os_wait_stats
WHERE wait_type = 'BACKUPIO'
OR wait_type = 'ASYNC_IO_COMPLETION';
```

The results of the query against the sys.dm_os_wait_stats DMV can be seen in Figure 7-6.

	wait_type	waiting_tasks_count	wait_time_ms	max_wait_time_ms	signal_wait_time_ms
1	ASYNC_IO_COMPLETION	4	1036	1034	0
2	BACKUPIO	366	39	6	6

Figure 7-6. *ASYNC_IO_COMPLETION and BACKUPIO waits*

As you can see in Figure 7-6, the database backup caused both wait types to be generated, and the most time has been spent on the ASYNC_IO_COMPLETION wait, which is responsible for reading the data pages that need to be written to the backup file. Since my backup destination is on an SSD disk, we didn't encounter very high BACKUPIO wait times.

Lowering BACKUPIO Waits

Tweaking the BUFFERCOUNT and MAXTRANSFERSIZE options does not have as much impact on the BACKUPIO wait type as they did on the BACKUPBUFFER wait type. When you see higher than normal wait times on the BACKUPIO wait type, the problem is most likely related to the throughput of either your storage subsystem or network location you are writing or reading your backup to/from. Make sure to check both locations for possible performance problems like high latency or network utilization.

Another possible option to explore is the use of striping backups across multiple files. Striping backup files will likely lower the duration of the backup operations, but may not lower the overall amount of BACKUPIO wait time.

BACKUPIO Summary

Just like the BACKUPBUFFER wait type, the BACKUPIO wait type occurs when a backup or restore operation is being performed. While the BACKUPBUFFER wait type is mostly related to the speed at which the backup operation can access the backup buffers, the BACKUPIO wait type is related to the speed at which those backup buffers can be written to disk. BACKUPIO waits frequently occur together with ASYNC_IO_COMPLETION waits when performing full database backups or restores. When seeing higher than normal wait times for the BACKUPIO wait type, check the performance metric of the location you are writing or reading the backup file to or from. Lowering BACKUPIO wait times will not have an impact on the query performance of your system but will help speed up backup and restore operations.

BACKUPTHREAD

The **BACKUPTHREAD** wait type is frequently seen when performing restore operations on a database but also occurs during a backup operation. It occurs when another thread is waiting for the backup/restore operation to finish so it can continue processing.

What Is the BACKUPTHREAD Wait Type?

When you see BACKUPTHREAD waits occurring, it means another thread wants to access a resource currently being accessed by a backup or restore operation. During the time the thread has to wait for the backup/restore to complete, BACKUPTHREAD wait time is recorded. An example of this type of wait would be a thread needing to access the database data file while it is being restored, for instance, the ASYNC_IO_COMPLETION wait type that is writing the data file to disk.

BACKUPTHREAD waits are not usually a cause for concern. They only indicate other threads are waiting for the backup/restore operation to complete, and they frequently have the same duration as the time it took for your backup or restore to complete. They do, however, give you a hint there are other waits occurring which might deserve investigation if the wait times are higher than expected.

Because a picture says more than a thousand words, Figure 7-7 shows the relation of the BACKUPTHREAD wait type with a restore operation and other waits occurring.

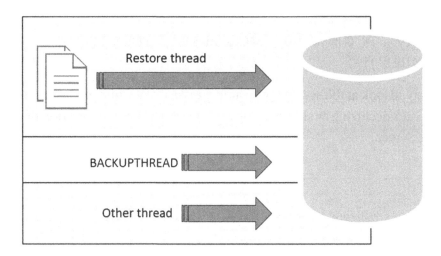

Figure 7-7. *BACKUPTHREAD relation to other threads*

In Figure 7-7, you see the BACKUPTHREAD wait is occurring because another thread also wanted to access a resource that was currently owned by the restore operation.

BACKUPTHREAD Example

An easy way to demonstrate BACKUPTHREAD waits is by performing a restore operation. When you perform a restore, other processes will need to access the database data files to write the information from the backup file to the database data files.

Listing 7-5 shows a script to restore a backup file I made earlier of the GalacticWorks database on my test SQL Server.

Listing 7-5. Restore AdventureWorks database

```
-- clear sys.dm_os_wait_stats
DBCC SQLPERF('sys.dm_os_wait_stats', CLEAR);
-- Restore database
USE [master]
RESTORE DATABASE [GalacticWorks]
FROM DISK = N'C:\TeamData\GWorks.bak'
WITH  FILE = 1, REPLACE;
-- Query BACKUPBUFFER waits
SELECT *
```

```
FROM sys.dm_os_wait_stats
WHERE wait_type IN ('BACKUPIO','BACKUPTHREAD', 'PREEMPTIVE_OS_
WRITEFILEGATHER');
```

If we were to look at the sys.dm_os_waiting_tasks DMV while the backup is running, we see the waits occurring as shown in Figure 7-8, which shows a selection of waits on my test SQL Server.

	wait_type	waiting_tasks_count	wait_time_ms	max_wait_time_ms	signal_wait_time_ms
1	BACKUPIO	713	1363	74	2
2	BACKUPTHREAD	10	1464	1462	0
3	PREEMPTIVE_OS_WRITEFILEGATHER	1	1466	1466	0

Figure 7-8. *BACKUPTHREAD and other waits*

As you see in Figure 7-8, the wait time of the BACKUPTHREAD wait type is close to the PREEMPTIVE_OS_WRITEFILEGATHER wait type. This wait type is responsible for writing data to the file system, and we will dive deeper into this specific wait type in Chapter 11, "Preemptive Wait Types."

Lowering BACKUPTHREAD Waits

While the BACKUPTHREAD wait type itself doesn't indicate any problems, its combination with other wait types can be a reason for some additional research. Basically, every method you can use to speed up your backup or recovery process will have an impact on the BACKUPTHREAD wait time.

Some good pointers to start with are the BufferCount and MaxTransferSize options that you can specify on the BACKUP and RESTORE T-SQL commands. We touched upon these settings when we discussed the BACKUPBUFFER and BACKUPIO wait types. Tweaking these settings can make your backups and restores take less time, resulting in lower BACKUPTHREAD wait times.

Another setting that can dramatically improve backup and restore times is the instant file initialization option that we discussed in Chapter 6, "IO-Related Wait Types," in the ASYNC_IO_COMPLETION section.

BACKUPTHREAD Summary

The BACKUPTHREAD wait time doesn't indicate access to a specific resource but rather indicates that another process is waiting for a backup or restore operation to complete. It is very common to see this wait type, especially during restore operations. Lowering the duration of backup and restore operations will also be reflected in the wait times of the BACKUPTHREAD wait type. One of the methods you can use to lower BACKUPTHREAD wait times is checking whether instant file initialization is enabled. This setting does not directly impact the BACKUPTHREAD wait type, but it will impact other wait types, which will in turn impact the BACKUPTHREAD wait time.

CHAPTER 8

Lock-Related Wait Types

Locking is a fundamental part of every relational database or Relational Database Management System (RDBMS). SQL Server is based on the relational database model and therefore utilizes locking when data is accessed. Even though we frequently relate locking to performance problems, it plays a vital role in making sure your data is reliable during concurrent workloads. The way SQL Server, or any other RDBMS for that matter, ensures data reliability is by following the "ACID" properties, which were originally defined by Jim Gray in the 1970s but received their name in 1983 from Andreas Reuter and Theo Härder. These ACID properties are enforced upon single operations, which we commonly know as *transactions*. The acronym ACID consists of four characteristics which guarantee data reliability inside transactions. The following list describes each of these characteristics:

- **Atomicity** – The atomicity characteristic requires transactions to be considered a single unit, and the unit either fails or succeeds completely. This means if one part of the transaction fails, the complete transaction fails, and every change done inside the transaction needs to be changed back to the state before the transaction started.

- **Consistency** – The consistency characteristic requires data written to the database by the transaction is valid. This means the data must be stripped of illegal or bad input.

- **Isolation** – The isolation characteristic requires transactions are hidden from other concurrent transactions. From a transaction point of view, this means concurrent transactions leave the database in the same state as if the transactions ran sequentially.

© Thomas LaRock, Enrico van de Laar 2023
T. LaRock and E. van de Laar, *Pro SQL Server 2022 Wait Statistics*,
https://doi.org/10.1007/978-1-4842-8771-2_8

- **Durable** – The durable characteristic requires every committed transaction remains committed, even in the event of a power failure or disaster.

As you might have guessed from reading the different ACID properties, locking inside SQL Server is closely related to the isolation characteristic.

Since this chapter is dedicated to lock-related wait types, we won't go into detail about ACID properties besides isolation. If you are interested in learning more about the ACID properties and database theory, a good place to start would be the "Principles of Transaction-Oriented Database Recovery" research paper by Andreas Reuter and Theo Harder, which describes the ACID properties in detail. You can find the paper here `https://slrwnds.com/ba7klg`.

To get a better understanding of how the isolation characteristic works, we need to understand transactions. A transaction represents an interaction with the database, it may consist of multiple actions, and it operates separate from other transactions.

To make sure our transactions do not conflict with other concurrent transactions, SQL Server uses **locks**. These locks make sure no other transaction will modify data your transaction is processing at the same time. For example, if you make a $100 withdrawal from your bank account, you do not want another concurrent withdrawal to modify the amount. Other transactions will wait for their withdrawals until your transaction is completed. Inside SQL Server, this process works the same way. When you request data from your database, you want the data you asked for, without running the risk the data was modified between the time it was requested and the time it was returned.

When you run your transaction, it will be protected by a lock SQL Server places on the object you are accessing. If another transaction wants to interact with the same object, a block will occur. When this block occurs, the latter transaction will have to wait until the lock on the object is removed. The transaction can then place its own lock on the object and start its interaction.

There are many options available to us within SQL Server to control the behavior of locking, and most are related to changing the isolation level of specific or all transactions against a database. There is a lot of information we can access inside SQL Server about locking and blocking, not the least of these are inside wait statistics. The time a transaction is waiting to access a locked object is recorded as wait time for specific, lock-related wait types (depending on the type of lock the transaction intends to place).

In this chapter, we will discuss the various wait types related to locking and blocking and how we can lower or even resolve them. This requires some knowledge of how SQL Server uses locks, and for this reason I included a section to familiarize ourselves with locking and blocking before we dive into the lock wait types.

Introduction to Locking and Blocking

As we just discussed, SQL Server uses locks to isolate different concurrent transactions from each other, so data is only accessed or modified by one transaction at a time. There are different lock types, or lock modes, SQL Server can use, and there are various object levels SQL Server can place locks on. To make it even more complex, different lock modes are not necessarily compatible with each other, and when two incompatible locks meet, a block occurs.

Lock Modes and Compatibility

To start off, let's get ourselves familiar with the different types of locks, or lock modes, inside SQL Server. The following list describes the most common lock modes. There are more lock modes inside SQL Server, but those only occur when you perform very specific actions. A complete list of the different lock modes can be found here `https://slrwnds.com/m664d1`.

SQL Server uses acronyms to indicate which lock mode is being used inside SQL Server. These acronyms are shown in parentheses:

- **Shared (S)** – A Shared lock will be placed on a resource when a query is reading data from that resource. For instance, a SELECT * FROM [table].

- **Update (U)** – The Update lock mode is used when a query wants to modify a resource. It was introduced to prevent "deadlocks," a situation where locks are waiting on each other to release in concurrent transactions which need to modify the same resource.

- **Exclusive (X)** – An Exclusive lock is placed when a transaction is modifying the resource. When an Exclusive lock is in place, no other transactions can modify the resource. For instance, INSERT, UPDATE, or DELETE T-SQL statements will result in Exclusive locks.

207

- **Schema (Sch)** – Schema locks are used when a table is being modified. An example of this would be adding a column to a table.

- **Intent (I)** – Intent locks are used to indicate locks placed at a lower level in the locking hierarchy. We will go into more detail on the lock hierarchy later.

When different locks need to interact with each other, SQL Server performs a lock compatibility check on the different lock modes involved. Not all of the lock modes are compatible with each other, which means when two different transactions are not able to access the resource at the same time because of incompatible locks, a block will occur. For instance, when a Shared lock is placed to read from a row, and another transaction wants to modify the row by placing an Exclusive lock, the Exclusive lock will have to wait until the Shared lock is removed. Table 8-1 shows the lock mode compatibility for the Shared, Update, and Exclusive lock modes.

Table 8-1. *Lock compatibility*

Lock mode	Shared	Update	Exclusive
Shared	Yes	Yes	No
Update	Yes	No	No
Exclusive	No	No	No

Let's go through an example to illustrate lock compatibility. Say you want to read from a row inside a table by executing a SELECT statement against the table. When you execute your query, SQL Server will check if there is an existing lock already in place on the row you want to access and if it is compatible with the lock you want to place on the row. Let's assume there isn't a lock in place when you run your query. In this case, a Shared lock will be placed on the row, indicating your query is reading data from that row. Right after you execute your query, another transaction is issued by another user who wants to modify data inside the row you are accessing. SQL Server will detect there is a Shared lock in place on the row, making the second transaction wait before placing its Exclusive lock, since Shared and Exclusive locks are incompatible. The user who ran the second transaction might experience a delay, since the transaction is waiting for the Shared lock to be removed before its Exclusive lock can be placed. If a third transaction is started which wants to read the same row as your transaction, no lock conflict will occur. Shared locks are compatible with other Shared locks, meaning the third transaction does not have to wait to place its lock, and it directly receives the results it asked for.

Figure 8-1 shows the example where the dotted line indicates an incompatible lock which has to wait.

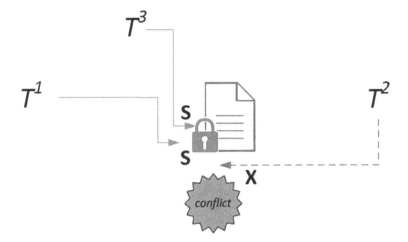

Figure 8-1. *Concurrent lock situation*

Locking Hierarchy

SQL Server uses multi-granular locking to allow different locks for different-level objects. It does this to minimize the overhead cost of locking. The lowest possible object where a lock can be placed is a row, and the largest is the database. There are many levels between those two granularity levels, and SQL Server automatically decides on what level the lock should be placed to minimize locking overhead. The following list shows the most common lock levels, ordered from the highest granularity to the smallest:

- Database
- Database file
- Table/object
- Extent
- Page
- RID (row inside a heap)/KEY (row inside a clustered index)

The Intent locks we discussed earlier play an important part in the placement of locks upon the different granularity levels. SQL Server will place Intent locks on objects on a higher granularity to indicate a lock has been placed at a lower level. This protects the lower level locks from changes on objects at a higher granularity level. All the Intent locks placed, from the highest granularity level to the actual lock on an object, when looked at together are called the locking hierarchy.

Figure 8-2 shows a graphical representation of a locking hierarchy for the modification of data inside a row, which will require an Exclusive lock on the row and Intent Exclusive locks higher in the hierarchy.

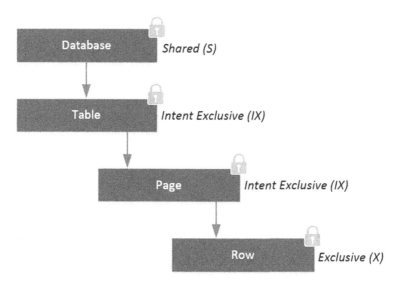

Figure 8-2. *Lock hierarchy example*

Note the Shared lock on the database level. Every request will always place one to protect changes to the database, while transactions are active. This makes sure that, for instance, you cannot delete a database, while transactions are still active. Also note the Intent locks will use the same lock mode on the lowest object, in this case Intent Exclusive (IX). If a Shared lock was placed, the lock mode of the Intent lock would change as well, in this case to Intent Shared (IS). We will go a little deeper into Intent locks a bit further on in this chapter.

Isolation Levels

We can exercise a certain level of control over what locks are placed by a transaction by changing the Isolation level. The Isolation level defines the degree to which transactions are isolated from each other during concurrent operations. We can change the Isolation level on either a connection or a transaction basis. Changing the Isolation level will only change the behavior of Shared locks; Exclusive locks needed for data modification are not affected. Changing the Isolation level will also introduce certain phenomena. These phenomena have an impact on the results of your read transaction and occur because of the changes to how Shared locks are placed and held during the transaction. The list that follows shows the various Isolation levels, from the lowest form of Isolation to the highest, available in SQL Server and the phenomena related to them:

- **Read Uncommitted**: This Isolation level will allow reads to occur while another transaction is performing modifications on the same object. It will not wait until the Exclusive lock on the object is released. This makes it possible to read uncommitted values called "dirty reads." Dirty reads can be bad (if you do not expect them) because they can return a value no longer in the database. For instance, if someone is updating a value to "B" while it was "A" at the start of the transaction, other users querying the same data at the same time can get the old value of "A" back instead of the updated "B" value.

- **Read Committed** – This is the default Isolation level in SQL Server. Using this Isolation level will make read transactions wait until concurrent write transactions are completed. A Shared lock will be placed on a row and will be released right after the row has been read. The phenomenon associated with this Isolation level is called "inconsistent analysis." This means it is possible to receive different results from the same read query if the data were modified by another transaction in the time between both read transactions.

- **Repeatable Read** – Setting the Isolation level to Repeatable Read will lock rows being read by a transaction. But instead of releasing the Shared lock on the row after it has been read, Repeatable Read will keep the lock in place until the entire transaction is completed.

A Repeatable Read makes it possible for "phantom reads" to occur. Phantom reads occur whenever data is added or changed by another transaction which has not yet been locked by the read transaction.

- **Serializable** – The Serializable Isolation level is the highest possible Isolation level you can use, and it will place the most locks to ensure the data you are reading is not modified during the time the transaction is running. It does this by locking the entire range of data (for instance, an entire table) you are selecting, making it impossible to make changes. Since the entire range of data you are selecting is being locked right at the start of the transaction, there are no phenomena possible.

SQL Server 2005 added another method for isolating transactions called Row Versioning. Row Versioning uses versions of data modification and returns them to read queries without causing blocking. When a transaction modifies data, the change will be recorded as a version. When a read transaction accesses the same data, it will receive the version of the change before the modification transaction is committed. More information about Row Versioning can be found on Books Online at `https://slrwnds.com/87n21i`.

Nerd Note   The READ UNCOMMITTED Isolation level is often achieved through the use of the NOLOCK query hint. Many developers have made the mistake of thinking their queries will run faster with the use of the magical NOLOCK hint. Not only is this myth wrong, but it is a bad practice for important queries which rely upon accurate data.

Because Isolation levels, and their locking behavior, can be complex to understand, I added Figure 8-3, which shows the way the various Isolation levels implement locking during a read operation. The boxes represent rows inside a table, and a row with a lock means a Shared lock is active on that row.

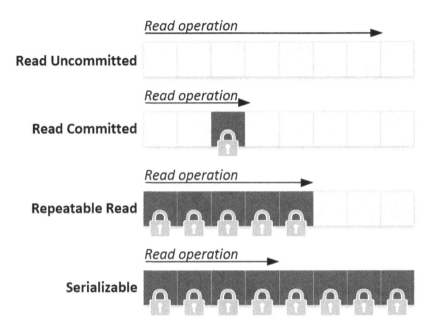

Figure 8-3. *Isolation levels and locking behavior*

There are various reasons why you would use a different Isolation level than the default of Read Committed. In many cases, these reasons are related to the amount of locking/blocking you expect with your workload or how "correct" the data returned by your transaction should be. For instance, with the default Isolation level of Read Committed, it is possible that data is modified by other transactions, while your transaction is running, which means that the results at the end of the transaction are not the same as they were at the start of your transaction. To make sure no data can change while your transaction is running, you could use the Serializable Isolation level, but this means more locks need to be placed and maintained, resulting in more blocking in concurrent SQL Server environments.

We change the default Isolation level of Read Committed by either configuring a different Isolation level in the connection string or by supplying a table hint (an exception is snapshot isolation, which is configured at the database level).

Nerd Note   The READ COMMITTED SNAPSHOT Isolation level (RCSI) is set at the database level, which means all transactions requesting READ COMMITTED will automatically use RCSI. This database level setting allows for the benefits of RCSI to be used without needing to make any changes to existing code.

For instance, the two queries that follow show two different methods of executing a query using the Read Uncommitted Isolation level. The first query sets the transaction Isolation level for the entire session:

```
SET TRANSACTION ISOLATION LEVEL READ UNCOMMITTED;
BEGIN TRANSACTION
SELECT *
FROM Person.Person
COMMIT TRANSACTION;
```

Another method is to use a table hint to set the Isolation level to Read Uncommitted:

```
SELECT *
FROM Person.Person
WITH (READUNCOMMITTED);
```

Both of these methods will achieve the same effect, but keep in mind setting the Isolation level for the session will result in using the selected Isolation level for all the queries that are being executed in this specific session after setting it.

Querying Lock Information

To take a look at currently placed locks, we can use the **sys.dm_tran_locks** DMV. This DMV will return a row for every active lock inside the SQL Server instance, along with information like the type of lock, the resource type, the session ID that placed the lock, and whether the lock is granted or is waiting to be placed. Figure 8-4 shows a (small) portion of the output of the DMV on my test SQL Server machine.

	resource_type	resource_subtype	resource_database_id	resource_description	resource_associated_entity_id	resource_lock_partition	request_mode	request_type	request_status
45	KEY		5	(36154064afaf)	72057594050052096	0	X	LOCK	GRANT
46	PAGE		5	1:20446	72057594045333504	0	IX	LOCK	GRANT
47	PAGE		5	1:20447	72057594045333504	0	IX	LOCK	GRANT
48	PAGE		5	1:20432	72057594045333504	0	IX	LOCK	GRANT
49	PAGE		5	1:20432	72057594045333504	0	S	LOCK	WAIT
50	KEY		5	(bdeab116bd74)	72057594050052096	0	X	LOCK	GRANT
51	KEY		5	(16336afdf6ae)	72057594050052096	0	X	LOCK	GRANT
52	KEY		5	(8194443284a0)	72057594045333504	0	X	LOCK	GRANT
53	KEY		5	(d8b6f3f4a521)	72057594045333504	0	X	LOCK	GRANT
54	KEY		5	(b9b173bbe8d5)	72057594045333504	0	X	LOCK	GRANT

Figure 8-4. *sys.dm_tran_locks output*

If we look at Figure 8-4, we see a number of Exclusive locks (X) granted and placed at the Key lock level. This means a transaction is currently modifying data inside a clustered index. There is also an Intent Exclusive lock on the Page level, which is above the Key lock level, indicating there is an Exclusive lock lower down in the hierarchy. Also note a Shared lock is currently waiting to get placed on the same data page (1:20432). The lock cannot be granted just yet, as there is an incompatible Intent Exclusive lock in place.

Since the Shared lock has to wait before it can be placed on the data page, we can view the time it has been waiting by looking at the wait statistics. Figure 8-5 shows a part of the results of a query against the sys.dm_os_waiting_tasks DMV.

	waiting_task_address	session_id	exec_context_id	wait_duration_ms	wait_type	resource_address	blocking_task_address
7	0x0000008261B5D088	17	0	110116	SP_SERVER_DIAGNOSTICS_SLEEP	0x0000000000000001	NULL
8	0x0000008261B5DC28	26	0	55911991	HADR_NOTIFICATION_DEQUEUE	0x000000810155F150	NULL
9	0x000000825DD004E8	23	0	1335703	BROKER_EVENTHANDLER	NULL	NULL
10	0x000000825DD01468	9	0	55911597	BROKER_TRANSMITTER	NULL	NULL
11	0x000000825DD01848	27	0	570	SLEEP_TASK	NULL	NULL
12	0x0000008261B5CCA8	55	0	147659	LCK_M_S	0x0000008252962940	NULL
13	0x0000008266027088	12	0	3115	XE_TIMER_EVENT	NULL	NULL
14	0x0000008266027848	1	0	55912386	WAIT_XTP_HOST_WAIT	NULL	NULL
15	0x0000008266027C28	20	0	48706900	ONDEMAND_TASK_QUEUE	0x000000832FC9EB50	NULL

Figure 8-5. *Lock information inside sys.dm_os_waiting_tasks*

By using the sys.dm_os_waiting_tasks DMV, we see session ID 55 is currently waiting on a resource named LCK_M_S. This represents a Shared lock resource type. Session ID 55 is currently blocked by session ID 53, which happens to be the same session with the Exclusive and Intent Exclusive locks placed on the objects session ID 55 is trying to query. The sys.dm_os_waiting_tasks DMV will also return information we can use as input for the sys.dm_tran_locks DMV. This information will be available in the resource_ description column of the sys.dm_os_waiting_tasks DMV, as shown in Figure 8-6.

blocking_session_id	blocking_exec_context_id	resource_description
NULL	NULL	NULL
NULL	NULL	NULL
NULL	NULL	NULL
NULL	NULL	NULL
NULL	NULL	NULL
53	NULL	pagelock fileid=1 pageid=20432 dbid=5 subresource=FULL id=lock8258467e00 mode=IX associatedObjectId=72057594045333504

Figure 8-6. *resource_description column of the sys.dm_os_waiting_tasks DMV during a block*

If we copy the associatedObjectID and use it as input in the WHERE clause against the sys.dm_tran_locks DMV, we receive more information about why, and on what, this task is waiting. The following query will retrieve all the rows inside the sys.dm_tran_locks DMV with a resource_associated_entity_id of 72057594045333504:

```
SELECT *
FROM sys.dm_tran_locks
WHERE resource_associated_entity_id = ' 72057594045333504';
```

On my test SQL Server, the query returned 32 locks, 26 of which are Exclusive locks on rows inside a clustered index; there are also a number of Intent Exclusive locks on data pages and one Shared lock that is waiting to be placed on a page. The waiting Shared lock is the one returned by the sys.dm_os_waiting_tasks DMV. A portion of the results is displayed in Figure 8-7.

	resource_type	resource_subtype	resource_database_id	resource_description	resource_associated_entity_id	resource_lock_partition	request_mode	request_type	request_status
1	KEY		5	(e222ff2f116e)	72057594045333504	0	X	LOCK	GRANT
2	KEY		5	(0932b31cce2f)	72057594045333504	0	X	LOCK	GRANT
3	KEY		5	(8bc081279a03)	72057594045333504	0	X	LOCK	GRANT
4	KEY		5	(98ec012aa510)	72057594045333504	0	X	LOCK	GRANT
5	KEY		5	(a0c936a3c965)	72057594045333504	0	X	LOCK	GRANT
6	KEY		5	(e8a66f387cfa)	72057594045333504	0	X	LOCK	GRANT
7	KEY		5	(d08358b1108f)	72057594045333504	0	X	LOCK	GRANT

Figure 8-7.   *Lock information from sys.dm_tran_locks*

Finding lock information and figuring out who is blocking whom by querying the sys.dm_tran_locks DMV can be a challenge on systems where you have many locks and blocks occurring, since the DMV will return a row for every lock placed. An easy way to get these details is to enable and use the blocked process report (https://slrwnds.com/emsjqo). To do this, you must first enable the blocked process threshold in the configuration options for SQL Server. You do this with the following code:

```
sp_configure 'show advanced options', 1 ;
RECONFIGURE
GO
sp_configure 'blocked process threshold', 20 ;
RECONFIGURE
GO
```

The threshold is set to seconds, and the minimum you can report on are blocked sessions for five seconds. Once you have configured the instance, you then capture details using SQL Trace; the easiest way to do this is with SQL Profiler. You will find the blocked process report inside the "Errors and Warnings" event:

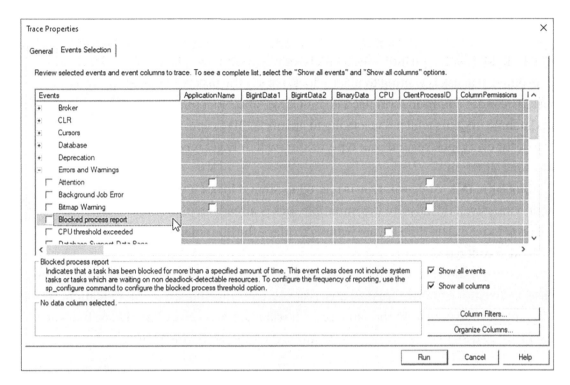

Figure 8-8. *Blocked process report*

The trace will return details in XML format, including details for blocked process and blocking process.

Another simple way to discover blocking is to query the sys.dm_os_waiting_tasks DMV and examine the blocking_session_id column.

Now that we have discussed many aspects of locking and blocking, from lock modes and hierarchies to analyzing locks and blocks, we should be ready to take a look at the lock-related wait types inside SQL Server. Keep in mind that this introduction to locking and blocking is far from a complete guide to the topic, as going into more detail on how locking and concurrency works inside SQL Server would fill a book by itself.

LCK_M_S

The first lock-related wait type is the **LCK_M_S** wait type. This wait type represents a task waiting to place a Shared lock on a resource. For example, if the resource currently has an Exclusive lock, the Shared lock task will wait.

What Is the LCK_M_S Wait Type?

The LCK_M_S wait type indicates a task is, or was, waiting to place a Shared lock on a resource. If a task is waiting to place a lock, we say the task is "blocked" by another task. The more common term used is "blocking," and blocking is a natural occurrence in database systems which use locking to ensure ACID properties are maintained. This is true for every lock-related wait type, as they will only get recorded when there is a blocking situation.

Since the LCK_M_S wait type is related to Shared locks, it will occur when a read action must wait because an incompatible lock is already in place on the resource we want to read. The time we are waiting to place the Shared lock is recorded as the LCK_M_S wait type.

Figure 8-9 shows a common situation resulting in LCK_M_S waits occurring. In this case, an Exclusive lock was placed on a page by T1, indicating a data modification. When T2 wants to read data from the same page, it will need to place a Shared lock, but since Exclusive and Shared locks are incompatible, the LCK_M_S wait occurs.

Figure 8-9. *LCK_M_S wait occurring*

LCK_M_S Example

Creating an example of a LCK_M_S wait occurring is not difficult; we will create a block situation between a data modification query and a data read query.

For this example, we will run the query in Listing 8-1 against the GalacticWorks database. This query will begin a transaction and modify a few rows but will not commit or rollback the transaction. Since we explicitly indicated this transaction by supplying a BEGIN TRAN, SQL Server will keep the locks in place until we explicitly execute a COMMIT or ROLLBACK command.

Listing 8-1. Start a modification transaction

```
BEGIN TRAN
UPDATE Sales.SalesOrderDetail
SET CarrierTrackingNumber = '4E0A-4F89-AD'
WHERE SalesOrderID = '43661';
```

When we execute the query, we receive a result very quickly; in my case, 15 rows were updated. But like I said before, the transaction is not yet finished (committed), so it will remain open, leaving locks on the objects it modified.

So far we aren't causing any blocking, since this is the test SQL Server and no other queries are running. Let's change that and create a blocking situation.

For this, we will open a second window in SQL Server Management Studio (SSMS) and execute the query seen in Listing 8-2. This will perform a SELECT against the Sales. SalesOrderDetail table, the same table in which we are currently modifying data.

Listing 8-2. Select data from a table where a modification is being performed

```
SELECT *
FROM GalacticWorks.Sales.SalesOrderDetail;
```

As soon as we run this SELECT query, we notice no results are returned and the query will keep executing. This is a typical example of a blocking operation where a transaction is modifying data we want to read inside another transaction.

If we query the sys.dm_os_waiting_tasks DMV, we will see the LCK_M_S wait type, as shown in Figure 8-10.

	waiting_task_address	session_id	exec_context_id	wait_duration_ms	wait_type	resource_address	blocking_task_address	blocking_session_id
1	0x0000020E94516CA8	63	0	13724	LCK_M_S	0x0000020E983A2B40	NULL	73

Figure 8-10. *LCK_M_S wait occurring*

The only way the LCK_M_S wait is resolved is when the incompatible lock is removed. In this case, we will roll back the modification transaction started in the first SSMS window. We do this by running the ROLLBACK command in the same session window. Immediately after performing the transaction rollback, we receive the results the SELECT query asked for. Querying the sys.dm_os_waiting_tasks also showed the LCK_M_S wait was resolved.

Lowering LCK_M_S Waits

Seeing LCK_M_S waits occur does not necessarily mean something is wrong. It does, however, indicate blocking is occurring. If you notice high wait times on the LCK_M_S wait type, it means a read transaction is running long to complete because it must wait to place the Shared lock. So the first step is to identify the query causing the block. We do this by using the sys.dm_os_waiting_tasks DMV and looking at the blocking_session_id column. This is relatively quick to do when there is a single block active but is complex when many concurrent queries are blocked by other transactions. In complex cases, we must follow the blocking chain until we find the head (also called the root or lead) blocker (which is the first lock on an object).

After we isolate the query causing the blocking, we will analyze the query to see if it is a candidate for optimization. Maybe the query is requesting more locks than it needs and thus requires a long time to complete. One way to optimize the query would be to look at whether any indexes should be added, resulting in fewer rows required to be locked. Or maybe you could cut the single transaction into multiple transactions, each accessing fewer objects. Another possible issue causing more locking than necessary is out-of-date statistics. Statistics are used as input for a query plan, and if they do not accurately reflect the contents of the table or index, they can lead to a bad query plan, which in turn can lead to more locks than necessary.

Another option would be to change the Isolation level of the read transactions, so no Shared locks are needed in order to read the data. For instance, setting the Isolation level to Read Uncommitted will not place Shared locks, and the read transaction will not be blocked. This does introduce another problem related to the Isolation level, dirty reads, which we discussed in the "Locking and Blocking Introduction" section of this chapter. Next to using Read Uncommitted, you could also use snapshot isolation, which will result in fewer Shared locks but will not cause dirty reads. Snapshot isolation does put more load on the TempDB database, since it must maintain versions of data if many concurrent transactions are modifying that data.

LCK_M_S Summary

The LCK_M_S wait type occurs when an incompatible lock exists on a resource and another transaction wants to place a Shared lock on the same resource. Seeing the LCK_M_S wait type means transactions are being blocked. You should try to identify which queries are causing the block to occur and see if these can be optimized to result in fewer locks or locks that have a shorter duration. As a final resort, you could choose to change the Isolation level of your read transactions, though this does introduce other side effects, like dirty reads or increased load inside TempDB.

LCK_M_U

LCK_M_U wait types are related to locks using the Update (U) mode. When a task wants to place an Update lock on a resource but an incompatible lock is already in place, LCK_M_U waits occur.

What Is the LCK_M_U Wait Type?

The Update lock type is a special type of lock mode indicating a data modification is about to occur. Even though its name might suggest it is only related to UPDATE queries, Update locks also appear when performing INSERT or DELETE statements.

Update locks primarily exist to minimize deadlocks from occurring. Deadlocks indicate two transactions needing to modify the same resource are waiting indefinitely on each other to acquire an Exclusive lock on the resource. To understand how a deadlock situation occurs, and how Update locks help prevent deadlocks, let's review the following scenario when no Update locks are used.

When two concurrent transactions want to perform a modification on the same resource, both transactions would first place a Shared lock on the resource, while the data they intended to modify was located. Since Shared locks are compatible with other Shared locks, the transactions would not block each other. When one of the two transactions found the data it needed to modify, it would convert its Shared lock to an Exclusive lock, and now we have a problem. Since Shared locks are incompatible with Exclusive locks, and since the other transaction would also have a Shared lock on the resource, the conversion from Shared lock to Exclusive lock could not occur. The transaction would need to wait until the Shared lock of the other transaction was removed before it could convert its own Shared lock to an Exclusive lock, but since the other transaction also wants to convert its Shared lock to an Exclusive lock, both transactions would end up waiting on each other, and a deadlock would occur. SQL Server will automatically detect deadlock situations and choose one of the deadlocked transactions as a victim and perform a rollback of that transaction, ending the deadlock situation. Figure 8-11 shows a graphical representation of that situation.

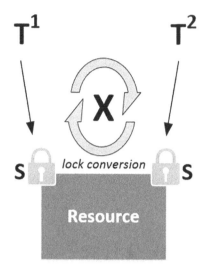

Figure 8-11. *Deadlock during lock conversion*

When Update locks are used inside SQL Server, deadlock situations are minimized. Update locks are compatible with Shared locks, but not with Exclusive or other Update locks. In the preceding scenario, the first transaction would not directly convert to an Exclusive lock but rather would convert to an Update lock first. Since Update and Shared locks are compatible, there would be no problem converting to an Update lock, even though there was a Shared lock in place from the other transaction. The Update lock would then get converted to an Exclusive lock so the data modification could occur. Figure 8-12 shows this lock behavior.

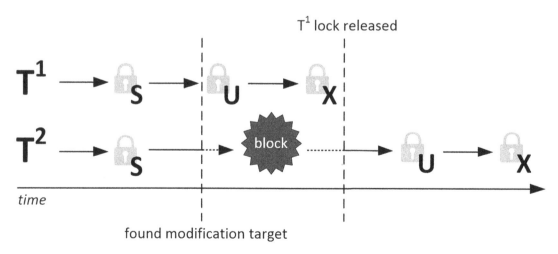

Figure 8-12. *Update locks during concurrent data modifications*

When a transaction wants to place an Update lock but there is an incompatible lock already in place on the object, for instance, an Exclusive lock, the LCK_M_U wait type will be recorded.

LCK_M_U Example

To show an example of LCK_M_U waits occurring, we will create a situation where concurrent transactions want to modify the same resource. For this we will make use of the Ostress utility to execute an identical query using multiple connections. The query is in Listing 8-3. This will perform an UPDATE against the Person.Address table inside the GalacticWorks database. I saved the query inside a .sql file named LCK_M_U.sql.

Listing 8-3. Modify the Person.Address table

```
UPDATE Person.Address
SET City = 'Los Angeles'
WHERE StateProvinceID = 9;
```

After saving the file, I run the Ostress utility using the following command:

```
"C:\Program Files\Microsoft Corporation\RMLUtils\ostress.exe" -S.\SQL2022
-E -dGalacticWorks -i"C:\TeamData\lck_m_u.sql" -n150 -r5 -q
```

This will create 150 concurrent connections, each one executing the query in Listing 8-3 5 times. This should be enough to create some blocking.

While the Ostress utility is running, I query the sys.dm_os_waiting_tasks DMV to find out what tasks are waiting. A small portion of the results are shown in Figure 8-13.

	waiting_task_address	session_id	exec_context_id	wait_duration_ms	wait_type	resource_address	blocking_task_address	blocking_session_id
1	0x0000020E9AAFC8C8	75	0	704	LCK_M_U	0x0000020E9A98D700	0x0000020E9C10A108	169
2	0x0000020E9AAFD468	59	0	683	LCK_M_U	0x0000020E96329C40	0x0000020E9C10A108	169
3	0x0000020E9AA408C8	207	0	657	LCK_M_U	0x0000020E98CDADC0	0x0000020E9C10A108	169
4	0x0000020E9AAFCCA8	91	0	99	LCK_M_U	0x0000020E8C142F80	0x0000020E9C10A108	169
5	0x00000211560DA108	140	0	1519	LCK_M_U	0x0000020E9820A140	0x0000020E9C10A108	169
6	0x0000020E95280CA8	142	0	1434	LCK_M_U	0x0000020E9BB93D80	0x0000020E9C10A108	169
7	0x0000020E94255468	163	0	1327	LCK_M_U	0x0000020E94162BC0	0x0000020E9C10A108	169
8	0x0000020E95246CA8	192	0	1301	LCK_M_U	0x0000020E9BD71F40	0x0000020E9C10A108	169
9	0x0000020E9C1764E8	194	0	1253	LCK_M_U	0x0000020E9C4A8DC0	0x0000020E9C10A108	169
10	0x0000020E930C8CA8	170	0	1231	LCK_M_U	0x0000020E9C4F7380	0x0000020E9C10A108	169

Figure 8-13. *LCK_M_U waits occurring*

As you can see in Figure 8-13, many different sessions are waiting to acquire an Update lock but are blocked by session ID 169. If we query the sys.dm_tran_locks DMV for lock information about this session, we can see it is granted an incompatible Intent Exclusive lock, as shown in Figure 8-14.

	request_mode	request_type	request_status	request_reference_count	request_lifetime	request_session_id
1	IX	LOCK	GRANT	1	33554432	169
2	S	LOCK	GRANT	1	0	169
3	IU	LOCK	GRANT	1	0	169
4	U	LOCK	WAIT	1	0	169

Figure 8-14. *Session ID 169 holding an Intent Exclusive lock*

All the other sessions will have to wait until the Intent Exclusive lock of session ID 161 is removed. Then one of those sessions will acquire the Update lock it is requesting, convert it into an Exclusive lock, and perform its modification. That cycle will repeat until all the sessions are done with their modifications.

Lowering LCK_M_U Waits

Lowering LCK_M_U waits uses the same approach as lowering LCK_M_S wait types: try to identify the transaction causing the blocking to occur and optimize its locking behavior.

Changing the Isolation level will have little effect on LCK_M_U wait times since other Isolation levels have the most impact on transactions that perform reads. This makes optimizing your queries and/or indexes the way to go if you need to lower higher-than-normal wait times on the LCK_M_U wait type.

LCK_M_U Summary

The LCK_M_U wait type is related to locks using the Update lock mode. Update locks are used to prevent deadlocks from occurring when concurrent transactions try to convert their Shared locks to Exclusive locks. Lowering LCK_M_U wait times is primarily achieved by optimizing potential blocking queries or indexes.

LCK_M_X

Another common lock-related wait type is the **LCK_M_X** wait type. Just like both lock-related wait types already discussed, the LCK_M_X wait type is related to a specific lock type, in this case the Exclusive lock. And just like the other lock-related wait types, seeing this wait type means there is some form of blocking occurring.

What Is the LCK_M_X Wait Type?

The LCK_M_X wait type occurs when a task is waiting to place an Exclusive lock on a resource. Since Exclusive locks are not compatible with just about every other lock mode, including other Exclusive locks, seeing blocking occur when there are many concurrent modifications is pretty common. This means seeing LCK_M_X waits is pretty common, especially in systems with a high amount of concurrent transactions.

LCK_M_X Example

To demonstrate LCK_M_X waits, we will execute a SELECT statement without committing it. Before we run the SELECT, we will set the Isolation level to Repeatable Read. Doing so makes sure the Shared locks are not removed while the transaction is still running. Since we do not commit the transaction, the locks will remain on the objects until we either kill the transaction or perform a COMMIT or ROLLBACK. The query in Listing 8-4 shows the SELECT statement we will execute against the GalacticWorks database:

Listing 8-4. Begin transaction on the HumanResources.Employee table

```
SET TRANSACTION ISOLATION LEVEL REPEATABLE READ
BEGIN TRANSACTION
SELECT *
FROM HumanResources.Employee;
-- COMMIT
```

Notice we commented out the COMMIT section to make sure the locks remain in place. Executing the query returns results quickly; after just 1 second, I got all the rows of the HumanResources.Employee returned. If we query the sys.dm_tran_locks DMV, we should see that all the Shared locks are still in place, as shown in Figure 8-15.

	resource_type	resource_subtype	resource_database_id	resource_description	resource_associated_entity_id	resource_lock_partition	request_mode	request_type
12	KEY		5	(2c018b24d2a1)	72057594039173120	0	S	LOCK
13	KEY		5	(ad3225e45be9)	72057594039173120	0	S	LOCK
14	KEY		5	(e68f1a16c0ff)	72057594039173120	0	S	LOCK
15	KEY		5	(2e66d7a5c130)	72057594039173120	0	S	LOCK
16	KEY		5	(af5579654878)	72057594039173120	0	S	LOCK
17	KEY		5	(27e646084986)	72057594039173120	0	S	LOCK
18	KEY		5	(ef0f8bbb4849)	72057594039173120	0	S	LOCK
19	KEY		5	(6e3c257bc101)	72057594039173120	0	S	LOCK
20	KEY		5	(ed68d73a5bd3)	72057594039173120	0	S	LOCK

Figure 8-15. *Shared locks still in place*

While the locks are still in place, we run another query inside a new window in SSMS. The query in Listing 8-5 will perform an UPDATE on a single row inside the same HumanResources.Employee table:

Listing 8-5. Updating the HumanResources.Employee table

```
UPDATE HumanResources.Employee
SET JobTitle = 'Tester'
WHERE BusinessEntityID = 5;
```

As soon as we execute the preceding query, we'll notice a block occurring since the query keeps running without returning any results. This is as expected since there is a Shared lock in place on the row, or specifically the index key, preventing us from updating it.

When we look at the sys.dm_os_waiting_tasks DMV, shown in Figure 8-16, we will notice the query in the second window is waiting to place an Exclusive lock, indicated by the LCK_M_X wait type.

	waiting_task_address	session_id	exec_context_id	wait_duration_ms	wait_type	resource_address	blocking_task_address	blocking_session_id
1	0x0000020E9AAFC8C8	63	0	34791	LCK_M_X	0x0000020E9C4EA6C0	NULL	73

Figure 8-16. *LCK_M_X waits occurring*

If we end the SELECT query, by either executing the COMMIT statement or by closing the windows inside SSMS, the Shared locks are removed and the second query will be able to execute its UPDATE command, ending the LCK_M_X wait.

Lowering LCK_M_X Waits

To lower LCK_M_X wait times, use the same approach as for lowering other lock-related wait types. Identify queries causing the blocking and see if you can optimize them so they cause less blocking.

LCK_M_X Summary

The LCK_M_X wait type is related to Exclusive locks being blocked by other locks already in place on the same resource. Since Exclusive locks are incompatible with just about every other lock type, seeing LCK_M_X waits occurring is not uncommon for SQL Server instances that experience concurrent query execution.

LCK_M_I[xx]

Seeing the **LCK_M_I[xx]** wait type means a task is blocked when placing an Intent lock. Since we already discussed the various lock modes on objects, I replaced the lock mode used for the Intent lock as [xx] when discussing this wait type. The [xx] can be replaced by a variety of different lock modes; for instance, a block on an Intent Shared lock would be represented by the LCK_M_IS wait type, while a block on an Intent Exclusive lock would be shown as LCK_M_IX.

What Is the LCK_M_I[xx] Wait Type?

LCK_M_I[xx] wait types indicate a task is waiting to place an Intent lock on a resource. As we learned from the "Introduction to Locking and Blocking" section at the start of this chapter, Intent locks indicate a lock of the same type is placed on an object lower down in the locking hierarchy. This doesn't mean Intent locks are only there to warn SQL Server there is a lock further down the hierarchy. Intent locks behave just like any other lock, and it is entirely possible one Intent lock can block another, incompatible, Intent lock. Intent locks do have more flexibility regarding other incompatible Intent locks. For instance, it is possible for two Intent Exclusive locks to exist on the same page resource, indicating a row will be modified. It is also possible to have an Intent Shared lock on a page resource together with an Intent Exclusive, because both of the locks can read and/ or modify different rows.

Next to indicating the type of lock which exists lower down in the locking hierarchy, Intent locks have a few "special" modes the other lock modes do not have. It is possible for Intent locks to represent more than one lock mode on lower levels of the locking hierarchy. The list that follows describes these three Intent lock modes:

- **Shared with Intent Exclusive (SIX)** – This lock mode represents there are Shared locks on all objects at a lower level and Intent Exclusive locks on some of these objects. These locks are acquired by one transaction which wants to read data and plans to modify other data at the same time. When a task is blocked while trying to place the SIX lock, it will be recorded by the LCK_M_SIX wait type.

- **Shared Intent Update (SIU)** – This lock mode is a combination of Shared and Intent Update locks. Again, it is possible for a single transaction to acquire, and hold, both these lock modes at the same time at a lower level. If a block occurs while trying to place this lock, the LCK_M_SIU wait type will be used to record the wait time.

- **Update Intent Exclusive (UIX)** – This lock mode is another combination of two other lock modes, Update and Intent Exclusive. Blocks on this lock mode will be represented by the LCK_M_UIX wait type.

Seeing high wait times on Intent locks is not very common, since Intent locks are more flexible regarding their incompatibility with each other. There is generally less blocking on the Intent level than there is further down the locking hierarchy.

LCK_M_I[xx] Example

In this example we will generate a wait of the LCK_M_IX wait type. This means a transaction is waiting to acquire an Intent Exclusive lock on a higher level in the locking hierarchy.

We will use a similar example as we did for the LCK_M_X wait type by running a SELECT statement using the REPEATABLE READ Isolation level and not completing the transaction. The query that follows is the query I will be running against the GalacticWorks database, Person.Address table:

```
SET TRANSACTION ISOLATION LEVEL REPEATABLE READ
```

```
BEGIN TRAN
SELECT * FROM Person.Address;
--COMMIT
```

The COMMIT command has been commented out to leave the transaction open.

If we look at the sys.dm_tran_locks DMV, shown by Figure 8-17, we see while the query is running there is only one lock currently active, a Shared lock on the OBJECT resource type. This indicates the entire table is locked. Since this lock exists on this high level, there is no need for other Shared locks further down the hierarchy.

	resource_type	resource_subtype	resource_database_id	resource_description	resource_associated_entity_id	resource_lock_partition	request_mode	request_type	request_status
1	OBJECT		5		757577737	0	S	LOCK	GRANT
2	DATABASE		5		0	0	S	LOCK	GRANT
3	DATABASE		5		0	0	S	LOCK	GRANT

Figure 8-17. *Shared lock on a table*

If another transaction wants to update a row inside the same table, it would first try to acquire an Intent Exclusive lock on the table and page level before it could acquire an Exclusive lock on the row level. The next query is such a transaction, and in this case we will try to update a single row:

```
UPDATE Person.Address
SET AddressLine1 = '1227 Shoe St.'
WHERE AddressID = 5;
```

You'll notice the preceding query "hangs" as long as the SELECT query still has its Shared lock on the table. Even though Intent locks are in most cases compatible with other Intent locks on the same object, having, in this case, a Shared lock on the table level while trying to perform a data modification lower in the hierarchy will cause a block to occur. Shared locks and Intent Exclusive locks are not compatible.

If we look at the sys.dm_os_waiting_tasks DMV, we will see the task to place the Intent Exclusive lock is waiting, as shown in Figure 8-18.

	waiting_task_address	session_id	exec_context_id	wait_duration_ms	wait_type	resource_address	blocking_task_address	blocking_session_id
1	0x0000020E9AA92CA8	63	0	24123	LCK_M_IX	0x0000020E967A8480	NULL	73

Figure 8-18. *LCK_M_IX waits occurring*

Lowering LCK_M_I[xx] Waits

Just like with the other lock-related wait types discussed earlier, focus on queries causing the blocking when trying to lower LCK_M_I[xx] wait times. Because LCK_M_I[xx] waits only occur when incompatible locks are held on objects higher in the locking hierarchy, it is worth the time to investigate why those locks are placed so high in the hierarchy. **Lock escalation** can cause this to happen. Lock escalation occurs when it is more efficient for SQL Server to place a single lock higher in the locking hierarchy instead of locking many objects lower down. For instance, instead of placing thousands of Shared locks on rows, SQL Server can decide to place a single Shared lock on the table level. This requires far less resources to place and maintain than thousands of single locks. As a matter of fact, this is exactly what is occurring in the example I have shown you of the LCK_M_IX wait type. The Person.Address table we are querying with the SELECT query has more than 19,000 rows inside it. When we ran our SELECT * query against the table, it would mean that at least 19,000 row locks would be needed. Because placing and holding that many locks would take a great deal of resources, SQL Server decided to place a single Shared lock on the table instead of 19,000 locks on the rows.

If we rewrite the query so it requires fewer locks, for instance, by only selecting the first x rows instead of everything, SQL Server would probably choose to lock the rows again, instead of the entire table.

LCK_M_I[xx] Summary

The LCK_M_I[xx] wait type is related to Intent locks or, rather, cases when another incompatible lock is blocking the placement of an Intent lock. Intent locks are placed on higher-level objects to indicate a lock was placed on a lower level in the locking hierarchy. Unlike the lock modes we discussed earlier that only represent one type of lock, Intent locks can represent different lock modes lower down in the locking hierarchy. One common cause of high wait times on LCK_M_I[xx] wait types is cases when SQL Server escalates lower-level locks to a higher-level lock. In this situation Intent locks will be blocked and cannot be acquired.

LCK_M_SCH_S and LCK_M_SCH_M

The last two lock-related wait types in this chapter are the LCK_M_SCH_S and LCK_M_SCH_M wait types. Both of these wait types are related to locks placed on tables, the so-called Schema locks. We didn't give a lot of attention to Schema locks earlier in this chapter, but since they have a big impact on wait times when they occur, I wanted to include them.

What Are the LCK_M_SCH_S and LCK_M_SCH_M Wait Types?

The LCK_M_SCH_S and LCK_M_SCH_M wait types are both related to Schema locks. Schema locks are placed at the table object level to protect the table from modifications while queries access the table or to prevent queries from accessing the table while it is being modified. There are two different types of Schema lock, Schema Stability (Sch-S) and Schema Modification (Sch-M). Each of them has a different wait type associated with them. The LCK_M_SCH_S wait type (to indicate read access to the table) is recorded when a Schema Stability lock has to wait before it can get placed, and the LCK_M_SCH_M wait type (to indicate the table schema will be changed) is recorded when a Schema Modification lock is waiting to get placed.

Both Schema locks have extreme compatibility with other lock types. The Schema Stability lock is compatible with all other types of locks except for the Schema Modification lock. The Schema Modification lock, on the other hand, is incompatible with every other lock type, including Intent locks.

When using Schema Stability locks, it is impossible to modify or change the table in any way while queries are currently reading or writing from or to the table. Because Schema Stability locks are compatible with every lock mode (except for Schema Modification), it is completely normal to see a Schema Stability lock on the table level together with, for example, an Intent Exclusive lock to indicate data modification is occurring on a lower level inside the table.

Schema Modification locks are the opposite from Schema Stability locks, as they prevent any queries from accessing a table while a modification to the table is being performed.

LCK_M_SCH_S and LCK_M_SCH_M Example

For the first example, I will add a new column to an existing table, and just as we did in the examples earlier in this chapter, I will keep the transaction open by not supplying a COMMIT or ROLLBACK command. The following query adds an extra column to the Person.Address table in the GalacticWorks database, and I left the ROLLBACK command commented so the locks stay in place:

```
BEGIN TRAN
ALTER TABLE Person.Address
  ADD
  Test VARCHAR(10);
--ROLLBACK
```

In a new window in SSMS, I will execute a SELECT query against the Person.Address table, like the one here:

```
SELECT *
FROM Person.Address;
```

If we look at the sys.dm_tran_locks DMV while both queries are running, we should see if there is any blocking going on. Figure 8-19 shows a part of the output of a SELECT * query against the sys.dm_tran_locks DMV.

	resource_type	resource_subtype	resource_database_id	resource_description	resource_associated_entity_id	resource_lock_partition	request_mode	request_type	request_status
1	OBJECT		5		757577737	0	Sch-M	LOCK	GRANT
2	OBJECT		5		757577737	0	Sch-S	LOCK	WAIT

Figure 8-19. *Sch-M and Sch-S locks*

As you can see from Figure 8-19, the first query we started, with the goal of adding a column to the Person.Address table, resulted in a Sch-M lock on the table. The second SELECT query is waiting to receive a Sch-S lock on the same table.

If we query the sys.dm_os_waiting_tasks DMV, we see a task waiting on the LCK_M_SCH_S wait type. Figure 8-20 shows the output of sys.dm_os_waiting_tasks, while both queries are running.

	waiting_task_address	session_id	exec_context_id	wait_duration_ms	wait_type	resource_address	blocking_task_address	blocking_session_id
1	0x0000020E928A24E8	63	0	160433	LCK_M_SCH_S	0x0000020E967A8280	NULL	73

Figure 8-20. *LCK_M_SCH_S wait occurring*

Just as we expected, the SELECT query is waiting to acquire its Schema Stability lock.

If we were to reverse the example by starting a read transaction and leaving it open and then try to modify the same table, we should run into a LCK_M_SCH_M wait, since we can only acquire a Schema Modification lock when there are no active transactions inside the table we want to modify.

To show this situation, I executed the following query. This starts a SELECT query with the Repeatable Read Isolation level, but I leave the transaction open so the locks stay in place:

```
SET TRANSACTION ISOLATION LEVEL REPEATABLE READ
BEGIN TRANSACTION
SELECT * FROM
Person.Address;
-- COMMIT
```

In a new window inside SSMS, I will execute the table modification query used earlier to demonstrate the LCK_M_SCH_S wait type, but without leaving the transaction open:

```
ALTER TABLE Person.Address
  ADD
  Test VARCHAR(10);
```

As you will probably notice when executing the second query, nothing is returned and the query keeps running, a clear indication of a block occurring.

Let's look at the sys.dm_tran_locks DMV again to see what we can find out. Figure 8-21 shows the output on my test SQL Server.

	resource_type	resource_subtype	resource_database_id	resource_description	resource_associated_entity_id	resource_lock_partition	request_mode	request_type	request_status
1	OBJECT		5		757577737	0	S	LOCK	GRANT
2	OBJECT		5		757577737	0	Sch-M	LOCK	WAIT

Figure 8-21. *Sch-M lock waiting to be acquired*

In this case, the table has a Shared lock on it from the SELECT query. Because we are selecting information from a large table, SQL Server decided to place a table lock instead of placing locks on a lower level. Because a Schema Modification lock is incompatible with every other lock type, a block occurs, and we will wait until the Shared lock is gone before we can perform our table modification.

Looking at the sys.dm_os_waiting_tasks DMV shows us the results we are expecting, a LCK_M_SCH_M wait, as shown in Figure 8-22.

	waiting_task_address	session_id	exec_context_id	wait_duration_ms	wait_type	resource_address	blocking_task_address	blocking_session_id
1	0x0000020E9CF3C8C8	63	0	157465	LCK_M_SCH_M	0x0000020E99E8A440	NULL	73

Figure 8-22. *LCK_M_SCH_M waits occurring*

Lowering LCK_M_SCH_S and LCK_M_SCH_M Waits

When you see waits occurring for either the LCK_M_SCH_S or LCK_M_SCH_M wait type, there is probably a transaction actively wanting to modify the table. In the case of high wait times on the LCK_M_SCH_S wait type, the table modification transaction is already running; when seeing LCK_M_SCH_M waits, the modification is waiting for all active transactions to remove their locks on the table.

Modifying a table is not something that happens every day on production SQL Server instances (hopefully). Changing large tables is especially problematic and a cause for high LCK_M_SCH_S wait times, and users trying to query the table being modified will notice delays. If, however, you absolutely need to modify a table, but there are long-running queries retrieving information from the table, you should expect LCK_M_SCH_M waits.

Lowering the wait times of both wait types is directly related to performing modifications to tables. A suggestion would be to perform the table modification during a defined maintenance window, or when there are as few as possible concurrent transactions accessing the table, instead of doing the modification when there are many transactions active against the table.

LCK_M_SCH_S and LCK_M_SCH_M Summary

The LCK_M_SCH_S and LCK_M_SCH_M wait types are the result of Schema Stability or Schema Modification locks blocked by other locks. Seeing high wait times of either wait type indicates that either a table modification is waiting for all active locks on that table to be removed or a table modification is currently running and other transactions are being blocked by it.

CHAPTER 9

Latch-Related Wait Types

In Chapter 8, "Lock-Related Wait Types," we reviewed locking and blocking inside SQL Server, together with different wait types which indicate blocking is occurring. Latches look a lot like the locks we discussed earlier; in some cases, they appear to use the same modes as the locks discussed in Chapter 8. Make no mistake though; *latches are different from locks*, even though they seem to share some features. While locks are used to guarantee transactions consistency, latches are used to guarantee the consistency of in-memory objects.

Latches, just like locking and blocking, are a complex subject inside SQL Server. Latches even have their own latch-statistics DMV which records how much time has been spent waiting on specific latch types.

Because of the complexity of latches and their function inside SQL Server, I believe they require an introduction to better understand how to troubleshoot latch-related wait types later in this chapter. For this reason, we will start this chapter with an introduction to latches, just as we did with the introduction to locking inside Chapter 8, "Lock-Related Wait Types."

Introduction to Latches

Microsoft describes latches as "lightweight synchronization primitives that are used by the SQL Server engine to guarantee consistency of in-memory structures" on Books Online. This description is pretty vague, and there is a lot more depth to latches than the description would initially suggest.

The first thing to understand about latches, which we touched upon in the introduction of this chapter, is how latches are different from locks. Latches, at first glance, do look similar to locks as regards their behavior and naming conventions within SQL Server. Just like locks, latches have various "modes," and some of the acronyms to indicate the type of mode used are the same as for some lock modes. Another thing locks

© Thomas LaRock, Enrico van de Laar 2023
T. LaRock and E. van de Laar, *Pro SQL Server 2022 Wait Statistics*,
https://doi.org/10.1007/978-1-4842-8771-2_9

and latches have in common are both objects play a role in keeping SQL Server objects consistent, and the way they manage this seems identical. While locks are used to make sure transactions are consistent, protecting the transaction for the entire duration it is running, latches are only used for the duration they are necessary and are not bound to the duration of a transaction. During the duration of one transaction, many different latches will be acquired and released again. Figure 9-1 visualizes this behavior.

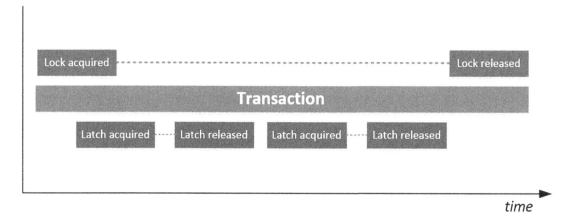

Figure 9-1. *Lock-and-latch behavior during transactions*

Nerd Note   An easy way to consider latches in a logical fashion, SQL Server uses buffer latches to protect pages *already in the buffer pool* and IO latches to protect pages *not yet loaded into the buffer pool.* This distinction will help you understand the different latch wait types and where the latch is happening.

Placing and maintaining locks on SQL Server objects is an expensive operation, as the locks need to stay in place during the entire transaction. Because latches are needed for specific operations and are released again, they are less costly to use than locks. This explains the "lightweight" part in the latch definition Microsoft uses.

The second part of the latch definition, "synchronization primitives," we discussed earlier in this book, but not under that exact name. If you have read through this book so far, you should have noticed, especially in Chapter 6, "IO-Related Wait Types," that SQL Server uses various methods to handle concurrent threads accessing objects. In Chapter 6, "IO-Related Wait Types," we talked about mutual exclusion, which makes sure only one thread at a time can access a memory object. In the same chapter, we also discussed semaphores that implement gates to limit concurrent access to memory. Latches are another method to make sure concurrent threads do not threaten the consistency of in-memory objects, and it does this in a way that looks a lot like locking.

Latch Modes

Latches have five different modes available for accessing objects. The following list describes these five modes, some of which might look familiar:

- **SH** – The SH mode represents a Shared latch. This mode is used when the latch is reading page data.

- **UP** – The UP latch mode is used by Update latches that are used whenever a resource needs to be modified. By using the Update latch, the resource can still be read by other latches.

- **EX** – The EX latch mode, or Exclusive latch, is also used when resource modification occurs. Unlike the Update latch, the Exclusive latch does not allow read or write access by other latch modes.

- **KP** – The KP latch mode is used by Keep latches. Keep latches are used to protect the resource so it cannot be destroyed by the Destroy latch. They are compatible with every other latch mode except for the Destroy mode.

- **DT** – The DT latch mode indicates Destroy latches. Destroy latches are used when removing contents from memory; for instance, when SQL Server wants to free up a data page in-memory.

As you see in this list, the first three modes look a lot like those used by locks and function more or less the same way. And just like lock modes, latch modes are compatible or incompatible with other latch modes. Table 9-1 shows the latch compatibility matrix and whether the different modes are compatible with each other or not.

Table 9-1. *Latch compatibility matrix*

	SH	UP	EX	KP	DT
SH	Yes	Yes	No	Yes	No
UP	Yes	No	No	Yes	No
EX	No	No	No	Yes	No
KP	Yes	Yes	Yes	Yes	No
DT	No	No	No	No	No

Unlike locks, which are partly controlled by Isolation levels and query hints, latches are completely controlled by the SQL Server engine. This means we cannot modify latch behavior like we can for locks.

Latch Waits

Whenever a latch has to wait because its request couldn't be granted immediately, a latch wait occurs. These waits are tracked and recorded by SQL Server inside the sys.dm_os_wait_stats DMV and also inside a dedicated DMV recording specific latch wait times, sys.dm_os_latch_waits, which we will discuss in more detail later in this chapter.

Figure 9-2 shows a situation in which a latch wait occurs. In this example, we are waiting for a data page to be read from the storage subsystem into the buffer cache. Latches are used to make sure the same data page on the storage subsystem is not being read into the buffer cache by multiple threads. While the latch is waiting for the page to read into memory, the PAGEIOLATCH_SH wait type will be recorded.

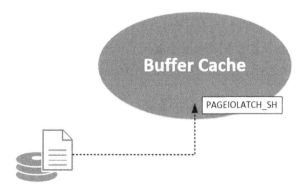

Figure 9-2. *PAGEIOLATCH_SH occurring*

There are three different latch wait types defined in SQL Server which are accessed by querying the sys.dm_os_wait_stats DMV, and they are described in the following list:

- **Buffer latches** – Buffer latches are used to protect data pages inside the buffer cache. They are used not only for user-related data pages but also for system pages like the Page Free Space (PFS) page that tracks free space inside data pages. Inside the sys.dm_os_wait_stats DMV, they are indicated by the PAGELATCH_[xx] wait type, where the [xx] indicates the latch mode used.

- **Non-buffer latches** – These latches are used to protect data structures outside of the buffer cache. They are indicated by the LATCH_[xx] wait type inside the sys.dm_os_wait_stats DMV.

- **IO latches** – IO latches are used when data pages are read from the storage subsystem into the buffer cache. This type is indicated by the PAGEIOLATCH_[xx] wait type.

Figure 9-3 shows the number of different latch wait types recorded by the sys.dm_os_wait_stats DMV.

	wait_type	waiting_tasks_count	wait_time_ms	max_wait_time_ms	signal_wait_time_ms
1	LATCH_DT	0	0	0	0
2	LATCH_EX	0	0	0	0
3	LATCH_KP	0	0	0	0
4	LATCH_NL	0	0	0	0
5	LATCH_SH	0	0	0	0
6	LATCH_UP	0	0	0	0
7	PAGEIOLATCH_DT	0	0	0	0
8	PAGEIOLATCH_EX	41	36	2	1
9	PAGEIOLATCH_KP	0	0	0	0
10	PAGEIOLATCH_NL	0	0	0	0
11	PAGEIOLATCH_SH	312	255	5	13
12	PAGEIOLATCH_UP	46	46	2	0
13	PAGELATCH_DT	0	0	0	0
14	PAGELATCH_EX	1047	8909	88	372
15	PAGELATCH_KP	0	0	0	0
16	PAGELATCH_NL	0	0	0	0
17	PAGELATCH_SH	41	2	1	0
18	PAGELATCH_UP	1	0	0	0
19	PWAIT_LATCH_ONLY	0	0	0	0
20	TRAN_MARKLATCH_DT	0	0	0	0
21	TRAN_MARKLATCH_EX	0	0	0	0
22	TRAN_MARKLATCH_KP	0	0	0	0
23	TRAN_MARKLATCH_NL	0	0	0	0
24	TRAN_MARKLATCH_SH	0	0	0	0
25	TRAN_MARKLATCH_UP	0	0	0	0

Figure 9-3. *Latch wait types inside sys.dm_os_wait_stats*

Whenever you see the LATCH_[xx] wait type inside the sys.dm_os_wait_stats DMV, you are viewing a summary of the wait times for non-buffer latches. There are various non-buffer latch classes inside SQL Server, and to make it easier to analyze these non-buffer latch classes in more detail, the sys.dm_os_latch_stats DMV was added.

sys.dm_os_latch_stats

The sys.dm_os_latch_stats closely resembles the sys.dm_os_wait_stats DMV. The sys.dm_os_latch_stats DMV shows the number of times a wait inside the latch class occurred, the total wait time, and the maximum wait time. The only column missing compared to the sys.dm_os_wait_stats DMV is signal_wait_time_ms; this is missing because latches do not follow the same execution process (RUNNING, SUSPENDED, RUNNABLE) as requests do.

Figure 9-4 shows a part of the sys.dm_os_latch_stats DMV. There are many more non-buffer latch classes, totaling 179, in SQL Server 2022.

	latch_class	waiting_requests_count	wait_time_ms	max_wait_time_ms
1	ACCESS_METHODS_DATASET_PARENT	0	0	0
2	ACCESS_METHODS_HOBT_FACTORY	0	0	0
3	ACCESS_METHODS_HOBT	12	1	1
4	ACCESS_METHODS_HOBT_COUNT	1	1	1
5	ACCESS_METHODS_HOBT_VIRTUAL_ROOT	2	0	0
6	ACCESS_METHODS_CACHE_ONLY_HOBT_ALLOC	0	0	0
7	ACCESS_METHODS_BULK_ALLOC	0	0	0
8	ACCESS_METHODS_SCAN_RANGE_GENERATOR	0	0	0
9	ACCESS_METHODS_KEY_RANGE_GENERATOR	0	0	0
10	ACCESS_METHODS_IOAFF_KEY_RANGE_GENERATOR	0	0	0
11	ACCESS_METHODS_IOAFF_KEY_TARGET_PAGE_CNT	0	0	0
12	ACCESS_METHODS_IOAFF_QUEUE	0	0	0
13	ACCESS_METHODS_IOAFF_READAHEAD_QUEUE	0	0	0
14	ACCESS_METHODS_IOAFF_READAHEAD	0	0	0
15	ACCESS_METHODS_IOAFF_WAITING_WORKER_QUEUE	0	0	0
16	APPEND_ONLY_STORAGE_INSERT_POINT	0	0	0

Figure 9-4. *sys.dm_os_latch_waits*

Just like the sys.dm_os_wait_stats DMV, the sys.dm_os_latch_stats DMV is cumulative since the start of the SQL Server service. This means it is reset to 0 when your SQL Server service is restarted. We also use the DBCC SQLPERF command against the sys.dm_os_latch_stats DMV to reset the wait times manually by executing this command:

```
DBCC SQLPERF('sys.dm_os_latch_stats', CLEAR)
```

Page-Latch Contention

One of the most common problems encountered regarding latches is page-latch contention. Page-latch contention occurs when concurrent latches try to acquire a latch, but there already is a latch in place with an incompatible mode, causing a latch wait. Because this problem can occur on every SQL Server instance subjected to concurrent workloads, I want to provide you with the knowledge needed to identify page-latch contention before we discuss the various latch-related wait types.

There are a variety of scenarios which cause page-latch contention to occur, and even though we have little influence on the latch behavior (remember, latches are placed and held by an internal process inside the SQL Server engine), the design of our database will impact latch behavior. One common cause for latch contention is when concurrent queries access so-called hotspots inside your database. For example, a small table holding a few rows which need to be accessed by an application for configuration information can be a potential hotspot. If many concurrent requests need data from this table, latches will probably run into other, incompatible latches, causing latch waits to occur and slowing down the application's performance. I have seen this problem occurring various times for different clients, making this a real-world scenario, and I will show you an example of page-latch contention based on one of those cases.

In this case, the client ran an application and at specific times would select large amounts of data and place the results into temporary tables. The application used a large amount of concurrent connections to speed up the creation of these temporary tables. To show the effects of this example, I will reproduce the scenario using Ostress to select rows from a table and then insert them into a temporary table.

As input for the Ostress utility, I save a .sql file named latch_contention.sql with the query shown in Listing 9-1.

Listing 9-1. Select rows from Sales.SalesOrderDetail into a temporary table

```
SELECT TOP (20000) *
INTO #tmptable
FROM Sales.SalesOrderDetail;
```

This query selects the top 20,000 rows from the Sales.SalesOrderDetail table inside the GalacticWorks database and inserts them into a temporary table (#tmptable).

The next step is to use Ostress and execute the latch_contention.sql script with 300 concurrent connections. The Ostress command line I use is shown here:

```
"C:\Program Files\Microsoft Corporation\RMLUtils\ostress.exe" -S.\RC0 -E
-dGalacticWorks -i"C:\TeamData\latch_contention.sql" -n300 -r1 -q
```

While the Ostress utility is running, let's look at the sys.dm_os_waiting_tasks DMV to see if anything is running into waits. Figure 9-5 shows a part of the results that are returned when the query that follows is executed:

```
SELECT
```

```
   session_id,
   wait_duration_ms,
   wait_type,
   resource_description
FROM sys.dm_os_waiting_tasks
WHERE session_id > 50;
```

	session_id	wait_duration_ms	wait_type	resource_description
24	187	91	PAGELATCH_EX	2:1:2411 (LATCH 0x000001B37D7B0518: Class: BUFFER...
25	165	91	PAGELATCH_EX	2:1:2411 (LATCH 0x000001B37D7B0518: Class: BUFFER...
26	188	91	PAGELATCH_EX	2:1:2411 (LATCH 0x000001B37D7B0518: Class: BUFFER...
27	94	4	PAGELATCH_SH	2:1:25321 (LATCH 0x000001B37D7D02D8: Class: BUFFE...
28	118	4	PAGELATCH_SH	2:1:25321 (LATCH 0x000001B37D7D02D8: Class: BUFFE...
29	197	64	PAGELATCH_EX	2:1:2411 (LATCH 0x000001B37D7B0518: Class: BUFFER...
30	143	89	PAGELATCH_EX	2:1:30912 (LATCH 0x000001B37D524AD8: Class: BUFFE...
31	139	89	PAGELATCH_EX	2:1:30912 (LATCH 0x000001B37D524AD8: Class: BUFFE...
32	140	90	PAGELATCH_EX	2:1:30912 (LATCH 0x000001B37D524AD8: Class: BUFFE...
33	153	90	PAGELATCH_EX	2:1:30912 (LATCH 0x000001B37D524AD8: Class: BUFFE...

Figure 9-5. *PAGELATCH_[XX] waits*

We are running into a lot of PAGELATCH_[XX] waits, indicating a latch is waiting to update a page in-memory. The resource_description column is useful here since it indicates the page ID the latch wants to access. The first number represents the database ID, which is the tempdb database. The second number indicates the file ID (the tempdb database on my test system consists of multiple data files). Finally, the last number indicates the page ID.

Because we are running inserts into a temporary table using many concurrent connections, we need to find, or allocate, data pages with free space to hold our rows inside the tempdb. All this space usage needs to be updated, and latches are used to make sure only one thread gets access at a time.

This is a classic example of the page-latch contention inside the tempdb database which can occur when many concurrent queries are creating objects inside tempdb. One way to resolve this specific case of latch contention is by adding more (equally sized) tempdb data files. Fortunately, starting with SQL Server 2016, the installation included the ability to create multiple tempdb files during setup.

Additional tempdb improvements since 2016 include the following:

- Adding trace flags T1117 and T1118 as default behavior (2016)

- Improvements to optimistic latching (2017)

- Use of round-robin for PFS pages (2017)

- Memory-optimized tempdb metadata (2019)

- Concurrent PFS updates (2019)

- System page-latch (GAM, SGAM) concurrent improvements (2022)

Now that we have discussed what latches are and how they work and looked at an example of latch contention, let's move on and look at latch-related wait types.

PAGELATCH_[xx]

The first latch-related wait type for review is the **PAGELATCH_[xx]** wait type, where the [xx] indicates the latch mode used (e.g., SH for Shared). Since we already discussed the various latch modes in the introduction of this chapter, we won't describe them again in this chapter.

What Is the PAGELATCH_[xx] Wait Type?

PAGELATCH_[xx] waits occur whenever a latch must wait before it can access a page in-memory. The main cause for these waits are other latches already in place on the page and are incompatible with the latch mode of our request. Just like with locks, the latch will wait until the incompatible latch is removed from the page. As long as the incompatible latch is in place, our request will record PAGELATCH_[xx] wait time. Figure 9-6 shows a graphical representation of a PAGELATCH_UP wait occurring. I used a cogwheel icon to indicate a latch is already in place on the page to avoid confusion with SQL Server locks.

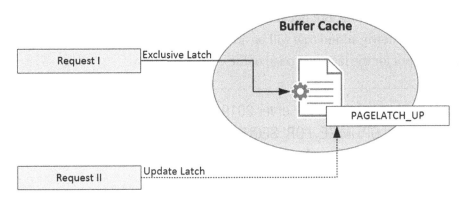

Figure 9-6. *PAGELATCH_UP wait occurring*

It's easy to confuse PAGELATCH_[xx] waits with PAGEIOLATCH_[xx] waits. Even though they look alike in name, they are completely different latch wait types. The former indicates access to pages already in-memory, while the latter indicates pages are being read from disk into memory. We will go into detail regarding the PAGEIOLATCH_[xx] wait type later in this chapter.

PAGELATCH_[xx] Example

In the introduction to this chapter, we took a look at page-latch contention inside the tempdb database when many concurrent queries are loading data in temporary queries. This isn't the only form of latch contention inside SQL Server. Another form of latch contention is "last-page insert contention." Just like the page-latch contention scenario discussed earlier, last-page insert contention is identified by noticing a high number of PAGELATCH waits. Let's go through an example of last-page insert contention.

Chances are, perhaps while attending a database design class, you were told every table should have a clustered index. You also were told the best candidate for a clustered index key was a narrow, unique, ever-increasing value, perhaps an integer. While these design options are useful for many scenarios, there are cases where this design will cause a performance issue known as last-page insert contention.

Last-page insert contention will occur on databases experiencing a heavy insert workload against a table with relatively small rows; for instance, a table with an ID column (Integer data type, auto increasing) and a Name column (Varchar data type). From a best-practice point of view, we would create a clustered index on the ID column since it fits the description of a good index key perfectly. It is narrow, unique for every row, and always increasing. But because of the ever-increasing nature of the auto increment, every newly added row will be added at the end of the clustered index, creating a hotspot for the last data page of the clustered index.

Nerd Note   Starting with SQL Server 2019, the CREATE INDEX statement added a new option called OPTIMIZE_FOR_SEQUENTIAL_KEY, which alleviates (but does not eliminate) the last-page insert scenario discussed here. You can read more about this option at `https://slrwnds.com/hn4nih`.

Figure 9-7 shows the insert behavior of rows into data pages inside a clustered index, inside the form of a so-called B-tree structure, which is the data structure SQL Server uses to sort indexes.

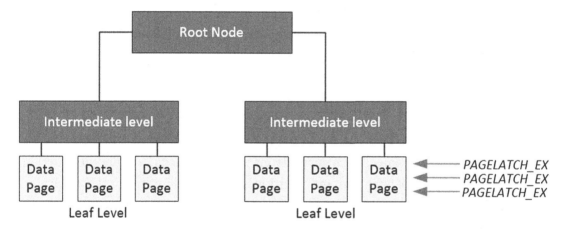

Figure 9-7. *Last-page insert contention on the last page in a clustered index*

Even if the current data page is full, and a new data page is added, the target of the inserts will change to the new page, switching the hotspot to the new data page.

Locks will not prevent this contention from happening. By default, SQL Server will use Exclusive row-level locks to insert data, as opposed to issuing a page-level lock. And you will recall it is possible to have multiple Exclusive row-level locks on a page.

However, access to the page in-memory still needs to occur serially, so latches are used to make sure only one thread has access to the page at any time. Figure 9-8 shows an enlarged view of the data pages at the leaf level of the clustered index with locks in place.

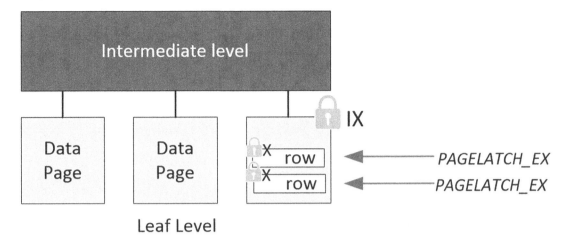

***Figure 9-8.** Leaf page of clustered index with locks in place*

To show an example of last-page insert contention, let's create a new table inside the GalacticWorks database using the query that follows:

```
CREATE TABLE Insert_Test
  (ID INT IDENTITY (1,1) PRIMARY KEY,
  RandomData VARCHAR(50));
```

As you see, this is a small table with an ID column which automatically increases for every new row inserted and a RandomData column to hold some data. I indicate the ID column is the primary key of this table, which will automatically create a clustered index using the ID column as the index key.

The next step is running Ostress with a highly concurrent workload that inserts new rows into the Insert_Test table. This time I don't create a .sql input file for Ostress but rather enter the following query in the Ostress command line:

```
INSERT INTO Insert_Test
  (RandomData)
VALUES
  (CONVERT(varchar(50), NEWID()))
```

Now we create the following Ostress command line to connect to the GalacticWorks database and execute the query we supplied using 500 concurrent connections, each connection performing the query 100 times. This should create enough concurrent inserts to demonstrate last-page insert contention:

```
"C:\Program Files\Microsoft Corporation\RMLUtils\ostress.exe" -S.\
RC0 -E -dGalacticWorks -Q"INSERT INTO Insert_Test (RandomData) VALUES
(CONVERT(varchar(50), NEWID()))" -n500 -r100 -q
```

While Ostress is running, I query the sys.dm_os_waiting_tasks DMV:

```
SELECT
  session_id,
  wait_duration_ms,
  wait_type,
  resource_description
FROM sys.dm_os_waiting_tasks;
```

This query filters out some columns, so a screenshot of the results will fit on the page. Figure 9-9 shows a portion of the results.

	session_id	wait_duration_ms	wait_type	resource_description
1	378	12	PAGELATCH_EX	5:1:25848 (LATCH 0x000001B37D32FE18: Class: BUFFE...
2	100	5	PAGELATCH_EX	5:1:25848 (LATCH 0x000001B37D32FE18: Class: BUFFE...
3	442	6	PAGELATCH_EX	5:1:25848 (LATCH 0x000001B37D32FE18: Class: BUFFE...
4	147	5	PAGELATCH_EX	5:1:25848 (LATCH 0x000001B37D32FE18: Class: BUFFE...
5	160	5	PAGELATCH_EX	5:1:25848 (LATCH 0x000001B37D32FE18: Class: BUFFE...
6	92	6	PAGELATCH_EX	5:1:25848 (LATCH 0x000001B37D32FE18: Class: BUFFE...
7	408	6	PAGELATCH_EX	5:1:25848 (LATCH 0x000001B37D32FE18: Class: BUFFE...
8	151	5	PAGELATCH_SH	5:1:25848 (LATCH 0x000001B37D32FE18: Class: BUFFE...
9	168	5	PAGELATCH_SH	5:1:25848 (LATCH 0x000001B37D32FE18: Class: BUFFE...
10	97	5	PAGELATCH_SH	5:1:25848 (LATCH 0x000001B37D32FE18: Class: BUFFE...
11	112	5	PAGELATCH_SH	5:1:25848 (LATCH 0x000001B37D32FE18: Class: BUFFE...
12	428	4	PAGELATCH_SH	5:1:25848 (LATCH 0x000001B37D32FE18: Class: BUFFE...
13	427	4	PAGELATCH_SH	5:1:25848 (LATCH 0x000001B37D32FE18: Class: BUFFE...
14	93	3	PAGELATCH_SH	5:1:25848 (LATCH 0x000001B37D32FE18: Class: BUFFE...

Figure 9-9. *PAGELATCH_EX waits on the same page*

As expected, the insert workload caused a hotspot to appear on a page inside the clustered index, in this case the page with a page ID of 25848. All of those tasks shown in Figure 9-9 (and there were around 200 more not shown) are all waiting to place a page latch, indicated by the PAGELATCH_[XX] wait types, on the page so they can perform their insert operation.

Next, let's use the undocumented DBCC IND command to learn more about page 25848. DBCC IND will return a row for every page associated with the table we supply as a parameter to DBCC IND and, among other things, will show us the page type of every page returned. The following table shows the page types returned by DBCC IND:

Table 9-2. *Page types returned by DBCC IND*

Page type	Page
1	Data page
2	Index page
3,4	Text pages
8	GAM page
9	SGAM page
10	IAM page
11	PFS page

Running the following command will execute DBCC IND against the GalacticWorks database's Insert_Test table. Before we run the actual DBCC IND command, we enable traceflag 3604 so the results of the DBCC IND command are returned in the SQL Server Management Studio (SSMS) results tab:

```
DBCC TRACEON (3604);
DBCC IND (GalacticWorks, Insert_Test, 1);
```

Figure 9-10 shows the results of the DBCC IND command. Highlighted is page 25848, the insert hotspot page during the Ostress workload.

	PageFID	PagePID	IAMFID	IAMPID	ObjectID	IndexID	PartitionNumber	PartitionID	iam_chain_type	PageType
623	1	25845	1	24797	1895677801	1	1	72057594065715200	In-row data	1
624	1	25846	1	24797	1895677801	1	1	72057594065715200	In-row data	1
625	1	25847	1	24797	1895677801	1	1	72057594065715200	In-row data	2
626	1	25848	1	24797	1895677801	1	1	72057594065715200	In-row data	2
627	1	25849	1	24797	1895677801	1	1	72057594065715200	In-row data	1
628	1	25850	1	24797	1895677801	1	1	72057594065715200	In-row data	1
629	1	25851	1	24797	1895677801	1	1	72057594065715200	In-row data	1

Figure 9-10. *DBCC IND results*

The information we are interested in resides in the IndexID and PageType columns. The IndexID column returns the Index ID this page is associated with. We only have one index on the Insert_Test table, and it has an ID of 1. The PageType column returns the page type of the specific page. In this case, the PageType of page 25848 is 2, which indicates the page is an index page.

Remember, DBCC IND is an undocumented SQL Server command, and I included it here to show you information about the page where the last-page insert contention was occurring. I strongly advise against using it on production servers.

Lowering PAGELATCH_[xx] Waits

So far we have seen two examples where PAGELATCH_[xx] waits occur, page-latch contention in the tempdb database and last-page insert contention. There is another latch contention problem also identified by PAGELATCH_[xx] waits occurring, but it also has a connection with the LATCH_[xx] wait type. For this reason, I am saving the explanation and example of this specific case of latch contention for the next section of this chapter where we discuss the LATCH_[xx] wait type.

Lowering PAGELATCH_[xx] waits is challenging. Frequently, they are related to the design of your database and your workload, and these are difficult to change in production environments. There are, however, a number of factors which contribute to latch contention and are worth taking the time to check.

It is common to scc latch contention occurring on systems with a large number of logical processors (16+) and high concurrent OLTP workloads. However, having fewer logical processors does not mean latch contention cannot occur. The examples of latch contention shown so far have all been generated on a virtual machine with four logical processors. Having more logical processors means there are more threads available to perform work, which results in more concurrent latches being placed, increasing the chances of latch contention. Adding logical processors when experiencing latch contention can, in this specific case, cause even more latch contention to occur instead of resolving it. Lowering the number of logical processors isn't an option either, because this will slow down all your other workloads.

The best way to resolve latch contention is by identifying where the contention is occurring and what type of contention you are dealing with.

If you are dealing with PFS page contention, a good first step would be to check if you are using one or multiple database data files. If you are using one database data file, the first step would be to add additional, equally sized data files and measure if this lowers the amount of PAGELATCH_[xx] waits occurring. If you already have multiple database data files, you could try adding more, but be careful not to add too many, because having this can introduce other performance problems. Your goal should be to find a database data file "sweet spot" where you have enough database data files to minimize the impact of latch contention, but not so many as to cause the overhead to become too high. This depends entirely on your workload, so it is impossible to give a generalized recommendation.

When dealing with last-page insert contention, you could consider changing the index key to something else instead of a sequentially increasing value, like a GUID. Using a GUID as an index key will result in a larger index because of the byte requirements of a GUID. Also, because GUIDs are entirely random, keeping the index in order requires more work than when dealing with an ever-increasing, sequential value. It can also have consequences for your applications or queries if they need to be rewritten to accommodate the change in data type.

Other factors to consider are indexing strategies, page fullness, and the number of concurrent connections to the database. Also, identifying and optimizing the access patterns to the data inside the database can help immensely. For instance, if you know your workload consists of many very small inserts against a single table, it might be worth taking the time to combine some of the small inserts into a larger batch, effectively lowering the number of latches needed.

Another option for resolving latch contention is a method called hash partitioning. Hash partitioning splits up a table or index into various partitions based on a value generated with a computed column. Partitioning is a method that can minimize, or completely prevent, latch contention.

Hash partitioning works by cutting up tables or indexes into partitions, with each partition holding a set of the data. Partitioning is frequently used for archiving data from inside a table to another filegroup residing on other (cheaper) storage, while the current data resides on fast storage. In the case of hash partitioning, we calculate a value for every row inside the table using a computed column. Based on the value, we move the row to a partition.

The great advantage of using this method of partitioning indexes is every partition has its own index tree. So even though the insert statements will still occur on the last (right-most) page of the index, it will be spread across the partitions. If we look at Figure 9-11, we see a case of last-page insert contention, where concurrent queries are trying to insert rows into an index as we discussed in the preceding example.

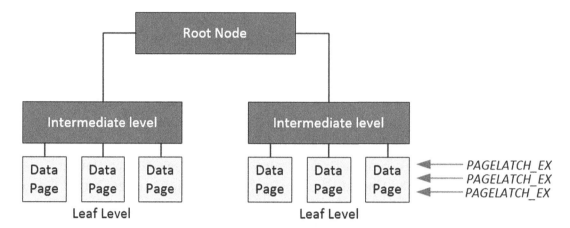

Figure 9-11. *Last-page insert contention on the right-most data page of an index*

If we use partitioning to cut the index into multiple parts (three in this case), we would get the situation shown in Figure 9-12, multiple B-trees, each spanning a part of the data.

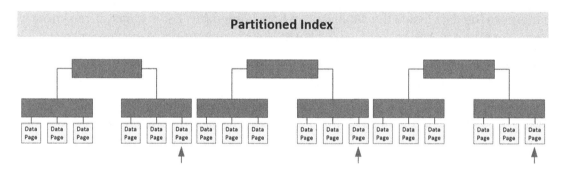

Figure 9-12. *Last-page inserts spread across partitions*

Let's look at the effects of hash partitioning when we run the workload to generate last-page insert contention, like we did in the example earlier in this chapter.

The first thing we do is create a Partition function. This will map rows inside the table or index to partitions based on the value of a column. The following script will create a Partition function named LatchPartFunc that will divide rows into nine partitions based on the value of a column (which we will create a bit later). See the following:

```
CREATE PARTITION FUNCTION [LatchPartFunc] (INT)
AS RANGE LEFT FOR VALUES
  (0,1,2,3,4,5,6,7,8);
```

The next step is to create a Partition scheme that will map the partitions to a filegroup:

```
CREATE PARTITION SCHEME [LatchPartSchema]
AS PARTITION [LatchPartFunc] ALL TO ([PRIMARY]);
```

In this case, I used the PRIMARY filegroup, but you are free to create an additional filegroup to hold the partitions.

Next up is creating a new table called Insert_Test3 using the query that follows. Notice the ID_Hash column. This is a computed column which will calculate a value between 0 and 8 based on the value of the ID column:

```
CREATE TABLE Insert_Test3
  (ID INT IDENTITY(1,1),
  RandomData VARCHAR(50),
  ID_Hash AS (CONVERT(INT, abs(binary_checksum(ID) % (9)), (0)))
  PERSISTED);
```

The last step is to create a clustered index and map it to the Partition scheme:

```
CREATE UNIQUE CLUSTERED INDEX idx_ID
ON Insert_Test3
  (ID ASC, ID_Hash)
ON LatchPartSchema(ID_Hash);
```

Now with our partitioned table in place, let's repeat the Ostress workload which caused last-page insert contention in our previous example. I changed the target table for the inserts to our new, partitioned Insert_Test3 table.

```
"C:\Program Files\Microsoft Corporation\RMLUtils\ostress.exe" -S.\
RCO -E -dGalacticWorks -Q"INSERT INTO Insert_Test3 (RandomData) VALUES
(CONVERT(varchar(50), NEWID()))" -n500 -r100 -q
```

During both Ostress workloads, I used Perfmon to monitor the number of latch waits occurring every second. Figure 9-13 shows the Perfmon graph for the first Ostress workload against a non-partitioned index and the second against the partitioned index we just created.

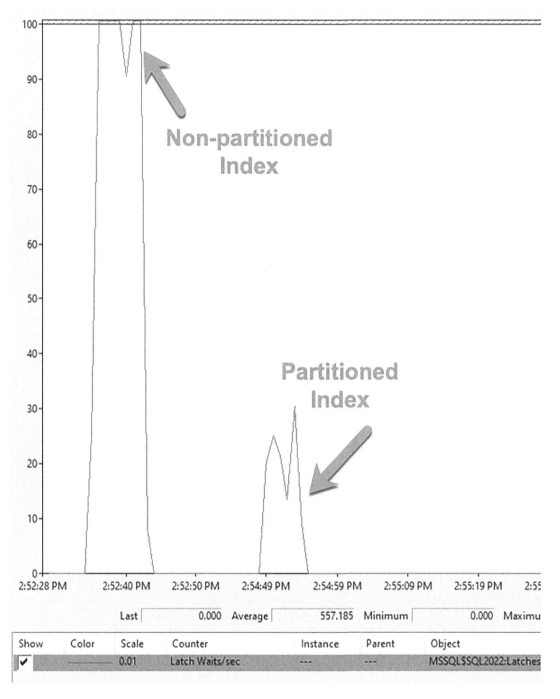

Figure 9-13. *Latch waits/sec against both a non-partitioned and a partitioned index*

As you can see, the number of latch waits occurring dropped drastically after configuring hash partitioning! We can view the distribution of rows across the different partitions we created by running this query:

```
SELECT *
FROM sys.partitions
WHERE object_id = OBJECT_ID('Insert_Test3');
```

Figure 9-14 shows the results of this query on my test SQL Server instance.

	partition_id	object_id	index_id	partition_number	hobt_id	rows	filestream_filegroup_id	data_compression	data_compression_desc
1	72057594065911808	1943677972	1	1	72057594065911808	5555	0	0	NONE
2	72057594065977344	1943677972	1	2	72057594065977344	5556	0	0	NONE
3	72057594066042880	1943677972	1	3	72057594066042880	5556	0	0	NONE
4	72057594066108416	1943677972	1	4	72057594066108416	5556	0	0	NONE
5	72057594066173952	1943677972	1	5	72057594066173952	5556	0	0	NONE
6	72057594066239488	1943677972	1	6	72057594066239488	5556	0	0	NONE
7	72057594066305024	1943677972	1	7	72057594066305024	5555	0	0	NONE
8	72057594066370560	1943677972	1	8	72057594066370560	5555	0	0	NONE
9	72057594066436096	1943677972	1	9	72057594066436096	5555	0	0	NONE
10	72057594066501632	1943677972	1	10	72057594066501632	0	0	0	NONE

Figure 9-14. *Rows distribution across partitions*

In Figure 9-14, we see the nine partitions we created on the Insert_Test3 table, numbered 1 to 9 by the partition_number column. The rows column shows the number of rows inside each partition, and as you can see, they are distributed very evenly across the nine partitions! The hobt_id returns the ID of the B-tree where two rows of this partition are stored; all the partitions have different IDs, meaning they each have their own B-tree structure.

Even though partitioning is a great way to resolve latch contention issues, it does come with its own unique challenges and drawbacks. One such drawback is partitioning can impact the generation of query execution plans, resulting in a suboptimal plan. You will want to test thoroughly before implementing in production.

One final option worth mentioning is the use of In-Memory OLTP as a possible remedy, if your workload and design allow for this feature.

PAGELATCH_[xx] Summary

The PAGELATCH_[xx] wait type indicates buffer latches, which are used to protect in-memory pages and are running into other, noncompatible, buffer latches. Just like locks, latches have different modes they use when protecting pages, and not all of these are compatible with each other. Seeing a large amount of PAGELATCH_[xx] waits occurring can indicate a case of latch contention. Resolving latch contention can be challenging and frequently requires making changes to the database design or queries.

LATCH_[xx]

Another latch-related wait type is the **LATCH_[xx]** wait type. Just like the PAGELATCH_[xx] wait type discussed in the previous section, LATCH_[xx] waits are related to a specific latch class. While the PAGELATCH_[xx] wait type is related to latches that protect data structures inside the buffer cache, the LATCH_[xx] wait type is related to latches which protect data structures outside of the buffer cache (but still inside the SQL Server memory).

What Is the LATCH_[xx] Wait Type?

When you see the LATCH_[xx] wait type occurring, a specific class of non-buffer latches is running into a wait. The LATCH_[xx] is a summary of the wait time of the different non-buffer latch classes and not a latch type of its own. All of the different non-buffer latch classes which add to the wait time shown by the LATCH_[xx] wait type are recorded inside their own DMV, sys.dm_os_latch_stats. There are many different latch classes that the LATCH_[xx] wait type represents, totaling 179 in SQL Server 2022. Figure 9-15 shows the memory area where LATCH_[xx] waits can occur.

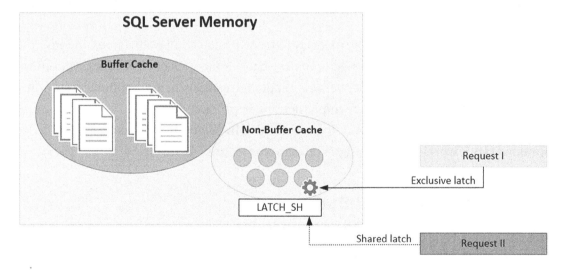

Figure 9-15. *LATCH_SH waits*

Because the LATCH_[xx] wait type is a cumulative view of waits occurring on a specific latch class, you will need to look inside the sys.dm_os_latch_stats DMV to find the exact cause of the LATCH_[xx] wait. We described the inner workings and columns of the sys.dm_os_latch_stats DMV in the "Introduction to Latches" section at the start of this chapter.

LATCH_[xx] Example

There is one case of latch contention which will result in LATCH_[xx] waits. This problem occurs on small tables with a shallow B-tree structure (we will explain more about the B-tree structure a bit further down in this section) during a large volume of concurrent insert operations. A typical use case of such a table could be a messaging table acting as a queue and is truncated when messages are sent. The script in Listing 9-2 will create a test table, named Insert_Test2, together with a non-clustered index on the table.

Listing 9-2. Test contention table with non-clustered index

```
-- Create the table
CREATE TABLE Insert_Test2
  (ID UNIQUEIDENTIFIER,
  RandomData VARCHAR(50));
-- Create a non-clustered index on the ID column
CREATE NONCLUSTERED INDEX idx_ID
ON Insert_Test2 (ID);
```

The ID column has a data type of UNIQUEIDENTIFIER to make sure random, nonsequential values are generated. By creating a non-clustered index on this column, inserts will happen randomly across the B-tree associated with the non-clustered index.

Once the table is created, we start Ostress with a workload consisting of a query which will insert a single row inside the table. We run the workload with 500 concurrent connections, each connection executing the query 5000 times. The command that follows shows the Ostress command:

```
"C:\Program Files\Microsoft Corporation\RMLUtils\ostress.exe" -S.\RCO
-E -dGalacticWorks -Q"INSERT INTO Insert_Test2 (ID, RandomData) VALUES
(NEWID(), CONVERT(varchar(50), NEWID())))" -n500 -r5000 -q
```

While the workload is running, we query the sys.dm_os_waiting_tasks DMV using the following query, so the resource_description column will fit on the screenshot:

```
SELECT
  session_id,
  wait_duration_ms,
  wait_type,
  resource_description
FROM sys.dm_os_waiting_tasks;
```

Figure 9-16 shows a part of the results of this query on my test SQL Server instance.

	session_id	wait_duration_ms	wait_type	resource_description
9	258	4	LATCH_SH	ACCESS_METHODS_HOBT_VIRTUAL_ROOT (0x000001B292266...
10	145	4	LATCH_SH	ACCESS_METHODS_HOBT_VIRTUAL_ROOT (0x000001B292266...
11	324	4	LATCH_SH	ACCESS_METHODS_HOBT_VIRTUAL_ROOT (0x000001B292266...
12	347	3	LATCH_SH	ACCESS_METHODS_HOBT_VIRTUAL_ROOT (0x000001B292266...
13	121	5	LATCH_SH	ACCESS_METHODS_HOBT_VIRTUAL_ROOT (0x000001B292266...
14	322	5	LATCH_SH	ACCESS_METHODS_HOBT_VIRTUAL_ROOT (0x000001B292266...
15	343	5	LATCH_SH	ACCESS_METHODS_HOBT_VIRTUAL_ROOT (0x000001B292266...
16	92	4	LATCH_SH	ACCESS_METHODS_HOBT_VIRTUAL_ROOT (0x000001B292266...
17	125	4	LATCH_SH	ACCESS_METHODS_HOBT_VIRTUAL_ROOT (0x000001B292266...
18	330	2	LATCH_SH	ACCESS_METHODS_HOBT_VIRTUAL_ROOT (0x000001B292266...
19	271	1	LATCH_SH	ACCESS_METHODS_HOBT_VIRTUAL_ROOT (0x000001B292266...

Figure 9-16. *LATCH_SH waits*

The resource_description column of the sys.dm_os_waiting_tasks DMV helps identify the latch class associated with the LATCH_[xx] wait. In this case, we are running into the ACCESS_METHODS_HOBT_VIRTUAL_ROOT latch class.

Next we can query the sys.dm_os_latch_stats DMV to find out the number of waits and the total wait time for this specific latch class using the following query:

```
SELECT *
FROM sys.dm_os_latch_stats
WHERE latch_class = 'ACCESS_METHODS_HOBT_VIRTUAL_ROOT';
```

Figure 9-17 shows the results of this query on my test SQL Server instance.

	latch_class	waiting_requests_count	wait_time_ms	max_wait_time_ms
1	ACCESS_METHODS_HOBT_VIRTUAL_ROOT	10078	68908	183

Figure 9-17. *ACCESS_METHOD_HOBT_VIRTUAL_ROOT latch wait*

With the identified latch class causing the LATCH_SH wait to occur, we start troubleshooting it. According to Books Online, the ACCESS_METHODS_HOBT_VIRTUAL_ROOT latch class is used to "synchronize access to the root page abstraction of an internal B-tree." Even though the description is pretty limited, it gives an idea of where to start looking when troubleshooting this specific problem. I included a list of the different latch classes that are described on Books Online, including some extra information whenever possible, in Appendix III of this book.

Apparently, something happened to the B-tree structures associated with indexes. Since we only have one non-clustered index on the table we created (idx_ID), we assume something happened to the B-tree of that index. Let's refresh our memory a little bit about what a B-tree index structure looks like by looking at Figure 9-18.

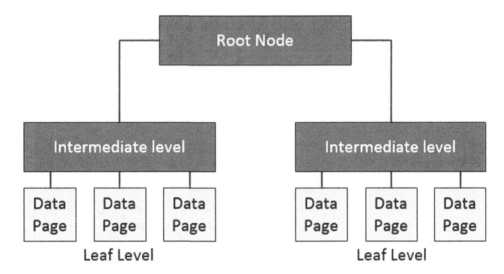

Figure 9-18. *B-tree index structure*

The B-tree structure we see in Figure 9-18 is shallow, as it only has three levels. The first one is the Root Node (level 0), the second is the Intermediate level (level 1), and finally at the bottom of the B-tree are the data pages holding the index keys (or in case of a clustered index, the entire row). In Figure 9-18, we have one level of intermediate nodes, but depending on the number of data pages inside the index, it is possible to have more Intermediate levels. When the table is very small, it is possible to have the data pages inside the Intermediate level instead of a level further down the B-tree.

Whenever SQL Server needs to navigate through the B-tree, it will start at the Root page inside the Root Node. The Root page will help navigate down to the index page which holds the information it needs inside the Intermediate level. In turn, the Intermediate page sends the request further down the B-tree if the page is not inside the Intermediate level but is rather at the Leaf level. The Leaf level is the last level in an index; it cannot navigate further down than that. Figure 9-19 shows how SQL Server navigates through the B-tree. In this case, I used numbers as the index key to make it a bit easier.

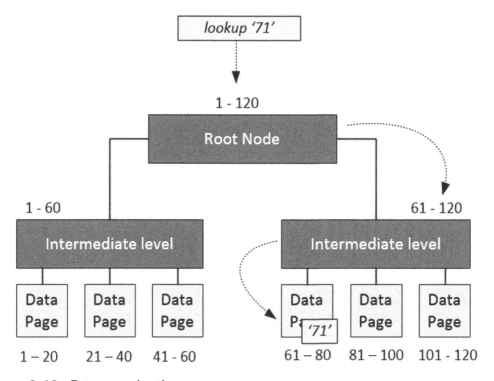

Figure 9-19. *B-tree navigation*

When data is added to the index, the index will allocate new data pages at the Leaf level to hold the index keys (remember, clustered indexes hold rows at the Leaf level). Whenever enough data is inserted and a new index level needs to be created, a Root page split occurs so the new level inside the index is accessed. This Root page split doesn't cut your Root page into two new ones, there is always one Root page, but it needs to be updated so we can use it to navigate through the B-tree to the new data.

The ACCESS_METHODS_HOBT_VIRTUAL_ROOT latch class is the latch wait class that is associated whenever a Root page split occurs in order to create another level inside the B-tree. Whenever a Root page split occurs, the B-tree will acquire an Exclusive latch. All threads wanting to navigate down the B-tree will have to wait for the Root page split to finish since they use Shared latches which are incompatible with the Exclusive latch. But we see LATCH_SH waits occurring when running our Ostress workload, instead of seeing Exclusive latches, since we are performing inserts. The reason why is pretty simple: before SQL Server knows where to place the new index key inside the index, it first has to navigate through the B-tree to locate where the new index key needs to be placed, and it uses Shared latches during its navigation.

To show you another level was added to the non-clustered index during our Ostress workload, I will use the INDEXPROPERTY function to retrieve the depth of the non-clustered index we created.

First, let's empty our Insert_Test2 table using the TRUNCATE command:

```
TRUNCATE TABLE Insert_Test2;
```

If we use the INDEXPROPERTY function against the non-clustered index on this table, we see the current depth of the B-tree. The query which follows shows how to use the INDEXPROPERTY function to retrieve this information:

```
SELECT INDEXPROPERTY(OBJECT_ID('Insert_Test2'), 'idx_ID', 'indexDepth');
```

Since we truncated the table, the index depth should be 0 as there are no rows inside the table yet.

We run the Ostress workload again, and after it has finished, review the index information again. Instead of using the INDEXPROPERTY function, we use the sys. dm_db_index_physical_stats DMF to return additional information about the number of index and data pages inside the index. This query returns such information:

```
SELECT
  index_id,
  index_type_desc,
  index_depth,
  index_level,
  page_count,
```

```
  record_count
FROM sys.dm_db_index_physical_stats
    (DB_ID(N'GalacticWorks'), OBJECT_ID(N'Insert_Test2'), NULL, NULL ,
    'DETAILED');
```

Figure 9-20 shows the results of this query on my test SQL Server instance.

	index_id	index_type_desc	index_depth	index_level	page_count	record_count
1	0	HEAP	1	0	20387	2500000
2	2	NONCLUSTERED INDEX	3	0	13765	2500000
3	2	NONCLUSTERED INDEX	3	1	91	13765
4	2	NONCLUSTERED INDEX	3	2	1	91

Figure 9-20. *sys.dm_db_index_physical_stats results*

As you see in this image, the non-clustered index now has three levels as indicated by the index_depth column. The index_level and page_count columns show how many pages exist on each level of the B-tree. The highest index_level number is the Root level, the lowest the Leaf level.

While the new levels were created inside the B-tree, the concurrent insert queries had to wait before they could navigate the B-tree, resulting in the LATCH_SH waits.

Lowering LATCH_[xx] Waits

In the previous example, I presented a specific case of latch contention that occurs when index Root page splits occur so as to extend the B-tree structure. As I mentioned before, there are many more latch classes reported by the LATCH_[xx] wait type. This makes describing "one-size-fits-all" suggestions impossible. I can describe a general approach though, using the list here:

- Query sys.dm_os_waiting_tasks if LATCH_[xx] waits are occurring. The resource_description column shows additional information about the specific latch class. If you are in a situation where the LATCH_[xx] waits do not show in sys.dm_os_waiting_tasks but high wait times are visible in sys.dm_os_wait_stats DMV, the sys.dm_os_latch_waits DMV should be your starting point.

- Another helpful DMV can be the sys.dm_exec_requests DMV. Joined together with the sys.dm_exec_sql_text DMF, it may help you to find the query that is causing the LATCH_[xx] wait.

- Query sys.dm_os_latch_waits to see if this correlates with the latch class shown in the resource_description column of the sys.dm_os_waiting_tasks DMV.

- Check Books Online or Appendix III in this book for more information about the specific latch class.

Thankfully, it is not very common to see consistent high wait times for the LATCH_[xx] wait type since the cases that can cause the LATCH_[xx] waits to occur are frequently related to specific workloads and database design.

LATCH_[xx] Summary

The LATCH_[xx] wait type represents waits encountered by a large selection of different, non-buffer-related latch classes inside SQL Server. These non-buffer-related latch classes have their own latch wait DMV, sys.dm_os_latch_waits, that returns the wait times of those latch classes. Troubleshooting LATCH_[xx] waits can be difficult since the latch classes that are associated with the wait type are minimally documented. Thankfully, it is not very common to see high wait times on the LATCH_[xx] wait type since they only occur for very specific situations and workloads.

PAGEIOLATCH_[xx]

The final latch-related wait type we will discuss in this chapter is the **PAGEIOLATCH_[xx]** wait type. The PAGEIOLATCH_[xx] wait type is by far the most common latch-related wait type and together with the CXPACKET wait type is the most common wait type to see on any SQL Server instance.

Just like the two previous latch wait types we discussed, the PAGEIOLATCH_[xx] has different access modes that I replaced with [xx] in this chapter. Since we already described the different latch modes in the introduction, we won't discuss them further in this chapter.

The PAGELATCH_[xx] wait type is related to latches being placed on memory pages inside the buffer cache, and the LATCH_[xx] wait type is related to latches on non-buffer objects. The PAGEIOLATCH_[xx] wait type also indicates the use of latches on a specific area in SQL Server, in this case the IO latches.

What Is the PAGEIOLATCH_[xx] Wait Type?

Disk operations inside SQL Server are very expensive. Accessing the disk subsystem of your system requires extra resources and is always slower than accessing information inside the memory of your system. Because SQL Server is a database, and accessing and storing data inside the database is its primary function, the way SQL Server accesses data is extremely important. If data access is slow, SQL Server will perform slower as well, and this will result in noticeable performance degradation inside your queries or applications. To make IO interactions as efficient as possible, SQL Server uses a buffer cache to cache data pages previously accessed into the memory of your system. By caching data pages, SQL Server only has to access the disk subsystem once, when the first query requests those specific data pages. When later queries require the same data pages as the first query, SQL Server will detect those pages are already inside the buffer cache, through the Buffer Manager, and will access the data pages from inside the buffer cache instead of performing extra interactions with the disk subsystem. Figure 9-21 shows the buffer cache behavior when a query requires data pages from the storage subsystem.

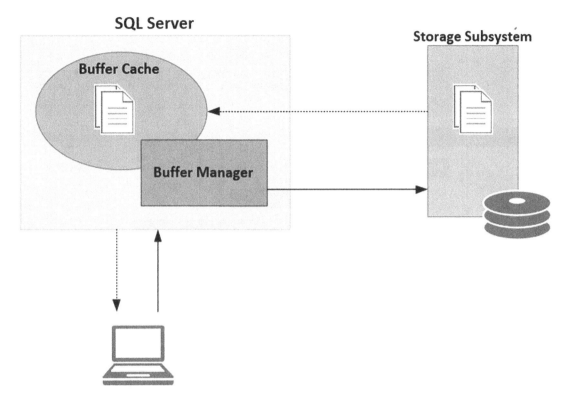

Figure 9-21. *Moving a page from the storage subsystem to the buffer cache*

During the movement of data pages from the storage subsystem to the buffer cache, latches are used to "reserve" a buffer page for the data page on the storage subsystem. This makes sure no other concurrent transactions allocate the same buffer page or simultaneously attempt to transfer the same data page from the storage subsystem to the buffer cache.

While SQL Server is transferring the data page from the storage subsystem into the buffer cache, an Exclusive latch will be placed on the buffer page. Because Exclusive latches are incompatible with almost every other latch mode (save for the Keep mode), it is guaranteed no other latch can access the buffer page while it is transferred. From the user perspective, a PAGEIOLATCH_[xx] wait will be recorded for the duration of the transfer of the data page. The mode of the latch depends on the action which initiated the movement of the data page from the storage subsystem to the buffer cache. A PAGEIOLATCH_SH will be recorded if the data is being moved for read access, and a PAGEIOLATCH_UP or PAGEIOLATCH_EX will be used if the data page is being moved for a modification. Figure 9-22 shows the data page movement including latches and latch waits.

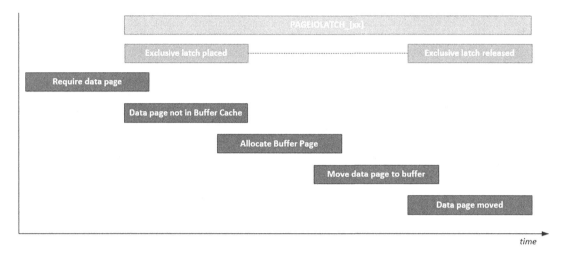

Figure 9-22. *Movement of data page*

To summarize the preceding section, if you see PAGEIOLATCH_[xx] waits occurring, it means your SQL Server instance is reading data from your storage subsystem into your buffer cache. Because this is a very common operation to perform, it is easy to see why the PAGEIOLATCH_[xx] wait type is one of the most common wait types on any SQL Server instance.

PAGEIOLATCH_[xx] Example

Creating an example for PAGEIOLATCH_[xx] waits is extremely easy – just run a SELECT query against a freshly restarted SQL Server instance. A restart of the SQL Server service will empty the buffer cache of all data pages. This will leave you with a buffer cache without any user data inside it. There is, however, another way to clear the buffer cache without needing to restart the SQL Server service. Running the DBCC DROPCLEANBUFFERS command will remove all the unmodified data pages from the buffer cache. Combining it with the CHECKPOINT command will ensure the modified pages are also written to disk, leaving you with an empty, or "cold," buffer cache.

The query in Listing 9-3 will perform a CHECKPOINT, followed by a DBCC DROPCLEANBUFFERS. It will then reset the sys.dm_os_wait_stats DMV and run a query against the GalacticWorks database. After the query against some of the tables inside the GalacticWorks database, we will query the sys.dm_os_wait_stats DMV for PAGEIOLATCH_[xx] waits.

Listing 9-3. Generate PAGEIOLATCH_SH waits

```
CHECKPOINT 1;
DBCC DROPCLEANBUFFERS;
DBCC SQLPERF('sys.dm_os_wait_stats', CLEAR);
SELECT
  SOD.SalesOrderID,
  SOD.CarrierTrackingNumber,
  SOH.CustomerID,
  C.AccountNumber,
  SOH.OrderDate,
  SOH.DueDate
FROM Sales.SalesOrderDetail SOD
INNER JOIN Sales.SalesOrderHeader SOH
ON SOD.SalesOrderID = SOH.SalesOrderID
INNER JOIN Sales.Customer C
ON SOH.CustomerID = C.CustomerID;

SELECT *
FROM sys.dm_os_wait_stats
WHERE wait_type LIKE 'PAGEIOLATCH_%';
```

Figure 9-23 shows the results of the last query against the sys.dm_os_wait_stats DMV on my test SQL Server instance.

	wait_type	waiting_tasks_count	wait_time_ms	max_wait_time_ms	signal_wait_time_ms
1	PAGEIOLATCH_NL	0	0	0	0
2	PAGEIOLATCH_KP	0	0	0	0
3	PAGEIOLATCH_SH	13	16	3	0
4	PAGEIOLATCH_UP	0	0	0	0
5	PAGEIOLATCH_EX	0	0	0	0
6	PAGEIOLATCH_DT	0	0	0	0

Figure 9-23. *PAGEIOLATCH_SH wait time information*

It makes sense to see only PAGEIOLATCH_SH waits recorded, since we are executing a SELECT query instead of performing data modification. If we were to perform some form of data modification against the rows, we would see PAGEIOLATCH_EX waits in the results.

Lowering PAGEIOLATCH_[xx] Waits

If you read the previous section, you would understand PAGEIOLATCH_[xx] waits are completely normal behavior inside SQL Server. In many cases, your databases are larger in size than the available amount of RAM inside your system, and some interaction with the storage subsystem is to be expected. Even if your databases are smaller than the amount of RAM in your system, and they can fit entirely inside the buffer cache, you will still notice PAGEIOLATCH_[xx] waits occurring during the startup of SQL Server, since this is the time SQL Server will start moving data pages from the storage subsystem into the buffer cache (if there is any query activity, SQL Server won't move data from the storage subsystem into the buffer cache by itself).

Since seeing PAGEIOLATCH_[xx] waits occur is completely normal for every SQL Server instance, it is important to maintain a baseline of the wait times (Chapter 4, "Building a Solid Baseline," can help you with that). When the wait times stay within the range of the baseline values for this wait type, there shouldn't be any cause for concern. If wait times are much higher than you expect them to be, investigation into the source of the higher-than-normal wait times might be necessary. There are quite a few possible causes for seeing higher-than-normal PAGEIOLATCH_[xx] wait times, and I will describe some of the more common ones.

The first place I look when noticing higher-than-normal PAGEIOLATCH_[xx] wait times is the SQL Server log to find out if SQL Server was restarted. SQL Server can restart due to a crash but also when a failover occurs. These events will cause high PAGEIOLATCH_[xx] wait times which might not be reflected in your baseline, especially since SQL Server restarts do not frequently occur. Since our baseline's measurements are calculated using average values, the PAGEIOLATCH_[xx] wait times during SQL Server startup are lower when more measurements are taken inside the average baseline. If you create your baseline on measurements taken between a specific time range, and SQL Server hasn't had a restart during the time range, your baseline measurements will also be considerably lower. As we read in the example section, a DBCC DROPCLEANBUFFERS will also remove data pages from the buffer cache, resulting in higher PAGEIOLATCH_[xx] wait times after the command completes.

Nerd Note   Sadly, unlike the DBCC FREEPROCCACHE command, the execution of the DBCC DROPCLEANBUFFERS command is not recorded in the SQL Server log.

One common piece of advice I see about lowering PAGEIOLATCH_[xx] wait times is to focus attention on the storage subsystem. Since the PAGEIOLATCH_[xx] wait type indicates data movement from your storage subsystem to your buffer cache, it is logical the storage subsystem plays a vital role in the wait times, but do not automatically assume this is the root cause! If you do have storage-related problems, this can show in the PAGEIOLATCH_[xx] wait time, so checking the performance of your storage subsystem is worth the effort.

A good place to start for monitoring storage performance is Perfmon. Perfmon has a variety of counters that will show you the current performance of your storage subsystem. Those in the following list are the ones I use the most when monitoring storage performance:

- **PhysicalDisk\Avg. Disk sec/Read** – This will show you the average read latency on the disk you are monitoring. Less latency is better, and as a general guideline, latency values should be below 20 milliseconds (0.020 within Perfmon, as it reports the latency in seconds).

- **PhysicalDisk\Avg. Disk sec/Write** – This will return the average write latency on the disk you are monitoring. Just like the read latency, write latency should, as a general guideline, be below 20 milliseconds.

- **PhysicalDisk\Disk Reads/sec** – This shows the amount of read IOPS (Input Output Operations) per second. This information can be helpful if you are running into capacity issues on the disk.

- **PhysicalDisk\Disk Writes/sec** – The same as the PhysicalDisk\Disk Reads/sec, but this one shows the amount of write IOPS.

- **PhysicalDisk\Disk Read Bytes/sec** – This counter shows the amount of bytes read from the disk per second. Again, this information can be useful for detecting possible capacity problems.

- **PhysicalDisk\Disk Write Bytes/sec** – This is identical to the PhysicalDisk\Disk Read Bytes/sec, but this counter shows the amount of bytes written to disk per second.

Using the information these Perfmon measurements provide, you should be able to identify possible storage-related bottlenecks. This information can also be helpful to the storage administrator (if there is one) who can compare these measurements to the measurements of the storage they manage.

Next to the performance of your storage subsystem, the behavior of your queries will impact the wait times of the PAGEIOLATCH_[xx] wait type. The more data your queries are requesting (and not already in the buffer cache), the larger the amount of data to be read from the storage subsystem into the buffer cache. For instance, if we were to modify the query of Listing 9-3 to be more selective so less data is returned, the amount of PAGEIOLATCH_[xx] wait time would also be less.

However, you don't always have the luxury of being able to modify every query so it is more selective. Maybe the queries are generated by an application and you can't modify them, or the queries simply need the large result set. Thankfully, as a DBA, we can also play a part in minimizing PAGEIOLATCH_[xx] wait times by performing database maintenance. Index fragmentation and out-of-date statistics also increase the PAGEIOLATCH_[xx] wait times drastically. If indexes are fragmented, more disk IOs need to take place to retrieve the data requested, which means IO latches will need to stay in place longer, which results in higher PAGEIOLATCH_[xx] wait times. Out-of-date statistics can also result in more disk IOs, because SQL Server expects a different number of rows to be returned instead of the actual number of rows. So, make sure you are performing index and statistics maintenance to limit the amount of disk interaction as small as possible.

The final area impacting PAGEIOLATCH_[xx] wait time is the memory of your system. SQL Server will remove data pages from inside the buffer cache if they have not been accessed within a specific time frame to free up room inside the buffer cache. The interval at which SQL Server performs this cleanup depends on the amount of data coming into the buffer cache and the amount of free space inside the buffer cache. If the request for data pages inside the buffer cache is very high, SQL Server will be forced to swap data pages accessed the least (or haven't been accessed for a while) for pages required now. This movement of data pages in and out of the buffer cache will result in more PAGEIOLATCH_[xx] waits. In an ideal world, your database would fit completely inside the buffer cache of your SQL Server instance. In this case, SQL Server will only need to move the data pages from the storage subsystem into the buffer cache once, where they will stay until SQL Server restarts again. Even though we do have access to very large amounts of RAM these days, in many cases we cannot simply fit our entire database into the buffer cache of our SQL Server instance, and some swapping of data pages from the buffer cache back to the storage subsystem can be expected. Adding more RAM to your system will increase the number of data pages the buffer cache stores and helps the buffer cache keep those pages in-memory longer.

There are two Perfmon counters to help you get some insight into the buffer cache usage: **SQLServer:Buffer Manager\Buffer cache hit ratio** and **SQLServer:Buffer Manager\Page life expectancy**. The SQLServer:Buffer Manager\Buffer cache hit ratio will show you what percentage of pages are located in the buffer cache and do not require a physical read on the storage subsystem. The SQLServer:Buffer Manager\Page life expectancy counter will show you the number of seconds a data page stays inside the buffer cache. If you see continuously low values on both these counters, compared to your baseline, it could mean SQL Server is running into memory pressure and needs to move data pages from the buffer cache back to disk again to free up memory.

These two counters are not perfect, though, and much has been written about their workings (and specifically their ideal values). Instead of viewing these values as separate entities, I prefer to combine them into what I call the "Buffer Pool IO Rate" metric. This is a measure of data pages being cycled through the buffer pool.

To get the Buffer Pool IO Rate, use the following code in Listing 9-4.

Listing 9-4. Buffer Pool IO Rate

```
SELECT counter_name, (1.0*cntr_value/128) /
(SELECT 1.0*cntr_value
FROM sys.dm_os_performance_counters
WHERE object_name like '%Buffer Manager%'
AND lower(counter_name) = 'Page life expectancy')
AS [BufferPoolRate]
FROM sys.dm_os_performance_counters
WHERE object_name like '%Buffer Manager%'
AND counter_name = 'Target pages';
```

It is not possible to tell you a defined "good" throughput rate, as it depends upon your system memory and workload. For example, a server with 56GB of RAM available for the buffer pool and if you want pages kept in the pool for an hour or so (3600 seconds), then we have 56000MB/3600sec, or about 15.5 MB/sec as a target throughput.

This is, again, why baselines are important. You will want to measure frequently for the IO rate and look for spikes.

PAGEIOLATCH_[xx] Summary

The PAGEIOLATCH_[xx] wait type is, by far, the most common latch-related wait type. Together with the CXPACKET wait type, the PAGEIOLATCH_[xx] wait type is probably the most common wait type on any SQL Server instance. The PAGEIOLATCH_[xx] wait type is directly related to the movement of data pages on the storage subsystem into the buffer cache memory of your SQL Server instance. SQL Server uses the buffer cache to minimize the number of interactions to the (much slower) storage subsystem so as to maximize performance. Whenever a data page is read into the buffer cache, the PAGEIOLATCH_[xx] wait type will be recorded for the time it took to do so. There are many methods available to lower the amount of PAGEIOLATCH_[xx] wait time. The frequently advised "get faster storage" doesn't always hold true, even though fast storage will indeed directly influence the PAGEIOLATCH_[xx] wait times. Optimizing queries so they require fewer data pages to be moved to the buffer cache, performing maintenance on indexes and statistics, and analyzing memory performance could all lead to lower PAGEIOLATCH_[xx] wait times.

CHAPTER 10

High-Availability and Disaster-Recovery Wait Types

SQL Server has provided several options for high availability and disaster recovery. Just like with performing regular database backups to ensure you can revert to a previous state of your database should a crash or data corruption occur, planning and maintaining highly available database environments is part of the job of a database administrator (or site reliability engineer).

As the need for highly available database servers grows, many DBAs find themselves managing SQL Server instances inside a high-availability solution, like AlwaysOn Availability Groups, or a disaster-recovery configuration, like log shipping. With these types of SQL Server high-availability and disaster-recovery configurations comes a group of dedicated wait types directly related to the health of your high-availability and disaster-recovery (HA/DR) configuration.

In this chapter, we will look at some of the common wait types in HA/DR configurations. The main focus of the wait types inside this chapter are AlwaysOn Availability Groups, because Microsoft is deprecating many of the previous installments of features (such as database mirroring) which now fall under the name AlwaysOn Availability Groups. As an exception to this rule, I selected one mirroring-related wait type which is relatively common on highly used mirroring configurations. All the other wait types are related to AlwaysOn Availability Groups.

For the examples inside this chapter, I used several virtual machines to create a mirroring and an AlwaysOn Availability Group configuration. The configuration of these VMs can be found in Appendix I, "Example SQL Server Machine Configurations."

© Thomas LaRock, Enrico van de Laar 2023
T. LaRock and E. van de Laar, *Pro SQL Server 2022 Wait Statistics*,
https://doi.org/10.1007/978-1-4842-8771-2_10

DBMIRROR_SEND

The first wait type in this chapter is the **DBMIRROR_SEND** wait type. As you might suspect from the name, DBMIRROR_SEND is related to database mirroring.

Database mirroring is a feature introduced in SQL Server 2005 but was deprecated with SQL Server 2012. This doesn't mean you cannot use database mirroring in SQL Server, but it does mean it is scheduled for removal. The entire feature will be replaced with AlwaysOn Availability Group, which offers the same configuration options as database mirroring.

Database mirroring is a solution which increases the availability of SQL Server databases, and unlike failover clustering, it can be configured on a per-database basis. Database mirroring works by redoing every data modification operation which occurs on the primary database (called the *principal* in database mirroring terms) on the mirror database. The redoing of every database modification operation is achieved by streaming active transaction log records to the mirror server, which perform the operations on the mirror database in the sequence in which they were inserted into the transaction log on the principal database.

Database mirroring offers two different operating modes which impact the availability and performance of the mirror configuration: synchronous (or high-safety) mode and asynchronous (or high-performance) mode. Even though both modes perform identical actions to ensure data modification operations are also performed on the mirror database, there can be a large difference in performance and thus in waits occurring.

The synchronous mirror mode makes sure every data modification action performed on the principal is also directly performed on the mirror. It does this by waiting on sending a transaction confirmation message to the client until the transaction is successfully written to disk on the mirror. Figure 10-1 depicts synchronous mirroring.

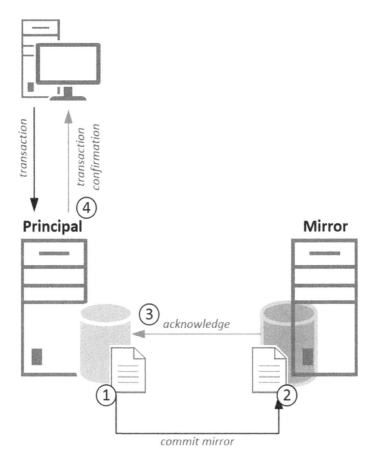

Figure 10-1. *Synchronous mirroring*

Even though synchronous mirroring makes sure data on the principal and mirror are 100% identical, it comes with a few drawbacks. One of those is the performance of your database inside a synchronous mirroring configuration is highly dependent on the speed the mirror can process data modification operations, since every transaction has to be committed on the mirror first.

The flow of a data modification transaction is described in the steps that follow:

1. When the transaction is received, the principal will write the transaction to the transaction log, but the transaction is not yet committed.

2. The principal will send the log record to the mirror.

3. The mirror will harden the log record to disk and send an acknowledgment to the principal.

4. After the principal receives the acknowledgment, it will send a confirmation message to the client showing the transaction was completed, and the transaction gets committed to the transaction log on the principal.

The asynchronous mode works in much the same way; the exception is it will not wait on an acknowledgment message from the mirror before sending the transaction confirmation message to the client. This means transactions are committed to disk on the principal before they are written to disk on the mirror. Using asynchronous mirroring will improve mirror performance, since the latency overhead of synchronous mirroring is removed. The trade-off for this increase in performance is that asynchronous replication can lead to data loss in the case of a disaster, since it is possible that transactions were not yet committed on the mirror. Figure 10-2 shows the transaction log flow on an asynchronous mirror; the dotted lines indicate the actions are not performed directly.

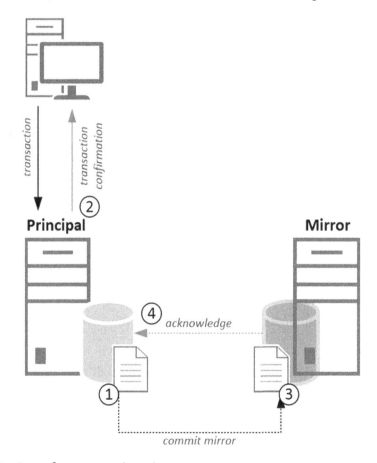

Figure 10-2. *Asynchronous mirroring*

What Is the DBMIRROR_SEND Wait Type?

The DBMIRROR_SEND wait type is most frequently related to synchronous mirroring configurations. The description of the DBMIRROR_SEND wait type on Books Online is "Occurs when a task is waiting for a communications backlog at the network layer to clear to be able to send messages. Indicates that the communications layer is starting to become overloaded and affect the database mirroring data throughput." In this case, the Books Online definition is quite descriptive, but the network is not the only thing to impact DBMIRROR_SEND wait times. Having a slow disk subsystem connected to the mirror database will also lead to an increase in DBMIRROR_SEND wait times.

Another important point to remember is high DBMIRROR_SEND wait times will frequently only be recorded on the mirror instance, and not on the principal. It is common to see waits occur on the DBMIRROR_SEND wait type on both the principal and the mirror, but these will normally be lower on the principal. They can still reach high values on the mirror since, generally, there is always some latency between both SQL Server instances. Because of expected latency, I advise you to use baseline measurements to identify higher-than-normal wait times for the DBMIRROR_SEND wait type.

DBMIRROR_SEND Example

For this example, I have built a synchronous mirror between two of my test SQL Server instances, using the GalacticWorks database as the database mirrored between both instances.

Inside the GalacticWorks database, I create a simple table using the script in Listing 10-1.

Listing 10-1. Create the Mirror_Test table

```
USE [GalacticWorks];
CREATE TABLE Mirror_Test
  (ID UNIQUEIDENTIFIER PRIMARY KEY,
  RandomData VARCHAR(50));
```

After the table is created, I clear the sys.dm_os_wait_stats DMV and insert 10,000 rows into the Mirror_Test table using the query in Listing 10-2. I also make sure to clear the sys. dm_os_wait_stats DMV on the mirror as well before running the script in Listing 10-2.

Listing 10-2. Insert 10,000 rows into Mirror_Test table

```
DBCC SQLPERF('sys.dm_os_wait_stats', 'CLEAR');
INSERT INTO Mirror_Test
  (ID,
  RandomData)
VALUES
  (NEWID(),
  CONVERT(VARCHAR(50), NEWID()))
GO 10000
```

While the script is running, I look at the DBMIRROR_SEND wait times on both the mirror and the principal using the following query:

```
SELECT *
FROM sys.dm_os_wait_stats
WHERE wait_type = 'DBMIRROR_SEND'
```

The results of this query can be seen in Figure 10-3, which shows the DBMIRROR_SEND wait times on the mirror. Figure 10-4 shows the DBMIRROR_SEND wait times on the principal server.

	wait_type	waiting_tasks_count	wait_time_ms	max_wait_time_ms	signal_wait_time_ms
1	DBMIRROR_SEND	21072	81309	57119	187

Figure 10-3. *DBMIRROR_SEND wait times on the mirror*

	wait_type	waiting_tasks_count	wait_time_ms	max_wait_time_ms	signal_wait_time_ms
1	DBMIRROR_SEND	0	0	0	0

Figure 10-4. *DBMIRROR_SEND wait times on the principal*

As you can see, we spend quite some time waiting on the DBMIRROR_SEND wait type on the mirror vs. no DBMIRROR_SEND waits on the principal.

Lowering DBMIRROR_SEND Waits

One common piece of advice for lowering DBMIRROR_SEND wait time is changing the mirror mode from synchronous (high-safety) to asynchronous (high-performance). While this will lower the DBMIRROR_SEND wait time, it also means you can potentially lose data when a disaster occurs on the principal. Lowering the wait time for the DBMIRROR_SEND wait type will have a positive effect on the duration of your queries. For instance, in the example in the previous section, the insert of 10,000 rows took around 30 seconds on my test SQL Server mirror configuration. When I changed the mirror mode from synchronous to asynchronous, not only did the wait times on the DBMIRROR_SEND wait type go down, but the total execution time of 10,000 inserts went down to 3 seconds. That's an improvement of almost 30 seconds!

While this improvement might sound attractive, changing the mirror mode is not always an option. For instance, your company's disaster-recovery strategy can require a synchronous mirror configuration. Changing the mirror mode from synchronous to asynchronous should, in my opinion, be the last option (if it is a viable option). There are other resources which influence DBMIRROR_SEND wait times, like the storage configuration on the mirror or the network connection between the principal and mirror SQL Server instances. Both resources act like a bottleneck between instances, contributing to the DBMIRROR_SEND wait time.

SQL Server also has a database mirroring monitor providing the status about the mirroring configuration. You can find the database mirroring monitor by right-clicking the database that is part of a mirror, selecting Tasks ➤ Database Mirroring Monitor. Figure 10-5 shows the monitor against my test mirror configuration.

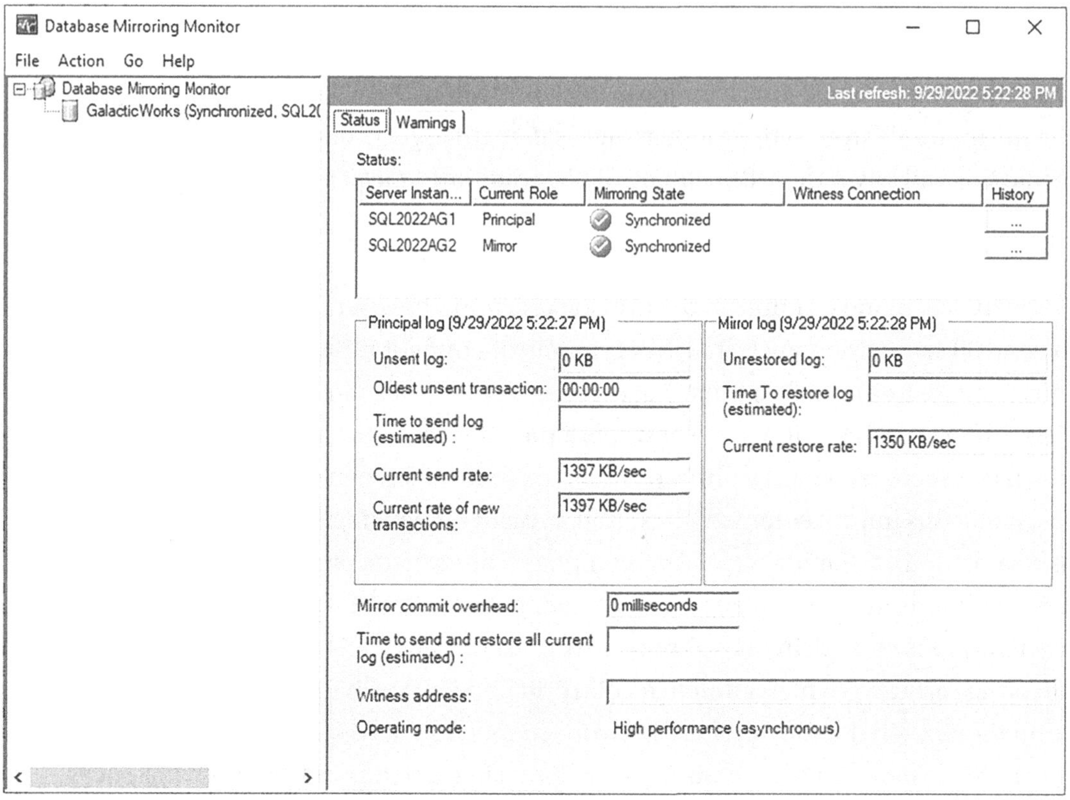

Figure 10-5. *Database mirroring monitor*

As you see, the database mirroring monitor provides some very interesting additional information like the volume of log records still needing to be sent or restored, how far behind the mirror currently is, and the send and restore rates. In many of my dealings with database mirroring, the database mirroring monitor is the first place I'll check when there are performance issues involving the mirror configuration.

DBMIRROR_SEND Summary

The DBMIRROR_SEND wait type is directly related to database mirroring. Seeing DBMIRROR_SEND waits occur is pretty normal on most mirror configurations. This makes using a baseline to identify wait time spikes a necessity. The mirroring mode plays a huge part in the DBMIRROR_SEND wait times. When using synchronous mirroring, DBMIRROR_SEND wait times will frequently be higher than when using asynchronous mirroring. Not only the mirroring mode influences DBMIRROR_SEND

280

wait times, though. Having a storage subsystem on the mirror SQL Server instance which cannot keep up with the load will have an effect on DBMIRROR_SEND waits, just like the network connection between the principal and the mirror.

HADR_LOGCAPTURE_WAIT and HADR_WORK_QUEUE

The **HADR_LOGCAPTURE_WAIT** and **HADR_WORK_QUEUE** wait types are both related to AlwaysOn Availability Groups. All wait types related to AlwaysOn can easily be identified by the HADR_ prefix in the wait type name. AlwaysOn Availability Groups were introduced in SQL Server 2012 as a replacement for various SQL Server high-availability and disaster-recovery features such as replication, log shipping, and database mirroring. There are quite a few different wait types associated with AlwaysOn, totaling 70 in SQL Server 2022. Not all of them indicate performance problems somewhere in your AlwaysOn configuration. The HADR_LOGCAPTURE_WAIT and HADR_WORK_QUEUE are both perfect examples of benign wait types which occur naturally over time and do not directly indicate a performance problem. Since both these wait types have high wait times associated with them on every AlwaysOn configuration, and are thus very common, I wanted to include them in this chapter to help you better understand what function they have.

What Are the HADR_LOGCAPTURE_WAIT and HADR_WORK_QUEUE Wait Types?

As I mentioned in the preceding section, both the HADR_LOGCAPTURE_WAIT and HADR_WORK_QUEUE wait types occur in AlwaysOn configurations. They occur in different places inside your AlwaysOn configuration and have slightly different functions.

According to Books Online, the HADR_LOGCAPTURE_WAIT wait type indicates that SQL Server is "waiting for log records to become available. Can occur either when waiting for new log records to be generated by connections or for I/O completion when reading log not in the cache. This is an expected wait if the log scan is caught up to the end of log or is reading from disk." The HADR_LOGCAPTURE_WAIT wait type occurs on the SQL Server hosting the primary database inside an AlwaysOn Availability Group. Think of the primary database as the principal inside a database mirroring configuration.

AlwaysOn Availability uses a similar log transport mechanism as database mirroring and also provides two different modes (called Availability modes inside AlwaysOn): Synchronous-commit and Asynchronous-commit. Both these Availability modes work in the same way as their database mirroring counterparts we were discussing earlier in this chapter do. This means in Synchronous-commit mode, the primary replica waits to commit transactions to the transaction log until the secondary replica has completed its own log hardening, while in Asynchronous-commit mode, the primary replica will directly commit the transaction to the transaction log without waiting for a confirmation from the secondary replica.

While the primary replica is waiting for work, SQL Server will record the time it has spent on waiting for new transactions to become available as the HADR_LOGCAPTURE_WAIT wait type. High wait times on the HADR_LOGCAPTURE_WAIT wait type means that SQL Server is waiting on new transactions to become available so they can be transferred to the secondary replica. This is not dependent on the Availability mode you configured for your AlwaysOn Availability Group. The HADR_LOGCAPTURE_WAIT wait type will always occur, no matter your AlwaysOn configuration. Figure 10-6 shows an AlwaysOn Availability Group configuration together with the HADR_LOGCAPTURE_WAIT wait type on the primary replica, which occurs while waiting for new transactions to be sent to the secondary replica.

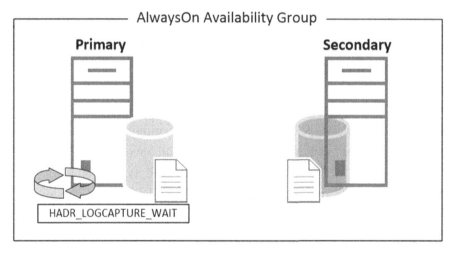

Figure 10-6. *AlwaysOn Availability Group and the HADR_LOGCAPTURE_WAIT wait type*

Even though I placed the HADR_LOGCAPTURE_WAIT wait type on the primary replica in Figure 10-6, it will also log the HADR_LOGCAPTURE_WAIT wait type on the secondary replica, although those values will normally be much lower than on the primary replica.

The HADR_WORK_QUEUE wait type is almost identical in function to the HADR_LOGCAPTURE_WAIT wait type. Books Online gives an excellent description of this wait type: "AlwaysOn Availability Groups' background worker thread waiting for new work to be assigned. This is an expected wait when there are ready workers waiting for new work, which is the normal state." The main difference between both wait types is the HADR_LOGCAPTURE_WAIT wait type is dedicated to waiting until new transactions become available, while the HADR_WORK_QUEUE indicates free threads waiting for work. Just like the HADR_LOGCAPTURE_WAIT wait type, the HADR_WORK_QUEUE occurs on both the primary and the secondary replicas, but the HADR_WORK_QUEUE wait type is much more prevalent on both replicas. As a matter of fact, the HADR_WORK_QUEUE wait type will frequently be the top AlwaysOn-related wait type on every SQL Server that is part of an AlwaysOn Availability Group, especially if the workload is low.

Figure 10-7 shows an AlwaysOn Availability Group like the one in Figure 10-6, but this time I added the HADR_WORK_QUEUE wait type to the image as well.

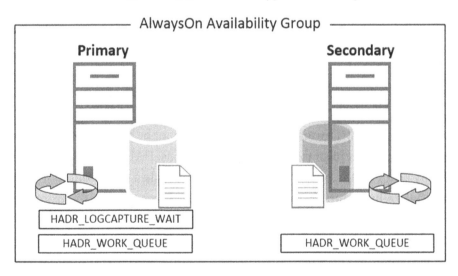

Figure 10-7. *HADR_LOGCAPTURE_WAIT and HADR_WORK_QUEUE wait types*

Since both the HADR_LOGCAPTURE_WAIT and HADR_WORK_QUEUE wait types occur naturally over time, I did not include an example of both the wait types. Also, because both these wait types are not directly related to performance problems, there is no use including a section on lowering the wait times of both these wait types.

HADR_LOGCAPTURE_WAIT and HADR_WORK_QUEUE Summary

Both the HADR_LOGCAPTURE_WAIT and HADR_WORK_QUEUE wait types are benign wait types that occur on every SQL Server that is part of an AlwaysOn Availability Group. Because the HADR_LOGCAPTURE_WAIT and HADR_WORK_QUEUE wait types are not directly related to performance problems, there is no direct need to focus attention on lowering them, and they can, in most cases, be safely ignored.

HADR_SYNC_COMMIT

The **HADR_SYNC_COMMIT** wait type is another AlwaysOn-related wait introduced with SQL Server 2012. In many ways, the HADR_SYNC_COMMIT wait type closely resembles the DBMIRROR_SEND discussed earlier in this chapter. There are some differences, however, between both wait types, which we will discuss in the following section.

What Is the HADR_SYNC_COMMIT Wait Type?

The HADR_SYNC_COMMIT wait type indicates the time the primary replica spends waiting for a secondary replica to harden the log records. HADR_SYNC_COMMIT waits will only occur on the primary replica and only inside a synchronous-replication AlwaysOn Availability Group. As soon as a transaction is received by the primary replica and is sent to the secondary replica for hardening, the HADR_SYNC_COMMIT wait time will start recording. The HADR_SYNC_COMMIT wait time will only stop recording when the secondary replica has sent its confirmation the write to the secondary's transaction log was completed. Figure 10-8 shows the HADR_SYNC_COMMIT wait time generation inside a timeline.

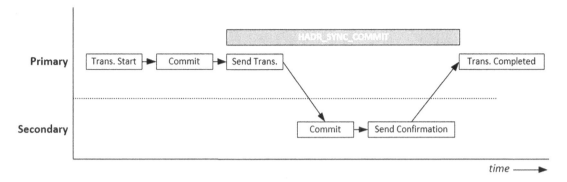

Figure 10-8. *HADR_SYNC_COMMIT and synchronous replication*

Since the HADR_SYNC_COMMIT wait type will always occur in every synchronous AlwaysOn Availability Group, it is normal to expect a certain amount of wait time. But just like the DBMIRROR_SEND wait type, the wait time of the HADR_SYNC_COMMIT wait type is highly dependent on the speed at which the secondary replica can process the log records. This means that a slow network connection between both replicas or the performance of the storage subsystem on the secondary replica can impact HADR_SYNC_COMMIT wait times. For this reason, it is important to understand what the normal wait times for the HADR_SYNC_COMMIT wait type are for your AlwaysOn configuration so you can identify higher-than-normal wait times easily.

HADR_SYNC_COMMIT Example

For this example, I have built an AlwaysOn Availability Group configured to use synchronous replication. The configuration of the test machines is found in Appendix I, "Example SQL Server Machine Configuration." I won't go into detail on how to configure an AlwaysOn Availability Group, as there is plenty of information available on the Internet to help you configure AlwaysOn. A good starting point is the "Getting Started with AlwaysOn Availability Groups" article on Books Online, which you can find here: https://slrwnds.com/yowojf. I used the GalacticWorks database as the database replicated inside my AlwaysOn Availability Group.

After configuring my AlwaysOn Availability Group, I added an extra table named AO_Test to the GalacticWorks database using the script in Listing 10-3.

Listing 10-3. Create AO_Test table

```
USE [GalacticWorks];
CREATE TABLE AO_Test
  (ID UNIQUEIDENTIFIER PRIMARY KEY,
  RandomData VARCHAR(50));
```

After the table is created, I clear and then query the sys.dm_os_wait_stats DMV to check the current wait times on the HADR_SYNC_COMMIT wait time on both the primary and secondary replicas using the following query:

```
SELECT *
FROM sys.dm_os_wait_stats
WHERE wait_type = 'HADR_SYNC_COMMIT';
```

Even after waiting for a couple of minutes, the wait time of the HADR_SYNC_ COMMIT wait type stays 0, as you can see in Figure 10-9. This is what I expected since we have not performed any data modifications on the primary replica so far.

	wait_type	waiting_tasks_count	wait_time_ms	max_wait_time_ms	signal_wait_time_ms
1	HADR_SYNC_COMMIT	0	0	0	0

Figure 10-9. *HADR_SYNC_COMMIT wait information during no activity on both the primary and the secondary mode*

This is different compared to HADR_LOGCAPTURE_WAIT and HADR_WORK_ QUEUE, which will accumulate wait times even though (or because) there is no user activity inside the AlwaysOn Availability Group.

Now with the table in place, let's generate some transactions by performing a number of inserts. The script in Listing 10-4 will insert 10,000 rows into the AO_Test table we created earlier.

Listing 10-4. Insert 10,000 rows into the AO_Test table

```
INSERT INTO AO_Test
  (ID,
  RandomData)
VALUES
  (NEWID(),
```

```
CONVERT(VARCHAR(50), NEWID()))
GO 10000
```

When the script in Listing 10-4 has completed, I check the wait statistics information inside the sys.dm_os_wait_stats DMV again on both the primary and secondary replicas. Figure 10-10 shows the results of this query on the primary, and Figure 10-11 on the secondary.

	wait_type	waiting_tasks_count	wait_time_ms	max_wait_time_ms	signal_wait_time_ms
1	HADR_SYNC_COMMIT	10000	15695	7	156

Figure 10-10. *HADR_SYNC_COMMIT waits on the primary replica*

	wait_type	waiting_tasks_count	wait_time_ms	max_wait_time_ms	signal_wait_time_ms
1	HADR_SYNC_COMMIT	0	0	0	0

Figure 10-11. *HADR_SYNC_COMMIT waits on the secondary replica*

The first thing you will notice when looking at both figures is the HADR_SYNC_COMMIT waits occur only on the primary replica and not on the secondary, which is expected behavior. The second interesting thing is the number of waits. This so happens to be the exact same amount as the number of rows inserted. Again, this is expected behavior. Since we performed a single insert and repeated it 10,000 times, every insert generated a single transaction log record to be replicated.

Nerd Note   While we did 10,000 single inserts, if you recreate the demo, it is possible to have less than 10,000 waiting tasks count due to network latency and storage speeds.

Using the number of waits and the wait time, it is possible to calculate the average time it took for one insert operation to be committed on the replica. In this case, it is 1.57 milliseconds (15695/10000) which is a pretty decent value.

Lowering HADR_SYNC_COMMIT Waits

Seeing HADR_SYNC_COMMIT waits occur does not necessarily mean there is a problem. HADR_SYNC_COMMIT waits will always occur whenever there are data modifications performed on your primary replica. They can indicate a problem if the wait times are much higher than your baseline measurements.

Changing the AlwaysOn operation mode to asynchronous replication will remove HADR_SYNC_COMMIT waits, but at the risk of losing data when a disaster occurs. Also, to reach your company's disaster-recovery or high-availability needs, you frequently do not have the luxury of just changing the AlwaysOn operating mode, and I advise you not to change it just to lower HADR_SYNC_COMMIT wait times.

Thankfully, there are many different methods you can use to monitor the performance of your AlwaysOn Availability Group, including the AlwaysOn Dashboard, DMVs, and Perfmon counters.

You view the AlwaysOn Dashboard by right-clicking your AlwaysOn Availability Group and selecting the "Show Dashboard" option. The AlwaysOn Dashboard, by default, gives you some general information, like the servers inside the Availability Group and the synchronization state, about your AlwaysOn Availability Group, as shown in Figure 10-12.

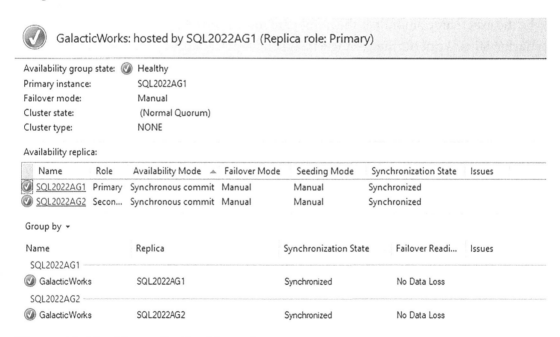

Figure 10-12. AlwaysOn Dashboard

The default view of the AlwaysOn Dashboard doesn't provide much information for troubleshooting. Thankfully, you are able to configure the view to suit your own needs by right-clicking the column bars and selecting the information you are interested in, as shown in Figure 10-13.

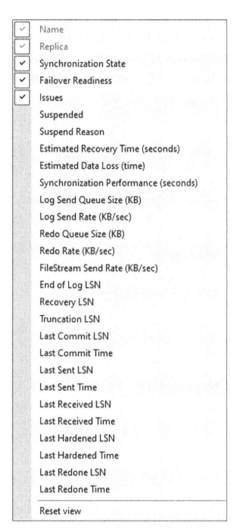

Figure 10-13. *AlwaysOn adding columns*

There are many interesting columns for troubleshooting synchronization issues, and I recommend taking the time to understand them to determine which columns are most applicable to your situation.

The information shown by the AlwaysOn Dashboard is originally recorded inside various AlwaysOn-related DMVs. This makes it possible to query this information yourself. All of the AlwaysOn-related DMVs are identified by the **dm_hadr** prefix in the DMV name, like the sys.dm_hadr_database_replica_states DMV contains a large part of the information you can access inside the AlwaysOn Dashboard.

Next to the AlwaysOn and DMVs that are related to AlwaysOn, there are Perfmon counters for AlwaysOn performance. These counters are grouped in the Perfmon **SQLServer:Availability Replica** and **SQLServer:Database Replica** groups. Figure 10-14 shows a part of the counters available in the SQLServer:Database Replica group.

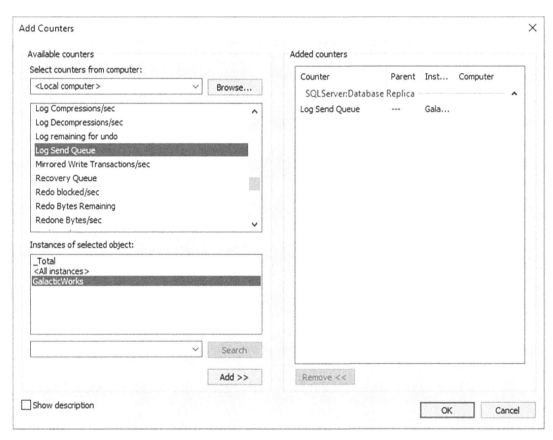

Figure 10-14. *Perfmon counters related to AlwaysOn*

As you have read so far, there are plenty of options available to you for analyzing the AlwaysOn performance between replicas.

Using the information from the various sources, you can check the general health of your AlwaysOn Availability Group. You then combine this information with other metrics for things impacting the performance of your secondary replica, like the performance of your storage subsystem and your network connection. Since the HADR_SYNC_COMMIT wait type is strictly related to the secondary replica, you should focus your analysis on the SQL Server hosting the secondary replica. For instance, if your storage subsystem cannot keep up with the number of transactions that need to be committed on the secondary replica, you will notice this in higher HADR_SYNC_COMMIT wait times and also in the various counters inside the AlwaysOn Dashboard, DMVs, or Perfmon.

It is difficult to give a general recommendation on how to lower HADR_SYNC_COMMIT wait times since they are highly dependent on variables and also depend on your workload. When you have a workload consisting of a large number of read queries, you will notice lower HADR_SYNC_COMMIT wait times than workloads performing many data modification operations. This means analyzing and optimizing your query workload can also contribute to the lowering of HADR_SYNC_COMMIT wait times.

HADR_SYNC_COMMIT Summary

The HADR_SYNC_COMMIT wait type will only occur on AlwaysOn Availability Groups consisting of replicas configured to use the synchronous-replication mode. The HADR_SYNC_COMMIT wait type will give you insight on how long it took for the secondary replica to commit the transaction to disk. Since the HADR_SYNC_COMMIT will always record wait times inside synchronous replication, you should only worry about the wait times when they are far higher than expected. Thankfully, there are various methods available to you to analyze the performance of your AlwaysOn Availability Group, including an AlwaysOn Dashboard, DMVs, and Perfmon counters.

Since the performance of the secondary replica has the largest impact on the HADR_SYNC_COMMIT wait times, your attention should focus on the secondary replica when troubleshooting this wait type. The storage subsystem and network connection both play a large role in the speed at which the secondary replica can write log records to its transaction log. Your workload also impacts HADR_SYNC_COMMIT wait times, and optimizing it so data modifications are better spread out will result in lower HADR_SYNC_COMMIT wait times.

REDO_THREAD_PENDING_WORK

The last wait type in this chapter is the **REDO_THREAD_PENDING_WORK** wait type. And even though it misses the characteristic HADR_ prefix identifying AlwaysOn-related wait types, it is related to AlwaysOn. The REDO_THREAD_PENDING_WORK wait type is, just like the HADR_LOGCAPTURE_WAIT and HADR_WORK_QUEUE wait types, a wait type accumulating over time when there is no work to be done. And just like the HADR_LOGCAPTURE_WAIT and HADR_WORK_QUEUE wait types, in most cases, it can be ignored since it does not indicate a performance problem.

Even though this is a wait type safely ignored in 99% of the cases, I wanted to include it in this chapter for two reasons. It is usually one of the top wait types on an AlwaysOn Availability Group secondary replica, and understanding its related process inside SQL Server will give you a better understanding of the inner workings of AlwaysOn.

What Is the REDO_THREAD_PENDING_WORK Wait Type?

The REDO_THREAD_PENDING_WORK wait type is related to a process which occurs only on the secondary replica inside an AlwaysOn Availability Group, the Redo Thread.

Up to this point in the chapter, we discussed how the secondary replica inside an AlwaysOn Availability Group processes log records, hardens them to its own transaction log, and sends a confirmation to the primary replica. When using synchronous replication, the primary replica will wait before sending a transaction complete message to the client which started the transaction, and when using asynchronous replication, the message is sent without waiting for the hardening on the secondary. But until now, we haven't discussed the process of performing the modifications inside the secondary database described in the log records. This is where the Redo Thread on the secondary comes in. This thread is responsible for performing the data modifications recorded in the log records the primary replica sent. There is one important concept associated with the Redo Thread: it does not impact the commit confirmation from the secondary replica. This means the Redo Thread might be performing work long after the transaction has been communicated as committed to the client (both the primary and secondary replica have hardened the log record, and the AlwaysOn Availability Group has the synchronized status).

This means even though your AlwaysOn Availability Group is synchronized, the data inside the secondary database is not necessarily identical to the primary database. This matters less than you might think, because the secondary hardened the log records to its own transaction log on disk, and it has all the information it needs to perform the redo operation. Transactions will not be lost if a failure occurs on the primary since the secondary has all the transactions performed in its own transaction log and can redo all the transactions. This works much the same as a standalone SQL Server instance where transactions are also hardened to disk first before data is actually changed. If SQL Server were to crash in this situation, SQL Server would use the transaction log to redo or undo the data modifications. Figure 10-15 shows an example of synchronous replication together with the Redo Thread. Note that the Redo Thread is a separate operation and does not impact the duration of the transaction complete message.

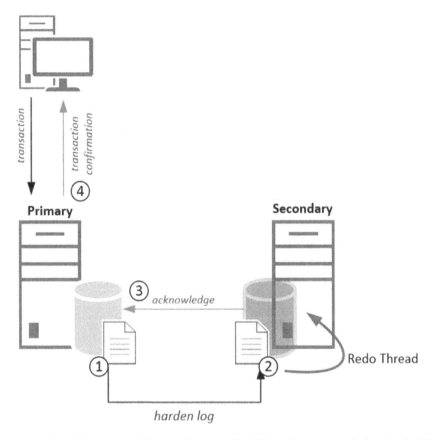

Figure 10-15. *Synchronous AlwaysOn Availability Group and the Redo Thread*

While the Redo Thread is waiting for work to arrive, it will record the time it is inactive as wait time on the REDO_THREAD_PENDING_WORK wait type. This will occur on both synchronous and asynchronous-replication modes, but only on the secondary replica.

Because the wait indicates the Redo Thread is not performing any work, it can, save for extremely rare cases, be safely ignored. And because the wait time for the REDO_THREAD_PENDING_WORK wait type will accumulate naturally when there is no work to be done, there is no need to write an example demonstrating the wait type. A simple query to retrieve REDO_THREAD_PENDING_WORK wait type information against the sys.dm_os_wait_stats DMV on a secondary replica will show you that the wait time increases, especially when there is no user activity against the AlwaysOn Availability Group, as shown in Figure 10-16.

	wait_type	waiting_tasks_count	wait_time_ms	max_wait_time_ms	signal_wait_time_ms
1	REDO_THREAD_PENDING_WORK	47179	4977971	148	1675

Figure 10-16. *REDO_THREAD_PENDING_WORK wait information*

REDO_THREAD_PENDING_WORK Summary

The REDO_THREAD_PENDING_WORK wait type is an AlwaysOn-related wait type which accumulates wait time naturally over time when there is no data modification activity against an AlwaysOn Availability Group. The REDO_THREAD_PENDING_WORK wait type is related to the Redo Thread on the secondary replica inside an AlwaysOn Availability Group, and it indicates that the Redo Thread is currently waiting for work. Since this wait type will occur on every secondary replica, especially when there is minimal to no user data modification occurring, it can safely be ignored.

CHAPTER 11

Preemptive Wait Types

In Chapter 1, "Wait Statistics Internals," we reviewed SQL Server's non-preemptive scheduling model used for thread scheduling and management. Unlike SQL Server, the Windows operating system uses *preemptive* scheduling to schedule and manage threads. Sometimes, SQL Server has to use Windows functions to perform specific actions through the operating system, for instance, when checking Active Directory permissions. When this occurs, SQL Server will ask for a thread from the Windows operating system, outside of SQL Server, thus making it impossible for SQL Server to manage that thread. While SQL Server is waiting for the preemptive thread inside the operating system to complete, SQL Server will record a wait on a preemptive wait type.

There are many different preemptive wait types inside SQL Server; at the time of writing this book, SQL Server 2022 has 240 different preemptive wait types. The preemptive wait type recorded when a thread is requested outside SQL Server depends on the function the thread is accessing. Each of the preemptive wait types inside SQL Server represents a different Windows function (save for some exceptions which act as a catch-all wait type for different functions), and in many cases, the name of the wait type is identical to the name of the Windows function. This is helpful because you can search for the specific Windows function on MSDN and learn what the function does. If you know what the function does, you also know why, or on what, SQL Server is waiting. For example, if you notice high wait times on the PREEMPTIVE_OS_WRITEFILEGATHER wait type, you can remove the PREEMPTIVE_OS_ part and search MSDN for the WRITEFILEGATHER function. Figure 11-1 shows the result for the WRITEFILEGATHER function.

© Thomas LaRock, Enrico van de Laar 2023
T. LaRock and E. van de Laar, *Pro SQL Server 2022 Wait Statistics*,
https://doi.org/10.1007/978-1-4842-8771-2_11

Windows / Apps / Win32 / API / Data Access and Storage / Fileapi.h /

WriteFileGather function (fileapi.h)

Article • 06/01/2022 • 4 minutes to read

Retrieves data from an array of buffers and writes the data to a file.

The function starts writing data to the file at a position that is specified by an OVERLAPPED structure. The **WriteFileGather** function operates asynchronously.

Figure 11-1. *WriteFileGather Windows function*

By reading the article, we learn a lot about this function; apparently this function is used when writing data to a file and has to occur outside SQL Server. I won't spoil anything else here, since we will go into more detail about the PREEMPTIVE_OS_ WRITEFILEGATHER wait type a bit further down in this chapter.

I won't describe every possible preemptive wait type in this chapter, since there are simply too many of them. Instead I have focused on the most common preemptive wait types. If you run into a preemptive wait type not discussed in detail in this chapter, I suggest you use the preceding method to find more information about the Windows function on MSDN. Hopefully, the information can help you figure out why the wait is occurring.

SQL Server on Linux

Starting with SQL Server 2017, SQL Server is no longer limited to the Microsoft Windows operating system. In a revolutionary announcement in March of 2016, Microsoft announced the next release of SQL Server (2017) would also be available on Linux. Needless to say, the announcement stirred up quite a bit of dust as it was something nobody would ever expect to happen.

The reason why support of SQL Server on Linux is important are preemptive waits occuring inside SQL Server are platform independent. Meaning calls to functions available in the Windows operating system are recorded when looking at the wait statistics of a SQL-on-Linux instance. The reason why has everything to do with the underlying technology Microsoft used to bring SQL Server to Linux.

To make SQL Server run on Linux, Microsoft adopted a concept called a Platform Abstraction Layer (or PAL for short). The idea of PAL is to separate the code needed to execute SQL Server with the code needed to interact with the operating system. Without PAL, rewriting SQL Server to run on Linux would take enormous amounts of time due to all the operating system dependencies. So the SQL Server team looked for different approaches to resolve this issue and found its answer in a Microsoft research project called Drawbridge. The definition of Drawbridge can be found on its project page at `https://slrwnds.com/izvn8c` and reads

> *Drawbridge is a research prototype of a new form of virtualization for application sandboxing. Drawbridge combines two core technologies: First, a picoprocess, which is a process-based isolation container with a minimal kernel API surface. Second, a library OS, which is a version of Windows enlightened to run efficiently within a picoprocess.*

The main part which attracted the SQL Server team to the Drawbridge project was the Library OS technology. This technology could handle a wide variety of Windows operating system calls and translate them to the operating system of the host, which in this case is Linux. Now, the SQL Server team did not adapt the Drawbridge technology one-on-one as there were some challenges involved with the research project. One of them was the research project itself was officially completed, and there was no support on the project. Another one was a large overlap of technologies inside the SQL Server OS (SOS) and Drawbridge. Both solutions have their own functionalities to handle memory management and threading/scheduling. It was decided to merge the SQL Server OS and Drawbridge into a new platform layer called the SQLPAL (SQL Platform Abstraction Layer). Using SQLPAL, the SQL Server team can develop code as they have always done and leave the translation of operating system calls to SQLPAL. Figure 11-2 shows the interaction between the various layers while running SQL Server on Linux.

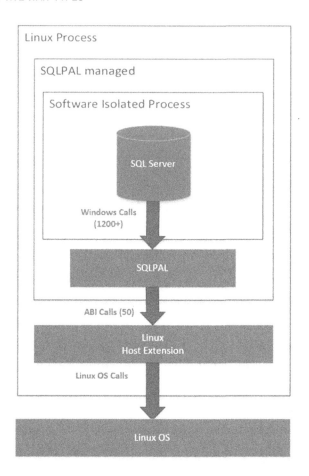

Figure 11-2.   *PAL layer interaction on SQL-on-Linux*

More information is available on various Microsoft blogs covering the functionality and design choices of SQLPAL. A good recommendation is the "SQL Server on Linux: How? Introduction" article over at `https://slrwnds.com/8ldyuz`.

For the remainder of this chapter, I will refer only to functions used by the Windows operating system. If you are running SQL Server on Linux, remember the functionality described in this chapter is handled by SQLPAL on Linux but has the same functionality as on Windows.

PREEMPTIVE_OS_ENCRYPTMESSAGE and PREEMPTIVE_OS_DECRYPTMESSAGE

The first preemptive wait types in this chapter are PREEMPTIVE_OS_ ENCRYPTMESSAGE and PREEMPTIVE_OS_DECRYPTMESSAGE. As you can probably guess from the names, the functions are related to either encrypting or decrypting messages through the operating system.

What Are the PREEMPTIVE_OS_ENCRYPTMESSAGE and PREEMPTIVE_OS_DECRYPTMESSAGE Wait Types?

As noted in the previous section, the **PREEMPTIVE_OS_ENCRYPTMESSAGE** and **PREEMPTIVE_OS_DECRYPTMESSAGE** wait types are related to the encryption and decryption of messages. More specifically, they are related to encrypting and decrypting network traffic to and from the SQL Server instance. One case where this is used is when connecting to your SQL Server instance using certificates to encrypt data sent between the client and the SQL Server instance. In this case, SQL Server will access the Windows operating system to perform the encryption of the messages sent to the client or to decrypt the messages received from the client. This encryption and decryption does not happen inside SQL Server, unlike, for instance, Transparent Data Encryption (TDE), where the encryption/decryption process happens entirely inside SQL Server.

Both the PREEMPTIVE_OS_ENCRYPTMESSAGE and PREEMPTIVE_OS_ DECRYPTMESSAGE wait types do not necessarily indicate any performance problems. They just show encryption is being used, so there is no real need to troubleshoot these wait types. The overhead of encrypting and decrypting messages is small and rarely causes any serious issues (I have yet to come across a case where using certificates to connect to SQL Server caused performance problems, but anything is possible I suppose).

PREEMPTIVE_OS_ENCRYPTMESSAGE and PREEMPTIVE_OS_DECRYPTMESSAGE Example

To show an example of both the PREEMPTIVE_OS_ENCRYPTMESSAGE and PREEMPTIVE_OS_DECRYPTMESSAGE wait types, we will configure a certificate for encrypting the connection to SQL Server. To make this example reproducible,

299

I have included the steps for creating a self-signed certificate. Normally, in production environments, you will use a certificate issued by a certificate authority, but for testing purposes, a self-signed certificate is fine.

The first step in this example is to install Internet Information Services (IIS) on my test virtual machine. IIS makes generating a self-signed certificate very simple.

After the installation of IIS is completed, open the IIS Manager from Administrative Tools. Then click the name of your machine and select the Server Certificates option in the Features View, as shown in Figure 11-3.

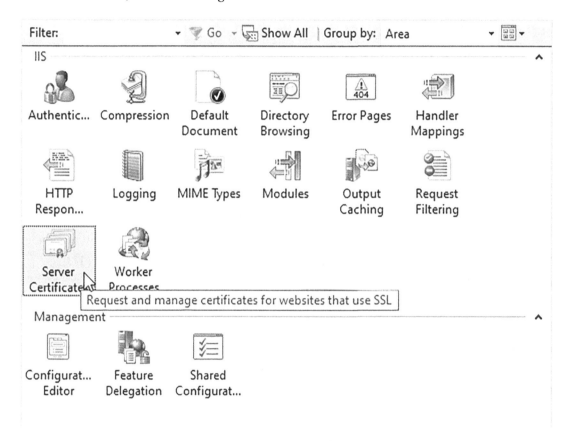

Figure 11-3. *Features View inside the IIS Manager*

This opens a new Server Certificates view inside the IIS Manager. Inside the Action Pane, click the Create Self-Signed Certificate option. We need a name for the certificate, so I filled in the name of my test virtual machine as you can see in Figure 11-4.

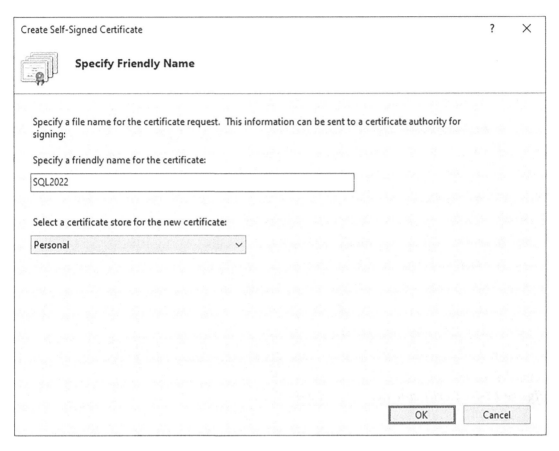

Figure 11-4. *Create self-signed certificate*

Click OK, and the self-signed certificate is created and automatically placed inside the correct certificate store on my machine (Local Machine ➤ Personal Certificates).

Now with the self-signed certificate inside the certificate store, we verify if the account the SQL Server service is running under has permissions to access the certificates. I open the Microsoft Management Console (MMC) by clicking Start ➤ Run, entering MMC, and pressing OK. With the MMC console open, add the Certificates snap-in by clicking File ➤ Add/Remove Snap-in, selecting the Certificates snap-in, and clicking Add. When prompted for the account I want to manage certificates, I select Computer account, as shown in Figure 11-5, and click Next and Finish.

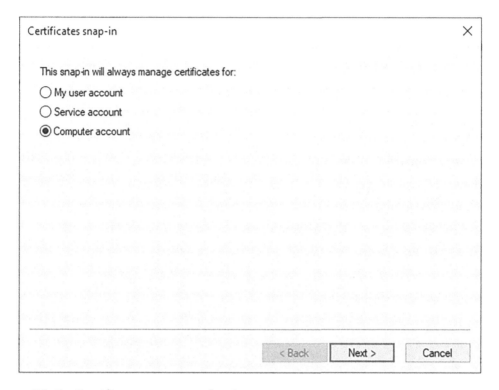

Figure 11-5. *Certificate account selection*

Inside the Certificates console, open the folder Certificates (Local Computer) ➤ Personal ➤ Certificates. If the generation of the self-signed certificate inside IIS was correct, I should see the certificate here. Figure 11-6 shows the certificates on my test virtual machine.

Issued To	Issued By	Expiration Date	Intended Purposes	Friendly Name
SQL2022.bacon.com	SQL2022.bacon.com	9/28/2023	Server Authentication	SQL2022
Windows Azure CRP Certificate Gen...	Windows Azure CRP Certificate Gen...	9/28/2023	<All>	TenantEncryptionCert

Figure 11-6. *Self-signed certificate*

Right-click the self-signed certificate and select All Tasks ➤ Manage Private Keys. A permissions dialog opens. Add the account under which the SQL Server service is running. If you run your SQL Server service under a different account, the account only needs read permission on the certificate, as shown in Figure 11-7.

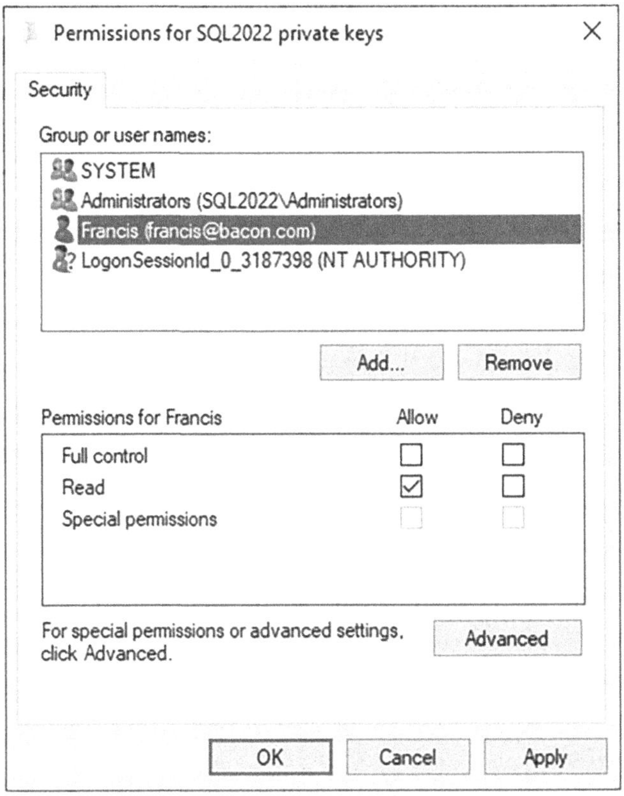

Figure 11-7. *Self-signed certificate permissions*

After adding the account and selecting the right permission, click OK to close the dialog. With the permissions correct and the SQL Server service account being able to access the certificate, add the self-signed certificate to the network configuration of the SQL Server instance. Open the SQL Server Configuration Manager and click the SQL Server Network Configuration option. Right-click the SQL Server instance and select Properties. Next, open the Certificates tab and select the self-signed certificate created earlier. Figure 11-8 shows the dialog on my test virtual machine.

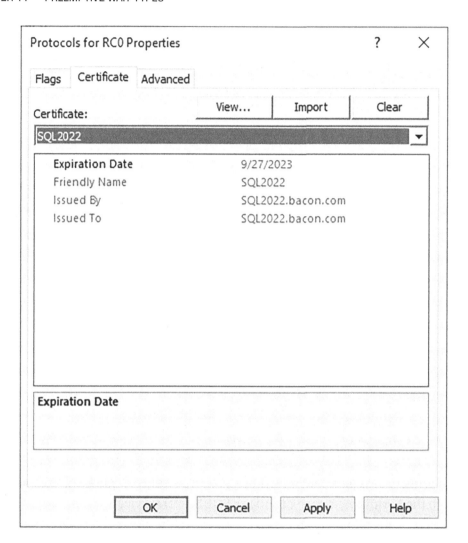

Figure 11-8. Certificate selection

After selecting the self-signed certificate, click OK to close the dialog. I am notified the certificate will become active after a restart of the SQL Server service, so we perform a restart of the SQL Server service.

Right now SQL Server can use the self-signed certificate, but to make sure my network messages are encrypted, I must connect to the SQL Server instance and tell it I want to use encryption. For this example, I will use the SQL Server Management Studio (SSMS) on the same virtual machine as my SQL Server instance to connect to the SQL Server instance. If you connect to your SQL Server instance from another machine, you need to make sure the self-signed certificate is available on that machine. When the

Connect to Server dialog appears inside SSMS, I click the Options button at the bottom right of the dialog. This opens up additional properties for the connection to my SQL Server instance. I select the Encrypt connection checkbox as shown in Figure 11-9 and connect to my SQL Server instance.

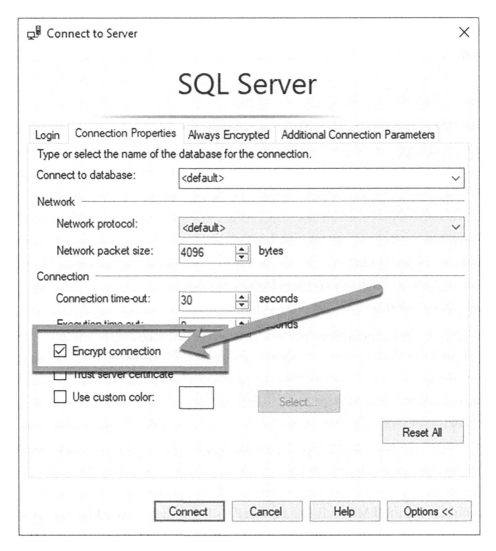

Figure 11-9. *Connection properties in SQL Server Management Studio*

Right now we have configured everything I need to make sure SQL Server will use the self-signed certificate to encrypt messages between the SQL Server instance and SSMS, so we can finally take a look at the PREEMPTIVE_OS_ENCRYPTMESSAGE and PREEMPTIVE_OS_DECRYPTMESSAGE wait types!

Generating the PREEMPTIVE_OS_ENCRYPTMESSAGE and PREEMPTIVE_OS_ DECRYPTMESSAGE waits is very simple. Every query I execute from SSMS right now will be encrypted, even if I run SSMS on the same machine as the SQL Server instance. I use the query in Listing 11-1 to reset the sys.dm_os_wait_stats DMV, connect to the GalacticWorks database, perform a simple query, and then look at the waits occurring on the PREEMPTIVE_OS_ENCRYPTMESSAGE and PREEMPTIVE_OS_DECRYPTMESSAGE wait types.

Listing 11-1. Select query using encrypted connection

```
DBCC SQLPERF('sys.dm_os_wait_stats', CLEAR);

USE GalacticWorks;

SELECT *
FROM Sales.SalesOrderDetail;

SELECT *
FROM sys.dm_os_wait_stats
WHERE wait_type = 'PREEMPTIVE_OS_ENCRYPTMESSAGE'
OR wait_type = 'PREEMPTIVE_OS_DECRYPTMESSAGE';
```

The results of these queries on my test SQL Server instance are shown in Figure 11-10.

	wait_type	waiting_tasks_count	wait_time_ms	max_wait_time_ms	signal_wait_time_ms
1	PREEMPTIVE_OS_DECRYPTMESSAGE	1	0	0	0
2	PREEMPTIVE_OS_ENCRYPTMESSAGE	2356	328	2	0

Figure 11-10. *PREEMPTIVE_OS_DECRYPTMESSAGE and PREEMPTIVE_OS_ ENCRYPTMESSAGE waits*

As you see, the PREEMPTIVE_OS_ENCRYPTMESSAGE wait time has more waits and wait time associated with it. This is logical since I performed a select query and it had to decrypt the acknowledgement network messages from the client. The results of the query are encrypted by SQL Server, which leads to higher waits on the PREEMPTIVE_ OS_ENCRYPTMESSAGE wait type.

Lowering PREEMPTIVE_OS_ENCRYPTMESSAGE and PREEMPTIVE_OS_DECRYPTMESSAGE Waits

Under normal circumstances, there should be no need to focus attention on lowering the PREEMPTIVE_OS_ENCRYPTMESSAGE and PREEMPTIVE_OS_DECRYPTMESSAGE wait types. They indicate encryption is occurring, which is probably a choice made when configuring the SQL Server instance. Disabling encryption will lower the PREEMPTIVE_OS_ENCRYPTMESSAGE and PREEMPTIVE_OS_DECRYPTMESSAGE wait times, but at the cost of security.

PREEMPTIVE_OS_ENCRYPTMESSAGE and PREEMPTIVE_OS_DECRYPTMESSAGE Summary

The PREEMPTIVE_OS_ENCRYPTMESSAGE and PREEMPTIVE_OS_DECRYPTMESSAGE wait types indicate encryption is occurring between the SQL Server instance and a client. These wait types can generally be ignored since they do not directly indicate a performance problem. Lowering them can be achieved by disabling the use of encryption, but this comes at the cost of security.

PREEMPTIVE_OS_WRITEFILEGATHER

The **PREEMPTIVE_OS_WRITEFILEGATHER** wait type is related to storage interactions, more specifically writing of files through the Windows operating system.

What Is the PREEMPTIVE_OS_WRITEFILEGATHER Wait Type?

The PREEMPTIVE_OS_WRITEFILEGATHER wait type is related to the WriteFileGather function inside the Windows operating system. From the definition of this function on Books Online, "Retrieves data from an array of buffers and writes the data to a file," from this description, we assume the function is called when SQL Server needs to write data to a file. This does not count for every storage subsystem write operation inside SQL Server, however. Generally there is no need for SQL Server to move outside its own engine to wait for a preemptive operation. There are some exceptions, however, which result in

PREEMPTIVE_OS_WRITEFILEGATHER waits (depending on the Windows function used to perform the storage subsystem interaction). One specific operation inside SQL Server which will always result in PREEMPTIVE_OS_WRITEFILEGATHER waits is the growing of data files. Whenever SQL Server needs to grow a data file, it will allocate extra space on the storage subsystem and "zero out" the new space. The allocation of the extra space does not happen inside the SQL Server engine; thus, a preemptive operation takes place, which leads to preemptive waits on the WriteFileGather function.

PREEMPTIVE_OS_WRITEFILEGATHER Example

To show an example of PREEMPTIVE_OS_WRITEFILEGATHER waits occurring, let's use the situation described in the previous section, growing a database data file. For this example, I will restore a backup of the GalacticWorks database, which has a single database data file with a size of 194 MB, as shown in Figure 11-11.

Database files:

Logical Name	File Type	Filegroup	Size (MB)	Autogrowth / Maxsize
GalacticWorks_Data	ROWS ...	PRIMARY	194	By 16 MB. Unlimited
GalacticWorks_Log	LOG	Not Applicable	2	By 16 MB. Unlimited

Figure 11-11. *Default database file configuration of GalacticWorks*

I will grow the single database data file to a size of 10 GB. Because the allocation of the extra space needed for the data file is performed outside SQL Server, this should result in PREEMPTIVE_OS_WRITEFILEGATHER waits.

Nerd Note   This example relies on the Instant File Initialization option disabled. More on that in the next section. But it warrants mentioning here, before you attempt this example.

To perform the action of enlarging the database data file, I used the script shown in Listing 11-2. This script will clear the sys.dm_os_wait_stats DMV, enlarge the GalacticWorks data file, and then query the sys.dm_os_wait_stats DMV for PREEMPTIVE_OS_WRITEFILEGATHER.

Listing 11-2. Enlarge AdventureWorks database data file

```
DBCC SQLPERF('sys.dm_os_wait_stats', CLEAR);

USE [master];

ALTER DATABASE [GalacticWorks]
  MODIFY FILE
  (NAME = N'GalacticWorks_Data',
  SIZE = 10240000KB);

SELECT *
FROM sys.dm_os_wait_stats
WHERE wait_type = 'PREEMPTIVE_OS_WRITEFILEGATHER';
```

The query in Listing 11-2 is almost instantly completed on my test SQL Server instance; it has very fast storage and results in the wait information shown in Figure 11-12 for the PREEMPTIVE_OS_WRITEFILEGATHER wait type.

	wait_type	waiting_tasks_count	wait_time_ms	max_wait_time_ms	signal_wait_time_ms
1	PREEMPTIVE_OS_WRITEFILEGATHER	1	447	447	0

Figure 11-12. *PREEMPTIVE_OS_WRITEFILEGATHER waits*

Notice that there was only one single wait on the PREEMPTIVE_OS_WRITEFILEGATHER wait type, and the duration was practically as long as it took to perform the enlargement of the data file.

Lowering PREEMPTIVE_OS_WRITEFILEGATHER Waits

When you notice higher-than-normal wait times on the PREEMPTIVE_OS_WRITEFILEGATHER wait type, it means a process from inside SQL Server is performing actions on the storage subsystem through the Windows operating system. The first matter of action should be to investigate what process initiated the action that resulted in PREEMPTIVE_OS_WRITEFILEGATHER waits. Very frequently, this will be the (automatic) growth of a database data or log file. If you allow the data or log files to grow automatically, you should expect to see PREEMPTIVE_OS_WRITEFILEGATHER waits occur whenever an auto-growth event occurs. This does not necessarily mean there is a problem, but if auto-growth events take a long time to complete because, for instance, the storage subsystem is experiencing performance problems, your queries might experience performance degradation as well.

There is one Windows setting available I frequently see not configured, instant file initialization. We discussed this setting, and how you can enable it, already in Chapter 6, "IO-Related Wait Types," under the ASYNC_IO_COMPLETION wait type, so I won't go into detail on how to enable the setting again. Figure 11-13 shows the results of the query in Listing 11-2 with instant file initialization enabled, and as you can see, the amount of wait time spent on the PREEMPTIVE_OS_WRITEFILEGATHER wait time disappeared completely.

	wait_type	waiting_tasks_count	wait_time_ms	max_wait_time_ms	signal_wait_time_ms
1	PREEMPTIVE_OS_WRITEFILEGATHER	0	0	0	0

Figure 11-13. PREEMPTIVE_OS_WRITEFILEGATHER waits with instant file initialization turned on

Next to using instant file initialization, the performance of the storage subsystem plays a large part in the PREEMPTIVE_OS_WRITEFILEGATHER wait times. The better your storage subsystem performs, the lower the wait times on the PREEMPTIVE_OS_WRITEFILEGATHER wait type.

Another SQL Server action that can cause higher-than-normal PREEMPTIVE_OS_WRITEFILEGATHER wait times is performing database restores. Much like expending a data file, before SQL Server can restore a database, it needs to allocate free storage for it. This is also related to instant file initialization, which will also speed up database restores just like file enlargements.

PREEMPTIVE_OS_WRITEFILEGATHER Summary

The PREEMPTIVE_OS_WRITEFILEGATHER wait type indicates SQL Server is asking the Windows operating system to perform an operation on the storage subsystem. Not all operations are handled from inside the SQL Server engine and actions; for example, the growing of a data file requires the execution of a Windows function to allocate the desired space on the storage subsystem. Instant file initialization is a setting in Windows which can lower the amount of PREEMPTIVE_OS_WRITEFILEGATHER wait time drastically, but the performance of the storage subsystem itself also plays a large role in PREEMPTIVE_OS_WRITEFILEGATHER wait times.

PREEMPTIVE_OS_AUTHENTICATIONOPS

The PREEMPTIVE_OS_AUTHENTICATIONOPS is related to security interactions, waiting at OS level to authenticate a user or login.

What Is the PREEMPTIVE_OS_AUTHENTICATIONOPS Wait Type?

The **PREEMPTIVE_OS_AUTHENTICATIONOPS** wait type is recorded whenever SQL Server performs an account authentication, for instance, to authenticate the SQL Server Windows login when it connects to SQL Server. Seeing PREEMPTIVE_OS_AUTHENTICATIONOPS waits occur is to be expected, especially when using mixed-mode authentication and Windows logins inside your SQL Server instance.

One common misconception about the PREEMPTIVE_OS_AUTHENTICATIONOPS wait type is PREEMPTIVE_OS_AUTHENTICATIONOPS is only related to SQL Server logins using Windows authentication inside a domain. This is not entirely correct. While it is true that PREEMPTIVE_OS_AUTHENTICATIONOPS wait times will frequently be higher when using Active Directory accounts to connect to SQL Server, PREEMPTIVE_OS_AUTHENTICATIONOPS waits will also occur if the SQL Server instance is installed on a machine outside of a domain; the wait times will generally be lower though.

Figure 11-14 shows a simplified image of how SQL Server connects to an Active Directory domain controller to validate the SQL Server Windows login. Keep in mind the Windows operating system takes care of the communication between the domain controller and the SQL Server, hence the preemptive wait type.

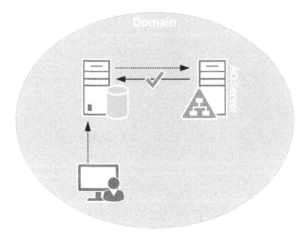

Figure 11-14. *SQL Server Windows login authentication inside domain*

On a machine with a SQL Server instance installed but is not part of a domain, the authentication of the Windows login will occur on the machine itself (local accounts).

Because it will generally take a longer time to authenticate a Windows login through a domain controller (the request has to travel across the network and authenticate on another machine), the wait times for the PREEMPTIVE_OS_AUTHENTICATIONOPS wait type will generally be higher for a SQL Server instance inside a domain.

PREEMPTIVE_OS_AUTHENTICATIONOPS Example

To generate an example of PREEMPTIVE_OS_AUTHENTICATIONOPS waits occurring, we do not need to perform any complex actions. Opening a new connection to the SQL Server instance using Windows authentication should be enough. One way to make this easy to measure is by connecting to the SQL Server instance with SQL Server Management Studio (SSMS), using Windows authentication. Figure 11-15 shows the SSMS connect dialog to my test SQL Server instance. Note that my test SQL Server instance is not inside a domain and that I use the local administrator account on my machine to connect.

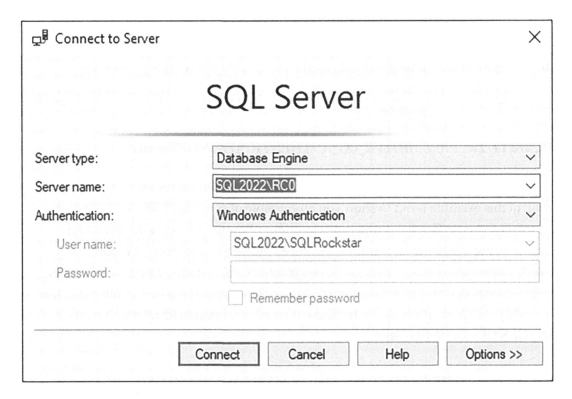

Figure 11-15. *Connect SQL Server Management Studio using local Windows authentication*

The next step I perform is opening a new Query Window inside SSMS and performing the steps inside the query shown in Listing 11-3.

Listing 11-3. Generate PREEMPTIVE_OS_AUTHENTICATIONOPS waits

```
-- Step 1 Clear sys.dm_os_wait_stats
DBCC SQLPERF('sys.dm_os_wait_stats', CLEAR);

-- Step 2 Open a new Query Window inside
-- SQL Server Management Studio
-- Step 3 go back to this Query Window
-- and run the query below

SELECT *
FROM sys.dm_os_wait_stats
WHERE wait_type = 'PREEMPTIVE_OS_AUTHENTICATIONOPS';
```

If you follow the steps commented inside the script in Listing 11-3, you should see PREEMPTIVE_OS_AUTHENTICATIONOPS waits occurring after running the query in step 3. Figure 11-16 shows the results of the query in step 3 on my test machine.

	wait_type	waiting_tasks_count	wait_time_ms	max_wait_time_ms	signal_wait_time_ms
1	PREEMPTIVE_OS_AUTHENTICATIONOPS	12	1	0	0

Figure 11-16. *PREEMPTIVE_OS_AUTHENTICATIONOPS waits*

As you see, the number of waits occurring and their wait times are very low. The point of this example is not to show you an example of very high PREEMPTIVE_OS_AUTHENTICATIONOPS wait times but rather how they occur naturally when connecting to a SQL Server instance. Because I opened a new Query Window inside SSMS, a new connection to the SQL Server instance will be made using the Windows login I used to connect to my SQL Server instance. Because it is a new connection, the account I used to connect had to be authenticated, resulting in PREEMPTIVE_OS_AUTHENTICATIONOPS waits.

Lowering PREEMPTIVE_OS_AUTHENTICATIONOPS Waits

In the example, we saw how PREEMPTIVE_OS_AUTHENTICATIONOPS waits occur naturally whenever you connect to a SQL Server instance. Now imagine a situation where your SQL Server instance is part of a domain environment and it uses Windows authentication to authenticate domain users (or groups) against an Active Directory. In this case, your authentication request will travel across the network to perform the authentication of the login account. There are many factors involved which impact the speed of the authentication request; for instance, if your domain controller is under a lot of stress, it can take longer to perform the authentication, or if your network experiences performance degradation, it will also impact the authentication request. These factors also contribute to the PREEMPTIVE_OS_AUTHENTICATIONOPS wait type and can result in higher wait times.

I would like to describe to you a case I encountered at a client that involved the PREEMPTIVE_OS_AUTHENTICATIONOPS wait type to give you an idea of how you can lower PREEMPTIVE_OS_AUTHENTICATIONOPS wait times.

At this client, they used an application which connected to SQL Server using the Windows account logged in on the computer which ran the application. The computers and the SQL Server were all part of a domain. From a security perspective, the application was well designed, as it did not require separate SQL Server users who needed permission on the database and also didn't use a generic account to connect to the SQL Server instance and execute queries. Inside, the database-specific objects (like tables) were also secured based on domain users and groups.

The client started to experience server performance problems inside the application after deploying it to every (3000+) computer inside the company. The DBA at the client couldn't find any problems, there were no infrastructure-related performance problems on the SQL Server instance, and executing the queries on the SQL Server instance itself revealed no issues. When we looked at the wait statistics, we noticed that the most prevalent wait type was the PREEMPTIVE_OS_AUTHENTICATIONOPS wait type. We also noticed that the application would connect to the SQL Server instance, run a query, and then disconnect again. Because so many concurrent users were using the application, it resulted in a high amount of Windows authentication requests, so many that the domain controller couldn't handle them, resulting in the slower processing of authentication requests.

In this case, the domain controller was a virtual machine, and after adding more processor and memory resources, it was able to keep up with the high amount of authentication requests.

As you can see from this example, seeing high PREEMPTIVE_OS_AUTHENTICATIONOPS wait times does not necessarily mean your SQL Server instance is running into problems, especially in a domain environment, as the performance of your domain controller also plays a large role in PREEMPTIVE_OS_AUTHENTICATIONOPS wait times.

The moral of the story is, if you notice higher-than-normal PREEMPTIVE_OS_AUTHENTICATIONOPS wait times, you will need to investigate more than just the SQL Server instance. Make sure to check the performance of your domain controllers if you are using Windows authentication inside a domain. Check every infrastructure part between your SQL Server instance and the domain controller, like network switches, firewalls, and so on. All of these infrastructure parts will add additional latency for each authentication request, which will result in higher PREEMPTIVE_OS_AUTHENTICATIONOPS wait times, making it a difficult wait type to troubleshoot.

PREEMPTIVE_OS_AUTHENTICATIONOPS Summary

The PREEMPTIVE_OS_AUTHENTICATIONOPS wait type is related to performing authentication requests by the Windows operating system. It is normal to see PREEMPTIVE_OS_AUTHENTICATIONOPS waits occur, especially when your SQL Server instance is part of a domain and uses Windows authentication to authenticate users. Higher-than-normal wait times can indicate that authentication requests are taking longer than normal to complete. This does not necessarily mean that your SQL Server instance is running into a performance problem. If the domain controller cannot process the authentication requests fast enough, it will result in higher PREEMPTIVE_OS_AUTHENTICATIONOPS wait times. A slow network connection to the domain controller, firewall, or switch configurations can also impact PREEMPTIVE_OS_AUTHENTICATIONOPS wait times.

PREEMPTIVE_OS_GETPROCADDRESS

The final wait type in this chapter is the **PREEMPTIVE_OS_GETPROCADDRESS** wait type. The PREEMPTIVE_OS_GETPROCADDRESS wait type is related to the execution of extended stored procedures inside SQL Server.

Extended stored procedures allow you to create external routines in a language other than T-SQL; for instance, using the C# programming language. These extended stored procedures are loaded into SQL Server using .dll files and expand the capabilities of SQL Server programming by allowing actions impossible in T-SQL, like reading/writing Windows Registry entries.

Extended stored procedures are marked as deprecated since SQL Server 2008 and Common Language Runtime (CLR) should be used instead of them. However, there are still cases inside SQL Server which require extended stored procedures, and some third-party software vendors still rely on them.

What Is the PREEMPTIVE_OS_GETPROCADDRESS Wait Type?

The PREEMPTIVE_OS_GETPROCADDRESS wait type is recorded whenever the entrypoint inside an extended stored procedure is loaded. The entrypoint is called upon whenever SQL Server loads or unloads the extended stored procedure .dll file. Under normal conditions, the loading of the entrypoint should complete quickly, resulting in very low PREEMPTIVE_OS_GETPROCADDRESS wait times. However, depending on the extended stored procedure (or problems related to loading the .dll file), it is possible to notice higher wait times. The PREEMPTIVE_OS_GETPROCADDRESS wait type records the time it took to load the entrypoint of the .dll file, not the execution time of the extended stored procedure. Figure 11-17 shows a (simplified) overview of how extended stored procedures are executed by SQL Server.

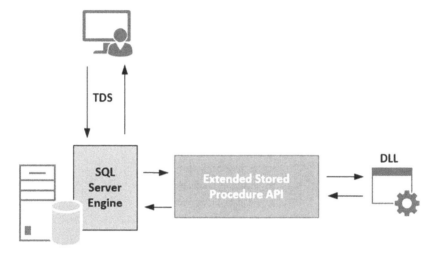

Figure 11-17. *Executing an extended stored procedure*

In addition to writing your own custom extended stored procedures, SQL Server ships with many extended stored procedures. Most of these are recognized by the xp_ prefix in the extended stored procedure name, though not all of them have this prefix. Figure 11-18 shows a selection of the 293 extended stored procedures inside the master database of my test SQL Server 2022 RC0 instance using the following T-SQL:

```
SELECT name
FROM master.dbo.sysobjects AS so
WHERE so.type = 'X';
```

Figure 11-18. *Selection of extended stored procedures inside the SQL Server 2022 RC0 master database*

Probably the most notorious extended stored procedure is the xp_cmdshell extended stored procedure. The xp_cmdshell extended stored procedures makes it possible to execute a command inside a Windows command shell from within SQL Server. This is a huge security risk if your SQL Server instance is compromised, since it gives access to commands that can affect the entire Windows operating system. Thankfully, it is impossible to run the xp_cmdshell extended stored procedure by default; you have to specifically allow its use by configuring an advanced configuration setting.

PREEMPTIVE_OS_GETPROCADDRESS Example

For this example, we execute an extended stored procedure already present inside SQL Server, xp_getnetname, instead of writing a custom extended stored procedure, which is beyond the scope of this book. The xp_getnetname is an undocumented extended stored procedure which returns the NETBIOS name of the machine hosting your SQL Server instance. Before executing the xp_getnetname extended stored procedure, we clear the sys.dm_os_wait_stats DMV, and after the execution of xp_getnetname, we query the DMV for PREEMPTIVE_OS_GETPROCADDRESS wait information. Listing 11-4 shows the entire query I executed on my test SQL Server instance.

Listing 11-4. Execute xp_getnetname and query wait statistics

```
USE [master];

DBCC SQLPERF('sys.dm_os_wait_stats', CLEAR);

exec xp_getnetname;

SELECT *
FROM sys.dm_os_wait_stats
WHERE wait_type = 'PREEMPTIVE_OS_GETPROCADDRESS';
```

The results of the query in Listing 11-4 can be seen in Figure 11-19.

	Server Net Name
1	SQL2022

	wait_type	waiting_tasks_count	wait_time_ms	max_wait_time_ms	signal_wait_time_ms
1	PREEMPTIVE_OS_GETPROCADDRESS	1	0	0	0

Figure 11-19. *PREEMPTIVE_OS_GETPROCADDRESS wait*

The results aren't spectacular. Apparently, the xp_getnetname extended stored procedure doesn't cause any problems when loading the .dll entrypoint, since there is no wait time recorded. A wait still did occur though; as you can see in the waiting_tasks_count column, it just took SQL Server less than a millisecond to load the entrypoint.

Lowering PREEMPTIVE_OS_GETPROCADDRESS Waits

Since the PREEMPTIVE_OS_GETPROCADDRESS wait type is directly related to executing extended stored procedures, the first step in your investigation should be to detect if the extended stored procedure is being executed and what its function is.

I have seen PREEMPTIVE_OS_GETPROCADDRESS waits occur because a third-party backup application used extended stored procedures to perform a database backup, but there are many more possible causes for high PREEMPTIVE_OS_GETPROCADDRESS wait times. Knowing which extended stored procedure is being executed can help you trace the process executing the extended stored procedure.

There have been known bugs inside SQL Server 2008 and 2008R2 which reported higher-than-normal PREEMPTIVE_OS_GETPROCADDRESS wait times because the execution time of the extended stored procedure was also recorded in the wait times, instead of only the entrypoint loading. If you are still using SQL Server 2008 or 2008R2 and experience very high PREEMPTIVE_OS_GETPROCADDRESS wait times, it might be worth your while to upgrade to the latest Service Pack and check if the PREEMPTIVE_OS_GETPROCADDRESS wait times go down. Or even better, upgrade to a higher version of SQL Server since SQL Server 2008R2 is marked end-of-life as of July 9, 2019.

PREEMPTIVE_OS_GETPROCADDRESS Summary

The PREEMPTIVE_OS_GETPROCADDRESS wait type is directly related to the execution of extended stored procedures. Extended stored procedures can be written in a variety of programming languages like C# and allow you to perform actions that would otherwise be impossible in T-SQL. Wait time for the PREEMPTIVE_OS_GETPROCADDRESS wait type is recorded whenever the entrypoint inside an extended stored procedure .dll is loaded. In normal situations, wait times for the PREEMPTIVE_OS_GETPROCADDRESS wait type are very low. Seeing high PREEMPTIVE_OS_GETPROCADDRESS wait times can indicate that the entrypoint loading is running into problems. There have also been bugs related to the calculation of the PREEMPTIVE_OS_GETPROCADDRESS wait type inside SQL Server 2008 and 2008R2. If you are running SQL Server 2008 or 2008R2 and experience high PREEMPTIVE_OS_GETPROCADDRESS wait times, it might be worth your time to upgrade to the latest Service Pack or move to a higher version of SQL Server since SQL Server 2008R2 is marked end-of-life as of July 9, 2019.

CHAPTER 12

Background and Miscellaneous Wait Types

SQL Server has different internal processes, and so far we have discussed quite a few of them. Some of these internal processes are constantly running inside SQL Server, waiting until there is work for them to do. While these processes, frequently called background processes, are waiting for work to arrive, SQL Server will record the time they are waiting for work as specific wait types related to these background processes. While these background wait types are not directly related to performance problems, they frequently have the highest wait time and will show up at the top of the list when you query for top wait types ordered by wait time.

Frequently these background wait types can safely be ignored because they simply indicate an internal process is waiting for work to arrive. This logic is also true for the wait types we discuss in this chapter, but instead of just telling you to ignore them when analyzing wait statistics, I want to give some background information about them so you know what they measure and why it is safe to ignore them. Keep in mind we are still talking about SQL Server here, which means "it depends" on many factors as to whether you can completely ignore these background wait types. You wouldn't be the first person to run into a performance problem only to find out an ignored background process was actually the cause of the issue. So my advice is to ignore but to not forget about them!

Next to the background wait types I also added a number of miscellaneous wait types difficult to place in an earlier chapter because they didn't quite fit in with the chapter's wait type category.

© Thomas LaRock, Enrico van de Laar 2023
T. LaRock and E. van de Laar, *Pro SQL Server 2022 Wait Statistics*,
https://doi.org/10.1007/978-1-4842-8771-2_12

Since the background wait types inside this chapter record wait time constantly when their associated processes are waiting for work to do, I did not include an example section or a lowering wait time section for these wait types.

CHECKPOINT_QUEUE

The first wait type in this chapter is one of those background wait types which accumulate large amounts of wait time over time. The **CHECKPOINT_QUEUE** wait type can (in many cases) be safely ignored, but understanding what the wait type stands for and why it has such high wait times won't hurt.

What Is the CHECKPOINT_QUEUE Wait Type?

The CHECKPOINT_QUEUE wait type is a background wait related to the checkpoint process in SQL Server responsible for writing "dirty" (modified) data pages from the buffer cache to the data file on disk. In Chapter 6, "IO-Related Wait Types," we reviewed the checkpoint process when we discussed the SLEEP_BPOOL_FLUSH wait type, so I won't repeat all the information again here. What is important to know, and the reason why this wait type is often ignored, is the CHECKPOINT_QUEUE wait type indicates the checkpoint process is waiting for work. This means wait times on the CHECKPOINT_QUEUE wait type don't indicate any performance issues; they just indicate the time the checkpoint processes spent waiting on work. On SQL Server instances which aren't very busy, or don't see many data modification operations, the wait time can reach very high values.

The recording of CHECKPOINT_QUEUE wait times inside the sys.dm_os_wait_stats and sys.dm_os_waiting_tasks DMVs goes through a specific internal routine which might return unexpected wait times (like sudden spikes inside your baseline). Figure 12-1 shows the results of queries against the sys.dm_os_wait_stats and sys.dm_os_waiting_tasks DMVs for wait information of the CHECKPOINT_QUEUE wait type on my test SQL Server instance.

	wait_type	waiting_tasks_count	wait_time_ms	max_wait_time_ms	signal_wait_time_ms
1	CHECKPOINT_QUEUE	0	0	0	0

	waiting_task_address	session_id	exec_context_id	wait_duration_ms	wait_type	resource_address
1	0x0000025F07848108	32	0	13722882	CHECKPOINT_QUEUE	0x000000B65C7FE7C0

Figure 12-1. *CHECKPOINT_QUEUE waits*

What is interesting to notice here is the cumulative wait times inside the sys.dm_os_wait_stats DMV stay at 0, while the wait times inside the sys.dm_os_waiting_tasks DMV have a very high value. My test SQL Server instance doesn't perform much work in the background, so it is logical the checkpoint process spends most of its time waiting for work. The reason for the difference in wait times between both DMVs is related to the way SQL Server executes checkpoint operations. The wait times shown in both the DMVs are recorded by the automatic checkpoint process. A manual checkpoint execution does not impact the wait times. As part of the automatic checkpoint process, the wait times of the sys.dm_os_waiting_tasks DMV are moved to the sys.dm_os_wait_stats DMV and reset to 0. So, if you notice very high CHECKPOINT_QUEUE wait times inside the sys.dm_os_waiting_tasks, it means it was some time ago when the automatic checkpoint process last ran.

To show a simple demonstration of this behavior, create a table, reset the sys.dm_os_wait_stats DMV, insert a few rows inside the table, perform a manual checkpoint, and query the sys.dm_os_wait_stats and sys.dm_os_waiting_tasks DMV, as shown in Listing 12-1.

Listing 12-1. CHECKPOINT_QUEUE example

```
-- Create a table in the GalacticWorks database
USE [GalacticWorks];

CREATE TABLE check_test
  (ID UNIQUEIDENTIFIER,
  RandomData VARCHAR(50));

-- Clear sys.dm_os_wait_stats
DBCC SQLPERF('sys.dm_os_wait_stats', CLEAR);
-- Insert a few rows into our table
INSERT INTO check_test
  (ID,
```

```
  RandomData)
VALUES
  (NEWID(),
  CONVERT(varchar(50), NEWID()))
GO 100

CHECKPOINT 1;

-- Query Wait Statistics
SELECT *
FROM sys.dm_os_wait_stats
WHERE wait_type = 'CHECKPOINT_QUEUE';

SELECT *
FROM sys.dm_os_waiting_tasks
WHERE wait_type = 'CHECKPOINT_QUEUE';
```

Figure 12-2 shows the results of the queries made against the sys.dm_os_wait_stats and sys.dm_os_waiting_tasks DMVs.

	wait_type	waiting_tasks_count	wait_time_ms	max_wait_time_ms	signal_wait_time_ms
1	CHECKPOINT_QUEUE	0	0	0	0

	waiting_task_address	session_id	exec_context_id	wait_duration_ms	wait_type	resource_address
1	0x0000025F07848108	32	0	19351	CHECKPOINT_QUEUE	0x000000B65C7FE7C0

Figure 12-2. *CHECKPOINT_QUEUE waits*

As you can see, the manual checkpoint didn't generate any waits inside the sys.dm_os_wait_stats DMV. Also, an automatic checkpoint didn't occur, because inserting 100 rows generated too few log records to trigger an automatic checkpoint.

If we insert more rows, we should be able to trigger an automatic checkpoint. In this case, I ran the following query to insert 100,000 rows into the table created in Listing 12-1. While the insert was running, I queried the sys.dm_os_wait_stats and sys.dm_os_waiting_tasks DMVs repeatedly to see if anything changed. See the following:

```
INSERT INTO check_test
  (ID,
  RandomData)
VALUES
```

```
(NEWID(),
CONVERT(varchar(50), NEWID())))
GO 100000
```

After a few seconds, I noticed that the wait time for the CHECKPOINT_QUEUE wait type was moved to the sys.dm_os_wait_stats DMV, as shown in Figure 12-3.

	wait_type	waiting_tasks_count	wait_time_ms	max_wait_time_ms	signal_wait_time_ms
1	CHECKPOINT_QUEUE	1	174419	174419	0

	waiting_task_address	session_id	exec_context_id	wait_duration_ms	wait_type	resource_address
1	0x0000025F07848108	32	0	193	CHECKPOINT_QUEUE	0x000000B65C7FE7C0

Figure 12-3. *CHECKPOINT_QUEUE waits*

Apparently, we inserted enough log records to cause an automatic checkpoint to occur, and as you see from this example, only an automatic checkpoint will write the wait times of the CHECKPOINT_QUEUE to the sys.dm_os_wait_stats DMV.

You should keep this behavior in mind when you notice sudden, very high wait time values inside the sys.dm_os_wait_stats DMV. This will normally only occur in SQL Server instances that either have a very small workload or have a workload mainly consisting of read operations instead of data modification operations.

CHECKPOINT_QUEUE Summary

The CHECKPOINT_QUEUE wait type is related to checkpoint operations inside SQL Server. Wait time on the CHECKPOINT_QUEUE wait type is recorded, while SQL Server is waiting for an automatic checkpoint operation to take place. This is one of the wait types you can normally safely ignore because it doesn't indicate there are any performance issues. The wait times on the CHECKPOINT_QUEUE wait type are recorded differently between the sys.dm_os_wait_stats and sys.dm_os_waiting_tasks DMV, and this can cause sudden high wait times when querying the sys.dm_os_wait_stats DMV. Keep this behavior in mind when noticing high CHECKPOINT_QUEUE wait times inside the sys.dm_os_wait_stats DMV.

DIRTY_PAGE_POLL

The **DIRTY_PAGE_POLL** wait type was introduced in SQL Server 2012 with the indirect checkpoint feature and behaves a lot like the previous wait type we discussed, CHECKPOINT_QUEUE. While the automatic checkpoint process runs at a set interval of 1 minute, the indirect checkpoint feature allows you to configure a specific checkpoint interval on a per-database basis. Even if you are not using indirect checkpoint, the DIRTY_PAGE_POLL wait type will still accumulate wait time.

What Is the DIRTY_PAGE_POLL Wait Type?

The DIRTY_PAGE_POLL wait type is another background wait which is often safely ignored. The DIRTY_PAGE_POLL is related to the recovery writer process used by the indirect checkpoint feature running continuously in the background of your SQL Server instance. Because of this connection, let's review what indirect checkpoints are and how they work.

The checkpoint process inside SQL Server is responsible for writing modified data pages from the buffer cache to the database data file on disk. By default, the checkpoint process runs automatically every minute or when enough log records have been generated. The checkpoint process plays a vital part in the recovery duration of your SQL Server databases when a crash occurs. Take, for instance, the following scenario: while you are performing many modifications to a database in your SQL Server instance, a crash occurs. Luckily, you were able to simply restart the SQL Server service to get everything up and running again. The first thing SQL Server will do is start a recovery process. The recovery process will check the transaction log for any transactions not committed when the crash occurred and perform a rollback of those transactions. The recovery process will also check whether any data pages modified by a committed transaction received their modification inside the database data file.

If any of those pages are found, SQL Server will use the transaction log to redo these transactions. Now imagine you have a busy SQL Server instance where thousands of modifications are performed every minute. This means the chance there is a high number of dirty pages not written to disk is pretty high. If your SQL Server then crashes (or, for instance, a failover occurs), the recovery process will take more time to complete.

Indirect checkpoints help keep this recovery process as short as possible. By configuring this feature, we tell SQL Server to write modified data pages to disk faster, for instance, every 10 seconds. Figure 12-4 shows the location and name of the indirect checkpoint feature inside the properties of a database.

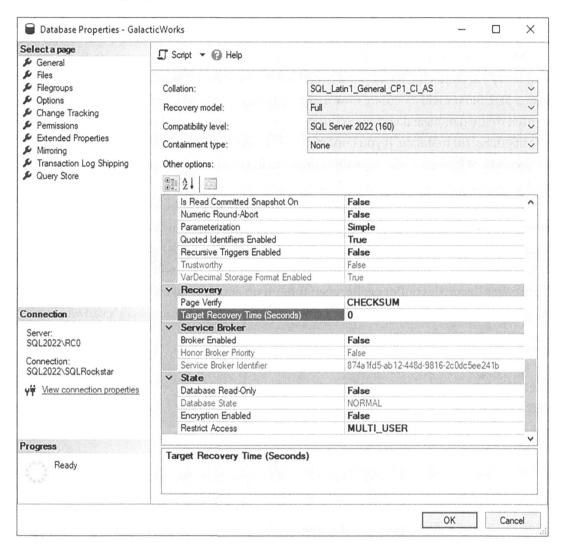

Figure 12-4. *Indirect checkpoint feature location and value*

By default, the value of the Target Recovery Time (Seconds) configuration option is 0. This means indirect checkpoints are not being used. If you modify the value to anything other than 0, an indirect checkpoint will occur at the interval in seconds you specified.

Nerd Note   Starting from SQL Server 2016, indirect checkpoints are automatically configured whenever you create a new database inside the SQL Server instance. In those cases, the Target Recovery Time (Seconds) will be set to a value of 60 instead of 0.

The time you configure in the Target Recovery Time (Seconds) option does not mean that every x seconds the checkpoint process will be executed, however. By setting this value, SQL Server will calculate how many dirty pages can exist before they need to be written to the database data file, so the recovery process never takes longer than the time specified. So, for instance, if you configure the Target Recovery Time (Seconds) option to 15 seconds, SQL Server will write dirty pages to the database data file at such an interval that when the SQL Server instance fails, it can be recovered within 15 seconds.

To monitor how many dirty pages are inside the buffer cache so SQL Server knows when the dirty-page threshold has been reached, the recovery writer was introduced. Even if you do not configure the Target Recovery Time (Seconds) option, DIRTY_PAGE_POLL waits will still occur because the recovery writer process will poll the number of dirty pages inside the buffer cache, even though no action is taken upon that number. As you can see in Figure 12-5, the wait times can reach high values easily even when not using indirect checkpoints.

```
-- Query Wait Statistics
SELECT *
FROM sys.dm_os_wait_stats
WHERE wait_type = 'DIRTY_PAGE_POLL';
```

	wait_type	waiting_tasks_count	wait_time_ms	max_wait_time_ms	signal_wait_time_ms
1	DIRTY_PAGE_POLL	16684	1679414	104	80

Figure 12-5. *DIRTY_PAGE_POLL waits*

Indirect checkpoints have a risk associated with them. Configuring the Target Recovery Time (Seconds) option to a very low value can lead to extra load on the storage subsystem because dirty pages are continuously written to disk. Be sure to test the setting extensively before configuring it on your production SQL Server instances.

DIRTY_PAGE_POLL Summary

The DIRTY_PAGE_POLL wait type was introduced in SQL Server 2012 with the introduction of the indirect checkpoint feature (which ended up being the default setting for new databases created in SQL Server 2016 or higher). Even if you do not use indirect checkpoints, the DIRTY_PAGE_POLL wait type will still accumulate wait time because of the new recovery writer process. Normally the DIRTY_PAGE_POLL wait type does not indicate a performance problem, and as such it can safely be ignored when analyzing wait statistics on your SQL Server instance.

LAZYWRITER_SLEEP

The **LAZYWRITER_SLEEP** wait type is, surprise, related to the SQL Server internal lazywriter background process. The lazywriter process shares some similarities with the checkpoint process discussed earlier in this chapter, as it also writes dirty pages from the buffer cache to the database data file. The similarities end here, though, because the reason why the lazywriter process writes these pages to the database data file is completely different than the checkpoint process.

What Is the LAZYWRITER_SLEEP Wait Type?

Just like with other wait types discussed so far in this chapter, the LAZYWRITER_SLEEP wait type occurs when an internal SQL Server process, in this case the lazywriter process, is waiting for work. The lazywriter process is a background process and will become active at a certain time interval. When it becomes active, it scans the size of the buffer cache to determine if there are enough free pages inside the buffer cache. It is important there are always a certain number of free pages inside the buffer cache, so new page requests can fit directly without first having to swap out other pages. If the lazywriter process determines there are enough free pages in the buffer cache, it will go back to sleep again and record the LAZYWRITER_SLEEP wait type while sleeping. However, if there are not enough free pages inside the buffer cache, the lazywriter process will detect, between checkpoints, which dirty pages in the buffer cache haven't been accessed for a while, write them to the database data file, and then remove them from the buffer cache. So, if there are more than enough free pages inside the buffer cache, the lazywriter process doesn't have much work to do. If your SQL Server instance is under memory pressure, the lazywriter process will be far busier while swapping out dirty pages and freeing up room inside the buffer cache. Figure 12-6 shows the relationship of the checkpoint and lazywriter processes with a flowchart.

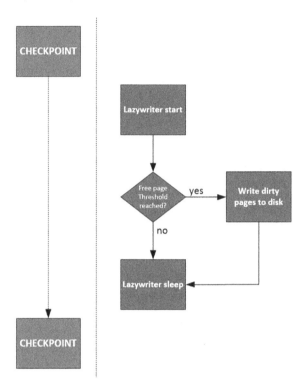

Figure 12-6. *Checkpoint and lazywriter processes*

Because the LAZYWRITER_SLEEP wait type indicates the time the lazywriter process spends sleeping, or waiting for work, it is another one of those wait types you can safely ignore. There is a catch however – if the lazywriter process is constantly working to move dirty pages from the buffer cache to the database data file, it might indicate your SQL Server instance is experiencing memory pressure. This is bad for performance because every page has to be moved to the buffer cache before it can get read or modified. This behavior can potentially result in lower-than-normal wait times on the LAZYWRITER_ SLEEP wait type.

LAZYWRITER_SLEEP Summary

The LAZYWRITER_SLEEP wait type is related to the lazywriter internal SQL Server process. The lazywriter process starts at a fixed time interval and is responsible for writing dirty data pages to the database data file if there are not enough free pages available inside the buffer cache. The LAZYWRITER_SLEEP wait type indicates that the lazywriter process is currently not running, or is sleeping, until it is signaled to wake up and check the buffer cache. Because the LAZYWRITER_SLEEP wait type only shows us how much time the lazywriter process spends being inactive, it can in most cases be ignored.

MSQL_XP

In the last section of Chapter 11, "Preemptive Wait Types," we discussed the PREEMPTIVE_GETPROCADDRESS wait type. We learned the PREEMPTIVE_GETPROCADDRESS wait type records the entrypoint time of an extended stored procedure. One important thing noted was the PREEMPTIVE_GETPROCADDRESS wait type does not record the execution time of the extended stored procedure, only the entrypoint loading. The execution time of an extended stored procedure is tracked by another wait type, **MSQL_XP**.

What Is the MSQL_XP Wait Type?

The MSQL_XP wait type records the execution time of extended stored procedures on your SQL Server instance. The MSQL_XP wait type is also used to detect deadlock situations when using Multiple Active Result Sets (MARS). MARS is a feature which allows for the execution of multiple (concurrent) batches through a single SQL Server connection. We won't go further into detail about MARS, but you can find some more information about it here `https://slrwnds.com/4y444e`.

The most common reason for seeing higher-than-normal wait times on the MSQL_XP wait type is the execution of extended stored procedures. This does not necessarily mean there is a problem as long as the execution time of the extended stored procedures stays the same. However, if an extended stored procedure takes more time than expected, you are sure to notice it in the increase of the MSQL_XP wait time when comparing the wait time against a baseline.

MSQL_XP Example

To demonstrate MSQL_XP waits occur when extended stored procedures are executed, create a simple example using the script in Listing 12-2. The script will reset the sys.dm_os_wait_stats DMV, execute an extended stored procedure (in this case the xp_dirtree extended stored procedure inside the master database), and query the sys.dm_os_wait_stats for MSQL_XP wait information.

Listing 12-2. MSQL_XP example

```
DBCC SQLPERF('sys.dm_os_wait_stats', CLEAR);

EXEC master..xp_dirtree 'c:\windows';

SELECT *
FROM sys.dm_os_wait_stats
WHERE wait_type = 'MSQL_XP';
```

The results of the query in Listing 12-2 on my test SQL Server instance can be seen in Figure 12-7. The top window shows the xp_dirtree results, the bottom window the results of the query against the sys.dm_os_waits_stats DMV.

	subdirectory	depth
1	ADFS	1
2	ar	2
3	bg	2
4	cs	2
5	da	2
6	de	2
7	el	2
8	en	2
9	en-GB	2
10	es	2
11	es-MX	2
12	et	2
13	fi	2
14	fr	2
15	fr-CA	2

	wait_type	waiting_tasks_count	wait_time_ms	max_wait_time_ms	signal_wait_time_ms
1	MSQL_XP	1	28159	28159	0

Figure 12-7. MSQL_XP wait

The information in the sys.dm_os_wait_stats DMV shows one wait occurred on the MSQL_XP wait type with a wait time of 28,159 milliseconds. This is almost identical to the time it took to execute the query in Listing 12-2, which was 28 seconds on my test SQL Server instance.

Lowering MSQL_XP Waits

When noticing higher-than-normal wait times for the MSQL_XP wait type, chances are extended stored procedures are taking longer than normal to complete. Your first point of action should be to identify which extended stored procedures are being used and why. Because extended stored procedures also perform tasks outside SQL Server, they can run into other Windows processes which can slow them down. Knowing what the extended stored procedure function is, and what it does, will help you quickly identify where it is running into issues.

If you are using MARS, you are probably running into MARS-connection deadlocks. There have been various SQL Server updates to reduce the chances of MARS deadlocks occurring, so make sure your SQL Server instance is patched. Also make sure to check the application code which executes queries using MARS for potential issues.

MSQL_XP Summary

The MSQL_XP wait type does two different things: it detects the time it takes to execute extended stored procedures and serves as deadlock detection for MARS connections. Seeing higher-than-normal wait times on the MSQL_XP wait type frequently indicates an extended stored procedure is taking longer than normal to complete. Try to detect which extended stored procedure is being executed and what its function is, as this will make troubleshooting the extended stored procedure easier.

OLEDB

The **OLEDB** wait type occurs whenever SQL Server has to access the Object Linking and Embedding Database (OLEDB) Client Provider. There are various reasons why SQL Server will use the OLEDB Client Provider, and whenever it does SQL Server will record wait time on the OLEDB wait type.

What Is the OLEDB Wait Type?

SQL Server uses the OLEDB Client Provider for many different actions inside SQL Server. For instance, linked server traffic will move through the OLEDB Client Provider and result in OLEDB waits. Other actions, especially when SQL Server has to retrieve data from an outside source, can also result in OLEDB Client Provider usage.

Some actions inside SQL Server will also use the OLEDB Client Provider, even though they occur internally. One good example of this is the DBCC command, which I will demonstrate in the following example section.

OLEDB Example

One interesting process using the OLEDB Client Provider is the DBCC command inside SQL Server. Whenever you execute a DBCC command, you are bound to see OLEDB

waits occur. Listing 12-3 shows an example of OLEDB waits occurring after a DBCC
CHECKDB. The example script will clear the sys.dm_os_wait_stats DMV, perform a
CHECKDB against the GalacticWorks database, and then query the sys.dm_os_wait_stats
DMV for OLEDB waits.

Listing 12-3. Generate OLEDB waits

```
DBCC SQLPERF('sys.dm_os_wait_stats', CLEAR);

DBCC CHECKDB('GalacticWorks');

SELECT *
FROM sys.dm_os_wait_stats
WHERE wait_type = 'OLEDB';
```

The results of the query in Listing 12-3 as performed against my test SQL Server
instance can be seen in Figure 12-8.

	wait_type	waiting_tasks_count	wait_time_ms	max_wait_time_ms	signal_wait_time_ms
1	OLEDB	112345	3930	27	0

Figure 12-8. *OLEDB waits*

As you can see from Figure 12-8, performing a DBCC CHECKDB will lead to
OLEDB waits.

Lowering OLEDB Waits

As you see in the previous example, performing a DBCC CHECKDB against a database
will result in OLEDB waits. This doesn't mean there is a problem related to the OLEDB
Client Provider, however; rather, it just indicates the DBCC CHECKDB command makes
use of the OLEDB Client Provider. Running DBCC CHECKDB is a vital part of making
sure your databases are healthy. Avoiding consistency checks just to lower OLEDB wait
times is bad practice, and I strongly advise against it. Seeing high OLEDB wait times
occur outside DBCC commands can indicate there is a performance issue somewhere
in your SQL Server environment. If you are dealing with remote sources, such as linked
servers or Excel files, you are also affected by the performance of the remote source.

For instance, if you are querying information from a linked server and the linked server is experiencing performance problems, it will probably also be reflected in the OLEDB wait time. Also, certain operations, like sorts, can also impact the query duration on the linked server. Network connections to the remote source can also play a role in higher-than-normal OLEDB wait times. If the network connection through which you are accessing your remote source experiences performance degradation, you will again notice this in the OLEDB wait times.

Because the OLEDB wait can occur for various reasons, some of which are benign like DBCC commands, and some that can be related to performance issues, I advise you not to ignore the OLEDB wait type but rather to monitor it like other performance-indicating wait types.

OLEDB Summary

The OLEDB wait type can occur due to various sources using the Object Linking and Embedding Database (OLEDB) Client Provider. Most of the sources are related to remote data sources, like linked servers. Some internal processes also use the OLEDB Client Provider, most notably the DBCC command. Seeing higher-than-normal wait times on the OLEDB wait type doesn't have to mean there is a performance problem, especially when they can be correlated to a planned DBCC command execution. Seeing higher-than-normal wait times outside DBCC command when you are using remote data sources like linked servers can mean that the remote data source is experiencing performance problems. In this case, focus on the data source; if the source has problems, it is bound to affect the OLEDB wait times as well.

TRACEWRITE

The **TRACEWRITE** wait type is a special wait type and only collects wait time when a trace is running, most commonly a SQL Server Profiler trace. A trace is a background process in SQL Server collecting various, often user-specified, information about the performance of a SQL Server instance. For example, it is possible to use SQL Server Profiler to capture currently executing queries, filtered against a single database, with runtime information. There are various trace methods available in SQL Server, but the most common one that affects the TRACEWRITE wait type is the SQL Server Profiler trace.

SQL Server Profiler is an application and starting from SQL Server 2016 separate from the SQL Server Management Studio (SSMS) product, allowing users to create and monitor traces against SQL Server instances. SQL Server Profiler was announced as deprecated by Microsoft with the introduction of SQL Server 2012, and Microsoft recommends using Extended Events to capture traces. Even though the SQL Server Profiler is deprecated, it is still available in SQL Server 2022 and is installed whenever you deploy the separate SSMS product. Many people still rely on SQL Server Profiler traces instead of Extended Events to troubleshoot and monitor query performance.

The bad news about using SQL Server Profiler is it can cause some performance overhead while a trace is being performed. Microsoft released an article which concluded running SQL Server Profiler traces on busy systems can have an impact of 10% on the amount of transactions per seconds; you can find the article at `https://slrwnds.com/j66us9`.

Because SQL Server Profiler traces can have such a big impact on the performance of your system, I believe it is important to monitor the TRACEWRITE wait time.

What Is the TRACEWRITE Wait Type?

The TRACEWRITE wait type will show up on your system when traces are performed against your SQL Server instance. Because SQL Server Profiler traces can have such an impact on the performance of your SQL Server instance, it is advisable you monitor the wait type to detect if any SQL Server Profiler traces are being performed.

There are a variety of reasons why you would want to run a SQL Server Profiler trace, for instance, if you want to troubleshoot a very specific query problem or when monitoring how many times a specific query gets executed. Even though there are alternatives to the SQL Server Profiler, like server-side traces and Extended Events, the SQL Server Profiler tool is very easy to use compared to the often complex Extended Events.

TRACEWRITE Example

To show you an example of TRACEWRITE waits, we will create a SQL Server Profiler trace. The SQL Server Profiler program is part of the Management Tools-Complete feature, which you can select when installing SQL Server versions lower than SQL Server 2016 or when adding features to an existing installation. If you install the separate SSMS product, the Profiler feature is automatically installed as well. Figure 12-9 shows the feature inside the SQL Server 2012 setup.

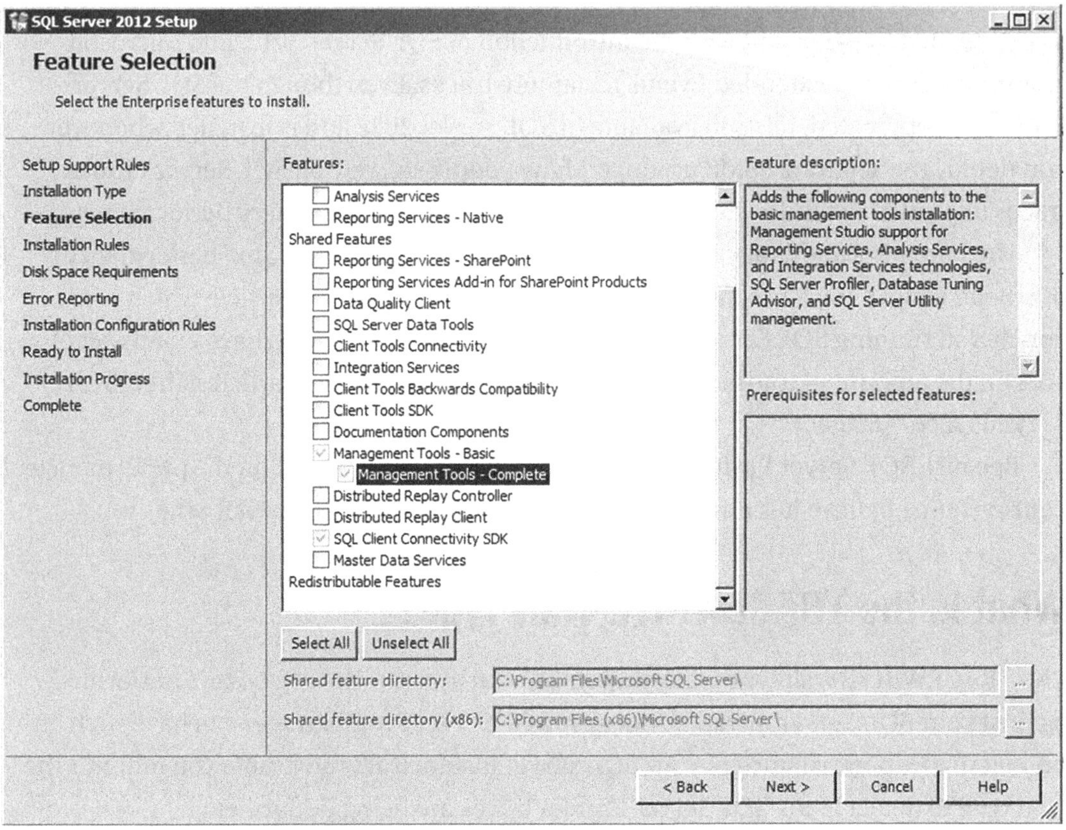

Figure 12-9. *Management Tools-Complete feature in SQL Server 2012 setup*

When you have installed the Management Tools-Complete feature, you will find the SQL Server Profiler in the SQL Server ➤ Performance Tools folder underneath the Start menu or in the C:\Program Files (x86)\Microsoft SQL Server\[edition number]\Tools\ Binn folder.

If you installed the separate SSMS product the Profiler is found in the C:\Program Files (x86)\Microsoft SQL Server\140\Tools\Binn folder.

After launching SQL Server Profiler, you start a new trace by clicking the New Trace button, shown in Figure 12-10, or selecting File ➤ New Trace.

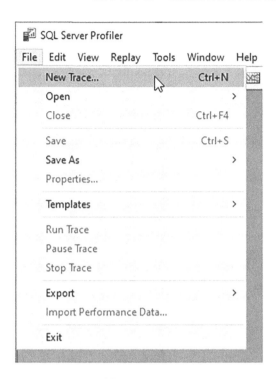

Figure 12-10. *New SQL Server Profiler trace*

When you start a new trace, you will need to connect to the SQL Server instance you want to trace. In this case, I connected to my test SQL Server instance. After logging on to the SQL Server instance, the Trace Properties window will open. This window provides a variety of options with which to configure your trace and how to store your trace. In this example, we are not going to change anything in the General tab but instead will go directly to the Events Selection tab. There we select the events we want to capture and optionally supply filters for those events.

For this example, we select the SQL:BatchCompleted event, as you can see in Figure 12-11. This will record all the T-SQL statements that are executed against the test SQL Server instance and capture all the information available for the event.

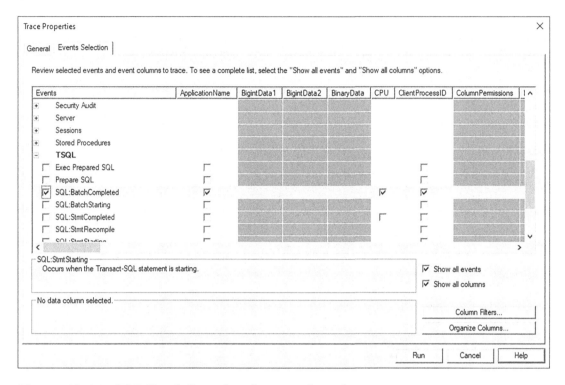

Figure 12-11. *SQL:BatchCompleted event selected*

We won't configure any filters on the event, so we will capture every T-SQL statement we execute against the SQL Server instance. We press Run to start the trace, which opens the trace window to show us the events as they take place on our SQL Server instance along with additional information about, in this case, the query.

Now that our SQL Server Profiler trace is running, we should be able to notice TRACEWRITE waits occurring. We execute the following query in SSMS against the sys. dm_os_waiting_tasks DMV:

```
SELECT *
FROM sys.dm_os_waiting_tasks
WHERE wait_type = 'TRACEWRITE';
```

The results of this query are shown in Figure 12-12.

	waiting_task_address	session_id	exec_context_id	wait_duration_ms	wait_type	resource_address
1	0x0000025F0FE11C28	60	0	5	TRACEWRITE	0x0000000000000001

Figure 12-12. *TRACEWRITE waits*

Even though we are not running any workload on the test SQL Server instance, the TRACEWRITE wait type will still be lógged. This is normal since the TRACEWRITE wait type will always be recorded as long as a SQL Server Profiler trace is active.

Lowering TRACEWRITE Waits

As mentioned before, if you notice TRACEWRITE waits occurring, it means someone is running a SQL Server Profiler trace against your SQL Server instance. Because a SQL Server Profiler trace can impact the performance of your SQL Server instance, it is important to know who is running the SQL Server Profiler trace and why.

Thankfully, there is a catalog view we can query to view trace activity – the sys.traces view. The sys.traces catalog view will give you an overview of traces that are either active or paused against the SQL Server instance. The following query will retrieve all the information inside the sys.traces catalog view:

```
SELECT *
FROM sys.traces;
```

Running this query against my test SQL Server instance returns the information shown in Figure 12-13 (some columns did not fit inside the image).

	id	status	path	max_size	stop_time	max_files	is_rowset	is_rollover
1	1	1	C:\Program Files\Microsoft SQL Server\MSSQL16.SQ...	20	NULL	5	0	1
2	2	1	NULL	NULL	NULL	NULL	1	0

Figure 12-13. *sys.traces*

Some important columns to highlight from the sys.traces catalog view are the status and reader_spid columns. The status column returns either a 0 or a 1, where a 0 indicates the trace is stopped or paused and a 1 indicates the trace is currently running. The reader_spid column returns the session ID of the session which started the trace. We can use this information to detect who is running the trace.

In our case, the trace started in the earlier example has an ID of 2, while the ID of 1 is reserved for the background SQL Server trace which is, by default, always active. This default trace collects specific information about the health of the SQL Server instance and can be used when troubleshooting. Because it is a so-called server-side trace, it does not record TRACEWRITE wait time while it is running.

Now we know the user running the trace, we can take action if the trace has a negative effect on the performance of your SQL Server instance.

Other than stopping SQL Server Profiler traces to lower the TRACEWRITE wait time, there are other methods available if you need to capture traces against your SQL Server instance. The most logical one is recreating your SQL Server Profiler trace within an Extended Event session. Extended Events allow more events and options while capturing traces.

If you still want to use SQL Server Profiler to analyze traces, it is a good idea to convert the trace you would normally run in the SQL Server Profiler application to a server-side trace. Let's convert the SQL Server Profiler trace created in the example section to a server-side trace and monitor the effects on the TRACEWRITE wait type.

The easiest way to convert a SQL Server Profiler trace is by defining the trace in the SQL Server Profiler application without starting it. Instead, select the File ➤ Export ➤ Script Trace Definition ➤ For SQL Server 2005 – SQL2019 option, as shown in Figure 12-14.

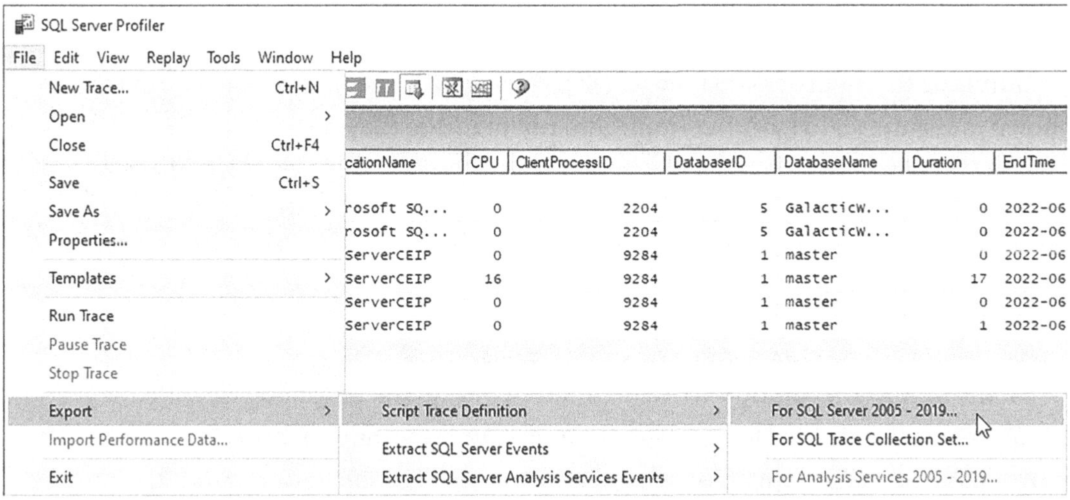

Figure 12-14. *Export SQL Server Profiler trace to trace definition*

After clicking the File ➤ Export ➤ Script Trace Definition ➤ For SQL Server 2005 – SQL2019 option, we are asked to save a .sql file. The entire trace definition will be scripted inside this .sql file. We then open this file in SSMS, modify the file location and some other options inside the script, and execute it. This will return the ID of the trace we just created and save the trace information to a file we specified at the top of the script. Figure 12-15 shows a part of the exported trace definition on our test SQL Server instance.

```
/******************************************************/
/* Created by: SQL Server 2019 Profiler        */
/* Date: 06/21/2022  03:10:35 PM        */
/******************************************************/


-- Create a Queue
declare @rc int
declare @TraceID int
declare @maxfilesize bigint
set @maxfilesize = 5

-- Please replace the text InsertFileNameHere, with an appropriate
-- filename prefixed by a path, e.g., c:\MyFolder\MyTrace. The .trc extension
-- will be appended to the filename automatically. If you are writing from
-- remote server to local drive, please use UNC path and make sure server has
-- write access to your network share

exec @rc = sp_trace_create @TraceID output, 0, N'c:\TeamData\', @maxfilesize, NULL
if (@rc != 0) goto error

-- Client side File and Table cannot be scripted

-- Set the events
declare @on bit
set @on = 1
```

Figure 12-15. *Trace definition*

After executing the script to create a server-side trace, we received a trace ID of 2. The trace ID is very important because it is the only way to either start or stop the server-side trace. After creation, the server-side trace is automatically started. If we query the sys.traces catalog view, we can see the server-side trace that was just created, as shown in Figure 12-16.

	id	status	path	max_size	stop_time	max_files	is_rowset	is_rollover
1	1	1	C:\Program Files\Microsoft SQL Server\MSSQL16.SQ...	20	NULL	5	0	1
2	2	1	c:\TeamData\.trc	5	NULL	1	0	0

Figure 12-16. *sys.traces*

The only way to interact with the server-side trace created is to execute the sp_trace_setstatus stored procedure and supply the trace ID and a status ID. For instance, executing the query that follows will stop the server-side trace with a trace ID of 2:

```
EXEC sp_trace_setstatus 2, 0
```

To start it again, we can execute this command:

```
EXEC sp_trace_setstatus 2, 1
```

And finally, to close the trace entirely, we can execute the following command:

```
EXEC sp_trace_setstatus 2, 3
```

This does not delete the server-side trace though. As a matter of fact, server-side traces are only removed by a restart of the SQL Server service.

Because a server-side trace can only output to a trace file, you must navigate to the file you supplied in the server-side trace definition and open the file in SQL Server Profiler. Thus, you can capture the same information as by using the SQL Server Profiler application but at a much lower performance price.

TRACEWRITE Summary

The TRACEWRITE wait type indicates a SQL Server Profiler trace is currently being performed against the SQL Server instance. SQL Server Profiler traces can have a pretty big impact on the performance of your SQL Server instance, and for this reason, it is important to monitor the number of traces running against your SQL Server instance. Thankfully, there are some alternatives to SQL Server Profiler traces. You can either choose to convert your SQL Server Profiler trace to an Extended Events session or execute the SQL Server Profiler trace using server-side tracing.

WAITFOR

The final wait type in this chapter is one of the few wait types directly related to a T-SQL command. The **WAITFOR** wait type doesn't indicate performance problems, though it definitely has an impact on the duration of the query executing the related WAITFOR T-SQL command.

What Is the WAITFOR Wait Type?

The WAITFOR wait type is recorded whenever a query is executed using the WAITFOR command. The WAITFOR T-SQL command will stop the execution of the query until a specific amount of time has passed or a specific point in time has been reached. When this happens, the query execution will continue. The WAITFOR command is frequently used inside queries or scripts to force a pause inside the query execution. For instance, in Chapter 4, "Building a Solid Baseline," we used the WAITFOR command to wait a specific amount of time to compare two measurements taken 15 minutes apart.

While pausing the query execution using the WAITFOR command, the transaction holding the WAITFOR command will remain open until the entire transaction has completed. This means threads held by the transaction cannot be used for other processes. SQL Server also reserves a dedicated thread just for the WAITFOR command; if too many threads are associated with WAITFOR commands and thread starvation occurs, SQL Server will select random WAITFOR threads and terminate them to free up more threads.

In many cases, the WAITFOR command is explicitly used by the person who wrote the query or script and in this sense only impacts the specific query or script; thus, there is no reason to be alarmed when seeing high WAITFOR wait times occur. It just indicates that queries are using the WAITFOR command.

WAITFOR Example

To show a quick example of the WAITFOR wait type, execute the query in Listing 12-4. The query will reset the sys.dm_os_wait_stats DMV, execute a WAITFOR DELAY statement which causes the script execution to wait for 30 seconds, and then query the sys.dm_os_wait_stats DMV for WAITFOR waits.

Listing 12-4. WAITFOR waits

```
DBCC SQLPERF('sys.dm_os_wait_stats', CLEAR);

WAITFOR DELAY '00:00:30';

SELECT *
FROM sys.dm_os_wait_stats
WHERE wait_type = 'WAITFOR';
```

When the query in Listing 12-4 finishes, you should see one WAITFOR wait occurred, having a total wait time of roughly 30 seconds, as you see in Figure 12-17.

	wait_type	waiting_tasks_count	wait_time_ms	max_wait_time_ms	signal_wait_time_ms
1	WAITFOR	1	30000	30000	0

Figure 12-17. *WAITFOR wait*

WAITFOR Summary

The WAITFOR wait type is one of the few background wait types directly related to the execution of a T-SQL command, in this case WAITFOR. The WAITFOR wait type doesn't indicate any performance problems with your SQL Server instance; it just indicates the WAITFOR command is being used by a query or script. The WAITFOR T-SQL command will only impact the execution time of the query or script that uses it; therefore, the only way to lower WAITFOR wait times is by removing the WAITFOR command inside queries.

CHAPTER 13

In-Memory OLTP–Related Wait Types

With the release of SQL Server 2014, Microsoft introduced a brand new SQL Server feature called In-Memory OLTP (codename Hekaton). In-Memory OLTP is a memory-optimized database engine directly integrated into the SQL Server engine. In-Memory OLTP is designed to improve performance – up to 20 times, according to Microsoft – by loading tables entirely into the memory of your SQL Server instance. These memory-optimized tables are fully durable and use lock-and-latch free structures to optimize concurrency control.

With the introduction of In-Memory OLTP, various new wait types have been added to SQL Server. Most of these are recognizable by the _XTP_ (or eXtreme Transaction Processing) section in the wait type name. In this chapter, we will review these In-Memory OLTP–related wait types.

Before we dive into the wait types though, let's first take a (simplified and short) look at what In-Memory OLTP is and how it works. I will focus on memory-optimized tables in this chapter. In-Memory OLTP also introduced other features, like natively compiled stored procedures and hash indexes, but these are beyond the scope of this chapter.

Introduction to In-Memory OLTP

The main difference between traditional (disk-based) tables and memory-optimized tables is that memory-optimized tables reside completely in the memory of your SQL Server instance. Unlike traditional tables, where data pages from the table are moved from disk into memory and back out again, memory-optimized tables are moved to your system's memory at SQL Server startup and never leave the memory (unless the memory-optimized table is removed, of course). While this might sound a bit scary at first, memory-optimized tables are, by default, fully durable. This means if your SQL

© Thomas LaRock, Enrico van de Laar 2023
T. LaRock and E. van de Laar, *Pro SQL Server 2022 Wait Statistics*,
https://doi.org/10.1007/978-1-4842-8771-2_13

Server instance crashes, memory-optimized table data is not lost. Of course, having an entire table reside in the memory of your SQL Server instance also has disadvantages. You need enough free memory to accommodate the entire memory-optimized table (and some extra memory to accommodate row versions used when accessing such tables). Calculating the memory requirements can be difficult, but the following article will help: `https://slrwnds.com/ecqxan`.

The memory reserved for memory-optimized tables is claimed by SQL Server and will not be wiped out; if your memory-optimized tables use too much memory, your SQL Server instance will run into memory starvation issues and cause performance degradation or, worst case, cause SQL Server to crash. This is a major difference compared to, for instance, the buffer cache, where pages are wiped out of memory when memory pressure occurs. Another disadvantage is many data types or SQL Server features are not supported for memory-optimized tables. The complete list of what can and cannot be used can be found at `https://slrwnds.com/939hqx` and `https://slrwnds.com/3cfwre`. With the release of SQL Server 2016, some of the major limitations were resolved, making the feature more attractive and less restrictive.

Let's take a look at some of the internals of In-Memory OLTP, how they work, and why they perform faster than traditional disk-based tables.

Checkpoint File Pairs (CFPs)

By default, memory-optimized tables are durable (you can choose to create a nondurable table with the contents cleared on a SQL Server service restart, but you must explicitly specify this). The way durability is achieved is through so-called checkpoint file pairs (CFPs). CFPs consist of two files, a data and a delta file, which exist inside a special memory-optimized filegroup created for the database where you use memory-optimized tables.

Unlike traditional tables which store row data inside data pages, CFP data files store the rows of **all** memory-optimized tables. I emphasize the word all because a single data file can hold the rows of many memory-optimized tables, unlike some data pages which store row data for a single table. The rows inside a data file are stored sequentially based on the time they were inserted into a memory-optimized table. This is different than with data pages, which hold row information inside extents for traditional tables. Because rows are stored sequentially inside the data files, there is a performance increase when reading rows since it eliminates the random reads which occur when reading rows from traditional tables. Figure 13-1 shows an abstract view of a data file and the row data it holds.

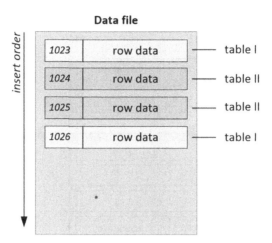

Figure 13-1. *Memory-optimized table's data file*

There are always multiple data files inside a memory-optimized filegroup. When you first create the memory-optimized filegroup, SQL Server automatically pre-allocates a number of data files in the file location of the memory-optimized filegroup. The data files will always have a fixed file size, either 128 MB on systems with more than 16 GB memory or 16 MB when there is less than or equal to 16 GB memory. When a data file is full, a new data file will automatically be created, and new rows will be inserted into the new data file. It is important to know that the data file keeps track of rows based on the transaction-commit timestamp which inserted the row into the data file (shown by the number inside Figure 13-1). Even if new data files are added and rows are spread across multiple data files, the data files will always have a contiguous range of transactions. Figure 13-2 shows multiple data files and the transaction-commit timestamps associated with those data files.

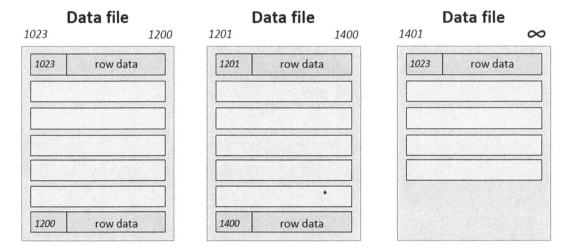

Figure 13-2. *Data files and transaction timestamps*

Notice in Figure 13-2 the last data file still has room for new rows – it doesn't have a transaction timestamp to indicate the file is full, so new rows will be added to that file.

Another important characteristic of the data file is the deleted rows are not directly removed from the file. Instead, they are tracked by the delta file associated with the data file. The delta file logs any deletes made in the data file and is connected to the data file by the transaction timestamp range. Row updates for memory-optimized tables are tracked as a delete and insert operation.

The population of the data and delta files is performed by a background thread – called the offline checkpoint thread – which runs constantly in the background of SQL Server. This is different from the checkpoint process used for traditional tables where pages are written to the database data files at intervals. The offline checkpoint thread monitors the transaction log for operations performed on memory-optimized tables and directly writes to the data and delta files.

Over time, when data files accumulate more deleted rows, a merge operation will take place which will merge multiple data files together into one data file. The merge operation will create new data and delta files and move the contents of one or more data and delta files into the new files, but it will not move the rows marked as deleted. The transaction-commit timestamps will be adjusted in the new data and delta files, so they match the timestamps of the files that were merged. Figure 13-3 shows a simplified view of a merge operation on a data file level. Keep in mind that a merge will also impact the delta file.

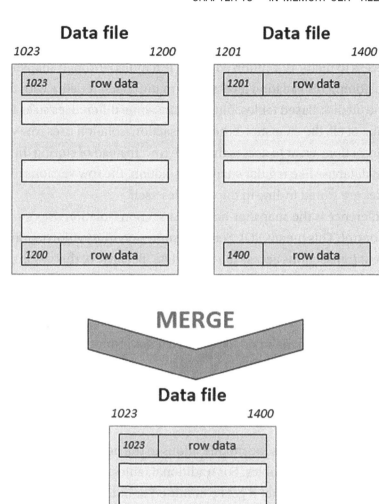

Figure 13-3. *Merge operation*

Isolation

Concurrent access to memory-optimized tables is handled through snapshot-based transaction isolation. This isolation level shares many characteristics with the snapshot isolation we use on disk-based tables, but there are some differences so as to optimize throughput. First of all, the snapshot-based transaction isolation uses row versions when concurrent transactions want to access the same row. Instead of storing the row versions in the TempDB database like regular snapshot isolation, the row versions for memory-optimized tables are stored in-line in the data files itself.

Another difference is the snapshot-based transaction isolation uses an optimistic concurrency control. This means SQL Server assumes no transaction conflict will occur when concurrent transactions access the same data. Because of this assumption, there is no need for locks or latches to protect the memory-optimized table data. There is a form of conflict detection active, however, and when it detects a conflict has occurred, it will end one of the transactions, and the transaction will need to be retried.

Not having to place and maintain locks and latches is another major contribution to the performance of In-Memory OLTP.

Transaction Log Changes

The final difference to discuss is the modifications to the behavior of the transaction log regarding memory-optimized tables. For traditional tables, a log record will be generated when a transaction starts whether it gets committed or not. For memory-optimized tables, the log record is generated when a transaction begins to commit processing. This means no information for transactions rolled back is recorded. This minimizes interaction with the transaction log on disk, thus improving performance.

Another modification is changes to indexes on memory-optimized tables are not logged in the transaction log. Since indexes created on memory-optimized tables are also maintained entirely in-memory, there is no need to record changes. Indexes on memory-optimized tables are regenerated on the start of the SQL Server service.

The final difference I want to mention is the grouping of multiple transactions into one log record. For traditional tables, every transaction will result in at least one log record. Transactions against memory-optimized tables are grouped together and then written as one log record (with a current maximum size of 24 KB). For instance, if you have 200 inserts against a traditional table, at least 200 log records would be generated.

If we could fit 100 inserts into one log record for the memory-optimized table, we would only have two log records instead of at least 200. Again, this improves throughput for memory-optimized tables.

Now with a (simplified and short) look at some of the inner workings of memory-optimized tables, let's review some of the wait types related to In-Memory OLTP. Most of the wait types in this chapter are related, one way or another, to the new offline checkpoint process introduced with In-Memory OLTP.

WAIT_XTP_HOST_WAIT

The first wait type in this chapter is **WAIT_XTP_HOST_WAIT**. This wait type shares some characteristics with the CHECKPOINT_QUEUE wait type discussed in Chapter 12, "Background and Miscellaneous Wait Types," as it seems to be running continuously but only writes wait information to sys.dm_os_wait_stats at specific conditions.

What Is the WAIT_XTP_HOST_WAIT Wait Type?

If we look up information on the WAIT_XTP_HOST_WAIT wait type on Books Online, we get a not-so-helpful definition: "Occurs when waits are triggered by the database engine and implemented by the host." This doesn't give us a lot of clues about the processes related to the WAIT_XTP_HOST_WAIT wait type, which means we have to do a little bit of digging ourselves.

Before we can start investigating the WAIT_XTP_HOST_WAIT wait type, we need to create a memory-optimized table. I used the script in Listing 13-1 to create a new database with a single memory-optimized table. There are some path references in this script you will need to change to make sure the database data and log files are created in the right location.

Listing 13-1. Create test database and memory-optimized table

```
-- Create database
-- Make sure to change the file locations if needed
USE [master];

CREATE DATABASE [OLTP_Test] CONTAINMENT = NONE
ON PRIMARY
```

```
        (NAME = N'OLTP_Test', FILENAME = N'E:\Data\OLTP_Test_Data.mdf' ,
SIZE = 51200KB , FILEGROWTH = 10%)
LOG ON
        (NAME = N'OLTP_Test_log', FILENAME = N'E:\Log\OLTP_Test_Log.ldf' ,
SIZE = 10240KB , FILEGROWTH = 10%);

-- Add the Memory-Optimized Filegroup
ALTER DATABASE OLTP_Test
ADD FILEGROUP OLTP_MO CONTAINS MEMORY_OPTIMIZED_DATA;

-- Add a file to the newly created Filegroup.
-- Change drive/folder location if needed.
ALTER DATABASE OLTP_Test
ADD FILE (name='OLTP_mo_01', filename='E:\data\OLTP_Test_mo_01.ndf')
TO FILEGROUP OLTP_MO;

-- Create our test table
USE [OLTP_Test];
CREATE TABLE OLTP
        (ID INT IDENTITY (1,1) PRIMARY KEY NONCLUSTERED,
        RandomData1 VARCHAR(50),
        RandomData2 VARCHAR(50),
        ID2 UNIQUEIDENTIFIER)
WITH (MEMORY_OPTIMIZED=ON);
```

Now with a memory-optimized table for testing, let's look at the WAIT_XTP_HOST_ WAIT wait type in the sys.dm_os_wait_stats and sys.dm_os_waiting_tasks DMV using the following query:

```
SELECT *
FROM sys.dm_os_waiting_tasks
WHERE wait_type = 'WAIT_XTP_HOST_WAIT';

SELECT *
FROM sys.dm_os_wait_stats
WHERE wait_type = 'WAIT_XTP_HOST_WAIT';
```

The results of this query on my test SQL Server instance can be seen in Figure 13-4.

	waiting_task_address	session_id	exec_context_id	wait_duration_ms	wait_type	resource_address
1	0x0000025F00397C28	12	0	44591	WAIT_XTP_HOST_WAIT	NULL

	wait_type	waiting_tasks_count	wait_time_ms	max_wait_time_ms	signal_wait_time_ms
1	WAIT_XTP_HOST_WAIT	4	93336678	93336386	0

Figure 13-4. *WAIT_XTP_HOST_WAIT waits*

The first thing to notice is the WAIT_XTP_HOST_WAIT wait type is constantly showing up in the sys.dm_os_waiting_tasks DMV, and over time the wait time increases. Also, the session_id related to the WAIT_XTP_HOST_WAIT wait type indicates it is an internal SQL Server thread recording the wait. From this information, we can already formulate some conclusions about the WAIT_XTP_HOST_WAIT wait type: it is related to an internal background process which continuously runs. What's also interesting is if I run the query a second time, the wait time in the sys.dm_os_waiting_tasks DMV increases but the wait time in the sys.dm_os_wait_stats remains the same. So far we have run into one other wait type sharing this characteristic, the CHECKPOINT_QUEUE wait time, which we discussed in Chapter 12, "Background and Miscellaneous Wait Types."

Since the CHECKPOINT_QUEUE wait type has interesting behavior in it only writes the accumulated wait time of the sys.dm_os_waiting_tasks DMV to the sys.dm_os_wait_stats DMV when an automatic checkpoint occurs, I decide to simply run a checkpoint command against the OLTP_Test database using Listing 13-1 and then query both the DMVs again. The impact on the wait times of the WAIT_XTP_HOST_WAIT wait type can be seen in Figure 13-5.

	waiting_task_address	session_id	exec_context_id	wait_duration_ms	wait_type	resource_address
1	0x0000025F00397C28	12	0	3279	WAIT_XTP_HOST_WAIT	NULL

	wait_type	waiting_tasks_count	wait_time_ms	max_wait_time_ms	signal_wait_time_ms
1	WAIT_XTP_HOST_WAIT	5	93637517	93336386	0

Figure 13-5. *WAIT_XTP_HOST_WAIT wait information after checkpoint*

As you see in Figure 13-5, the wait time in the sys.dm_os_waiting_tasks DMV is small, but the wait time in the sys.dm_os_wait_stats DMV has increased. Because of this behavior, I believe the WAIT_XTP_HOST_WAIT wait type has something to do with the offline checkpoint process related to memory-optimized tables.

We verify this by going to the location of the in-memory file created in Listing 13-1. The interesting thing about adding a file to an in-memory filegroup is it will create a directory, and inside this directory, there is a folder with a unique ID string. If you go further down the directory tree, you will end up in a folder with numbered files. Figure 13-6 shows a part of the contents of this folder on my test machine.

Name	Date modified	Type	Size
{3D2FD9F1-D6D7-427E-AF85-ABD9E1E4A0F0}.hkckp	6/22/2022 11:56 AM	HKCKP File	16,384 KB
{7DB18A63-F022-45C6-B265-93681A46DFDF}.hkckp	6/22/2022 11:56 AM	HKCKP File	2,048 KB
{10C83AF1-4F61-4817-BEAB-EC2767BB160B}.hkckp	6/22/2022 11:56 AM	HKCKP File	1,024 KB
{34D09375-6D1B-4C00-9590-4CEBC9E37841}.hkckp	6/22/2022 11:56 AM	HKCKP File	16,384 KB
{36C21B4E-931A-4B3B-B7E2-F4F3882E7CE5}.hkckp	6/22/2022 11:56 AM	HKCKP File	2,048 KB
{43EF56DA-D779-4BD3-A1C6-0755E545A550}.hkckp	6/22/2022 11:56 AM	HKCKP File	2,048 KB
{49C27142-0180-4687-A8D7-B19E7FA9EDE8}.hkckp	6/22/2022 11:56 AM	HKCKP File	1,024 KB
{74E48AAB-DDF4-430E-A62A-C10F209384C1}.hkckp	6/22/2022 11:56 AM	HKCKP File	4,096 KB
{89B08BE5-C6E0-4676-897B-FB20192A219C}.hkckp	6/22/2022 11:56 AM	HKCKP File	1,024 KB
{3017D1E4-A799-4606-B626-5E34A511CE2A}.hkckp	6/22/2022 11:56 AM	HKCKP File	16,384 KB
{66104FDA-D399-4ABB-A475-3DC0A2D840DC}.hkckp	6/22/2022 11:56 AM	HKCKP File	4,096 KB
{A41B60E4-7299-42AD-85AD-091B10C82677}.hkckp	6/22/2022 11:56 AM	HKCKP File	2,048 KB
{B60EEEAC-25AC-4A3F-A4AF-425C1D03427A}.hkckp	6/22/2022 11:56 AM	HKCKP File	1,024 KB
{BE9F30CE-C95E-43FD-A8CB-7D390FD684D4}.hkckp	6/22/2022 11:56 AM	HKCKP File	16,384 KB
{C2CCA2BE-886F-48EB-BF0D-573455546A6A}.hkckp	6/22/2022 11:56 AM	HKCKP File	4,096 KB
{E5034414-D590-407A-AF51-08CF3A644246}.hkckp	6/22/2022 11:56 AM	HKCKP File	16,384 KB
{EFA2C5FD-64E2-4A89-B40F-EF90BCB459C4}.hkckp	6/22/2022 11:56 AM	HKCKP File	1,024 KB

Figure 13-6. *In-memory filegroup files*

As a matter of fact, the files you are seeing here are the data and delta files that are associated with the memory-optimized table we created earlier.

Since I am guessing a checkpoint would create another CFP, I checked the number of files in the folder before executing a CHECKPOINT, which was 18 files. I then executed a CHECKPOINT command and looked at the number of files again, and it turned out there were now 21 files after the checkpoint.

WAIT_XTP_HOST_WAIT Summary

I believe the WAIT_XTP_HOST_WAIT wait type has a clear relation to the creation of new checkpoint file pairs. Running a manual CHECKPOINT statement will generate a new CFP for memory-optimized tables. Because the WAIT_XTP_HOST_WAIT wait type generates wait time constantly in the background and writes it to the sys.dm_os_wait_stats DMV, a new CFP was created (either by manual checkpoint, when an existing CFP was full, or when a Merge operation occurred), I believe the WAIT_XTP_HOST_WAIT

wait type does not directly indicate performance problems. It mostly indicates a new CFP has been added to the in-memory filegroup. This does not mean this is the only process that generates WAIT_XTP_HOST_WAIT waits, though. There can be other processes that can also cause the waits, but so far they only occurred whenever a new CFP needed to be added.

WAIT_XTP_CKPT_CLOSE

As the name suggests, the **WAIT_XTP_CKPT_CLOSE** wait type seems to be related to the offline checkpoint process introduced with the In-Memory OLTP feature.

What Is the WAIT_XTP_CKPT_CLOSE Wait Type?

The WAIT_XTP_CKPT_CLOSE wait type seems to be related to the offline checkpoint process introduced with the release of In-Memory OLTP. Analyzing the behavior of this wait type shows it records wait time only when a checkpoint occurs, no matter if it is an automatic or manual checkpoint. The wait time WAIT_XTP_CKPT_CLOSE represents seems to be the time it takes for the checkpoint operation to complete. We verify this by executing a CHECKPOINT command against the database and table created earlier when we discussed the WAIT_XTP_HOST_WAIT wait type. The script in Listing 13-2 will clear the sys.dm_os_wait_stats DMV, insert a few rows inside the memory-optimized table, perform a CHECKPOINT operation, and then query the sys.dm_os_wait_stats DMV for WAIT_XTP_CKPT_CLOSE wait type information.

Listing 13-2. Generate WAIT_XTP_CKPT_CLOSE waits

```
USE [OLTP_Test];

-- Clear sys.dm_os_wait_stats
DBCC SQLPERF('sys.dm_os_wait_stats', CLEAR);

-- Insert some rows
INSERT INTO OLTP
     (RandomData1,
      RandomData2,
      ID2)
```

```
VALUES
    (CONVERT(VARCHAR(50), NEWID()),
    CONVERT(VARCHAR(50), NEWID()),
    NEWID())
GO 1000

-- Perform a CHECKPOINT
CHECKPOINT;

-- Query sys.dm_os_wait_stats for WAIT_XTP_CKPT_CLOSE waits
SELECT *
FROM sys.dm_os_wait_stats
WHERE wait_type = 'WAIT_XTP_CKPT_CLOSE';
```

The results are seen in Figure 13-7.

	wait_type	waiting_tasks_count	wait_time_ms	max_wait_time_ms	signal_wait_time_ms
1	WAIT_XTP_CKPT_CLOSE	2	896	896	0

Figure 13-7. *WAIT_XTP_CKPT_CLOSE waits*

I don't believe seeing WAIT_XTP_CKPT_CLOSE waits occur is a direct cause for concern. They indicate checkpoints are being performed. I can imagine a sudden spike in wait times for the WAIT_XTP_CKPT_CLOSE could indicate a performance issue. As in the previous section, performing a checkpoint against a memory-optimized table will result in extra CFPs created. I am guessing if the allocation of CFPs takes a long time, the checkpoint operation will take longer to complete as well, resulting in higher WAIT_XTP_CKPT_CLOSE wait times. The amount of data a checkpoint has to process will probably also mean higher WAIT_XTP_CKPT_CLOSE wait times. Since the checkpoint writes data to the storage subsystem, the performance of your storage will probably also impact WAIT_XTP_CKPT_CLOSE wait times.

WAIT_XTP_CKPT_CLOSE Summary

The WAIT_XTP_CKPT_CLOSE wait type seems closely related to performing checkpoint operations. It indicates the time a checkpoint performed against a memory-optimized table took to complete. I don't believe this directly indicates performance issues, since it just records the time it took for the checkpoint to complete. The amount of work a checkpoint has to process will probably result in higher WAIT_XTP_CKPT_CLOSE wait times. Storage subsystem performance will probably also impact WAIT_XTP_CKPT_CLOSE wait times.

WAIT_XTP_OFFLINE_CKPT_NEW_LOG

The final In-Memory OLTP related wait type in this chapter is the WAIT_XTP_OFFLINE_CKPT_NEW_LOG wait type. This is another wait type related to the offline checkpoint process.

What Is the WAIT_XTP_OFFLINE_CKPT_NEW_LOG Wait Type?

The **WAIT_XTP_OFFLINE_CKPT_NEW_LOG** wait type appears to be a benign wait type recording the length of time the offline checkpoint process is waiting for work. This is confirmed by Books Online, which has the following definition: "occurs when offline checkpoint is waiting for new log records to scan."

As we discussed earlier in this chapter, the offline checkpoint process monitors the transaction log for transactions impacting memory-optimized tables, so those transactions are recorded in the data and delta files. This is a constantly running process in the background of SQL Server, which means you will see an internal process with the WAIT_XTP_OFFLINE_CKPT_NEW_LOG wait type when you query the sys.dm_os_waiting_tasks DMV, as you can see in Figure 13-8.

	waiting_task_address	session_id	exec_context_id	wait_duration_ms	wait_type	resource_address
34	0x0000025F1AAB3088	83	0	5152022	DISPATCHER_QUEUE_SEMAPHORE	NULL
35	0x0000025F19E788C8	39	0	4967595	DISPATCHER_QUEUE_SEMAPHORE	NULL
36	0x0000025F19E78CA8	63	0	3417230	DISPATCHER_QUEUE_SEMAPHORE	NULL
37	0x0000025F1260A108	72	0	3765	WAIT_XTP_OFFLINE_CKPT_NEW_LOG	NULL
38	0x0000025F078424E8	13	0	57	DIRTY_PAGE_POLL	NULL
39	0x0000025F078504E8	17	0	99	LOGMGR_QUEUE	0x000000B65D3FC3A0

Figure 13-8. *WAIT_XTP_OFFLINE_CKPT_NEW_LOG waits inside sys.dm_os_waiting_tasks*

Unlike the WAIT_XTP_HOST_WAIT wait type which only writes wait time information to the sys.dm_os_wait_stats DMV when specific conditions occur, the WAIT_XTP_OFFLINE_CKPT_NEW_LOG wait type appears to wait for around 5 seconds, adds the wait time to the sys.dm_os_wait_stats DMV, and then resets the wait time in the sys.dm_os_waiting_tasks DMV again. This suggests that the offline checkpoint process checks for new work at an interval of around 5 seconds.

Seeing this behavior makes me believe the WAIT_XTP_OFFLINE_CKPT_NEW_LOG wait type is harmless. It just indicates that the offline checkpoint process is waiting for work to arrive.

WAIT_XTP_OFFLINE_CKPT_NEW_LOG Summary

The WAIT_XTP_OFFLINE_CKPT_NEW_LOG wait type is related to the offline checkpoint process and indicates the process is waiting for work to arrive. Because the WAIT_XTP_OFFLINE_CKPT_NEW_LOG wait type only indicates the offline checkpoint process is waiting for work, I believe the wait type doesn't indicate any performance issues and can probably be safely ignored.

Example SQL Server Machine Configurations

This appendix will describe the configuration of systems used for the examples and wait type demonstrations in this book. If it was necessary to modify the system to demonstrate a specific wait type or situation occurring, those details are included in the text inside the chapter holding the demonstration.

All test systems are virtual machines created inside Microsoft Azure. Each VM was built, then SQL Server installed manually, followed by SQL Server Management Studio v19.0 Preview 1 (16.0.19024.0).

Another tool frequently used during examples is Ostress. Ostress is part of the RML utilities provided to manage your SQL Server's performance. You can download the RML utilities using this link: `https://learn.microsoft.com/en-US/troubleshoot/sql/tools/replay-markup-language-utility`.

Default Test Machine

The table that follows shows the virtual machine configuration used for the majority of the book, except for Chapter 10, "High-Availability and Disaster-Recovery Wait Types," which discusses high-availability and disaster-recovery wait types.

Configuration	Value
Computer name	SQL2022
vCPUs	2

(continued)

© Thomas LaRock, Enrico van de Laar 2023
T. LaRock and E. van de Laar, *Pro SQL Server 2022 Wait Statistics*,
https://doi.org/10.1007/978-1-4842-8771-2

Configuration	Value
Architecture	Standard D2s v3, 64-bit
Memory	8 GB
Storage	Premium SSD LRS
	127 GB
	Max IOPS 500
	Max throughput (MBps) 100
Operating system	Windows Server 2022 Datacenter Azure Edition
VM Generation	V2
SQL Server edition	Microsoft SQL Server 2022 (RC0) – 16.0.900.6 (X64) Enterprise Evaluation Edition (64-bit)
SQL Server features	Database Engine Services
SQL Server instance name	RC0

HA/DR Test Machines

The tables that follow show the configurations of the virtual machines used for demonstrating high-availability and disaster-recovery wait types as described in Chapter 10, "High-Availability and Disaster-Recovery Wait Types."

Configuration	Value
Computer name	BACONDC
Role	Domain controller (BACON)
vCPUs	2
Architecture	Standard D2s v3, 64-bit

(continued)

Configuration	Value
Memory	8 GB
Storage	Premium SSD LRS 127 GB Max IOPS 500 Max throughput (MBps) 100
Operating system	Windows Server 2022 Datacenter Azure Edition
VM Generation	V2

Configuration	Value
Computer name	SQL2022AG1
Role	Principal (mirroring) Primary (AlwaysOn) Failover node
vCPUs	2
Architecture	Standard D2s v3, 64-bit
Memory	8 GB
Storage	Premium SSD LRS 127 GB Max IOPS 500 Max throughput (MBps) 100
Operating system	Windows Server 2022 Datacenter Azure Edition
VM Generation	V2
SQL Server edition	Microsoft SQL Server 2022 (RC0) – 16.0.900.6 (X64) Enterprise Evaluation Edition (64-bit)
SQL Server features	Database Engine Services
SQL Server instance name	MSSQLSERVER (Default instance)

363

Configuration	Value
Computer name	SQL2022AG2
Role	Mirror (mirroring)
	Secondary (AlwaysOn) Failover node
vCPUs	2
Architecture	Standard D2s v3, 64-bit
Memory	8 GB
Storage	Premium SSD LRS
	127 GB
	Max IOPS 500
	Max throughput (MBps) 100
Operating system	Windows Server 2022 Datacenter Azure Edition
VM Generation	V2
SQL Server edition	Microsoft SQL Server 2022 (RC0) – 16.0.900.6 (X64) Enterprise Evaluation Edition (64-bit)
SQL Server features	Database Engine Services
SQL Server instance name	MSSQLSERVER (Default instance)

APPENDIX II

Spinlocks

Spinlocks are described as "lightweight synchronization primitives." The description looks a lot like the one used for latches, which are described as "lightweight synchronization objects." This is no coincidence, as spinlocks and latches have a lot in common and both are used to serialize access to internal data structures. Both latches and spinlocks are used when access to objects needs to be held for a very short amount of time.

While spinlocks and latches have an identical purpose, there is one large difference between them. Whenever you cannot acquire a latch because there is another incompatible latch already in place, for example, your request is forced to wait, it will leave the processor and is returned to the Waiter List (the request receives the "SUSPENDED" state). It is then forced to wait inside the Waiter List until the latch is acquired, and then it moves through the Runnable Queue until it can finally get back on the processor. Because latches are treated like a resource for query execution, they are closely related to wait statistics. SQL Server even records the time it has been waiting on acquiring different latch types and classes, which we discussed in Chapter 9, "Latch-Related Wait Types." There is a relatively large overhead associated with latches, because if a latch cannot be obtained immediately, it has to move through the different phases of the scheduler again before the request can acquire its latch and get executed on the processor.

Spinlocks work differently than latches, because whenever a spinlock has to wait out another spinlock already in place before it can get placed itself, the thread does not have to leave the processor. Instead, a spinlock will "spin" until it can be acquired.

The main advantage of spinlocks instead of latches to synchronize thread access is that spinlocks are even "lighter" synchronization objects than latches. Latches cause extra context switching to occur whenever a latch has to wait before it can get acquired. Spinlocks do not cause context switching because they never move away from the processor. Because spinlocks do not cause context switching, they are used to protect those areas of SQL Server used most intensely.

© Thomas LaRock, Enrico van de Laar 2023
T. LaRock and E. van de Laar, *Pro SQL Server 2022 Wait Statistics*,
https://doi.org/10.1007/978-1-4842-8771-2

Because spinlocks never move away from the processor, they consume processor time, even when they are waiting. To avoid spinlocks consuming too much processor time, every x time around the spinlock will stop spinning and sleep. The interval of the spinlock sleep is calculated by an internal algorithm.

On very busy systems, where many spinlocks are used, it is possible to encounter a phenomenon called spinlock contention. If the spinlock contention gets bad enough, you can notice an increase in processor time difficult to troubleshoot, since this will not always show by analyzing wait statistics.

Thankfully, just like latches, there is a spinlock DMV inside SQL Server that tracks the specific spinlock classes (470 in SQL Server 2022), the amount of time a spinlock had to wait before it was acquired, and the total number of spins that occurred for that spinlock class. We can access this information by querying the sys.dm_os_spinlock_stats DMV like the query here:

```
SELECT *
FROM sys.dm_os_spinlock_stats
ORDER BY spins DESC;
```

This returns results like those shown in Figure AII-1.

	name	collisions	spins	spins_per_collision	sleep_time	backoffs
1	LOCK_HASH	36986	936664	25.32483	55	9787
2	SOS_SCHEDULER	3080	557843	181.1179	0	22
3	RESQUEUE	29282	366235	12.50717	0	10
4	SOS_SUSPEND_QUEUE	9514	72496	7.619928	0	5
5	SPL_XE_BUFFER_MGR	5	29244	5848.8	1	14
6	SOS_TLIST	20	25133	1256.65	0	4
7	XDESMGR	161	20078	124.7081	1	27
8	BLOCKER_ENUM	1832	19596	10.69651	0	1
9	SESSION_MANAGER	157	6883	43.84076	0	1
10	BACKUP_CTX	1429	5884	4.117565	0	33

Figure AII-1. *sys.dm_os_spinlock_stats*

The columns returned by the sys.dm_os_spinlock_stats are described in the following list:

- **name** – Shows the name of the spinlock class.

- **collisions** – Returns the amount of time this spinlock class encountered a wait event because another spinlock was already in place.

- **spins** – When a spinlock has to wait, it performs a spin. The spins column shows the amount of times spins occurred for this specific spinlock class. You can think of a spin as the amount of time the spinlock had to wait before it could get acquired.

- **spins_per_collision** – The average number of spins per collision.

- **sleep_time** – Time that was spent sleeping for this spinlock class.

- **backoffs** – The number of times a spinlock went to sleep to allow other threads to use the processor.

While the columns returned by the sys.dm_os_spinlock_stats DMV provide valuable information, the backoffs column is the most interesting when you are suspecting a case of spinlock contention. If you notice very high CPU usage and cannot directly correlate the high CPU usage with queries or specific wait types, but the amount of backoffs for a specific spinlock class is very high and increasing quickly, you likely have a case of spinlock contention occurring.

Spinlock contention is difficult to troubleshoot since it has a very large number of causes. Also, information about specific spinlock classes is often lacking, increasing the difficulty of troubleshooting spinlock contention. One method to use during the analysis of spinlock contention is building a baseline of the sys.dm_os_spinlock_stats DMV by capturing the contents of the DMV at a specific interval, like I described in Chapter 4, "Building a Solid Baseline." This baseline can give you valuable insight into the usage of spinlocks inside your SQL Server instance. Another great tool to diagnose spinlock contention is Extended Events. By using Extended Events, you can trace various spinlock-related events, like spinlock backoffs.

To truly analyze why spinlock-class contention is occurring, you will have to dive even deeper by debugging SQL Server memory dumps and looking through the call stack to find what spinlock class is being accessed. Debugging SQL Server memory dumps to identify spinlock contention is beyond the scope of this book and requires a deep knowledge of the inner workings of SQL Server. Thankfully, there is a free Microsoft whitepaper available on spinlock contention that can give you a few pointers for what to do when dealing with spinlock contention. You can get the whitepaper at `https://slrwnds.com/1tvozd`.

APPENDIX III

Latch Classes

Latch class	Books Online description	Additional information
ALLOC_CREATE_RINGBUF	Used internally by SQL Server to initialize the synchronization of the creation of an allocation ring buffer	Used when creating a ring buffer. A ring buffer briefly holds internal event information in memory and is used for diagnostics
ALLOC_CREATE_FREESPACE_CACHE	Used to initialize the synchronization of internal free space caches for heaps	Allocates free space for heaps (tables without a clustered index)
ALLOC_CACHE_MANAGER	Used to synchronize internal coherency tests	
ALLOC_FREESPACE_CACHE	Used to synchronize access to a cache of pages with available space for heaps and binary large objects (BLOBs). Contention on latches of this class can occur when multiple connections try to insert rows into a heap or BLOB at the same time. You can reduce this contention by partitioning the object. Each partition has its own latch. Partitioning will distribute the inserts across multiple latches	

(continued)

© Thomas LaRock, Enrico van de Laar 2023
T. LaRock and E. van de Laar, *Pro SQL Server 2022 Wait Statistics*,
https://doi.org/10.1007/978-1-4842-8771-2

Latch class	Books Online description	Additional information
ALLOC_EXTENT_CACHE	Used to synchronize the access to a cache of extents that contains pages that are not allocated. Contention on latches of this class can occur when multiple connections try to allocate data pages in the same allocation unit at the same time. This contention can be reduced by partitioning the object of which this allocation unit is a part	
ACCESS_METHODS_ DATASET_PARENT	Used to synchronize child dataset access to the parent dataset during parallel operations	Used together with the ACCESS_ METHODS_SCAN_RANGE_ GENERATOR latch class during parallel operations to distribute the work among multiple threads
ACCESS_METHODS_ HOBT_FACTORY	Used to synchronize access to an internal hash table	
ACCESS_METHODS_ HOBT	Used to synchronize access to the in-memory representation of a HoBt	
ACCESS_METHODS_ HOBT_COUNT	Used to synchronize access to a HoBt page and row counters	Used for page and row count deltas for heaps and B-trees
ACCESS_METHODS_ HOBT_VIRTUAL_ROOT	Used to synchronize access to the root page abstraction of an internal B-tree	Used when accessing metadata regarding the index's root page. See Chapter 8, "Latch-Related Wait Types," for an example

(continued)

Latch class	Books Online description	Additional information
ACCESS_METHODS_ CACHE_ONLY_HOBT_ ALLOC	Used to synchronize worktable access	Used for synchronizing access to transparent, temporary tables that are created during query execution
ACCESS_METHODS_ BULK_ALLOC	Used to synchronize access within bulk allocators	
ACCESS_METHODS_ SCAN_RANGE_ GENERATOR	Used to synchronize access to a range generator during parallel scans	
ACCESS_METHODS_ KEY_RANGE_ GENERATOR	Used to synchronize access to read-ahead operations during key-range parallel scans	
APPEND_ONLY_ STORAGE_INSERT_ POINT	Used to synchronize inserts in fast append-only storage units	
APPEND_ONLY_ STORAGE_FIRST_ ALLOC	Used to synchronize the first allocation for an append-only storage unit	
APPEND_ONLY_ STORAGE_UNIT_ MANAGER	Used for internal data structure access synchronization within the fast append-only storage unit manager	
APPEND_ONLY_ STORAGE_MANAGER	Used to synchronize shrink operations in the fast append-only storage unit manager	
BACKUP_RESULT_SET	Used to synchronize parallel backup result sets	
BACKUP_TAPE_POOL	Used to synchronize backup tape pools	

(*continued*)

Latch class	Books Online description	Additional information
BACKUP_LOG_REDO	Used to synchronize backup log redo operations	
BACKUP_INSTANCE_ID	Used to synchronize the generation of instance IDs for backup performance monitor counters	
BACKUP_MANAGER	Used to synchronize the internal backup manager	
BACKUP_MANAGER_ DIFFERENTIAL	Used to synchronize differential backup operations with DBCC	
BACKUP_OPERATION	Used for internal data structure synchronization within a backup operation, such as database, log, or file backup	
BACKUP_FILE_HANDLE	Used to synchronize file open operations during a restore operation	
BUFFER	Used to synchronize short-term access to database pages. A buffer latch is required before reading or modifying any database page. Buffer latch contention can indicate several issues, including hot pages and slow I/Os This latch class covers all possible uses of page latches. sys.dm_os_wait_stats makes a difference between page latch waits that are caused by I/O operations and read and write operations on the page	Directly related to buffer latches. When seeing higher-than-expected wait times, check if you are running into buffer latch-related contention

(continued)

Latch class	Books Online description	Additional information
BUFFER_POOL_GROW	Used for internal buffer manager synchronization during buffer pool grow operations	
DATABASE_CHECKPOINT	Used to serialize checkpoints within a database	
CLR_PROCEDURE_HASHTABLE	Internal use only	
CLR_UDX_STORE	Internal use only	
CLR_DATAT_ACCESS	Internal use only	
CLR_XVAR_PROXY_LIST	Internal use only	
DBCC_CHECK_AGGREGATE	Internal use only	
DBCC_CHECK_RESULTSET	Internal use only	
DBCC_CHECK_TABLE	Internal use only	
DBCC_CHECK_TABLE_INIT	Internal use only	
DBCC_CHECK_TRACE_LIST	Internal use only	
DBCC_FILE_CHECK_OBJECT	Internal use only	
DBCC_PERF	Used to synchronize internal performance monitor counters	
DBCC_PFS_STATUS	Internal use only	
DBCC_OBJECT_METADATA	Internal use only	
DBCC_HASH_DLL	Internal use only	
EVENTING_CACHE	Internal use only	

(continued)

Latch class	Books Online description	Additional information
FCB	Used to synchronize access to the file control block	
FCB_REPLICA	Internal use only	
FGCB_ALLOC	Use to synchronize access to round-robin allocation information within a filegroup	
FGCB_ADD_REMOVE	Use to synchronize access to filegroups for ADD and DROP file operations	Latch is used when adding or removing files inside a filegroup, or when a file grows. Check auto-growth configuration if you are running into contention
FILEGROUP_MANAGER	Internal use only	
FILE_MANAGER	Internal use only	
FILESTREAM_FCB	Internal use only	
FILESTREAM_FILE_ MANAGER	Internal use only	
FILESTREAM_GHOST_ FILES	Internal use only	
FILESTREAM_DFS_ROOT	Internal use only	
LOG_MANAGER	Internal use only	Indicates transaction log growth because the log could not be cleared or truncated
FULLTEXT_DOCUMENT_ ID	Internal use only	
FULLTEXT_DOCUMENT_ ID_TRANSACTION	Internal use only	
FULLTEXT_DOCUMENT_ ID_NOTIFY	Internal use only	

(continued)

Latch class	Books Online description	Additional information
FULLTEXT_LOGS	Internal use only	
FULLTEXT_CRAWL_LOG	Internal use only	
FULLTEXT_ADMIN	Internal use only	
FULLTEXT_AMDIN_ COMMAND_CACHE	Internal use only	
FULLTEXT_LANGUAGE_ TABLE	Internal use only	
FULLTEXT_CRAWL_DM_ LIST	Internal use only	
FULLTEXT_CRAWL_ CATALOG	Internal use only	
FULLTEXT_FILE_ MANAGER	Internal use only	
DATABASE_MIRRORING_ REDO	Internal use only	
DATABASE_MIRRORING_ SERVER	Internal use only	
DATABASE_MIRRORING_ CONNECTION	Internal use only	Responsible for controlling the message flow between database mirrors
DATABASE_MIRRORING_ STREAM	Internal use only	
QUERY_OPTIMIZER_VD_ MANAGER	Internal use only	
QUERY_OPTIMIZER_ID_ MANAGER	Internal use only	
QUERY_OPTIMIZER_ VIEW_REP	Internal use only	

(continued)

Latch class	Books Online description	Additional information
RECOVERY_BAD_PAGE_ TABLE	Internal use only	
RECOVERY_MANAGER	Internal use only	
SECURITY_OPERATION_ RULE_TABLE	Internal use only	
SECURITY_OBJPERM_ CACHE	Internal use only	
SECURITY_CRYPTO	Internal use only	
SECURITY_KEY_RING	Internal use only	
SECURITY_KEY_LIST	Internal use only	
SERVICE_BROKER_ CONNECTION_RECEIVE	Internal use only	
SERVICE_BROKER_ TRANSMISSION	Internal use only	
SERVICE_BROKER_ TRANSMISSION_UPDATE	Internal use only	
SERVICE_BROKER_ TRANSMISSION_STATE	Internal use only	
SERVICE_BROKER_ TRANSMISSION_ERRORS	Internal use only	
SSBXmitWork	Internal use only	
SERVICE_BROKER_ MESSAGE_ TRANSMISSION	Internal use only	
SERVICE_BROKER_MAP_ MANAGER	Internal use only	
SERVICE_BROKER_ HOST_NAME	Internal use only	

(continued)

Latch class	Books Online description	Additional information
SERVICE_BROKER_ READ_CACHE	Internal use only	
SERVICE_BROKER_ WAITFOR_MANAGER	Internal use only	
SERVICE_BROKER_ WAITFOR_ TRANSACTION_DATA	Internal use only	
SERVICE_BROKER_ TRANSMISSION_ TRANSACTION_DATA	Internal use only	
SERVICE_BROKER_ TRANSPORT	Internal use only	
SERVICE_BROKER_ MIRROR_ROUTE	Internal use only	
TRACE_ID	Internal use only	
TRACE_AUDIT_ID	Internal use only	
TRACE	Internal use only	
TRACE_CONTROLLER	Internal use only	Related to SQL Trace. More information about SQL Trace can be found at https://msdn. microsoft.com/en-us/ hh245121.aspx. Seeing contention on this latch class can mean too many traces are running at the time
TRACE_EVENT_QUEUE	Internal use only	
TRANSACTION_ DISTRIBUTED_MARK	Internal use only	
TRANSACTION_ OUTCOME	Internal use only	

(continued)

Latch class	Books Online description	Additional information
NESTING_ TRANSACTION_ READONLY	Internal use only	
NESTING_ TRANSACTION_FULL	Internal use only	
MSQL_TRANSACTION_ MANAGER	Internal use only	
DATABASE_AUTONAME_ MANAGER	Internal use only	
UTILITY_DYNAMIC_ VECTOR	Internal use only	
UTILITY_SPARSE_ BITMAP	Internal use only	
UTILITY_DATABASE_ DROP	Internal use only	
UTILITY_DYNAMIC_ MANAGER_VIEW	Internal use only	
UTILITY_DEBUG_ FILESTREAM	Internal use only	
UTILITY_LOCK_ INFORMATION	Internal use only	
VERSIONING_ TRANSACTION	Internal use only	
VERSIONING_ TRANSACTION_LIST	Internal use only	
VERSIONING_ TRANSACTION_CHAIN	Internal use only	

(continued)

Latch class	Books Online description	Additional information
VERSIONING_STATE	Internal use only	
VERSIONING_STATE_ CHANGE	Internal use only	
KTM_VIRTUAL_CLOCK	Internal use only	

APPENDIX IV

Waits and DMVs

The list of wait events and DMVs used in this book is found here for your quick review.

Chapter	Wait event	Books Online description	Additional information
6	ASYNC_IO_COMPLETION	Occurs when a task is waiting for asynchronous non-data I/Os to finish	Examples include database backups, instant file initialization not configured
6	ASYNC_NETWORK_IO	Occurs on network writes when the task is blocked waiting for the client application to acknowledge it has processed all the data sent to it	Identify queries returning a large result set back to the application; examine your network for high utilization or low bandwidth
7	BACKUPBUFFER	Occurs when a backup task is waiting for data or is waiting for a buffer in which to store data	Expected behavior, can typically be ignored; can be lowered by altering BACKUP syntax to increase MAXTRANSFERSIZE
7	BACKUPIO	Occurs when a backup task is waiting for data or is waiting for a buffer in which to store data	Identify possible storage or network issues with transfer of backup data
7	BACKUPTHREAD	Occurs when a task is waiting for a backup task to finish. Wait times may be long, from several minutes to several hours	Expected behavior; examine instant file initialization settings

(*continued*)

Chapter	Wait event	Books Online description	Additional information
12	CHECKPOINT_QUEUE	Occurs while the checkpoint task is waiting for the next checkpoint request	Expected behavior and in many cases safely ignored
6	CMEMTHREAD	Occurs when a task is waiting on a thread-safe memory object	Look for large amounts of short, concurrent, ad hoc queries executed
5	CXCONSUMER	Occurs with parallel query plans when a consumer thread (parent) waits for a producer thread to send rows	Expected behavior and in many cases safely ignored
5	CXPACKET	Occurs with parallel query plans when waiting to synchronize the Query Processor Exchange Iterator and when producing and consuming rows	Identify queries running in parallel with skewed workloads; if applicable, tune system parallelism configuration options
10	DBMIRROR_SEND	Occurs when a task is waiting for a communications backlog at the network layer to clear to be able to send messages	Identify network bandwidth issues; consider changing to asynchronous mirror mode
12	DIRTY_PAGE_POLL	Internal use only	Expected behavior, can typically be ignored
10	HADR_LOGCAPTURE_ WAIT	Waiting for log records to become available	Expected behavior, can typically be ignored
10	HADR_SYNC_COMMIT	Waiting for a transaction commit processing on the synchronized secondary databases to harden the log	Expected behavior; higher wait times above your baseline could be an issue; consider changing to asynchronous mode

(continued)

Chapter	Wait event	Books Online description	Additional information
10	HADR_WORK_QUEUE	AlwaysOn Availability Groups' background worker thread waiting for new work to be assigned	Expected behavior, can typically be ignored
6	IO_COMPLETION	Occurs while waiting for I/O operations to complete	Identify queries and activities using non-data pages; examine storage subsystem for issues
9	LATCH_[xx]	Occurs when a task is waiting to acquire a non-buffer latch. The [xx] can be replaced by a variety of different latch modes	Latch waits are frequently related to specific workloads and database design
12	LAZYWRITER_SLEEP	Occurs when lazy writer tasks are suspended	Expected behavior, can typically be ignored
8	LCK_M_I[xx]	Occurs when a task is waiting to acquire an Intent lock. The [xx] can be replaced by a variety of different lock modes	Identify queries causing blocking. Optimize as necessary
8	LCK_M_S	Occurs when a task is waiting to acquire a Shared lock	Identify queries causing blocking. Optimize as necessary
8	LCK_M_SCH_M	Occurs when a task is waiting to acquire a Schema Modify lock.	Identify queries causing schema modification. Optimize as necessary
8	LCK_M_SCH_S	Occurs when a task is waiting to acquire a Schema Share lock.	Identify queries causing schema modification. Optimize as necessary
8	LCK_M_U	Occurs when a task is waiting to acquire an Update lock	Identify queries causing blocking. Optimize as necessary

(continued)

Chapter	Wait event	Books Online description	Additional information
8	LCK_M_X	Occurs when a task is waiting to acquire an Exclusive lock	Identify queries causing blocking. Optimize as necessary
6	LOGBUFFER	Occurs when a task is waiting for space in the log buffer to store a log record	Identify queries executing frequent small transactions; examine storage subsystem for issues
12	MSQL_XP	Occurs when a task is waiting for an extended stored procedure to end	Identify queries executing external stored procedures
12	OLEDB	Occurs when SQL Server calls the SNAC OLE DB Provider (SQLNCLI) or the Microsoft OLE DB Driver for SQL Server (MSOLEDBSQL)	Identify queries using the OLEDB providers such as linked server queries or CHECKDB statements
9	PAGEIOLATCH_[xx]	Occurs when a task is waiting on a latch for a buffer that is in an I/O request. The [xx] can be replaced by a variety of different latch modes	Latch waits are frequently related to specific workloads and database design
9	PAGELATCH_[xx]	Occurs when a task is waiting to acquire a buffer latch. The [xx] can be replaced by a variety of different latch modes	Latch waits are frequently related to specific workloads and database design
11	PREEMPTIVE_OS_ AUTHENTICATIONOPS	Internal use only	Expected behavior; check for issues with domain controllers, network devices, and firewalls

(*continued*)

Chapter	Wait event	Books Online description	Additional information
11	PREEMPTIVE_OS_DECRYPTMESSAGE	Internal use only	Expected behavior, can typically be ignored
11	PREEMPTIVE_OS_ENCRYPTMESSAGE	Internal use only	Expected behavior, can typically be ignored
11	PREEMPTIVE_OS_GETPROCADDRESS	Internal use only	Identify queries executing external stored procedures
11	PREEMPTIVE_OS_WRITEFILEGATHER	Internal use only	Identify processes writing to files outside SQL Server; verify instant file initialization configuration
10	REDO_THREAD_PENDING_WORK	Internal use only	Expected behavior, can typically be ignored
6	RESOURCE_SEMAPHORE	Occurs when a query memory request during query execution cannot be granted immediately due to other concurrent queries	Identify queries requiring large memory grants; add additional RAM if necessary
6	RESOURCE_SEMAPHORE_QUERY_COMPILE	Occurs when the number of concurrent query compilations reaches a throttling limit	Identify queries requiring large memory grants or a large number of concurrent queries requiring grants; add additional RAM if necessary
6	SLEEP_BPOOL_FLUSH	Occurs when a checkpoint is throttling the issuance of new I/Os in order to avoid flooding the disk subsystem	Verify configuration options available for recovery interval; verify storage subsystem issues
5	SOS_SCHEDULER_YIELD	Occurs when a task voluntarily yields the scheduler for other tasks to execute	Identify growth in transactions or user connections increasing volume of requests, or queries with complex calculations require large CPU time

(continued)

Chapter	Wait event	Books Online description	Additional information
5	THREADPOOL	Occurs when a task (query or login/logout) is waiting for a worker thread to execute it	Identify queries running in parallel, or a higher than usual number of connections
12	TRACEWRITE	Occurs when the SQL Trace rowset trace provider waits for either a free buffer or a buffer with events to process	Identify processes running a SQL Trace
13	WAIT_XTP_CKPT_CLOSE	Occurs when waiting for a checkpoint to complete	Expected behavior, can typically be ignored
13	WAIT_XTP_HOST_WAIT	Occurs when waits are triggered by the database engine and implemented by the host	Expected behavior, can typically be ignored
13	WAIT_XTP_OFFLINE_CKPT_NEW_LOG	Occurs when offline checkpoint is waiting for new log records to scan	Expected behavior, can typically be ignored
12	WAITFOR	Occurs as a result of a WAITFOR Transact-SQL statement	Identify queries using WAITFOR commands
6	WRITE_COMPLETION	Occurs when a write operation is in progress	Verify instant file initialization configuration; look for operations writing to disk such as data and log file growth or DBCC operations
6	WRITELOG	Occurs while waiting for a log flush to complete	Examine disk throughput; isolate data and log write activities; if applicable, enable Delayed Durability

(continued)

Chapter	DMV	Books Online description	Additional information
9	sys.dm_db_index_ physical_stats	Returns size and fragmentation information for the data and indexes of the specified table or view in SQL Server	Identify additional information about the number of index and data pages inside the index
6	sys.dm_exec_cached_ plans	Returns a row for each query plan that is cached by SQL Server for faster query execution	Identify the categories of cached plans (i.e., ad hoc) and their sizes
5	sys.dm_exec_query_plan	Returns the Showplan in XML format for the batch specified by the plan handle	Identify execution plan information for the executed batch statement
6	sys.dm_exec_query_ resource_semaphores	Returns the information about the current query-resource semaphore status in SQL Server	Identify if your system needs additional RAM to process queries and their associated memory grants
5	sys.dm_exec_query_stats	Returns the Showplan in XML format for the batch specified by the plan handle	Identify execution plan information for the executed batch statement
1,2	sys.dm_exec_requests	Returns information about each request that is executing in SQL Server	Identify all current requests
2	sys.dm_exec_session_ wait_stats	Returns information about all the waits encountered by threads that executed for each session	Identify wait events for each session
1,2	sys.dm_exec_sessions	Returns one row per authenticated session on SQL Server	Identify all current sessions

(*continued*)

Chapter	DMV	Books Online description	Additional information
5,9	sys.dm_exec_sql_text	Returns the text of the SQL batch that is identified by the specified sql_handle	Identify SQL text for the executed batch statement
10	sys.dm_hadr_database_replica_states	Returns a row for each database that is participating in an AlwaysOn Availability Group for which the local instance of SQL Server is hosting an availability replica	Identify Ag health status using a DMV instead of the AlwaysOn Dashboard
9	sys.dm_os_latch_waits	Detailed breakdown of cumulative wait information for non-buffer latches	Identify additional information related to lowering LATCH_[xx] waits
9	sys.dm_os_performance_counters	Returns a row per performance counter maintained by the server	Identify available Perfmon counters
1	sys.dm_os_schedulers	Returns one row per scheduler in SQL Server where each scheduler is mapped to an individual [logical] processor	Identify if your system is experiencing CPU pressure
5	sys.dm_os_sys_info	Returns a miscellaneous set of useful information about the computer and about the resources available to and consumed by SQL Server	Identify the resources SQL Server believes to be available or is currently using
1	sys.dm_os_tasks	Returns one row for each task that is active in the instance of SQL Server	Identify all current tasks; important for understanding parallel tasks and work

(continued)

Chapter	DMV	Books Online description	Additional information
2	sys.dm_os_wait_stats	Returns information about all the waits encountered by threads that executed	Identify aggregate amount of wait for all threads since last instant restart or wait stats refresh
2	sys.dm_os_waiting_tasks	Returns information about the wait queue of tasks that are waiting on some resource	Identify aggregate amount of wait for threads in SUSPENDED or RUNNABLE queues since last instant restart or wait stats refresh
1	sys.dm_os_workers	Returns a row for every worker in the system	Identify all current workers
8	sys.dm_tran_locks	Returns information about currently active lock manager resources in SQL Server	Identify all current requests for locks to be granted or have been granted
2	sys.dm_xe_map_values	Returns a mapping of internal numeric keys to human-readable text	Identify wait-related Extended Events available for the SQL Server instance
9	sys.partitions	Contains a row for each partition of all the tables and most types of indexes in the database	Identify distribution of rows across partitions
6	sys.sp_configure	Displays or changes global configuration settings for the current server	Set or display server-level configurations
12	sys.traces	The sys.traces catalog view contains the current running traces on the system	Identify traces that are either active or paused against the SQL Server instance

Index

A

AlwaysOn Availability Groups, 273, 281, 283, 291

ASYNC_IO_COMPLETION wait type
  backup operation, 143
  Books Online (BOL), 142
  definition, 142
  lowering waits
    backup-related waits, 144
    instant file initialization, 144, 147
    local policy, 146
    modification, 144
    Perfmon counters, 148, 149
    server configuration, 145
    volume maintenance task, 146
  storage subsystem, 141, 149
  visual representation, 142

ASYNC_NETWORK_IO wait type
  application requests, 153
  client application, 150
  graphical representation, 150
  lowering queries, 152, 153
  modification, 152
  network connection, 150
  networking tab, 152
  network utilization, 153
  SQL Server instance, 151

B

Background wait types
  CHECKPOINT_QUEUE, 322–325

DIRTY_PAGE_POLL wait type, 326–329
  internal processes, 321
  LAZYWRITER_SLEEP wait type, 329–331
  miscellaneous, 321
  MSQL_XP wait type, 331–334
  OLEDB wait type, 334–336
  TRACEWRITE wait type, 336–344
  WAITFOR wait type, 344–346

BACKUPBUFFER wait types
  additional information, 194
  buffer cache, 192
  buffer count/size parameter, 194
  code generation, 195
  database backup, 196
  definition, 192–197
  GalacticWorks database, 193, 195
  internals, 192
  lowering queries, 195, 196
  MAXTRANSFERSIZE option, 196, 197
  reader and writer buffers, 193
  sys.dm_os_wait_stats DMV, 196

BACKUPIO wait type
  database option, 200
  identical tasks, 197
  internals, 198
  modification, 198
  results, 199
  storage subsystem/network location, 199
  striping backup files, 199

391

E

F, G

H

Printed in the United States
by Baker & Taylor Publisher Services